Educational Sciences in the 1950s

STUDIA EDUCATIONIS HISTORICA

Studies in the History of Education

Vol. 10

PETER LANG

Tomáš Kasper, Iveta Kestere and Attila Nóbik (eds.)

Hour Zero – Educational Sciences in Central, Eastern and Southeastern Europe

PETER LANG
Berlin · Bruxelles · Chennai · Lausanne · New York · Oxford

Bibliographic Information published by the Deutsche Nationalbibliothek
The Deutsche Nationalbibliothek lists this publication in the Deutsche Nationalbibliografie; detailed bibliographic data is available online at http://dnb.d-nb.de.

Library of Congress Cataloging-in-Publication Data
Names: Kasper, Tomáš, 1974 editor | Ķestere, Iveta, 1960- editor | Nóbik, Attila, 1978- editor
Title: Hour Zero – Educational Sciences in Central, Eastern and Southeastern Europe/ editors, Tomáš Kasper, Iveta Kestere, Attila Nóbik.
Description: Berlin ; New York : Peter Lang, [2025] | Series: Studia educationis historica, 2195-5158 ; vol. 10 | Includes bibliographical references.
Identifiers: LCCN 2025022772 (print) | LCCN 2025022773 (ebook) | ISBN 9783631890615 hardback | ISBN 9783631940907 pdf | ISBN 9783631940914 epub
Subjects: LCSH: Education and state--Europe, Eastern--History--20th century | Education and state--Europe, Central--History--20th century | Education--Political aspects--Europe, Eastern--History--20th century | Education--Political aspects--Europe, Central--History--20th century
Classification: LCC LC93.E852 E377 2025 (print) | LCC LC93.E852 (ebook)
LC record available at https://lccn.loc.gov/2025022772
LC ebook record available at https://lccn.loc.gov/2025022773

The editors would like to thank the Technical University of Liberec and the Czech Science Foundation (GACR) for their financial support of the research project: Towards a New Model of Educational Sciences – Totalitarianism, Ideology, and Political Instrumentalization in Educational Sciences during the Communist Period, No. 25-16883S.

ISSN 2195-5158
ISBN 978-3-631-89061-5 (Print)
ISBN 978-3-631-94909-7 (ePDF)
ISBN 978-3-631-94091-4 (ePUB)
DOI 10.3726/b23071

Published by Peter Lang GmbH, Berlin (Germany)

info@peterlang.com

www.peterlang.com

Contact for General Product Safety Regulation (GPSR): gpsr@peterlang.com

Contents

PART ONE

Introduction

Hour Zero – Educational Sciences in Central, Eastern and Southeastern Europe between Continuity and Discontinuity, between Political Instrumentalization and Autonomous Development

Tomáš Kasper, Iveta Kestere and Attila Nóbik

Focus of the Book: Educational Sciences at Zero Hour after 1945

The book *Hour Zero – Educational Sciences in Central, Eastern and Southeastern Europe* aims to analyse the continuities and discontinuities in educational sciences[1] when formerly independent European countries were absorbed into the Soviet Union's sphere of influence at the end of World War II. We believe that cross-national case studies of "new beginnings" will yield material for more in-extensive transnational comparative analysis. The timeframe covers the period from the gradual seizure of power by communist leaders in the countries of Central, Eastern, and Southeastern Europe after 1945 to a certain "détente" associated with the death of Stalin and the condemnation of his "cult of personality"[2] at the 20th Congress of the Communist Party of the USSR in 1956.[3] We delimit our study to the period of 1944/45–1956 (but the periodization may be subject to country specificities). The case studies include

1 This book makes use of the terms 'educational sciences' and 'educational discussion', which are well established in the Anglophone educational research area. When the terms 'pedagogical sciences', 'pedagogical discussion', etc., are used, it is mainly to emphasize the original meaning of the term.

2 On the personality cult of Stalin see Jan Plamper, *The Stalin Cult: a Study in the Alchemy of Power* (Stanford, California: Stanford University, 2012), 119–220.

3 Polly Jones, "From the Secret Speech to the Burial of Stalin: Real and Ideal Responses to de-Stalinization," in *The Dilemmas of De-Stalinisation: a Social and Cultural History of Reform in the Khrushchev Era*, ed. Polly Jones (London: Routledge, 2006), 41–63.

Czechoslovakia, Hungary, Poland, the former German Democratic Republic and the former republic of Soviet Union – Latvia, as well as countries of the former Yugoslavia (contemporary Slovenia, Croatia, Bosnia and Herzegovina, Montenegro, Serbia and Macedonia).

The current academic scholarship on Soviet politics, culture, and education is not lacking. However, the Soviet Union's influence on a field of educational sciences so important for teachers, students, and general public has not been explored extensively, especially in this specific period, which we have labelled "zero hour". Some studies on Hungary[4], Poland[5], Ex-Yugoslavia[6], Ex-GDR[7],

---

4 Johanna Hopfner, András Németh and Éva Szabolcs, *Kindheit-Schule-Erziehungswissenschaft in Mitteleuropa 1948–2008* (Frankfurt a. M.: Peter Lang, 2009); András Németh, *Erziehungswissenschaft in Ungarn (1870–1952)* (Budapest: Gondolat, 2013); Andras Neméth and Éva Szabolcs, "Educational Science as an Academic Discipline in Hungary (1867–1953): Turns and Developmental Phases," in *Folds of Past, Present and Future: Reconfiguring Contemporary Histories of Education*, ed. Sarah Ruyskensvelde, Geert Thyssen, Geert, Frederik Herman, Angelo van Gorp and Pieter Verstraete (Berlin, München, Boston: De Gruyter Oldenbourg, 2021), 249–266.

5 Bogusław Śliwerski, "Main Development Lines of Polish Pedagogy from Socialist Orthodoxy to Postmodern Heterogeneity," *Polska Myśl Pedagogiczna*, no. 5 (2019): 17–51; Teresa Hejnicka-Bezwińska, *Zarys historii wychowania (1944–1989)* (Kielce: Wydawnictwo Pedagogiczne ZNP, 1996); Justyna Gulczynska, "The Student in the Polish Socialist Secondary School (1945–1989): a Cultural Context," *Paedagogica Historica* 53, no. 1–2, (2017): 170–188; Joanna Wojdon, "The System of Textbook Approval in Poland under Communist Rule (1944–1989) as a Tool of Power of the Régime," *Paedagogica Historica* 51, no. 1–2 (2015): 181–196.

6 Zdenko Medveš, "Socialist Pedagogy: Caught between the Myth of the Fairness of the Unified School and Cultural Hegemony," *Sodobna pedagogika. Journal of Contemporary Educational Studies* 66, no. 2 (2015): 14–41; Edvard Protner, ed., *Razvoj i aktualne tendencije pedagogije i školstva na području nekadašnje Jugoslavije* (Maribor: University of Maribor Press, 2020).

7 Jakob Benecke, ed., *Erziehungs – und Bildungsverhältnisse in der DDR* (Bad Heilbrunn: Klinkhardt, 2022); Andreas Malycha, *Die Akademie der Pädagogiachen Wissenschaften in der DDR 1970 bis 1990. Zur Geschichte einer Wissenschaftsinstitution im Kontext staatlicher Bildungspolitik* (Leipzig: Akademische Verlagsanstalt, 2008); Heinz Elmar Tenorth and Ulrich Wiegmann, *Pädagogische Wissenschaft in der DDR. Ideologieproduktion, Systemreflexion und Erziehungsforschung* (Bad Heilbrunn: Klinkhardt, 2022); Gert Geißler and Ulrich Wiegmann, *Schule und Erziehung in der DDR. Studien und Dokumente* (Neuwied: Luchterhand, 1995).

and Czechoslovakia[8] address this period in the history of education and our topic only partially. The studies of Baltic historians of education are collated in the book *History of Pedagogy and Educational Sciences in the Baltic Countries from 1940 to 1990: an Overview*, published in 2013. One part of that volume is devoted to the development of pedagogy as a scientific discipline in Latvia, Estonia, and Lithuania under Soviet rule.[9]

However, none of these studies has focused specifically on the period of transformations in educational sciences after World War II, hence the main question we pursue is how to regard "zero hour" – a post-1945[10] period, when the "old" order was dismantled to make way for a new political and ideological system represented by the Soviet Union. We are aware that the terms "new beginning" and "zero hour" require the most careful handling. Although the

---

8 Justyna Gulczynska, Magdolna Rébay and Dana Kasperová, "History of Education in Central and Eastern Europe: Past, Present, Future", *History of Education* 52, no. 2–3 (2023): 1–44; Tomáš Kasper, "The Field of History of Education – from Development to Stagnation, Crisis and Perhaps a 'New' Beginning: the Czech Example," *Paedagogica Historica* 58, no. 6 (2022): 920–943; Tomáš Kasper, "'Alles muss man umschreiben': Der Wille zum 'neuen Anfang' in der pädagogischen Diskussion in den Fünfzigerjahren," in *Fall des Eisernen Vorhangs 1989 und die Folgen, Europäische pädagogische Perspektiven*, ed. Henning Schluss et al. (Wien: Lit Verlag, 2020), 99–111; Blanka Kudláčová and Andrej Rajský, eds., *Education and "Pädagogik". Philosophical and Historical Reflections (Central, Southern and South-Eastern Europe)* (Berlin, Bratislava: Peter Lang, 2019); Blanka Kudláčová, ed., *Two Sides of the Same Coin. Examples of Free and Unfree Education in Slovakia during the Period of Socialism* (Berlin, Trnava: Peter Lang, 2023).

9 Aīda Krūze, "Development of Pedagogy as a Science in the Baltic Republics under Soviet Rule," in *History of Pedagogy and Educational Sciences in the Baltic Countries from 1940 to 1990: an Overview*, ed. Iveta Ķestere and Aīda Krūze (Riga: RaKa, 2013), 230–234.

10 The various chapters are focused on the development of educational sciences and educational discussion, especially after the Communist Party took power. Timewise, the communist authorities exercised the grip of totalitarian power differently in Central, Eastern, and Southeastern Europe and in the "new" countries of the Soviet Union. While in today's Latvia, it started already 1944, in most Central, Eastern, and Southeastern European countries the period "in between" without communist domination and Soviet control lasted mostly until 1948. Of course, the developments in defeated Germany, the USSR-controlled Eastern Zone (sector), and the future GDR were also time-specific. For these reasons, we speak of the 1945 transition point, when the end of World War II marked an "official" landmark in the political direction of Europe, and thus also of the states we have analysed in Central, Eastern and Southeastern Europe.

"new scientific elite" after 1945 wanted to write the "new" educational sciences and staged the "new beginning" in different ways, previous experience in the field was still present and could not simply be erased from educational theory and practice. We refer to these transformation processes of educational sciences, processes of continuity and discontinuity, as zero hour.[11]

Our studies focus on 1) the relationship between the "autonomy and heteronomy" of educational sciences under the control of state power, including communist ideology,[12] and 2) on the opportunities for and the development of debate in the shadow of the Soviet ideological "pattern", namely sovietization of educational sciences. We ask to what extent can sovietization processes exhaustively characterize the post-1945 developments in educational sciences, and to what extent were the "autonomous" development processes possible and relevant to national contexts and discourses? We are thus interested in a differentiated analysis of relationship between several trends – continuity and discontinuity, autonomy and heteronomy, and instrumentalization of political power, as well as in our own research endeavours. We ask about the processes of "enculturation" of the "new scientist" in radically changed political and social conditions, and we ask how to reconstruct their "new identity". We also ask about the rules, norms, and mechanisms of the "new order" that was established in educational sciences after 1945. We ask to what extent the perspective of instrumentalizing educational sciences for the political, economic and social goals or political "mission" of educational sciences of the "new world" is expressed in the educational debate after 1945. In this sense, an important question is to what extent, under ideological (Marxism-Leninism) "control", educational sciences lose their free critical view and instead prefer scientifically unfruitful dogmatic research methods, thereby experiencing a dramatic decline. This common focus allows us to

---

[11] Jürgen Schriewer, "Problemdimensionen sozialwissenschaftlicher Komparistik," in *Vergleich und Transfer. Komparatistik in den Geschichts-, Sozial- un Kulturwissenschaften*, ed. Jürgen Schriewer and Hartmut Kaelble (Frankfurt am Main, New York: Campus, 2003), 9–54.

[12] Jürgen Kocka, "Wissenschaft und Politik in der DDR," in *Wissenschaft und Wiedervereinigung. Disziplinen im Umbruch*, ed. Jürgen Kocka and Renate Mayntz (Berlin: Akademie Verlag, 1998), 435–460.

examine the post-1945 revisions in educational sciences in Central, Eastern, and Southeastern Europe from a transnational viewpoint.[13]

Setting the Context and Some Methodological Considerations

The idea for the book was conceived at a conference in Trnava, Slovakia, in 2019, where the three editors of this book from the Czech Republic, Latvia, and Hungary, who were familiar for years, met up again. We are all historians of education who have studied our national histories and grappled with the challenges of making them understandable to an international audience. After the collapse of the Eastern-European communist regimes, historians of education faced two old challenges: they had to reconstruct their national (educational) histories and, at the same time reconnect with their Western colleagues. The "new" Europeans' renewed sense of national identity and their enthusiastic presentations were received with some reservations in the West.[14]

We are still struggling with the telling of our story. The transnational turn in the history of education is one of the useful approaches, encouraging self-reflection in the research field, research that transcends local and national boundaries, revealing global trends.[15] How do the European countries that were excluded from the global sphere after World War II and remained behind the Iron Curtain, fit into this transnational perspective? We believe that a kind of transnationalism, still called "internationalisation" in the tradition of

[13] Marcelo Caruso, "Within, Between, Above, and Beyond: (Pre)Positions for a History of the Internalisation of Educational Practises and Knowledge," *Paedagogica Historica* 50, no. 1–2 (2014): 10–26.

[14] Iveta Ķestere, "The 'Nation' in the History of Education from a European 'Postness' Perspective," *Bildungsgeschichte. International Journal for the Historiography of Education* 6, no. 1 (2016): 109–111.

[15] Eugenia Roldán Vera and Eckhardt Fuchs, "Introduction: The Transnational in the History of Education," in *The Transnational in the History of Education. Concepts and Perspectives*, ed. Eckhardt Fuchs and Eugenia Vera Roldán (Palgrave: Macmillan, 2019), 1–47; Eckhardt Fuchs, "Transnational Perspectives in Historical Educational Research," in *Transnationalizing the History of Education*, ed. Eckhardt Fuchs (Leipzig: Leipziger Universitätsverlag, 2012), 7–14.

leftist movements, was also at work in this part of Europe.[16] Moscow was the central actor in the Eastern bloc's international networks coordinating and monitoring local processes in politics and society, including the educational sciences. Here, we can ask whether this can be called the internationalisation of education or whether the label of colonisation applies there.

Our common interest in incorporating educational sciences within the networks of the Soviet Union inspired us to seek out like-minded colleagues. We conceptualised our project by proposing a series of detailed questions that our collaborators could address in their research.

The first group of questions concerned the continuity and discontinuity of educational life in the interwar period and after 1945 in Central, Eastern, and Southeastern Europe: How justified is the reference to "zero hour" in the development of educational sciences and educational debate? Was it more a desire and goal of the new communist political elite in the field of education and science, or can we talk about the new beginning? What legacy did the interwar left-wing or communist pedagogical debate leave behind in the attempt to sovietize educational sciences after 1945? Can this be considered a continuity, or did communist power after 1945 foster fundamentally different conceptions of the man, of educational goals, and different methods and approaches in educational debate? How did the power struggles in the ranks of communist representation influence the direction of professional educational debate?

The second group of questions addressed the processes of sovietization of institutions[17] after 1945 in Central, Eastern and Southeastern Europe: What representative institutions of educational sciences were newly established or

---

16 Roldán Vera and Fuchs, "Transnational Perspectives in Historical Educational Research," 7–14.

17 On the role of institutions – especially universities – in the "transformation of science" according to the Soviet model, we find the following books important John Connelly, *Captive University: The Sovietization of East German, Czech, and Polish Higher Education, 1945–1956* (Chapel Hill: University of North Carolina Press, 2000); Natalia Tsvetkova, *Failure of American and Soviet Cultural Imperialism in German Universities, 1945–1990* (Leiden, Boston: Brill, 2013); Benjamin Tromly, *Making the Soviet Intelligentsia: Universities and Intellectual Life under Stalin and Khrushchev* (Cambridge: Cambridge University Press, 2014). To the key study of sovietization in Czechoslovakia please see Rachel Applebaum, *Empire of Friends: Soviet Power and Socialist Internationalism in Cold War Czechoslovakia* (NY: Cornell University Press, 2019).

renewed their pre-war activities? Who led these institutions, and what goals or program did they pursue? What models were essential for their programming and institutional definition? How were they related to Soviet science, e.g., contacts with Soviet educators, visits to Moscow or the USSR and *vice versa*?

The third group of questions pertained to the sovietization of educational media and the content of educational sciences promoted through subjected media: what topics dominated the educational sciences after 1945, namely were these topics and goals only the result of the exercised political and economic power, or can one consider certain autonomous academic educational debate? What names of Soviet pedagogy became the canon for pedagogy in the countries concerned? When were these works translated, if at all, into the languages of these countries? When and upon whose instigation were "domestic" writings modelled after Soviet educational sciences? Can these products be described as examples of Marxist pedagogy? Did they critically address Marxist philosophy (the teachings of Karl Marx, Friedrich Engels, or Vladimir Ilyich Lenin), or were they rather a list of some dogmatic instructions based on the efforts of communist power to manage and control education in the newly-established regimes? Did these writings lead to a critical analysis of the reference points and goals of Marxist pedagogy, or did they "drain" educational sciences by "stealing" the key questions of its professional education while trying to "publicize" the educational image of the "New (Soviet) Man"? What educational (especially academic) journals were founded, and did they disseminate the canon of Soviet pedagogy?

The fourth group of questions concerned personalities or actors who supported, condemned, or assumed a neutral position in the sovietization of educational sciences in Central, Eastern and Southeastern Europe: How did the exchange of the main figures of educational sciences in the period under research proceed? Who occupied the position of the "new communist elite" in the field of educational sciences? How was the denunciations or removals of domestic scientific elites of the interwar period handled? By what instruments and using what language was the scientific authority of the interwar domestic actors weakened so they could be replaced by the "new" elite?

We recognise that our sets of questions are wide-ranging and challenging, not answerable in one single study, but hopefully opening doors for further research. The articles collected in this volume are an attempt to explore this broad field from at least some national perspectives. We are grateful to those colleagues who responded to our call and look forward to cooperating with those who will also be inspired by the questions posed.

One Centre, Different Paths: Case Studies from Central, Eastern and Southeastern Europe

After World War II, the theoretical foundations, concepts and goals of education established in the inter-war debate were repositioned and/or their meanings revised to meet the demands of Soviet authorities. In some cases, in Central, Eastern, and Southeastern Europe, it was possible to maintain some continuity with the interwar educational debate, but it also implied the implementation of new goals and content in the educational sciences. This situation was determined by post-1945 political and social changes and driven by the international aspirations of communist power from the Soviet centre (see especially Kestere/Zigmunde), as well as from the "domestic" centres of communist power. The authors of the Latvian case study (Kestere/Zigmunde) used the biographical method to investigate the ambivalence or rewriting of the logic and rules of educational theory and practice, using the example of Soviet "missionaries". Similarly, complicated examples of the transformation of educational discourse are visible in the cases of Czechoslovakia (Kasper/Kasperová), the former GDR (Wiegmann), and Hungary (Garai/Pimenta/Németh), as well as in the former Yugoslavia, where sovietization took on quite specific forms due to the political relations between Stalin and Yugoslav leader Tito.

The Yugoslavian case represents a specific form of zero hour, as after the rift with the Stalin-led Soviet Union, Yugoslavia followed its own path not only in the political but also in the socio-cultural space. However, as Medveš' study indicates, the Yugoslavian way was still strongly inspired by Soviet models of educational theory. Marxism-based Yugoslav educational sciences pursued a course that on many levels diverged from the inter-war tradition and was primarily geared towards the political imperatives of the formation of a communist society, rather than trying to find its own path in educational theory. In this respect, the Yugoslav story did not differ so much from those of the other USSR-controlled states in Central, Eastern, and Southeastern Europe. Control and ideological pressure were exercised by the new domestic elites uncritically following Soviet models (Šušnjara).

The Marxist-oriented academic elites were driven more by socio-political than academic and scientific goals. Tito was a strong authority, authoritarian leader and his cult was not unlike that of a Soviet dictator. New institutions (universities, journals, educational research institutes) set the direction of Yugoslav educational thought, but it must always be remembered that different ethno-cultural approaches in Yugoslavia itself differed considerably.

All studies agree that educational research in the countries of Central, Eastern, and Southeastern Europe after 1945 was increasingly challenged by a fundamentally new political and social agenda, including the collective education of the New (Soviet) Man. According to the ideology of the time, the implementation of this collective education required the revolutionary dismantling of the old orders and erecting new rules of logic into scientific life, the rejection of existing educational traditions and the opening up to "proved" Soviet models. The goals of new communist education should have been achieved, inter alia, by forgetting the "old" rules and logic of educational sciences and advancing new models, namely, forcing the idea that the present is not conditioned by the past but by the achievement of a goal that lies in the future (Stępkowski). Rewriting history according to political agendas, re-evaluating ideas and people – erasing them from history or marginalising them on the periphery, ideologically and/or physically – became a priority.

The new tasks in the field of education required reliable actors who could quickly implement communist plans. This led to the creation of a new educational elite, closely associated with high positions in the political and social hierarchy (Kudláčová, Kestere/Zigmunde). This situation that could be called corrupt, weakened independent scientific approaches in educational sciences and made it easy to substitute educational theory with the ideological dogma of Marxism-Leninism.

The authors reconstructed the discursive practices by which the new leaders devalued interwar educational sciences. The study will examine the arguments of the new leaders who discredited inter-war pedagogical research, which allegedly failed to overcome the "bourgeois" presuppositions and was therefore unable to successfully address important pedagogical questions in the new communist reality. Therefore, only the "revolutionary changes" after 1945 could provide the opportunity and power to address truly "new ways" in educational theory and practice. However, a closer reading of the chapters shows that the "new ways", supported by rhetorical and visual propaganda of the "new world order" as well as the power of Marxism and Marxism-Leninism, could not completely neglect the long-established educational traditions at the ideological and personal levels of society (Szabó/Golnhofer/Szabolcs/Polyák/Ruzsa). Yet, the present chapters of the book also show that despite the constant propaganda underlining the revolutionary transformation of education after 1945, the new science continuously flagged the insufficient "progress" in the transformation of educational sciences and practice in the light of socio-political and economic needs of the communist "world order". The reasons for this "non-progressive" state of educational theory and reality were to be found at several levels, namely, in the lack of understanding and poor practical application of the true foundations of Marxist philosophy, in the neglect of Soviet educational models, and in the actions of the "hidden" enemies of the "new" and "better" world.

Marxist educational sciences also justified their legitimacy by corresponding changes in educational practice. The changes and the associated achievements in the educational field were publicly framed as the results of the transformation of educational sciences. Academic evaluation reports and political statements, proudly presented the increase in the number of experts in the educational field. The sources of the time claimed that a new generation of academics was trained, new scientific and specialized educational departments were established, institutes developing "friendly cooperation" with educational institutions in the USSR were supported, and Soviet canons of educational literature were translated. Public statements by academic and political elite at the time indicated that enrolments in secondary and tertiary education were rising, as were the number of teaching positions, the accessibility of higher education, and changes in teacher training.

However, the economic and social, as well as cultural, transformation according to the ideas of the communist authorities did not occur in the educational sphere as quickly and sufficiently as the plans and political statements envisaged. We should also remember the processes and their actors that have been central to the resilience against the "new" models of educational sciences. The failures to replace the "old" tradition of academia with the "new" tradition in many ways was due to the hidden resistance shown by actors at different levels of the educational space. Many actors were simply entrenched in the "self-evident old rules" and therefore could not implement the "new order" as directly and convincingly as they were expected to.

Although the task of implementing revolutionary transformations in education according to *homo sovieticus* unified the new “people’s democracies” under Soviet “patronage”, we must also note the many specifics that separated the various states of the “East”. This can be seen, inter alia, in the examples of curriculum reforms and the “new concept of learning” – polytechnic education. While in Hungary (Somogyvári), polytechnic education after 1956 was in many respects “finished” and recognised as a failed concept, in Czechoslovakia (Kasper/Kasperová), despite failures, ways and models were repeatedly sought to develop the principles of polytechnic education and to introduce them into educational theory and practice.

The speed of Soviet-inspired changes also often differed from one country to another (Garai/Pimenta/Németh), which points to the confusion and differences in the acceptance, advocacy, and implementation of new order in educational sciences and practice. We can also see the capacity of each country to resist the new socio-political conditions, e.g., the case of the East German revolt of 1953, as well as the Hungarian and Polish acts of resistance in 1956. Comparing the development of educational sciences in the Central, Eastern, and Southeastern European countries under study, we can conclude that, despite the extensive centralisation of academic and pedagogical life, it was not easy to regulate educational theory and practice centrally. Reality therefore was “lagging” behind the constantly innovating plans.

Thus, sovietization did not mean a unilateral and non-conflicting adoption of the Soviet educational model in different countries. It was impossible to avoid the specificities of these countries and their cultural, scientific and political traditions. The authors agree that the pressure to adopt Soviet models became more acute after 1945. This adoption was facilitated by the publication of Soviet educational canons and translated textbooks into the national languages, as well as by directly installing Soviet envoys as “new” leaders of educational sciences, e.g., in Latvia. On the other hand, clearly not everything went as the Soviet or communist leaders expected. The transfer and transition were accomplished by similar or identical procedures and methods, e.g., exchange of elites, prohibitions of interwar literature, denunciation of “bourgeois” relations to interwar science and alleged nationalism, cosmopolitanism, and idealism as opposed to the dialectic, materialism, and internationalism of Marxist educational sciences. Nevertheless, the transformation of educational sciences took place in each country with some peculiarities, namely with respect to the specific political, economic, social and cultural context. This context differed to a significant level in the Eastern German occupation zone (later the GDR), Hungary and Latvia in comparison to the "victorious" countries of World War II, such as Czechoslovakia or Poland. The national, conservative, or liberal traditions of each country also played an important role in how Soviet-imported ideas were read and received there.

The comparison of the development of educational theory and practice in various countries further shows that although political developments changed the atmosphere in society in the early 1960s after Stalin's death in 1953, the following "thaw" and "revision" in the Communist Party structures did not question the basic socialist/communist orientation of educational sciences in Central, Eastern, and Southeastern Europe in the coming years.

Although the space given to Marxist-Leninist dogmas and Stalinist declarations in educational debate weakened after the Congress of the Communist Party of the Soviet Union in 1956, the overall development of educational sciences remained true to both Marxist jargon and political instrumentalization (Wiegmann). While the tempo of the sovietization of educational theory, as well as related propoganda got slightly relaxed, the politicization of educational sciences remained unabated. That said, this period and the "liberation" or "pedagogical spring" require further attention from researchers.

Bibliography

Applebaum, Rachel. *Empire of Friends: Soviet Power and Socialist Internationalism in Cold War Czechoslovakia*. NY: Cornell University Press, 2019.

Benecke, Jakob, ed. *Erziehungs- und Bildungsverhältnisse in der DDR*. Bad Heilbrunn: Klinkhardt, 2022.

Caruso, Marcelo. "Within, Between, Above, and Beyond: (Pre)Positions for a History of the Internalisation of Educational Practises and Knowledge." *Paedagogica Historica* 50, no. 1–2 (2014): 10–26.

Connelly, John. *Captive University: The Sovietization of East German, Czech, and Polish Higher Education, 1945–1956*. Chapel Hill: University of North Carolina Press, 2000.

Fuchs, Eckhardt. "Transnational Perspectives in Historical Educational Research." In *Transnationalizing the History of Education*, edited by Eckhardt Fuchs, 7–14. Leipzig: Leipziger Universitätsverlag, 2012.

Geißler, Gert, and Ulrich Wiegmann. *Schule und Erziehung in der DDR. Studien und Dokumente*. Neuwied: Luchterhand, 1995.

Gulczynska, Justyna. "The Student in the Polish Socialist Secondary School (1945–1989): a Cultural Context." *Paedagogica Historica* 53, no. 1–2, (2017): 170–188.

Gulczynska, Justyna, Rébay Magdolna, and Daan Kasperová. "History of Education in Central and Eastern Europe: Past, Present, Future." *History of Education* 52, no. 2–3 (2023): 1–44.

Hejnicka-Bezwińska, Teresa. *Zarys historii wychowania (1944–1989)*. Kielce: Wydawnictwo Pedagogiczne ZNP, 1996.

Hopfner, Johanna, Németh, András, and Éva Szabolcs. *Kindheit-Schule-Erziehungswissenschaft in Mitteleuropa 1948–2008*. Bruxelles: Peter Lang, 2009.

Jonnes, Polly. "From the Secret Speech to the Burial of Stalin: Real and Ideal Responses to de-Stalinization." In *The Dilemmas of De-Stalinisation: a Social and Cultural History of Reform in the Khrushchev Era*, edited by Polly Jones, 41–63. London: Routledge, 2006.

Kasper, Tomáš. "The Field of History of Education – from Development to Stagnation, Crisis and Perhaps a 'New' Beginning: the Czech Example." *Paedagogica Historica* 58, no. 6 (2022): 920–943.

Kasper, Tomáš. "'Alles muss man umschreiben': Der Wille zum 'neuen Anfang' in der pädagogischen Diskussion in den Fünfzigerjahren." In *Fall des Eisernen Vorhangs 1989 und die Folgen, Europäische pädagogische Perspektiven*, edited by Henning Schluss et al., 99–111. Wien: Lit Verlag, 2020.

Ķestere, Iveta. "The 'Nation' in the History of Education from a European 'Postness' Perspective." *Bildungsgeschichte. International Journal for the Historiography of Education* 6, no. 1 (2016): 109–111.

Kocka, Jürgen. "Wissenschaft und Politik in der DDR." In *Wissenschaft und Wiedervereinigung. Disziplinen im Umbruch*, edited by Jürgen Kocka and Renate Mayntz, 435–460. Berlin: Akademie Verlag, 1998.

Krūze, Aīda. "Development of Pedagogy as a Science in the Baltic Republics under Soviet Rule." In *History of Pedagogy and Educational Sciences in the Baltic Countries from 1940 to 1990: an Overview*, edited by Iveta Ķestere, and Aīda Krūze, 230–234. Riga: RaKa, 2013.

Kudláčová, Blanka and Andrej Rajský, eds. *Education and "Pädagogik". Philosophical and Historical Reflections (Central, Southern and South-Eastern Europe)*. Berlin, Bratislava: Peter Lang, 2019.

Kudláčová, Blanka, ed. *Two Sides of the Same Coin. Examples of Free and Unfree Education in Slovakia during the Period of Socialism*. Berlin, Trnava: Peter Lang, 2023.

Malycha, Andreas. *Die Akademie der Pädagogiachen Wissenschaften in der DDR 1970 bis 1990. Zur Geschichte einer Wissenschaftsinstitution im Kontext staatlicher Bildungspolitik*. Leipzig: Akademische Verlagsanstalt, 2008.

Medveš, Zdenko. "Socialist Pedagogy: Caught between the Myth of the Fairness of the Unified School and Cultural Hegemony." *Sodobna pedagogika. Journal of Contemporary Educational Studies* 66, no. 2 (2015): 14–41.

Németh, András. *Erziehungswissenschaft in Ungarn (1870–1952)*. Budapest: Gondolat, 2013.

Németh, András and Éva Szabolcs. "Educational Science as an Academic Discipline in Hungary (1867–1953): Turns and Developmental Phases." In *Folds of Past, Present and Future: Reconfiguring Contemporary Histories of Education*, edited by Sarah Ruyskenvelde, Geert Thyssen, Frederik Herman, Angelo van Gorp and Pieter Verstraete, 249–266. Berlin, München, Boston: De Gruyter Oldenbourg, 2021.

Plamper, Jan. *The Stalin Cult: a Study in the Alchemy of Power*. Stanford: California: Stanford University, 2012.

Protner, Edvard, ed. *Razvoj i aktualne tendencije pedagogije i školstva na području nekadašnje Jugoslavije*. Maribor: University of Maribor Press, 2020.

Roldán Vera, Eugenia and Eckhardt Fuchs. "Introduction: The Transnational in the History of Education." In *The Transnational in the History of Education. Concepts and Perspectives*, edited by Eckhardt Fuchs and Vera Roldán Eugenia, 1–47, Palgrave: Macmillan, 2019.

Schriewer, Jürgen. "Problemdimensionen sozialwissenschaftlicher Komparistik." In *Vergleich und Transfer. Komparatistik in den Geschichts-, Sozial- un Kulturwissenschaften*, edited by Jürgen Schriewer and Hartmut Kaelble, 9–54. Frankfurt am Main, New York: Campus, 2003.

Śliwerski, Bogusław. "Main Development Lines of Polish Pedagogy from Socialist Orthodoxy to Postmodern Heterogeneity." *Polska Myśl Pedagogiczna*, no. 5 (2019): 17–51.

Tenorth, Heinz-Elmar, and Ulrich Wiegmann. *Pädagogische Wissenschaft in der DDR. Ideologieproduktion, Systemreflexion und Erziehungsforschung.* Bad Heilbrunn: Klinkhardt, 2022.

Tromly, Benjamin. *Making the Soviet Intelligentsia: Universities and Intellectual Life under Stalin and Khrushchev*. Cambridge: Cambridge University Press, 2014.

Tsvetkova, Natalia. *Failure of American and Soviet Cultural Imperialism in German Universities, 1945–1990*. Leiden, Boston: Brill, 2013.

Wojdon, Joanna. "The System of Textbook Approval in Poland under Communist Rule (1944–1989) as a Tool of Power of the Régime." *Paedagogica Historica* 51, no. 1–2 (2015): 181–196.

PART TWO

Sovietization of Educational Sciences: General

A New Beginning? Educational Sciences between Continuity and Discontinuity in Czechoslovakia, 1945–1960

Tomáš Kasper and Dana Kasperová

Abstract: The study focuses on processes of importing Soviet educational writing and Soviet ideological knowledge into the Czech educational debate after 1945, and particularly after the communist success in the Czechoslovakian election of 1948, focusing on questions of continuity and discontinuity. The central question is how Marxist educational doctrine and the Soviet educational canon were implemented in Czech educational sciences after 1945 and 1948 respectively, by which means and through which actors? We examine how the politicization and control of educational thought by the Czechoslovak Communist Party took place and how the state planned, designed and controlled the process and development of educational sciences. Finally, the chapter focuses on the question of the techniques employed to achieve the Marxist ideologization of Czechoslovak educational sciences.

Keywords: Ideologization of science, Sovietization of science, socialism, political instrumentalization of science, Marxist science, planning of science, Czechoslovakia

The Development of Educational Sciences and the Question of Continuity and Discontinuity – "Beginnings, Breakthroughs, Changes and Traditions"

Educational sciences in Czechoslovakia lived their "new beginning" several times in the 20th century. The collapse of the Austro-Hungarian monarchy and the creation of Czechoslovakia in 1918 were major political breakthroughs. This, of course, also changed social, cultural, educational and scientific life in the region, though to a somewhat lesser degree the educational thinking and focus of Czechoslovakian educational sciences. A much greater transition took place in 1938, after the signing of the Munich Agreement, the occupation of the Czech Sudetenland and the subsequent annexation of the remaining Czechoslovakian territory in March 1939. The period between 1939 and 1945 was characterised by major political and cultural change. This was intensified after 17 November 1939 when the Czech universities were closed and thus Czech cultural and scientific life in the Nazi-controlled Protectorate of Bohemia and Moravia was completely frozen. The free development of Czech educational thought in the public sphere was impossible.

The previous receptivity of Czech educational thinking to many foreign impulses and contacts, Czech-German scientific cooperation and exchanges and Czech-Slovak influences during the interwar period were challenged or interrupted by external factors in 1939–1945. This experience was reflected by the actions of the principal leaders of educational thought who disappeared into enforced silence, internal exile or even hidden resistance during World War II. 1945 can be seen as a major transition period, when the war experience significantly changed the perception of the interwar democratic socio-political order and previously held cultural-scientific positions, views and aspirations. 1948 saw the emergence of the tendency to discredit the 'dysfunctional' democratic order of the interwar period which resulted in a struggle over the future political and socio-cultural direction of Czechoslovakia. By this point, the competition was already influenced by the rivalry between the East and West.[1] At the same time, Czechoslovakia was incorporated - partly through its own decisions, partly due to external actions, Allied war-time agreements and post-war negotiations – into the sphere of influence of the Soviet Union.

After 1948, it was not in the interest of the new authorities that the cultural and scientific efforts of social reform of the interwar period should be reflected openly or praised in any way. The emphasis was on the interwar failings of all efforts to alter society, including the reform of education and the upbringing of children. After 1948, inter-war democracy was characterised by the communist authorities as having been unable to solve fundamental social and societal problems, and also as weak because it had "easily" given in to Nazi totalitarianism.

The failure to solve the social and economic problems of the interwar period and the war itself were deemed to prove that Czechoslovakia should leave the "old way of thinking, the old way of doing things" and embark on a radically "new" way. It was a call to "shine the light of success" and the revolutionary victory of communism based on the model of the Soviet

---

1 Christiane Brenner, *"Zwischen Ost und West": tschechische politische Diskurse 1945–1948* (München: Oldenbourg, 2009).

Union.[2] "New patterns, new actors with new leaders, new thinking embodied in new doctrine" were to guarantee the success of the transformation into a "new society" and guarantee the education and training of a "New Man"[3].

The fundamental changes brought about by the Bolshevik Revolution of 1917 and the subsequent Soviet way were to become the defining model for Czechoslovakia. This would, of course, mean revolutionary political change and fundamental cultural and social transformation. This change, despite of the support of a part of the public, and in spite of the aggression of the totalitarian communist power, could not take place as an "exchange" of one world for another, or as a transformation of one order for another. We ask, therefore, in what direction, according to what models and plans was the world of educational sciences changed in Czechoslovakia? Which actors constructed and controlled these transformation processes? How was this agenda and ways of the new educational sciences promoted and followed? How was it, in turn, rejected – publicly or covertly – and weakened by the power of the old scientific identity?[4]

Actors and the "Field" of Educational Sciences after 1948 in Czechoslovakia

After 1945, education was given a much more space to develop, shape and influence political and social changes. The politicization of education also changed the status and standing of educational sciences. This was increased even more after 1946 with the establishment of faculties of education at the universities, providing higher education for teachers. The establishment of these faculties of education and non-university scientific institutions allowed greater opportunities for the employment of more educational experts and,

---

2 Markéta Devátá et al., *Vědní koncepce KSČ a její institucionalizace po roce 1948* (Praha: Ústav pro soudobé dějiny AV ČR, 2010), 9–96. Markéta Devátá, *Marxismus jako projekt nové společnosti: Dvě studie ke společenským vědám (1945–1969)* (Praha: Ústav pro soudobé dějiny AV ČR, 2014).

3 Monica E. Mincu, "Communist Education as Modernisation Strategy? The Swings of the Globalisation Pendulum in Eastern Europe (1947–1989)," *History of Education* 45, no. 3 (2016): 319–334.

4 To the question of power and knowledge see Michel Foucault, *The Archaeology of Knowledge and the Discourse on Language* (New York: Pantheon, 1972).

to some extent, a new generation of teachers. However, despite these apparent improvements, it must be stressed that Law No. 58 on Higher Education of 1950 strongly instrumentalised higher education both politically and ideologically, "putting it at the service of the people" and explicitly led it in the spirit of "the new era and the educational requirements for a communist society". Moreover, this Law radically restricted the academic freedom of universities and colleges, as well as bringing their academic activities, both scientific and educational, under the control of the state power (e.g., the Ministry of Education) and the "supervision" of the Communist Party of Czechoslovakia (CPC).

Educational sciences marked a significant milestone in 1954, when the Pedagogical Cabinet (Pedagogical Department) was established within the Czechoslovak Academy of Sciences (CAS), founded in 1952.[5] In 1957 the Cabinet was transformed into the Pedagogical Institute of J. A. Comenius (PI JAC CSA) of the Czechoslovak Academy of Sciences. It also had collaborators in Slovakia in Bratislava at the Slovak Academy of Sciences (part of the CAS). An important partner of PI JAC CAS was the Research Institute of Education in Prague and later also in Brno (RIE Prague, RIE Brno)[6] and the State Educational Institute in Bratislava – SEI Bratislava, later renamed the Research Institute of Education in Bratislava (RIE Bratislava).[7] The scientific young generation in educational sciences was mainly developed by the Czechoslovak Academy of Sciences, which also provided the doctoral

5 Martin Franc and Věra Dvořáčková, *Dějiny Československé akademie věd I.* (Praha: Academia, 2019).

6 The Research Institute of Education in Prague was founded in 1945 by the Ministry of Education. The Institute had an office in Brno, and was managed by Josef Váňa, Dean of the Faculty of Education at Charles University in Prague and later an important figure in the PI JAC CAS. In 1956, according to the report on the control of research institutes, the RIE scientific staff numbered 93. In total, including the Brno office, it had 151 employees. Source: MÚA AV ČR, fund Presidium ČSAV, carton 6.

7 State Educational Institute in Bratislava – SEI Bratislava, later Research Institute of Education in Bratislava (RIE Bratislava), was established by a decree of the Slovak National Council in 1947. According to the report on the control of research institutes, RIE Bratislava had 48 employees, including 36 in scientific positions in 1956. Source: MÚA AV ČR, fund Presidium ČSAV, carton 6.

programme (aspirancy courses[8]) for the RIE (Prague, Brno) and for university staff.

These transformations offered greater space for educational research, but, at the same time, posed risks of overlapping research tasks and topics, as well as fragmentation or duplication of educational research. Multiple educational research institutions also required coordinated management and cooperation on research projects. If we compare the research tasks carried out at RIE Prague, Brno and SEI Bratislava and at the Pedagogical Cabinet and later at PI JAC CAS. It is clear that the research at RIE exhibited the character of applied research, more connected with educational practice, while at PI JAC CAS, they gave more emphasis to issues of basic educational research, history of education and the research to the work and thought of J. A. Comenius. Between 1950–1956, the RIE and SEI focused on research in the following areas: early writing and reading; the basic curriculum in Czech, Slovak, Russian and mathematics; school hygiene; research in physical education, aesthetic education and extracurricular activities. The solution of research tasks was to help in particular changes in school teaching, e.g. selection of curriculum, new textbooks, in the planning and implementation of after-school activities, in the functioning of schools (e.g. hygiene, school

---

8 The scientific *Aspirantship* is a specific term adopted from the language of Soviet science and *de facto* referred to the stage of scientific gradation – in contemporary terms, doctoral studies. Scientific aspirantships were introduced at the CAS soon after the establishment of the Academy in 1953. The aspirancy was to be for a maximum of 3 years, with the age limit of aspirants set to 40 years. Scientific aspirantships were managed by the Presidium of the Czechoslovak Academy of Sciences and by the Ministry of Education at universities. Both the CAS and the Ministry of Education worked conceptually and consistently, arranging changes to the organisational and study regulations of the aspirantry and sending aspirants to the USSR. The Aspirantship included the study of a chosen scientific discipline, Marxist philosophy, language instruction (compulsory Russian and a second language, usually English or German) and the defence of a dissertation prepared under the guidance of a supervisor.

furniture, etc.), and the field of polytechnic education.[9] As will be pointed out, the question of the selection of the basic curriculum and the production of new textbooks was not only one of the tasks of the RIE and SEI, but also one of the important research problems at the CAS. Thus, the staff of the Ministry of Education and associated research institutes came together with the staff of CAS to work on the design of new textbooks.

The position of the social sciences and humanities within the CAS was quite different from that of the natural sciences. Research in the field of technology and natural sciences was given expert space and autonomy, both from a scientific point of view and also regarding foreign cooperation with Western countries. This supportive position was adopted, because the results of technical and natural sciences research could quickly and successfully support the "victory of communist power" and thereby stimulate the development of a socialist state-planned economy. The development of these communist objectives was based on the power of technology and a technocratic approach to the world and man. The social sciences and humanities, on the other hand, were more ideologised and the key aim here was to break the connections with Western currents of thought, to make cooperation with Western colleagues difficult or impossible, and to replace any Western influence with Soviet models and Marxist philosophy, specifically the teachings of Marxism-Leninism.[10] The "progress" and "victory" of communism in the social sciences were conditional on the abandonment of traditions and the rapid ideological transformation of science. Therefore, translations of the "canons" of Soviet scientific works were required, as well as the institutional and personal interconnection of Czech and Soviet science, (both of the older scientific generation and especially of the young scientific community using the power of the asiprantship). Institutions of Czechoslovak-Soviet

9 Polytechnic education was the central task of the "new" socialist comprehensive school, as it was required to train pupils during compulsory schooling for practical work, for their eventual entry into employment or for their further education at secondary vocational institutes. Polytechnic education was also expected to embody an effort to link school and practice, to promote education for work experience. The terms and concept of polytechnic education and training became a central topic of socialist pedagogy in the 1950s and 1960s.

10 John Connelly, *Captive University: The Sovietization of East German, Czech, and Polish Higher Education, 1945–1956* (Chapel Hill: University of North Carolina Press, 2000).

"cooperation and friendship"[11] were also important agents of the sovietization of Czech/Czechoslovak science after 1948. In the case of CAS, this was the Czechoslovak-Soviet Institute of the CAS.[12]

The reorganization of scientific life, determined by the establishment of the CAS in 1952, came relatively late compared to the "reform" of higher education in 1950. We can conclude that the Academy was (in terms of time) spared the intense ideological transformation to which higher education was subjected. As noted above, however, the social sciences and humanities were also the focus of ideological indoctrination in the CAS, and the leaders of "the new" humanities were often ideologically and politically mindful and active political representatives loyal to, or closely associated with, the communist authorities.

Lastly, we are able to reconstruct the post-1948 discussion of educational science in the context of the development and transformation of primary and secondary education. In 1948, the Law on the Unified Socialist School, regulating the structure of the educational system in the Czechoslovak Republic, was adopted. The Law abolished the segregation of pupils into different types of secondary schools of the interwar period and instead introduced an educational institution within which the whole population was educated over a period of eight years, namely from six to fourteen years of age. Educational sciences received the task of making the transition of education to the challenges of people's democratic and socialist education – in the fields of curriculum design, school education, extracurricular activities, vocational education, and the reform of secondary education.

---

11 Rachel Applebaum, *Empire of Friends: Soviet Power and Socialist Internationalism in Cold War Czechoslovakia* (Ithaca: Cornell University Press, 2019).

12 The Czechoslovak-Soviet Institute (CSI) was founded at the Ministry of Education in 1950 and was not primarily a research institute. Since 1952 it had been incorporated into the Czechoslovak Academy of Sciences. The Institute's task was to "strengthen the scientific anchorage" of Czech-Soviet relations and their further development. On 1 January 1954, the Institute of Russian Language, Literature and History of the USSR was separated from the Institute. Since 1956, the CAS published the journal Czechoslovak Russian Studies (by fusing the journals *Soviet Linguistics*, *Soviet Literature* and *Soviet History*) and co-published several comprehensive publications, of which the literary and historical emphasized the cultural and historical interconnection of Czechoslovakia and the USSR (Cf. Czechoslovak-Soviet Institute of the Czechoslovak Academy of Sciences. MÚA AV ČR, fonds Presidium ČSAV, carton 11).

In summary, we can say that the post-1948 development of educational sciences in Czechoslovakia shows how the tasks of science were largely set by the requirements of educational practice, which was co-determined by the socio-political demands of the totalitarian power of communists. Furthermore, the tasks of science were conditioned by ideological starting points, e.g. Marxist-Leninist revolutionary doctrine, and the Soviet model of education. After 1948, it was very problematic, almost impossible, to defend the scientific independence and autonomy of educational thinking in Czechoslovakia.

The Pedagogical Department of the Czechoslovak Academy of Sciences (1954–1957): Science in the Context of Scientific Autonomy and Political Instrumentalization

The Act on the Establishment of the CAS[13] of 29 October 1952 and the opening of the CAS on 17 November 1952 should have marked the beginning of a "new science".[14] The replacement of the former scientific institutions[15] under one joint institution of CAS was to physically embody the centralization of science in communist Czechoslovakia, its state planning and the interconnection of science and the "reform" of the economy.[16] On the one hand, the authorities of the CAS were given significant autonomy in the

13 Act No. 52/1952 Coll.

14 Iveta Kestere and Manuel Joaquín Fernández González, "Educating the New Soviet Man: Propagated Image and Hidden Resistance in Soviet Latvia," *Historia scholastica* 7, no. 1 (2021): 11–32.

15 Section 1(2) of Act No. 52/1952 Coll. states that the CAS follows the tradition of Czech and Slovak science, in particular the institutions of the Royal Czech Society of Sciences, founded in 1784 (dissolved in 1945) and the Czech Academy of Sciences and Arts (founded in 1890). The Act does not mention the institutions of German science on Czech territory (German institutions of science led by so-called Czech Germans, i.e. inhabitants of Czech lands of German nationality, in the 19th and first half of the 20th century). Also, the law terminated the activities of the Masaryk Academy of Labour (founded in 1920, where applied research in the social sciences was developed).

16 Science (basic and applied research) becomes an independent field (a department with an institutional background, plan, programme, financial coverage, management and control of the state power) and an instrument for the successful development of society in the spirit of communist goals, as declared by the law and many conceptual materials on science in the 1950s in Czechoslovakia.

management of the institution; however, the management of the institution was controlled by the Ministry of Education, which was itself managed by the communist authorities. This is illustrated, among other, by the figure of the first chairman of the CAS, Zdeněk Nejedlý[17].

The CAS was divided into eight sections after its foundation. Within the sixth section (historical and philosophical) there was also the so-called Pedagogical Cabinet acting from 1 January 1954, which was transformed from 1 January 1957 into the Pedagogical Institute of J. A. Comenius CAS (PI JAC CAS).

The Pedagogical Cabinet initially had three employees, from 1 July 1954 a total of five employees and at the beginning of 1955 there were already seven employees. They worked both in educational sciences and in psychology. In 1956, the number of staff increased due to the expansion and fulfilment of tasks in J. A. Comenius studies (publishing the writings of J. A. Comenius). At the end of 1956, the Cabinet had a total of thirteen scientific and expert staff, as well as three assistant staff and one administrative staff member.[18] The programme of scientific research activities in the field of educational sciences was discussed in 1955 and 1956 by a commission set up for this purpose. The commission consisted of both experts and members of the Ministry of Education. Thus, both the educational as well as the socio-political tasks of educational sciences were emphasized.

An expert group was set up in the Pedagogical Cabinet. There was one researcher and two experts in the theory of education and teaching (the basic

---

17 The first director of the Czechoslovak Academy of Sciences was the communist leader Zdeněk Nejedlý (1878–1962), who was a representative of interwar left-wing intellectuals. He spent the period of Nazi occupation in exile in Moscow (also as a professor at Lomonosov University), where he joined the Communist Party. After the liberation of Czechoslovak territory, Nejedlý held high positions in the Communist Party for cultural and educational policy and was also Minister of Education from 1945–1946 and 1948–1953, then Minister without portfolio. Nejedlý thus demonstrates the direct connection between the communist power of the state and the CAS.

18 Cf. Transformation of the Pedagogical Cabinet of the Czechoslovak Academy of Sciences. Material prepared by Prof. Chlup in 1956 for the presidium of the CAS and discussed in the historical section in February 1957 (MÚA AV ČR, Presidium of the Czechoslovak Academy of Sciences, carton 10).

curriculum as a compulsory base for all pupils, new curricula)[19]. In the history of education and Comenius studies there were two researchers and six expert staff. In psychology there was one researcher and one expert staff member.[20] The primary task of the Pedagogical Cabinet was, according to the report of its Head, academician Prof. Otokar Chlup (1875–1965), to develop a new university textbook of educational sciences. However, this was not achieved in the period between 1954–1956. From 1954 Prof. Chlup also worked on the research of basic curriculum and textbook research for comprehensive schools, which was intended to support the implementation of the socialist school, the reform of the school system and teacher education in accordance with the intentions of Education Law No. 31 of 1953.[21] In fact, Chlup's research into the theory of education and teaching stagnated.[22] Anthologies on the

---

19 Not only the Pedagogical Cabinet of the Czechoslovak Academy of Sciences, but also the RIE Prague and the staff of the Faculties of Education worked on the task of designing the new curriculum.

20 The founding member of the psychological section was Dr. Jan Doležal. He officially advocated the importance of I. P. Pavlov's psychology for the development of socialist psychology in the 1950s.

21 Act No. 31 of 1953 replaced the Education Act No. 95 of April 1948 and significantly reformed the Czechoslovak school system away from existing educational traditions. The 1953 Law declared an aim to shape the school system according to the model and experience of the Soviet school and the Soviet educational system. It was therefore seen by the wider public as a manifestation of the Sovietization of Czechoslovak education. This initial itercation of the changed system soon proved to be a failure in the eyes of many reformers. Consequently, the system was again reformed by Law Act No. 186/1960 Coll., which returned in many respects to the form of the school system in force before the 1953 Act. Although the 1953 Act guaranteed secondary education for nearly everyone, as the lower secondary level was *de facto* called secondary school, it was not a qualitative change in education. The Law could be read as a norm supporting the formal completion of ideological-political goals of raising the level of education for the broad ("working class") population. Law No. 31 of 1953 also radically changed teacher education for the new school system.

22 Otokar Chlup, *Z teorie výchovy a vyučování: Sborník pedagogických studií* (Praha: Československá akademie věd, 1962). And Otokar Chlup, *Podmínky výchov a vzdělávání na národní škole* (Praha: SPN, 1960).

history of education[23] and selected works of Comenius were published, as well as research on aesthetic education.[24]

The transformation of the Pedagogical Cabinet at PI JAC CAS (requiring personnel expansion and the enlargement of academic premises) reflected the scientific development of the Cabinet with more systematic research in the theory of education and teaching, history of education and curriculum. Prof. Chlup, in his 1955 text for the presidium of the Czechoslovak Academy of Sciences regarding the state and development of educational sciences in the Czechoslovakia and the role of the Czechoslovak Academy of Sciences, supported the personnel expansion of the Pedagogical Institute for several reasons. First of all, the CAS was to play a (legally mandated) leading role in the coordination of scientific development in the spirit of communist ideology. The Pedagogical Institute was to study and monitor educational sciences in the USSR[25], but also in other "people's democratic" states and also in capitalist countries to develop scientific contacts. According to Chlup, the Pedagogical Institute at the CAS was to help plan and implement the transformation of education so that education would support the fulfilment of the goals of the communist society and socialist economy. The "success" of the formation of a socialist society should have been determined by a "new view" of general education, which should no longer emphasize only its linguistic aspect in classical languages (as in the interwar period), but should balance language, literary, natural sciences and, above all, mathematical education. It was also required to be in accordance with the demands of work – polytechnic education. The socialist school was to "stand close" to socialist everyday life to achieve a balance between intellectualism and practicality. Education was also expected to lead to the acquisition of work habits and manual skills, an overview of production and the demands of economic practice. The aim of educational sciences was also the development of the pupils' "scientific worldview" and understanding of Marx's dialectic (historical materialism).

---

23 Otokar Chlup, *Čítanka k dějinám pedagogiky pro pedagogické vyšší a vysoké pedagogické školy. Díl 1., K dějinám pedagogiky do vzniku marxismu* (Praha: SPN, 1955).

24 Otokar Chlup and Antonín Sychra, *O estetické výchově* (Praha: Státní nakladatelství dětské knihy, 1956).

25 In 1956, a delegation of "leading figures" of Soviet educational sciences – among others, Ivan Andreevich Kairov and Nikita K. Goncharov – visited the Pedagogical Cabinet of the Czechoslovak Academy of Sciences.

Education was to be developed in such a way that the distinctions between physical and mental work, industrial and agricultural labour "disappear".

It is clear, therefore, that the task of socialist educational sciences was to achieve the goals that were based on the requirements for the formation of a socialist society. Thanks to the new educational sciences, the school was to be more efficient – it was to educate the mass of pupils, to prevent failure and the repetition of grades, to modify (select and limit) the basic curriculum, to prepare pupils to enter quickly into public life and practice of socialist society; to enable them to participate quickly and successfully in the running and development of socialist production and economy, These principles would also influence the public and private lives of all citizens in the state. The tasks of educational sciences, the socialist school and the training of new teachers were derived from the tasks of building socialism. They were described and expressed in the same language of ideology, they were legitimized by the logic of "building a new world": "our primary task is (…) to instill our future teachers with enthusiasm for the role of educational collaborator and co-builder of this new society without human exploitation, building a life of peace and intensive labour".[26] It is thus clear that educational research was based on external and specific political, social and ideological goals. The official programmes of socialist educational sciences of CAS did not shy away from discussion of "the democratic educational way", "education for socialist humanism" and "building on the tradition of progressive educational ideals". This is also evidenced by the 1956 argument (supporting the creation of PI JAC CAS)[27], where Prof. Chlup speaks of the necessity of reconstructing the methodology of educational sciences on the basis of Marxism-Leninism, the necessity of overcoming the remnants of pedagogical reformism[28], positivist

[26] Pedagogical problems and tasks. Material by academician Prof. O. Chlup. MÚA AV ČR, Presidium ČSAV fund.

[27] The transformation of the Cabinet of Educational Sciences of the Czechoslovak Academy of Sciences. Material from Prof. Chlup for the Presidium of the CAS discussed in the Historical Section in February 1957. MÚA AV ČR, Presidium of the Czechoslovak Academy of Sciences, carton 10.

[28] This refers to the Czech and Slovak interwar educational reform movement.

and pragmatic philosophy and psychology from the "bourgeois period" of the First Republic[29].

At the same time, however, it is clear that the process was not entirely successful, in the eyes of the actors themselves: "The development of our educational sciences was obstructed, firstly, by the remnants of idealistic thinking, and secondly, by a misunderstanding or dogmatic application of the principles of Marxism-Leninism, which led, among other, to a one-sided emphasis on the social nature of educational phenomena without taking into account the biological and psychological principles of child development. Such a conception led to a 'pedagogy without children', to a disconnection between theory and practice, and was reflected in the neglect of certain research methods, especially experimental ones, which made it impossible to overcome speculativeness, voluntarism and normativism more effectively in the educational sciences."[30]

A similar situation emerges when examining the "victory" of Marxism in philosophy. Here, too, the ideological perspective did not seem to have established itself as quickly as was expected. In 1954, Miloš Kaláb (1920–1994)[31], a researcher in the field of philosophy and later a sociologist from the Department of Philosophy at the Czechoslovak Academy of Sciences, emphasized the fact that many scientists were slow and inconsistent in adopting the dialectical method and theory of materialism on the Soviet model,

---

29 Transformation of the Cabinet of Pedagogical Sciences of the Czechoslovak Academy of Sciences. Material from Prof. Chlup for the Presidium of the CAS and discussed in the Historical Section in February 1957. MÚA AV ČR, Presidium of the Czechoslovak Academy of Sciences, carton 10.

30 Transformation of the Cabinet of Pedagogical Sciences of the Czechoslovak Academy of Sciences. Material from Prof. Chlup for the Presidium of the CAS and discussed in the Historical Section in February 1957. MÚA AV ČR, Presidium of the Czechoslovak Academy of Sciences, carton 10.

31 Miloš Kaláb (1920–1994) belonged to the "cadres" of Marxist philosophy and Marxist sociology; he significantly developed sociology in this spirit in the 1960s. From 1957–62 he became Director of the Institute of Marxism-Leninism for Higher Education at Charles University in Prague. Between 1965–70 he was Director of the Institute of Sociology of the Czechoslovak Academy of Sciences. See Sociologická encyklopedie. "Kaláb Miloš." Accessed September 23, 2024. https://encyklopedie.soc.cas.cz/w/Kal%C3%A1b_Milo%C5%A1.

and persisting in idealistic views of philosophy and in dogmatism.[32] Kaláb adds: "Soviet philosophy must be for us a model of the connection between theory and practice, a model of how to relate to actual, living problems, these special problems of history, the problem of scientific communism. Soviet philosophy shows us what the application of the principles of the Party in the field of philosophy means. Partisanship – it is not something external to philosophy, it is its very essence, the basis of its scientific existence. (…) The consistent application of the principle of partisanship, the consistent orientation towards current issues, the connection of philosophical work with the needs of our building of socialism, this will be the best medicine against any dogmatism."[33]

The Pedagogical Institute of J. A. Comenius CAS (1957–60) – Science as a Part of Planning Social Changes in the Second Five-year Period

The Pedagogical Institute of J. A. Comenius was established on 1 January 1957 and had three departments. These were (1) the Department of Theory of Education (2) the Department of History of Education; and (3) the Department of Educational Psychology. The Department of Theory of Education focused on research on curriculum in the comprehensive school, on issues of basic curriculum, polytechnic education, as well as issues of aesthetic education. The Pedagogical Institute participated in the publication of "new" schoolbooks, where the content was revised in view of the educational needs of the New Socialist Man. The task of Department also included the development of a university textbook of education and translations of Soviet textbooks of education.[34]

The second department, the Department of History of Education, focused mainly on the Czech history of pedagogy and the publication of university

32 Discussion of the Philosophical and Historical Section of the Czechoslovak Academy of Sciences in 1954. MÚA AV ČR, fund PU JAK (1953) 1955–1960, cardboard 3.

33 Discussion of the Philosophical and Historical Section of the Czechoslovak Academy of Sciences in 1954. MÚA AV ČR, fund PU JAK (1953) 1955–1960, cardboard 3.

34 It was a follow-up to Goncharov's previously published work translated from Russian into Czech and Slovak: Nikolaj K. Gončarov, *Pedagogika* (Praha: SPN, 1952).

textbooks on the history of education[35], as well as on Comenius research (publications on Comenius' works, organising Comenius conferences[36], publishing the journal *Acta Comeniana*). The first and second departments were from 1956, also engaged in publishing the journal *Pedagogika* (founded in 1951)[37]. The third department, the Department of Educational Psychology, focused on psychological problems of education and teaching, (also publishing the journal *Czechoslovak Psychology*, and organising conferences).

The director of the Institute was academician Prof. Chlup and his deputy and head of the second department was Prof. Josef Váňa (1899–1966). In 1957, nine scientific and eleven expert colleagues were active in the PI JAC CAS. By the end of 1960, the number of staff in the three departments had been raised to a total of eighteen senior scientific and sixteen junior expert members of staff. At the end of the 1950s, various areas of science and research

---

[35] The work was a follow-up to the already published publications (strongly Marxist oriented) Josef Váňa et al., *Dějiny pedagogiky* (Praha: SPN, 1955). In addition, "illustrative" textbooks on the history of education were translated from Russian: Jevgenij N. Medynskij, *Dějiny pedagogiky* (Praha: SPN, 1950). Nikolaj A. Konstantinov, Jevgenij N. Medynskij and Maria F. Šabajeva, *Dějiny pedagogiky* (Praha: SPN, 1959).

[36] In particular, 1957 was the year of an important international conference of Comenius researchers (September 23–28, 1957) organized by the Czechoslovak Academy of Sciences. The conference was attended by 52 foreign participitants.

[37] From 1951 the journal *Pedagogika* was published by the Ministry of Education, Sciences and Arts. The journal heralded a "new" beginning of educational discussion. The founding of the journal demonstrated an intention to end the continuity with pre-war educational journals or with even older educational publications. The "patronage" of the Ministry of Education guaranteed political and ideological control over the journal. Cf. Růžena Váňová, "Vědy o výchově na stránkách Pedagogiky," *Pedagogika* 50, no. 4 (2000): 313–315. In 1956, the journal came under PI JAC CAS control. Its scientific character was underlined, which until then had "suffered" under the ideological-political control of the Ministry of Education. (State control was manifested in political editorials, texts from high political functionaries on educational issues, as well as discussions of "denunciation of bourgeois pedagogy, bourgeois nationalism and cosmopolitanism" and "reactionary" thinking in the pages of the journal.) On this, cf. Jan Průcha, "50 let časopisu Pedagogika – vývoj média české pedagogické vědy," *Pedagogika* 50, no. 4 (2000): 345. Under the leadership of the editorial board authorized by the Czechoslovak Academy of Sciences (the editorial board was chaired by Prof. Chlup), the journal *Pedagogika* published the results of educational research of PI JAC CAS, but it continued to be strongly ideologically loyal to the socialist system. This is clear both from the notes of the PI JAC CAS and from the content analysis of the journal *Pedagogika* itself.

at PI JAC CAS were dealt with in cooperation with other bodies – partly with institutes of the CAS, and also with other institutions outside the CAS (mainly with RIE Prague, SIE Bratislava, but also with the departments of education of universities and teachers colleges[38]).

According to the programme of the Institute, the task of educational sciences at PI JAC CAS was viewed and presented in the light of the political imperatives of building a communist or socialist society (the lower stage of communism), but also in the light of the Marxist view of historical development. Educational sciences were supposed to develop from a less progressive or even reactionary/stagnating stage (bourgeois education and school) to a higher, progressive stage (socialist education, socialist school). It was declared that the mission of educational sciences should be to follow and support the "political victory of the socialist people" on the road to building a communist society: "We must, of course, also deeply elaborate the basic theory, the system of educational sciences, the theory of education and their role in socialist society, if we are to get a view that controls the educational process."[39] Utopian visions and ideological challenges became official goals of the "new" educational sciences in the CAS. Questions of authenticity, individuation, and individual freedom receded to the objectification of educational processes interpreted in the materialistic and dialectical spirit of Marxism and determined by "historical development".

The "new educational style"[40] was to be developed not only in science (in academies and universities), but also in practice – in schools, as well as "in educational work in factories, which are educational institutions in many respects"[41], and also in the family. It is interesting that Prof. Chlup's writings on the objectives and programme of educational sciences at the

---

[38] In particular, selected staff members of the educational colleges and departments of education of the faculties of arts participated in educational research coordinated by PI JAC CAS. On the one hand, the expert capacities of these colleges and departments were used, and on the other, thanks to this connection, teacher training was to move in a "new" direction.

[39] Pedagogical problems and tasks. Material by academician Prof. Chlup. MÚA AV ČR, Presidium ČSAV fund, carton 6.

[40] Pedagogical problems and tasks. Material by academician Prof. Chlup. MÚA AV ČR, Presidium ČSAV fund, carton 6.

[41] Pedagogical problems and tasks. Material by academician Prof. Chlup. MÚA AV ČR, Presidium ČSAV fund, carton 6.

CAS, dating back to 1955 and 1956, do not directly mention the Soviet educational model, the translation of Soviet textbooks and publications, or the transfer of the results of scientific research on Soviet educational sciences to the Czechoslovak context. On the contrary, it speaks of the "own way" in defining and fulfilling the objectives of educational sciences. Also from the programme materials of the PI JAC CAS, especially between1958–60, it is clear that the tasks of educational sciences were planned, discussed and defined mainly during the meetings of the PI JAC CAS. Of course, these objectives of PI JAC CAS were loyal to communist party resolutions, government directives on school and communist society, etc. But it is clear that "accordance" with government and party policy was "guarded" by the expert staff of PI JAC CAS itself. The sources do not show the interference of external powers. However, the heads of social sciences in CAS and the Presidium of the CAS "consulted" and discussed the Academy's programme with representatives of the Ministry of Education, who "supervised" the party line in the progress of science. The materials used as a basis for the drafting and discussion of the programmatic tasks of educational sciences in the CAS in 1958–60 show that it was impossible for the educational sciences not to be shaped by political need.

Examining the Presidium reports of the CAS from 1952–1960[42], it is evident that all the departments were confronted with political-ideological imperatives and tasks as well as practical and everyday problems of scientific life. Finances were often lacking, stronger staffing was called for, and funds were requested for foreign trips – both to the Soviet Union[43] and to Western countries. However, the reports show that there were no specific requests from the government or the Communist Party Central Committee for the number and intensity of trips from/to the Moscow Academy, to scientific institutions in the USSR or to "people's democracies" (especially Poland, the GDR or Hungary). Also, the desired cooperation with the USSR Academy of

42 Report of the Presidium of the Czechoslovak Academy of Sciences of 14 October 1955. MÚA AV ČR, Presidium of the Czechoslovak Academy of Sciences, carton 6, pp. 1–6.

43 The visit of the Presidium of the Academy of Sciences of the USSR was to take place in 1956, but was postponed to 1957. The Soviet delegation did not include researchers of educational sciences. The members of the delegation were mainly from the field of natural or technical sciences, as well as from the Presidium of the Academy of Sciences of the USSR. A meeting was held with the President of the CAS, Prof. Nejedlý.

Sciences had a gradual development, which depended in part on the actors themselves in the USSR Academy of Sciences and the CAS, not exclusively on political instructions.[44] The intensity of direct scientific contacts between people from the CAS and the USSR Academy of Sciences was, however, relatively low, although demonstrative celebrations of Czechoslovak-Soviet cooperation and "pompous" declarations of scientific cooperation were part of scientific and wider social life.

The sovietization of educational sciences via foreign scientific visits (Czechoslovak-Soviet Union) was thus more demanded and promoted than implemented. Nobody from the experts of the PI JAC CAS questioned the importance and obviousness of Czechoslovak-Soviet scientific cooperation for the "correct development" of educational sciences. Although it cannot be documented from archival sources that Czech educational sciences in CAS formulated its programme and scientific questions according to Soviet academic instructions. Similarly, as mentioned above, no one rejected or openly questioned the "self-evident" assumption that Soviet educational sciences was a model for Czechoslovak science. Further, that it was necessary to "overcome the obscurity" of educational sciences from the interwar period and follow the Soviet experience. However, how this was interpreted and how it was practiced is another matter, though it is not particularly easy to substantiate via contemporary sources.

In 1954, psychologists made two trips to the USSR and declared the necessity to build Czechoslovak psychology on the Pavlovian school through close cooperation with the USSR. The visit of the leader of Soviet

---

[44] The cooperation between the Academy of Sciences and the Czechoslovak Academy of Sciences was governed by a bilateral cooperation agreement from 1956. The agreement covered cooperation between the institutes, leadership of the academies, study trips, exchange of publications, joint publications, conferences, meetings, congresses, discussions, and support in expanding membership in professional societies. This agreement was followed by annual updates and plans for Czechoslovak-Soviet cooperation. For example, in 1957 a "commitment" of 200 study weeks for 50 academics from the Academy of Sciences of the USSR to the CAS was agreed. Among the institutes establishing direct cooperation between the Czech and Soviet sides were 35 institutes – mostly in the field of chemical, natural, mathematical, technical, geological sciences. No direct cooperation was established in the field of educational sciences. MÚA AV ČR, Presidium of the Czechoslovak Academy of Sciences, carton 11.

educational sciences N.K. Goncharov to Prague in 1956, as well as the signing of the agreement between the Academy of Sciences of the USSR, and the Czechoslovak Academy of Sciences in 1956, can be seen as an important milestone in strengthening Czechoslovak-Soviet contacts in educational sciences. Conversely, educational sciences were not represented among the institutes that established direct cooperation between the CAS and Soviet Academy. Prof. Chlup, in a report from the end of 1957, where he evaluated the activities and results of the existence of the Pedagogical Cabinet of the CAS, stated that he himself had published only one article in the USSR journal *Soviet Science*. The transfer of Czech science to the USSR was thus minimal. If we follow the Soviet transfer to Czechoslovak science, the situation and "numbers" are different. In the journal *Pedagogika* a much larger number of articles by Soviet authors were published in the 1950s, and the importance given to their statements in discussions or editorials was considerable. The function of these articles was not only to make known the results of Soviet educational research. Mainly the editorials called for following the practices and themes developed by Soviet pedagogy and called for by Soviet party policy. In addition, these texts were "supplemented" with quotations from resolutions of the CPSU congresses or articles on education and training in communist society from the pens of the top leaders of Soviet power, including articles by Stalin or Lenin.

An important point in the development of scientific disciplines in the CAS was the evaluation of science and scientific outputs (lectures, publications, conferences, foreign cooperation, patents). Even in the area of science evaluation, foreign or Soviet schemes developed outside the Academy (Central Committee and other parts of the Communist Party of Czechoslovakia.) were not directly introduced to the CAS. Although the development of science was politically directed (laws, decrees, regulations, government and party concepts, etc.) and these documents were essential for the formation of the programme of scientific life in the CAS, there was an important debate about their concretization in the CAS. On the one hand, the scientific programme had to be in line with the party and government concept, while on the other, the members of the Presidium and the academics themselves tried to present a development programme according to scientific requirements. It was thus the area of the scientific programme that was most heavily ideologised and politicised – especially in the social sciences and humanities, and particularly in the educational sciences. We must also not forget the "cadre control" i.e. control of the CAS staff who formulated and implemented the programme.

The Pedagogical Institute of J. A. Comenius of the Czechoslovak Academy of Sciences until 1965 (until the End of the Third Five-year Period)

The Presidium of the Czechoslovak Academy of Sciences dismissed appealed at its own request Prof. Chlup from the position of Director of the Institute as of 30 June 1960 and agreed with Prof. Chlup's suggestion to appoint his deputy, corresponding member Dr. Josef Váňa[45] as Director of the Institute (named in 1961).[46]

After 1960, the activities of the PI JAC CAS were regulated by the Guidelines of the Scientific Research Plan of the CAS for the years 1961–65 (created in the Institute of Science Planning of the CAS) and the agreed state research

---

45 Josef Váňa was sufficiently "reviewed and tested" before his nomination and emerged from this assessment positively. Josef Váňa (1899–1966) studied philosophy at Charles University in Prague and at the Sorbonne in Paris. In the interwar period, he successfully, practically and theoretically, developed the field of psychotechnics. In 1945 (June 1, 1945) he joined the Communist Party of Czechoslovakia and became an active advocate of Marxism-Leninism in pedagogy and psychology – especially after 1948, when he was also a member of the education commission of the Central Committee of the Communist Party of Czechoslovakia. In 1945 he became director of the RIE Prague, in 1949 he was named Professor of Educational Sciences at the Faculty of Education of Charles University in Prague and also became its Dean. Later (after the reform of teacher education provided by the 1953 law) he became the Rector of the College of Education in Prague (which ceased its activity in 1959, when the educational reform gave rise to the so-called pedagogical institutes). From 1956 he worked at the PI JAC CAS Prague, from 1959 as Deputy Director and from 1961 as Director.

After 1948, J. Váňa worked intensively for the transformation of Soviet pedagogy into the Czech discourse, which headvocated, in the publication History of Pedagogy (1955 – 1st edition, four editions in total), for which he was awarded an honorary mention by the Czechoslovak government in 1956. Information obtained from the cadre evaluation of J. Váňa PI JAC and from the documents of PI JAC CAS for the proposal to award the Order of Labour to J. Váňa.

46 O. Chlup was thanked for his work, he was also awarded the Order of the Republic in 1955 on the nomination of the Presidium of the Czechoslovak Academy of Sciences and Josef Váňa was awarded the Order of Labour in 1960 by the Minister of Education.

plan for the 3rd five-year period (1961–65).[47] After internal discussion and acceptance, the CAS included the proposal from the PI in the so-called State Scientific Plan. The programme was named School Education in the Stage of Completion of Socialism and Transition to Communism.[48] This programme focused on achieving the stage of development of a fully-communist society in schools and teaching (the aims of education, the contents of the curriculum, the educational means and teaching methods). As stated in the background documents preceding the adoption of the research plans and programmes for 1959–60 and for the post-1960 period, educational science was to focus on: the analysis of the social needs of man and the needs of man in communist society with regard to education; the revision of the basic categories of educational theory; the theoretical foundations of the system of teaching courses; the elaboration of methods of moral education; the problem of education for a scientific world view; extra-curricular education; and the history of education. This was intended to meet several objectives. The first goal was formulated as a research task to develop a programme for the education of the Socialist Man (led by Prof. Váňa). The second task was the problem of the basic curriculum of the comprehensive school (led by Prof. Chlup). Another objective was to bring about the development and extension of polytechnic education. Furthermore, a textbook of education at university level was to be published in early 1960 and subsequently evaluated, corrected, completed and published by 1965. Also, all educational research from a "methodological" point of view was to be conducted in accordance with Marxist "perspectives in the field of education".[49]

In 1960 it was also planned to intensify the psychological section in the PI JAC CAS[50] by establishing an independent psychological cabinet, which was to become the basis for the future Psychological Institute of the CAS.

---

47 On the problem of planning and management in socialism see Vítězslav Sommer et al., *Řídit socialismus jako firmu: technokratické vládnutí v Československu, 1956–1989* (Praha: Ústav pro soudobé dějiny AV ČR, 2019).

48 The programme was a continuation of the previous and identically named State Plan of Scientific Research Work for 1959–60 for the field of education.

49 Main research plans up to 1975. Materials of the Historical Section of the Czechoslovak Academy of Sciences, 11 November 1959.

50 In 1960, the Laboratory for Child Psychology from the University of Education in Prague was incorporated under PI JAC CAS.

The activities of the psychological cabinet were to follow the work that had been carried out in Prague and Brno up to that time. In Prague, it was mainly concerned with questions of general psychology (Prof. Doležal) and in Brno with questions of educational psychology (Prof. Chmelař). The Psychological Cabinet was in existence from 1 January 1962.

To meet the objectives, an expansion of the scientific staff was also needed. The state development plan also foresaw for this in the CAS. The issue of new generation of researchers was also to be conceptually supported (Government Decree No. 183 of 1960), and the stability of scientific staff was to be financially and socially supported (Government Decree No. 929 of 1960 on the cadre, financial and material support for the further development of scientific and research activities of universities).

Planned Science

The centralization and planning of research after 1948 had to support the research efficiency and so support the transformation of socialist economic and communist-oriented society. This idea also stood behind the reform of science after 1952 and led to the establishment of the CAS. These goals were not so easy to achieve, so the problem of the efficiency of socialist science after 1950 continued to thwart progress in this field. Plans for the use of scientific practice, and cooperation between scientific institutions and practical institutions to benefit the national economy represented important points of discussion. These debates were held both in the Presidium of the CAS and in the various sections, as well as in the leadership of other scientific research institutions in the Czechoslovak Republic, government ministries, and the Central Committee of the Communist Party of Czechoslovakia. This discussion can betraced throughout 1955 and 1956 and in the period up to the end of the 1960s. The question of systematic, centralized coordination in the development of science for the "tasks of socialist society" came up repeatedly. Plans and concepts for the development of science (both annual and long-term) took up significant time and attention of senior officials of the CAS, as well as of individual section leaders and academics.

The situation was no different in the educational sciences. The "crisis" of the results and planning of science can be seen by the discussion over the material of Government Resolution No. 454 of 22 February 1956 on the tasks of science in providing for the development of the national economy and improving the technical level of Czechoslovak industry. The contemporary material points out the weakness in the conceptual planning of scientific research in Czechoslovakia. It also speaks of the need to coordinate research planning with the USSR and with the countries of the Eastern Bloc. Furthermore, attention is paid to the overlapping and duplication of research tasks[51], the lack of cooperation between research institutes, the inadequate professional level of researchers and the material resources of many research institutes, the poor coordination of research programmes, plans or tasks, and the lack of coherence between scientific research and the needs of practice, the economy and industry.[52] The government documents (motivated, among other things, by the significant problems of the socialist economy)[53] gave rise to many working panels at the CAS and the formulation of the so-called State Research Plan (under the supervision of the State Planning Institute – SPI).[54]

The CAS participated significantly in the formulation of the five-year state plan of scientific research work together with the SPI and the ministerial departments. The document conceptually and unified planned scientific work and supported in particular the development of technical or natural sciences. This plan was developed into two sub-plans – the State Plan of Scientific Research for 1957 and for the period 1958–1960. The state plans for scientific

---

51 The research was planned and implemented in the Czechoslovak Republic by CAS (Act of 1952), the Czechoslovak Academy of Agricultural Sciences, the departmental research institutes established under Act No. 14/1955 Coll.

The state research was regulated between 1949–1955 by Act No. 261/1949 Coll. on the organisation of research and technical development.

52 The state research plans and the research plans of the CAS were designed to synchronize the research work and research teams of the institutions of the Academy, universities, ministerial research organizations, and the organisations of the Communist Party of Czechoslovakia.

53 The lack of planning for science and its connection with economic progress (socialist progress) was related to the whole debate about the results of the first Five-Year Plan (1949–1953). These were not evaluated positively, and therefore one-year plans were introduced in 1954 and 1955. Then in 1956 the second Five-Year Plan (1956–1960) began, when production and other parts of social life were to be planned more extensively so that the goal of "transition and completion" of socialist life could be achieved.

54 Report on the activities of the CSAV in 1956. MÚA AV ČR, Presidium of the Czechoslovak Academy of Sciences, carton 11.

development took into account, among other things, the conclusions of the 11th Congress of the Communist Party of Czechoslovakia of June 1958.

The congress confirmed the government's 1956 resolution on the leading role of science and the importance of its centralization and systematization (planning) for the success of the socialist economy. The tasks resulting from the 11th congress were discussed by scientists in November 1958. The resolutions of the 11th Congress were followed by the Resolution of the Central Committee of the Communist Party of Czechoslovakia of 23 April 1959 "On the close connection between school and life and on further education and upbringing in Czechoslovakia" and by the Government Plan on Scientific Research Activities No. 751 of 20 August 1959. The document prepared the scientific and research tasks for the third five-year period (1960–1965).

This kind of practice led to a constant attention to the planning of tasks and to the planning of scientific programmes in the CAS (not excluding educational sciences). Furthermore, the list of specialisations for aspirant studies was defined. In 1956, a government resolution about new forms of "education of scientific cadres" was drawn up. The main task was to draw up state objectives and research plans, including their annual updating, to draw up personnel development plans, as well as plans for foreign cooperation (mainly with the USSR, but also within the area of the Council for Mutual Economic Assistance, COMECO, and possibly also with capitalist Western countries). Scientific planning also involved personnel reviews and personnel checks and the evaluation of the implemented plans. At the end of the 1950s, evaluation, critical reflection, and self-reflection of activities, became part of scientific life.

The longer the planning period of scientific activity, the more generally and ideologically formulated the plans were. The short-term plans were concrete. Among the short-term plans we find in educational sciences, for example, the elaboration of specific curricula, the publication of Comenius' writings, the production of school textbooks, university publications, etc. Long-term plans (e.g., the proposal of a scientific plan from 1960 to 1975) aim at "finishing of the cultural revolution" or achievement of the "transition of communist society". This is reflected, for example, in the main research plans up to 1975, which were discussed by the Historical Section of the Czechoslovak Academy of Sciences in November 1959. Here it states, "the basic aim of research until

1975 is a) to carry out the cultural revolution; b) to reach the moral-political unity of the people; c) to develop communist education".[55]

"New" Educational Sciences – Marxist Science?

The Marxist orientation of educational research and educational sciences became the official goal. But this was apparently not satisfactorily fulfilled in the eyes of the "guardians of the new science". The reports on the activities of the sixth section in PI CAS (the historical-philosophical section, which also included educational sciences) permanently repeat the necessity to advance the Marxist view of philosophical, historical, educational analysis: "…the most important measure is attention to the scientific youth, to the improvement of the professional and ideological-political level of the staff. Here it will be mainly a matter of systematically deepening their knowledge of Marxist ideology. Marxism-Leninism must not be a schematism for young scientists, but a living source of creative scientific method."[56]

The fundamental instrument of ideological control of science was the departments of Marxism-Leninism at universities and in the Academy of Science (departments of dialectical and historical materialism). The passing of courses in these departments was compulsory for university students or young scholars, as well as for other academics and scientists. However, the weakness of such a task soon became apparent. The task of the departments – "providing everyone with a Marxist view of science and society" – meant a great overloading of staff. At the same time, it was pointed out that lecturers often did not have a satisfactory academic background. As a result the level of teaching dropped, formalism and dogmatism won out, rather than the real acceptance of the Marxist world view. The "friendship with the USSR" should have become formal, the gap between philosophy (meaning

55 Main research objectives until 1975. Materials of the Historical Section of the Czechoslovak Academy of Sciences, 11 November 1959.

56 Report on the activities of the Philosophy Cabinet in the 6th Section of the Czechoslovak Academy of Sciences for the year 1956/57. MÚA AV ČR, fund PU JAK (1953) 1955–1960, carton 3.

Marxism-Leninism) and the sciences should have been growing.[57] In the CAS, these "weaknesses" were to be rectified by improving the Philosophy Cabinet staff, by strengthening the scientific cadets in the field of Marxist philosophy, and by closer cooperation with Soviet Marxist philosophy.

The Marxist and ideological orientation of science, the instrumentalisation of science for the goals of totalitarian society, did not only proceed one-way from the state level "downwards". Scientists themselves were closely interrelated as high officials with the "organs" of state and party power. For example, Prof. Chlup had been a member of the Education Commission of the Central Committee of the Czechoslovak Communist Party.[58]

The "dissemination" of the new science in the new generation of scientific youth as well as in university education was deemed successful thanks to the activities of academics. Prof. Chlup headed the Department of Education at the Faculty of Arts and History of Charles University in Prague. The academician in the Slovak section of the CAS, Ondrej Pavlík (1916–1996) was a Professor at the University of Education in Bratislava. Another important correspondent member of the psychology department Vilém Chmelař (1892–1988) was professor, vice-dean, head of the department of education and psychology at the Faculty of Arts in Brno. Corresponding member and head of PI JAC CAS Josef Váňa also held several political positions. At the end of the 1950s, he was chairman of the Czechoslovak Committee for the Care of Children, a member of the International Committee for the Care of Children, chairman of the Education Section of the Czechoslovak Commission for Cooperation with UNESCO, and chairman of the Central Pedagogical Commission.[59]

---

[57] Report on the activities of the Philosophy Cabinet in the 6th Section of the Czechoslovak Academy of Sciences for the year 1956/57. MÚA AV ČR, fund PU JAK (1953) 1955–1960, carton 3.

[58] O. Chlup was, from 1956, the director of the Central Pedagogical Commission at Research Institute of Education (RIE) Prague founded by the Minister of Education. The Commission was to develop new curricula and textbooks and to address the issue of the selection of the core curriculum. The aim was to develop curricula for all educational levels in the spirit of socialist education.

[59] The information about the positions of Prof. Dr. J. Váňa is taken from the proposal of PI JAC CAS for awarding J. Váňa with the Order of Labour from August 1959. The proposal was prepared and submitted by Dr. B. Kujal, Director of the RIE Prague.

The ideological character of science was also underlined in the evaluation of the outputs of science. As shown in the proceedings of the sixth section (historical and philosophical) in CAS, publications that carried an ideological goal and "charge" and helped science on "its path to socialism" were especially rewarded.

Science under "Cadre Control"

If the "new" educational sciences were to free themselves from "the influence of cosmopolitanism, bourgeois nationalism, idealism" and achieve a "victorious transformation", the "credible" actors themselves had to be well "selected". Their "loyalty and devotion" (i.e. submissiveness and discipline) had to be controlled. Whoever did not have "solid and credible" profile at the entry into the new scientific elites was not allowed into the community. Whoever, over time, "defected" or somehow distanced himself from the official party idea of the "new scientist" was forced in various ways not to publish, not to be scientifically active, or was ostracized and excluded from science altogether.

The "new management of science" used various ways to secure party loyalty and commitment to the cause of socialism. In educational sciences, this involved "cadre screening" of members joining the research institutions and academy, colleges of education/faculties of education, or postgraduate studies. There were also campaigns carried out to exclude particular individuals from the scientific community (especially those associated with "bourgeois" educational sciences). In the years between 1953–1955, a discrediting campaign was waged in the pages of the journal *Pedagogika* against the general teaching community and the scientific educational community in particular, both of which were seen as having been actively involved in or shaping the direction of the interwar educational reform movement in Czechoslovakia.[60] Although in many respects this reform movement followed leftist goals, both in the area

[60] Tomáš Kasper, "Alles muss man umschreiben. Der Wille zum „neuen Anfang," in der pädagogischen Diskussion in den Fünfzigerjahren," in *Fall des Eisernen Vorhangs 1989 und die Folgen: Europäische pädagogische Perspektiven*, ed. Henning Schluss and Hanna Holzapfel et al. (Wien: Lit Verlag, 2020), 99–111.

of school reform and the so-called reform of society, it was not seen as having sufficiently embraced or promoted communist ideas of the "new society".

Another instrument was the *de facto* physical exclusion of participation in the "new educational sciences" by the conviction of specific individuals. Such a case, which was certainly intended to terrify, was the impeachment and conviction of the prominent interwar pedagogue and psychologist Cyril Stejskal (1890–1969).[61]

Such harsh actions demonstrated that no one was protected, that anyone could be excluded (even if they were at the top of the science community) if they were deemed to be insufficiently loyal to the Party. Such examples were supposed to lead to increased ideological and party loyalty and to show that it did not "pay to go one's own way" and try to "take one's own direction in education". Another example was the case of the director of the Pedagogical Cabinet of the Slovak Academy of Sciences, Prof. Ondrej Pavlík, one of the main "architects" of the socialist school in Slovakia and a leading Slovak theoretician of polytechnic education, editor of the Slovak journal *Jednotná škola*. Pavlík can be seen as an important practitioner of cooperation between Slovak and Soviet educational sciences.[62] Despite all this, Pavlík was excluded from the Communist Party of Czechoslovakia in 1957[63] and his publishing activities were banned, his participation in conferences forbidden and he was also dismissed from his position as a professor at the college in Bratislava. However, his fall was not as steep as that of other representatives of science, because even after he was banned from teaching at the university, Pavlík was employed at the Educational Research Institute in Bratislava, where he could

---

61 Cyril Stejskal was a prominent interwar psychologist particularly in the fields of child studies (pedopsychology), experimental psychology and experimental pedagogy. He was imprisoned in 1950 and sentenced to 10 years in a staged court case. In an extraordinary amnesty in 1960 he was freed but barred from access to his property, denied his civil rights and exiled outside Prague. During the liberalization in the so-called 'Prague Spring' (1968), he was temporarily allowed to work at the Faculty of Arts of Charles University in Prague before the entry of Warsaw Pact troops into Czechoslovakia. He died in 1969, a year after the Warsaw Pact troops occupied Czechoslovakia.

62 In 1956, he stayed in the USSR for a 33-day work placement on the subject of ethical and polytechnic education. MÚA AV ČR, PU JAK fund (1953) 1955–1960, carton 3.

63 As Pavlik states in his report, he was a member of the UV KSS until June 1955 and a member of the Presidium of the UV KSS until June 1954. MÚA AV ČR, PU JAK fund (1953) 1955–1960, carton 3.

partly devote himself to his favoured scientific topics. He was engaged in polytechnic education as well as in ethical questions of education. He chose the topic: the formation of morals in "primitive society" and the fundamentals of Marxist ethics, the relationship between religion and morality. At the end of the 1950s, however, Pavlík was unable to publish his results in Czechoslovakia but he partly used the possibility of publishing in Polish journals. Reading Pavlik's reports in CAS (he was still a member of CAS) it is surprising how open he was about the "suspension" of his activities: "I believe that the Slovak Academy of Sciences was established to help develop science in Slovakia. And this also includes helping scientists to publish their work. Unfortunately, as can be seen from my case, the presidency of the Slovak Academy of Sciences is not fulfilling this basic task even towards its own members. The situation is simply such that I am not allowed to publish anything, not even under my full name, or even without one."[64]

Conclusions

If we look at the development of educational sciences in the years 1945–1960 in Czechoslovakia, we can see that there was an effort to make Marxism-Leninism, not just a philosophical matter, but a direction of "scientific development" of all the departments of the Czechoslovak Academy of Sciences. This meant that scientific disciplines should "cooperate" with Marxism-Leninism and be "methodologically" guided by it. This required the "cooperation" and ideological education of the members of the CAS. The "political-scientific synergy" required ideological constancy, strength, belief, class loyalty and the initiative of scientists. In this regard, it is not surprising to find that the ideological precision of scientific tasks and plans grew stronger in the late 1950s and early 1960s and was related to the consolidation of communist power. While in the early 1950s the plans of educational sciences were aimed at "overcoming the weaknesses of bourgeois science", the goal of finishing the communist reconstruction of society was advocated at the end of the 1950s. In this reconstruction, education, schooling and educational sciences played an essential role. The ideologization of educational sciences, as well as its

64 Report on Activities for 1958. Ondrej Pavlík. MÚA AV ČR, PU JAK fund (1953) 1955–1960, carton 3.

political instrumentalization, were important characteristics after 1948. At the end of the 1950s we observe a systematic effort to transform educational research and educational theory on the basis of political resolutions on education in communist society.

The basic characteristic of educational sciences in Czechoslovakia after 1948 was the "connection between school and life". This meant that the tasks of educational research were to be guided by social (political) tasks. They were to be seen in categories of the "development" of the school in the culmination of the communist development of society and the implementation of a "new" world view. At the forefront of educational sciences was not the pupil, but the goal was "social revolution", and the success of the socialist economy, In this respect, it was decided what man should know, how to behave in order to be ready for the "new" society and, of course, to build it himself. The autonomy of the educational goals was thus significantly undermined and neglected. The school under communist rule was to follow neither intellectualism (and the supposed formalism associated with it) nor flat practicalism, but the ideal of a communist, harmonious, classless and conflict-free society. Discussion centred on the education of an "all-round developed Socialist Man" who would fulfil the aims of communism with joy and elan. The school was based on the needs of communist society, linked to that society's political demands. In this iteraction the school based its teaching on "science" (materialistic, Marxist), on the "new" type of general education and on the priority of vocational education. Not only ideologization, but also utopianism was at the heart of such educational thinking, and the formulation of the goals of educational research. The standardization of goals, of a human personality became the basis of educational practice, theory and research.

Who was to set these norms? This was seen as the prerogative of political representatives and the "new elite of educational research", often anonymously through research plans, and educational programmes. Thus, the reality of educational research became limited to state educational research plans, evaluation of their implementation and proposals for further updating.

In the question of the sovietization of school and educational sciences, we find that, in some instances, the leading actors in educational sciences were allowed partial autonomy. Though often, their activities could only take place within a clearly demarcated space, which was defined by government and communist party resolutions that were required to be in line with Soviet models. Although the Presidium protocols of the CAS and the protocols of the sixth section of the CAS (which included educational sciences) do not show direct intervention by the Soviet leadership of science, the "authority and pattern" of Soviet science were unquestionable. "Ideological development and stability", "political maturity", "party experience" were all characteristics of Soviet science, which were to help the "new" orientation of Czechoslovak educational sciences.

This study was supported by the GACR project No. 25-16883S: For a New Model of Educational Sciences – Totalitarianism, Ideology and Political Instrumentalization in Educational Sciences in the Communist Period.

Bibliography

Applebaum, Rachel. *Empire of Friends: Soviet Power and Socialist Internationalism in Cold War Czechoslovakia*. Ithaca: Cornell University Press, 2019.

Brenner, Christiane. *"Zwischen Ost und West": tschechische politische Diskurse 1945–1948*. München: Oldenbourg, 2009.

Connelly, John. *Captive University: The Sovietization of East German, Czech, and Polish Higher Education, 1945–1956*. Chapel Hill: University of North Carolina Press, 2000.

Devátá, Markéta et al. *Vědní koncepce KSČ a její institucionalizace po roce 1948*. Praha: Ústav pro soudobé dějiny AV ČR, 2010.

Devátá, Markéta. *Marxismus jako projekt nové společnosti: dvě studie ke společenským vědám (1945–1969)*. Praha: Ústav pro soudobé dějiny AV ČR, 2014.

Foucault, Michel. *The Archaeology of Knowledge and the Discourse on Languag*. New York: Pantheon, 1972.

Franc, Martin and Věra Dvořáčková. *Dějiny Československé akademie věd I*. Praha: Academia, 2019.

Kasper, Tomáš. "Alles muss man umschreiben. Der Wille zum „neuen Anfang" in der pädagogischen Diskussion in den Fünfzigerjahren." In *Fall des Eisernen Vorhangs 1989 und die Folgen, Europäische pädagogische*

Perspektiven, edited by Henning Schluss and Hanna Holzapfel et al., 99–111. Wien: Lit Verlag, 2020.

Kestere, Iveta, and Manuel Joaquín Fernández González. "Educating the New Soviet Man: Propagated Image and Hidden Resistance in Soviet Latvia." *Historia scholastica* 7, no. 1 (2021): 11–32.

Mincu, Monica E. "Communist Education as Modernisation Strategy? The Swings of the Globalisation Pendulum in Eastern Europe (1947–1989)." *History of Education* 45, no. 3 (2016), 319–334.

Průcha, Jan. "50 let časopisu Pedagogika – vývoj média české pedagogické vědy." *Pedagogika* 50, no. 4 (2000): 340–364.

Sommer, Vítězslav et al. *Řídit socialismus jako firmu: technokratické vládnutí v Československu, 1956–1989*. Praha: Ústav pro soudobé dějiny AV ČR, 2019.

Tromly, Benjamin. *Making the Soviet Intelligentsia: Universities and Intellectual Life under Stalin and Khrushchev*. Cambridge: Cambridge University Press, 2014.

Váňová, Růžena. "Vědy o výchově na stránkách Pedagogiky." *Pedagogika* 50, no. 4 (2000): 313–339.

Sources

Gončarov, Nikolai K. *Pedagogika*. Praha: SPN, 1952.

Chlup, Otokar. *Čítanka k dějinám pedagogiky pro pedagogické vyšší a vysoké pedagogické školy. Díl 1., K dějinám pedagogiky do vzniku marxismu*. Praha: SPN – pedagogické nakladatelství, 1955.

Chlup, Otokar, and Antonín Sychra. *O estetické výchově*. Praha: Státní nakladatelství dětské knihy, 1956.

Chlup, Otokar. *Podmínky výchovy a vzdělávání na národní škole*. Praha: SPN, 1960.

Chlup, Otokar. *Z teorie výchovy a vyučování: Sborník pedagog. studií*. Praha: Československá akademie věd, 1962.

Konstantinov, Nikolaj A., Medynskij, Jevgenij N., and Maria F. Šabajeva. *Dějiny pedagogiky*. Praha: SPN, 1959.

Medynskij, Jevgenij N. *Dějiny pedagogiky*. Praha: SPN, 1950.

Sociologická encyklopedie. "Kaláb Miloš." Accessed September 23, 2024. https://encyklopedie.soc.cas.cz/w/Kal%C3%A1b_Milo%C5%A1.

Váňa, Josef. *Dějiny pedagogiky*. Praha: SPN, 1955.

MÚA AV ČR, fund Presidium ČSAV.

MÚ AV ČR, Presidium of the Czechoslovak Academy of Sciences.

MÚA AV ČR, fund PU JAK (1953) 1955–1960.

Zur Geschichte der Sowjetisierung und des sowjetpädagogischen Einflusses auf die Grundlagen pädagogischer Wissenschaft in der SBZ/DDR

Ulrich Wiegmann

Abstrakt: Der Beitrag bietet einen Abriss zur pädagogischen „Sowjetisierung“ und zum „sowjetpädagogischen“ Einfluss in der Sowjetischen Besatzungszone und nachfolgend in der DDR bis zu deren Ende. Diese Entwicklung begann mit dem Abbruch der in den ersten Nachkriegsjahren versuchten pädagogischen/erziehungswissenschaftlichen Selbstverständigung im Kontext der sog. Tendenzwende 1948/49. Sie setzte sich fort durch die Übernahme des „sowjetpädagogischen“ Paradigmas 1949–1953 und mündete sodann in die allmähliche, ebenso vorsichtige wie tendenziell selbstbewusstere Rezeption im Zusammenhang mit der gesellschaftspolitischen Stabilisierung nach dem Mauerbau und mündete schließlich in die Irritation über sowjetische und -pädagogische Entwicklungen in den 1980er Jahren. Der Prozess vollzog sich entlang der gesellschaftspolitischen Zäsuren in der DDR und unter dem Einfluss der globalen und nationalen Systemauseinandersetzung. Die nachhaltige Prägung der Pädagogik in der DDR durch „Sowjetisierung“ und „sowjetpädagogischen“ Einfluss blieb unabhängig von der Tatsache des Charakters der „Sowjetpädagogik“ als traditioneller national und „marxistisch-leninistisch“ modifizierter Lernschulpädagogik gleichwohl und schon angesichts ihres rezeptionsgeschichtlichen Zusammenhangs mit deutschen und europäischen Entwicklungen pädagogischen Denkens im 19. und 20. Jahrhundert auch am Ende der DDR in ihren Grundlagen präsent.

Schlüsselwörter: „Sowjetpädagogik“, Tendenzwende 1948/49, Stalins Tod 1953 und der 17. Juni 1953, Revisionismuskampagne, Gesellschaftspolitische Stabilisierung nach dem Mauerbau, Glasnost und Perestroika

Erziehungswissenschaftliche Neuorientierung in der Sowjetischen Besatzungszone

Die Geschichte der in der DDR überwiegend als pädagogische Wissenschaft bezeichneten Erziehungswissenschaft begann 1945 in der Sowjetischen Besatzungszone (SBZ) als Bilanzierung des desaströsen Endes einer pädagogischen Ära und als Nachdenken über Erziehung im Moment der gesellschaftlichen Katastrophe.[1] Die sowjetische Besatzung versprach die Chance, dominierende Theorien der Zwischenkriegszeit zu überwinden und anknüpfend an die vorfaschistische Ära eine sozialwissenschaftlichen Ansprüchen gerechte Pädagogik zu entwickeln. Mit der im Juni 1946 in Berlin erstmals erschienenen Zeitschrift „Pädagogik" stand ein Jahr nach Kriegsende ein Medium des erziehungswissenschaftlichen Austausches zur Verfügung, das bis zum Ende der DDR mit dem Anspruch einer erziehungstheoretischen Zeitschrift konkurrenzlos fortlebte.[2]

Redaktionell geleitet wurde die Zeitschrift bis 1950 gemeinsam von zwei Kennern Marxscher Schriften aus dem sozialdemokratischen Milieu der Weimarer Schulreformbewegung – Robert Alt und Max-Gustav Lange.[3] Beide gehörten weder zu den aus der Sowjetunion zurückgekehrten Emigranten noch zur kommunistischen „Kaderreserve" der in der UdSSR „umerzogenen" und „marxistisch-leninistisch" geschulten Kriegsgefangenen.[4]

Der jüdisch-herkünftige Robert Alt hatte als Häftling Auschwitz überlebt. Max-Gustav Lange entging nationalsozialistischen Sanktionen durch

---

1 Vgl. v. a. Heinrich Deiters, „Der deutsche Lehrer vor der Welt," in *Pädagogische Aufsätze und Reden* (Berlin: Volk und Wissen Volkseigener Verlag, 1957), 187–202. Deiters hatte die Zeit des Nationalsozialismus in „innerer Emigration" verbracht. Vgl. Ulrich Wiegmann, „Heinrich Deiters – berufliche Ausgrenzung und ‚erziehungswissenschaftliche Remigration'," *Zeitschrift für Pädagogik* H 40, no. 5 (1994): 765–780. Max Gustav Lange, „Zur Grundlegung der Erziehungswissenschaft," *Pädagogik* 1, no. 3 (1946): 16–26.

2 Die Zeitschrift überdauerte das Ende deutscher Zweistaatlichkeit unter dem Titel Pädagogik und Schulalltag mit den Jahrgängen 46 (1991) bis 52 (1997).

3 Vgl. Zur Biografie Robert Alts Ulrich Wiegmann, „Zur Geschichte des Lebensbildes von Robert Alt," in *Robert Alt (1905–1978)*, ed. Friedrich Bodo et al. (Frankfurt a.M.: Lang, Peter GmbH, 2006), 143–157. Ulrich Wiegmann, „Robert Alt," in *Klinkhardt Lexikon Erziehungswissenschaft (KLE)*, ed. Klaus-Peter Horn et al. (Bad Heilbrunn: Klinkhardt, 2012), 36. Zur Biografie Max-Gustav Langes vgl. Ulrich Wiegmann, „Max Gustav Lange," in *Klinkhardt Lexikon Erziehungswissenschaft (KLE)*, ed. Klaus-Peter Horn et al. (Bad Heilbrunn: Klinkhardt, 2012), 268–269; speziell zur Geschichte seiner sogenannten Republikflucht 1950 vgl. Ulrich Wiegmann, *Agenten – Patrioten – Westaufklärer. Staatssicherheit und Akademie der Pädagogischen Wissenschaften der DDR* (Berlin: Metropol, 2015), 22–28.

4 Vgl. Christa Uhlig, *Rückkehr aus der Sowjetunion: Politische Erfahrungen und pädagogische Wirkungen. Emigranten und ehemalige Kriegsgefangene in der SBZ und frühen DDR*. (Weinheim: Deutscher Studien Verlag, 1998).

eine Strategie der Anpassung an die gesellschaftspolitischen Verhältnisse. Sie schloss auch den späten, nach 1945 verheimlichten Beitritt zur NSDAP ein.[5]

Robert Alt wurde in den pädagogisch-soziologischen Debatten der Weimarer Zeit an der Berliner Universität neben seiner beruflichen Tätigkeit als Lehrer an einer reformpädagogischen Schule in Berlin akademisch sozialisiert.[6] Seine 1937 fertiggestellte Dissertation[7] reichte er auf Grund des im selben Jahr erlassenen Promotionsverbots für jüdisch-herkünftige Deutsche erst 1948 ein.

Max Gustav Lange promovierte 1946 mit der Arbeit „Der Junghegelianismus und die Anfänge des Marxismus" bei Peter Petersen in Jena. Nach seiner Übersiedlung 1950 nach Westberlin, die ihn in der DDR zur persona non grata werden ließ, beschrieb er sich als vertraut mit der „westlichen marxistischen Tradition" und als Kenner der „Schriften von Marx und Engels".[8] Sowohl Alt als auch sich selbst zählte er rückblickend zu jenen Leuten, die die „wissenschaftliche Begründung" der Schulreform in der SBZ besorgten. Dabei wollten sie „grundsätzlich etwas anderes … als die Besatzungsmacht und ihre deutschen Beauftragten". Mit der Sowjetpädagogik auf „marxistisch-leninistischer" Grundlage stalinistischer Prägung machten beide – wie andere der damals „namhafteren deutschen Pädagogen" auch – erst „im Laufe der Jahre 1946 und 1947 … Bekanntschaft".[9]

Alt publizierte im ersten Heft 1946 der Zeitschrift „Pädagogik" mit Marx und ohne Lenin und Stalin eine gesellschaftstheoretische, soziologisch

---

5 Vgl. Sonja Häder, „Sozialporträt der Pädagogischen Fakultät der Universität Halle-Wittenberg von ihrer Gründung 1946/47 bis zu ihrer Auflösung 1955," in *Strukturwandel vs. bürgerliche Kontinuität. Eliten im Sozialismus. Beiträge zur Sozialgeschichte der DDR*, editiert von Peter Hübner (Köln u.a.: Böhlau, 1999), 381–403, hier 395.

6 Vgl. Ulrich Wiegmann, „Über vergessene, verschwiegene und verdrängte Ursprünge des marxistischen Erziehungsbegriffs bei Robert Alt," in *Jahrbuch für Historische Bildungsforschung*, redigiert von Peter Dudek et al. (Bad Heilbrunn: Klinkhardt, 2004), 75–100.

7 Robert Alt, *Die Industrieschulen. Ein Beitrag zur Geschichte der Volksschule* (Berlin/Leipzig: Volk und Wissen Verlags, 1948).

8 Max Gustav Lange, *Totalitäre Erziehung. Das Erziehungssystem der Sowjetzone Deutschlands* (Frankfurt a.M.: Verl. d. Frankfurter Hefte, 1954), 273.

9 Max Gustav Lange, *Totalitäre Erziehung. Das Erziehungssystem der Sowjetzone Deutschlands* (Frankfurt a.M.: Verl. d. Frankfurter Hefte, 1954), 273.

geleitete Begründung der „sozialen" und „demokratischen" Schulreform in der SBZ.[10] Dennoch wurde der Text in der DDR als „theoretische Begründung der Schule auf marxistisch-leninistischer Grundlage" geadelt.[11] Nicht zuletzt wegen der von Lange eingeräumten „gewisse(n) formale(n) Übereinstimmung mit dem historischen Materialismus stalinistischer Prägung"[12] erwies sich Alts funktionales Erziehungsverständnis aus bildungspolitischer Perspektive dazu geeignet, im Kontext der bereits 1947 einsetzenden gesellschaftspolitischen Tendenzwende[13] unerwünschte Pädagogiken als gesellschaftssystemisch inkompatibel zurückzuweisen. Parteiideologisch zurechtgestutzt, bot Alts Erziehungsbegriff im Gründungszeitraum der DDR und der Hochzeit des Stalinismus eine willkommene gesellschaftstheoretisch legitimierte Formel dafür, allein die sog. Sowjetpädagogik als gesellschaftspolitisch vereinbare Pädagogik zu propagieren.

In den ersten vier Jahrgängen der „Pädagogik" engagierte sich vor allem Max Gustav Lange für eine „notwendige neuorientierung" der Erziehungswissenschaft. Wie Alt und Lange in ihrem Eröffnungsbeitrag der Zeitschrift betonten, ging es ihnen „um den ausbau einer strengen erfahrungswissenschaft, die weder das individuum noch die gesellschaft verabsolutiert, sondern den prozeß der erziehung als ein verhalten vergesellschafteter menschen in erscheinung treten läßt".[14]

---

10 Robert Alt, „Zur gesellschaftlichen Begründung der neuen Schule," *Pädagogik* 1, no. 1 (1946): 12–22. Nachdruck in: Karl-Heinz Günther, Helmut König und Rudi Schulz, *Alt, Robert: Erziehung und Gesellschaft. Pädagogische Schriften*, editiert von Karl-Heinz Günther, Helmut König und Rudi Schulz (Berlin: Volk und Wissen Verlag, 1975), 68–85.

11 Karl-Heinz Günther, Helmut König und Rudi Schulz, „Vorbemerkungen," in *Alt, Robert: Erziehung und Gesellschaft. Pädagogische Schriften*, ed. Karl-Heinz Günther, Helmut König und Rudi Schulz (Berlin: Volk und Wissen Verlag, 1975), 67–68, hier 68.

12 Lange, *Totalitäre Erziehung. Das Erziehungssystem der Sowjetzone Deutschlands*, 275.

13 Vgl. Gert Geißler, „Die bildungspolitische Tendenzwende 1947–1949," in *Schule und Erziehung in der DDR. Studien und Dokumente*, editiert von Gert Geißler, Ulrich Wiegmann (Neuwied: Luchterhand, 1995), 41–68. Vgl. auch Oskar Anweiler, *Schulpolitik und Schulsystem in der DDR* (Opladen: Leske & Budrich, 1988), 40–58.

14 Die Redaktion der Zeitschrift *Pädagogik*, „Zum Geleit," *Pädagogik* 1, no. 1 (1946): 1–2, hier 1. In den ersten vier Jahrgängen wurde in der *Pädagogik* Kleinschreibung praktiziert.

Dieser Anspruch, Erziehungsforschung als Sozialwissenschaft zu betreiben, ließ sich unter den Bedingungen des komplizierten wirtschaftlichen Wiederaufbaus in der Nachkriegszeit, angesichts drückender Reparationslast,[15] der zunehmenden Tendenz zur ineffektiven Planwirtschaft nach sowjetischem Vorbild und den zunehmenden Spannungen zwischen den Alliierten sowie nicht zuletzt auf Grund mangelnder Revisionsbereitschaft und -kompetenz des in der SBZ verbliebenen erziehungswissenschaftlichen Personals nicht durchsetzen. Im Dialog mit Bildungsoffizieren der Sowjetischen Militäradministration in Deutschland (SMAD) erlebte Lange, dass die Redaktion der „Pädagogik" gedrängt wurde, die Zeitschrift stärker praktisch auszurichten. Vor allem wurden Beiträge verhindert, „die der antiautoritären Richtung der Reformpädagogik Ausdruck verliehen".[16] Die SMAD habe jedoch Aufsätze geduldet, „die mit ‚Marxismus-Leninismus' nicht das geringste zu tun hatten", ebenso wie Beiträge auf der Grundlage eines „‚nichtstalinistischen Marxismus'".[17] Im ersten Jahrgang der „Pädagogik" mit fünf Monatsheften erschien lediglich ein kurzer Beitrag über Uschinski.[18]

Die neun Ausgaben des zweiten Jahrgangs 1947 enthalten drei kurze Aufsätze mit Bezug zur Sowjetpädagogik. Zusammen nehmen sie einen

---

15 Vgl. z. B. Jochen Laufer, „Von den Demontagen zur Währungsreform – Besatzungspolitik und Sowjetisierung Ostdeutschlands 1945–1948," in *Sowjetisierung und Eigenständigkeit in der SBZ/DDR*, Zeithistorische Studien, Bd. 13, ed. Michael Lemke (Köln/Weimar/Wien: Böhlau, 1999), 163–186.

16 Lange, *Totalitäre Erziehung. Das Erziehungssystem der Sowjetzone Deutschlands*, 276.

17 Lange, *Totalitäre Erziehung. Das Erziehungssystem der Sowjetzone Deutschlands*, 276–277.

18 Vgl. Sergej Maximowitsch Schabalow, „Uschinskij, der Vater der russischen Pädagogik," *Pädagogik* 1, no. 1 (1946): 29–33. Dem vorrevolutionären Traditionsbestand der seit den 1930er Jahren in der Sowjetunion herrschenden Pädagogik wurde Uschinskijs ‚kämpferische' Pädagogik, der in blumiger Sprache und stalinistischer Manier etwa wegen ihrer angeblichen materialistischen Tendenz, einer wissenschaftlich begründeten, nichtfunktionalistischen Psychologie und ihrer Nähe zum „dialektischen materialismus" zugerechnet.

Umfang von nur rund 13 der insgesamt 318 Seiten umfassenden einspaltigen Hauptbeiträge ein.[19]

Gegen Jahresende 1947 veröffentlichte die „Pädagogik“ erstmals eine vierseitige sowjetpädagogische Makarenko-Interpretation. Kaum vertraut mit dem etwa zeitgleich in der Sowjetunion entstehenden Makarenko-Mythos, kündigte die Redaktion einleitend die Übersetzung des Schlusskapitels von Jessipows Pädagogiklehrbuch an mit einem Bericht „über einen im Jahre 1945 allzufrüh (sic!) verstorbenen anerkannten vertreter der sowjetpädagogik“.[20] Der Beitrag wirkt wie ein pädagogisch-propagandistischer Fremdkörper inmitten der Selbstverständigungsbemühungen im östlichen Nachkriegsdeutschland. Gerahmt von einem kritischen Beitrag über Dilthey[21] und einem Aufsatz über die Entwicklung der „modernen deutschen Gesellschaftswissenschaft“[22] war die Darstellung im Modus pädagogischer Propaganda schwerlich dazu angetan, der Sowjetpädagogik bei der alten und neuen erziehungswissenschaftlichen Intelligenz in der SBZ Respekt

---

19 Hinzu kommen sechs annotationsartige Buchbesprechungen zu sowjetpädagogischen und außerpädagogischen sowjetischen Publikationen, zwei Berichte sowie eine Kurzinformation. Zwei der drei Aufsätze beschäftigen sich mit fachdidaktischen Diskussionen zum Biologie- und Geografieunterricht. Sie sollten in einer eigenwilligen Mischung von Nähe und Distanz zu sowjetpädagogischen Entwicklungen „manchen denkanlaß für die westeuropäische pädagogik“ bieten. Vgl. Paul Heimann, „Darwinismus und Schule. Naturkundliche Unterrichtsprobleme im Spiegel der Sowjetpädagogik,“ *Pädagogik* 2, no. 4 (1947): 18–22; Paul Heimann, „Mensch und Umwelt im Geographieunterricht. Probleme und Erfahrungen im Spiegel der Sowjetpädagogik“. *Pädagogik* 2, no. 5 (1947): 10–14, zit. 14.

20 B. P. Jessipow. „A.S. Makarenko, sein Wirken und seine pädagogischen Lehren“. *Pädagogik* 2, Nr. 8 (1947): 25–29, hier 25. Entgegen der redaktionellen Darstellung handelt es sich um das Schlusskapitel von B. P. Jesipow und N.K. Gontscharow, *Pädagogik. Lehrbuch für pädagogische Lehranstalten*, hier geprüft in der 1948 erschienenen deutschen Übersetzung der 3., vermehrten und verbesserten russischen Ausgabe (Berlin/Leipzig, 1948).

21 Karl Gerhard, „Diltheys Lebensphilosophie und die Pädagogik,“ *Pädagogik* 2, no. 8 (1947): 14–24.

22 Max Gustav Lange, „Die Hauptrichtungen der modernen deutschen Gesellschaftswissenschaft (Teil II),“ *Pädagogik* 2, no. 8 (1947): 29–37.

zu verschaffen. Ein Jahr später erschien das Buch von Jessipow und Gontscharow als erste deutsche Übersetzung eines Pädagogiklehrwerkes aus dem Russischen.[23]

Im Jahrgang 1948 schlug sich die gesellschaftspolitische Tendenzwende bereits deutlich in einer zunehmenden Nötigung zur „Parteilichkeit" und der Akzeptanz für die ökonomische Indienstnahme der Pädagogik sowie in einer gewachsenen Zahl von sowjetpädagogisch relevanten Beiträgen nieder. Im Ergebnis wurden die Leser der Zeitschrift ebenso mit prominenten sowjetischen Autoren und mit Grundlagen stalinistischer Sowjetpädagogik konfrontiert, wie mit einem akademisch befremdlichen Parteijargon. Inhaltlich bezogen sich die Beiträge im Interesse größerer Praxisnähe zum einen auf den (Schul-) Unterricht und zum anderen auf Fragen der „weltanschaulich" besonders sensiblen (pädagogischen) Psychologie. Im Jahrgang 1948 erhöhte sich der Umfang sowjetpädagogischer Abhandlungen bereits auf rund 20 Prozent – nicht eingerechnet ein längerer Bericht über die Entwicklung der Wissenschaft in der UdSSR[24] und die umfangreiche Besprechung einer Neuerscheinung zur Geschichte der Sowjetunion.[25]

Während sich eine Reihe deutscher Autoren noch immer um eine erziehungswissenschaftliche Selbstverständigung bemühten, brachte die „Pädagogik" parallel und vorgeblich zum Zwecke der „kritischen auseinandersetzung"[26] das sowjetpädagogische Paradigma und den Ausschließlichkeitsanspruch des stalinistischen „Marxismus-Leninismus" mit holprigen Übersetzungen in Stellung.

---

[23] Ein auf „marxistisch-leninistischer" Grundlage verfasstes deutsches Pendant stand erst 1953 mit Werner Dorst, *Erziehung, Bildung und Unterricht in der deutschen demokratischen Schule. Grundlagen* (Berlin: Volk und Wissen Verlag, 1953) zur Verfügung.

[24] „Die Entwicklung der Wissenschaft in der Sowjetunion seit der Oktoberrevolution," *Pädagogik* 3, no. 3 (1948): 44–46.

[25] Karl Gerhard und A. M. Pankratowa, „Geschichte der UdSSR (Moskau 1947)," *Pädagogik* 3, no. 8 (1948): 373–379.

[26] „Vorbemerkungen der Redaktion," in M. N. Skatkin, „Wissenschaft und Lehrfach (Teil I)," *Pädagogik* 3, no. 6 (1948): 249–257, hier 249. Vgl. auch Teil II, *Pädagogik* 3, no. 7 (1948): 309–317.

In einer Zeitschrift mit wissenschaftlichem Anspruch deplatziert wirkt vor allem der Text über Grundprinzipen „marxistisch-leninistischer“ Pädagogikgeschichtsschreibung. Der Autor mahnte, dass „nur von der marxistisch-leninistischen position aus … sich die vergangenheit wirklich verstehen“ ließe. Die Pädagogikgeschichtsschreibung habe „ihre leitenden grundsätze aus den werken“ von Marx, Engels, Lenin und Stalin sowie aus den Dokumenten der herrschenden Partei zu schöpfen und „parteigebunden“, zu sein. Die Geschichte der Pädagogik als „klassengeschichte“ habe „alles überlebte und für den aufbau des kommunismus nicht notwendige auszusondern“. Auffassungen von Stalin und anderen Autoritäten des „Marxismus-Leninismus“ müssten als „Anweisungen“ verstanden werden. Sie „verlangten die entfernung des schematismus, die (sic!) unwissenschaftlichen, abgedroschenen, schablonenmäßigen und nicht selten bei den bürgerlichen historikern entlehnten begriffe und redensarten“.[27]

Die im Jahrgang 1948 eigentümliche Gemengelage aus fortgesetzter Selbstverständigung und der sich inmitten des sich verschärfenden Ost-West-Konflikts vollziehenden gesellschaftspolitischen Ausrichtung an der sowjetischen Gesellschaftskonzeption und zunehmender Konfrontation mit Sowjetpädagogik ist exemplarisch in den Beiträgen zur Psychologie präsent. Einem Tagungsbericht zufolge debattierten ostdeutsche Experten über die Situation der psychologischen Forschung und befassten sich besonders eingehend mit der Psychoanalyse.[28] Zwei Ausgaben der „Pädagogik“ später erschien ein sowjetpädagogischer Beitrag über die auf Erziehung und Unterricht konzentrierte „richtige“, sich auf die „lehre des dialektischen materialismus“ stützende Psychologie und deren Kritik an der überlebten, klassengebundenen „idealistischen“ Psychologie im Allgemeinen und an der Psychoanalyse im Besonderen.[29] Zudem klang der Jahrgang 1948 mit einem Vorabdruck

---

27 E. N. Medinskij, „Grundprinzipien einer Geschichte der Pädagogik,“ *Pädagogik* 3 (1948): 35–39.

28 Vgl. „Die gegenwärtige Situation der psychologischen Forschung. Bericht über eine von der Volk und Wissen GmbH veranstaltete Psychologen-Zusammenkunft,“ *Pädagogik* 3, no. 6 (1948): 267–272.

29 Vgl. A. A. Smirnow, „Die Entwicklung der sowjetischen Psychologie,“ *Pädagogik* 3, no. 8 (1948): 349–359.

eines Kapitels von Rubinsteins „Grundlagen der allgemeinen Psychologie“ aus.[30]

1949 mündete die ost-west-deutsche Spaltung in die Gründung der Bundesrepublik und der DDR. Inmitten des verschärften Kalten Krieges kam die gesellschaftspolitische Tendenzwende in der SBZ/DDR zum Abschluss. Die Umbildung der SED zur „Partei neuen Typs“ nach dem Vorbild der „bolschewistischen“ KPdSU erhöhte den „politisch-ideologischen“ Gesinnungsdruck nicht nur auf Parteimitglieder. Auf dem 4. Pädagogischen Kongress im August 1949 manifestierte sich schließlich die Durchsetzung des doktrinär geleiteten gesellschaftspolitischen Führungsanspruchs der SED auch auf erziehungswissenschaftlichen Terrain.

Der 4. Jahrgang 1949 der „Pädagogik“ dokumentiert die Tendenz zu der mit politischer Macht beanspruchten Indienstnahme der Pädagogik für die Durchsetzung wirtschafts- und gesellschaftspolitischer Ziele. Damit einher ging die verstärkte Propagierung des sowjetpädagogischen Vorbilds, vor allem die Orientierung an einem Theorie-Praxis-Verständnis, das die pädagogisch-wissenschaftliche Konzentration auf Fragen der Optimierung institutioneller Erziehung und (schulischer) Unterrichtung einforderte. Der Anteil sowjetpädagogisch relevanter Aufsätze in den Beitragsteilen des Jahrgangs 1949 betrug nun mehr als ein Viertel. Hinzu kamen Aufsätze, Berichte und Buchbesprechungen mit ausdrücklichem Bezug zur Sowjetpädagogik von zum Teil größerem Umfang. Die Propagierung des sowjetpädagogischen Theorie-Praxis-Verständnisses mündete in die Behauptung, dass „eine erziehungstheorie … heute … wirkung nur dann erzielen (kann), wenn sie an die

---

30 S. L. Rubinstein, „Die Struktur des Psychischen (Teil I)“. *Pädagogik* 3, no. 9 (1948): 399–409. Die erste deutsche Übersetzung der russischen Erstauflage von 1940 erschien im Ostberliner Verlag Volk und Wissen erst 1958. Vgl. https://www.zvab.com/buch-suchen/titel/grundlagen-der-allgemeinen-psychologie/autor/rubinstein/. Die Bibliothek für Bildungsgeschichtliche Forschung (BBF) weist hingegen eine Ausgabe im Katalog mit „ca. 1953“ aus. Vgl. https://bbf.bsz-bw.de/cgi-bin/koha/opac-search.pl?q=Rubinstein+Grundlagen. Nachweislich wurden von der Abteilung Fernstudium der Pädagogischen Fakultät der Humboldt-Universität bereits 1957 als Studienmaterial zu Allgemeinen Psychologie Auszüge aus Rubinsteins „Grundlagen einer allgemeinen Psychologie“ herausgegeben. Vgl. ebd. Rubinsteins Monografie erlebte bis gegen Ende der DDR zahlreiche Auflagen.

lehrerpraxis anknüpft, wenn sie eine verallgemeinerung der gesamten unterrichts-erziehenden tätigkeit der demokratischen schule, die bereits fortschrittliche formen in ihrem wirkungsbereich aufzeigt, darstellen wird".[31] Ferner wurden umfängliche Buchvorstellungen etwa zur deutschen Erstausgabe des Pädagogiklehrbuches von Ogorodnikow und Schimbiriew,[32] zur Russischen Makarenko-Werkausgabe und zur russischen Uschinskij-Ausgabe publiziert.

Als Stützen der Sowjetisierung erwiesen sich vor allem in den sowjetischen Kriegsgefangenenlagern zu Stalinisten[33] „umerzogene" resp. disziplinierte und „marxistisch-leninistisch" geschulte „Heimkehrer". Zu ihnen zählte prominent der Direktor des 1949 gegründeten Deutschen Pädagogischen Zentralinstituts (DPZI) Werner Dorst[34]. Er wurde indessen noch in seinem Eifer von dem trotz alledem seitens der SED-Führung „politisch-ideologisch" beargwöhnten Westemigranten Hans Siebert[35] übertroffen.

Die Durchsetzung des sowjetpädagogischen Paradigmas während der Hochzeit des Stalinismus in der DDR (1949–1953)

Die seit 1949 konkurrenzlos zum Vorbild pädagogischer Wissenschaft erhobene Sowjetpädagogik charakterisierte Max Gustav Lange 1954 als „radikal von der traditionellen abendländischen Wissenschaft unterschiedene[n], vom Marxismus-Leninismus geprägte „Wissenschaft neuen Typs".[36] Leonard Froese kennzeichnete sie 1962 durch deren Selbstverständnis als „neue, ‚revolutionäre

---

31 Heinz Kelbert, „Die nächsten Aufgaben der Pädagogik". *Pädagogik*, no. 5 (1949): 218–224, hier 218. Mit einem Nachwort der Redaktion. Kelbert, „Die nächsten Aufgaben der Pädagogik," 224–226.

32 I. T. Ogorodnikow und P. N. Schimbiriew, *Lehrbuch der Pädagogik* (Berlin: Volk und Wissen Volkseigener Verlag, 1953. (1. Aufl. Berlin 1949, hier vorliegend in der unveränderten 5. Aufl. 1953).

33 Lange, *Totalitäre Erziehung. Das Erziehungssystem der Sowjetzone Deutschlands*, 283.

34 Vgl. die Kurzbiografie in Gert Geißler, „Dokumente und Personen," in *Schule und Erziehung in der DDR*, editiert von Gert Geißler und Ulrich Wiegmann (Neuwied: Luchterhand, 1995), 207–344, hier 305.

35 Vgl. zur Person: Gert Geißler, „Hans Siebert – zur erziehungsgeschichtlichen Spur eines emigrierten politischen Pädagogen," *Zeitschrift für Pädagogik*, no. 5 (1994): 781–799.

36 Lange, *Totalitäre Erziehung. Das Erziehungssystem der Sowjetzone Deutschlands*, 268.

Pädagogik' … frei vom ‚Ballast abendländischen Bildungsdenkens'".[37] Christa Uhlig beschrieb die „These" bzw. den „Mythos von der Sowjetisierung" als ein schwieriges Problem, das „in seiner erziehungsgeschichtlichen Relevanz noch längst nicht erfaßt" sei.[38] „Auf der Systemebene" räumte sie „sowjetische Einflußnahme und Kontrolle" ein, während ein mit der „‚Amerikanisierung' von Lebenswelten in der Bundesrepublik … vergleichbarer Prozeß" der Sowjetisierung „so nicht stattgefunden" habe.[39] Christine Lost erklärte Sowjetpädagogik zu einem deutschen Phänomen, das als „Konstrukt" zu verstehen sei und einen politisch-weltanschaulichen Typus „sozialistischer bzw. marxistisch-leninistischer Pädagogik in seiner sowjetrussischen bzw. sowjetischen Realisierungsform" bezeichne.[40]

Es fällt allerdings schwer, die so gefasste Sowjetpädagogik als neuartig zu akzeptieren. Zumal sie vorwiegend als Unterrichtslehre einer herkömmlichen und seitens von Reformpädagogen verachteten „Lernschule" in der SBZ/DDR publik wurde. Frei von abendländischer Tradition war Sowjetpädagogik allein schon dadurch nicht. Freigeräumt war sie seit den 1930er Jahren weithin von reformpädagogischen Einflüssen und der eigenen

---

[37] Leonhard Froese, *Die Sowjetisierung der deutschen Schule. Entwicklung und Struktur des mitteldeutschen Bildungswesens (Das Pädagogische Gespräch)* (Freiburg/Basel/Wien: Herder, 1962), 4.

[38] Vgl. Uhlig, *Rückkehr aus der Sowjetunion*, 28.

[39] Uhlig, *Rückkehr aus der Sowjetunion* 11, 13 u. 17.

[40] Vgl. Christine Lost, *Sowjetpädagogik. Wandlungen Wirkungen Wertungen in der Bildungsgeschichte der DDR* (Hohengehren: Schneider, 2000), 16–17. Die Empfehlung von Lost, auf den Begriff Sowjetisierung zu verzichten, wird unabhängig von der Frage, ob er als wissenschaftlicher Terminus zur Beschreibung und Erklärung der DDR-Bildungsgeschichte taugt, nicht geteilt. Zu berücksichtigen ist vielmehr die Tatsache sowohl der Adaption der sog. Sowjetpädagogik in ihren Grundlagen, d.h. speziell in ihren leitenden Begriffen, besonders zwischen 1947/48 und 1953 in der SBZ/DDR als auch die historische Präsenz als Kampfbegriff in der Bundesrepublik besonders zwischen 1950 und Mitte der 1960er Jahre. Selbst im Ergebnis einer gewollt vorurteilsfreien, politisch möglichst distanzierten erziehungswissenschaftlichen Beobachtung wurde der Terminus etwa durch Leonard Froese benutzt und bestätigt. Vgl. Leonhard Froese, *Die Sowjetisierung der deutschen Schule*. Vgl. Christine Lost, „Sowjetpädagogik. Zur Verabschiedung untauglicher Interpretationsmuster der Bildungs- und Pädagogikgeschichte der SBZ/DDR," *Jahrbuch für Historische Bildungsforschung*, no. 4 (1998): 299–341, hier 300.

reformpädagogischen Tradition des Jahrzehnts nach der Oktoberrevolution. Freilich war Sowjetpädagogik keine, wie es die wörtliche Übersetzung nahelegt, Rätepädagogik. Dass es sich um ein deutsches Konstrukt handelte, ist angesichts der Selbstbezeichnung[41] und ihrer Wirkungen in den sog. Volksdemokratien Mittel- und Osteuropas mehr als fraglich. Eine Pädagogik, die sich zu Recht auf die Marxsche Philosophie berufen kann, war Sowjetpädagogik ebenfalls nicht. Als geradezu idealtypische, intentionale, auf Belehrung in Verbindung mit „politisch-ideologischer" resp. sittlicher und „parteilicher" Erziehung angelegte, im engeren Sinne erziehliche Unterrichtslehre hält sie einer materialistischen Attribuierung schwerlich stand. Dies allein schon deshalb nicht, weil sie ein aus der „marxistisch-leninistischen" Doktrin abgeleitetes Ideal institutionalisierter Erziehung und Bildung zur Grundlage pädagogischer Wissenschaft erhob, anstatt der tätigen Selbstveränderung des Menschen den Vorzug zu geben. Auf der Grundlage der „Lehre Lenin-Stalins" (!), habe pädagogische Theorie die Frage zu beantworten: „Wie muß der Mensch des sozialistischen Zeitalters beschaffen sein, und wie ist er zu erziehen?"[42] Der Konflikt, der sich daraus ergab, dass die herrschende Partei und der Staat der Pädagogik die Ziele vorgaben und Erziehungswissenschaft genötigt war, diese als erziehungswissenschaftliche Grundlage und Aufgabe zu akzeptieren, blieb unberücksichtigt. Auch die autoritative Entwertung der Pädagogik durch die Stalinsche Auslegung des Verhältnisses von Sein und Bewusstsein/Erziehung wurde durch das sowjetpädagogische Selbstverständnis erziehungswissenschaftlich ignoriert.[43]

Sowjetpädagogik bezeichnet somit schlicht die aus der UdSSR seit der Tendenzwende in die SBZ/DDR importierte verbindliche, unter Stalin in den ersten 1930er Jahren in der Sowjetunion mit Macht auf der Basis der

---

41 Vgl. Jessipow und Gontscharow, *Pädagogik*, 16.

42 Vgl. Jessipow und Gontscharow, *Pädagogik*, 15.

43 „Die wirkliche stählung der kader erfolgt in der lebendigen arbeit, außerhalb der schule, im kampf mit schwierigkeiten, bei der überwindung von schwierigkeiten". Gustav Wilhelm Lehmbruck, „Stalin und die Entwicklung des sowjetischen Bildungswesens," *Pädagogik*, no. 4 (1949): 12, 1–9, hier 7.

herrschenden Parteidoktrin gegen reformpädagogische Tendenzen[44] durchgesetzte Pädagogik. Pädagogische Sowjetisierung charakterisiert eine in der Geschichte der pädagogischen Wissenschaft in der DDR nach Art und Intensität unterscheidbare Übernahme der Sowjetpädagogik, die sodann in der zweiten Existenzhälfte der DDR treffender als sowjetischer Einfluss begriffen werden kann.[45] Sowjetpädagogik wurde während der Hochphase der Sowjetisierung der Gesellschaft zwischen 1949 und 1953 in ihren Grundfesten, d.h. in ihrer Substanz adaptiert, ohne dass die ostdeutsche Rezeption das theoretische „Konstrukt" nicht nur nicht wesentlich modifizierte, sondern vielmehr ihre Grundbegriffe anerkannte und aufnahm. Manche der leitenden Termini mussten lediglich aus gebotenem Respekt vor einem revolutionstheoretisch gedeuteten Vorsprung der UdSSR den Verhältnissen in der DDR angepasst werden. Zudem verliefen beispielsweise Art und Ausmaß der Sowjetisierung des Bildungswesens anders als die Adaption des pädagogischen Paradigmas. Die sowjetpädagogische Antwort auf die Frage, wie Erziehung, Bildung und Unterricht zu verstehen seien, markierte die Säulen des „Konstrukts" Sowjetpädagogik.

Das sowjetpädagogische Paradigma wurde im Jahr vor der DDR-Gründung mit der Erstauflage der deutschen Übersetzung des Lehrbuchs für pädagogische Lehranstalten von Jessipow/Gontscharow aus dem Jahr 1946 eingeführt. Gleichsam nach Art eines Grundgesetzes wurde es in den Paragrafen 1 bis 16 fixiert.[46]

Paragraf 1 reduziert Pädagogik auf eine „Wissenschaft von der Erziehung der Kinder" und definiert sie als „Lehre von den Zielen und Aufgaben der Erziehung, ihrem Inhalt, ihren Methoden und ihrer Organisation". Pädagogische Forschung wird als Verallgemeinerung von Erziehungserfahrungen beschrieben, die zu einer regelgerechten Systematisierung bewährter Erziehung führe.

---

[44] Vgl. insbes. „Über die Grund- und Mittelschule. Beschluß des Zentralkomitees der KPdSU (B) vom 5. Sept. 1931," in *Die Sowjetische Bildungspolitik seit 1917. Dokumente und Texte*, ed. Oskar Anweiler und Klaus Meyer, (Heidelberg: Quelle & Meyer, 1961), 178–186 u. „Über die Lehrpläne und die Schulordnung der Grund- und Mittelschule. Beschluß des Zentralkomitees der KPdSU (B) vom 25. August 1932 (Auszug)," in *Die Sowjetische Bildungspolitik seit 1917*, 188–194.

[45] Vgl. zu den Begriffen Sowjetisierung, Bolschewisierung und sowjetischer Einfluss Michael Lemke, *Sowjetisierung und Eigenständigkeit*, 12–15.

[46] Vgl. zum Folg. Jessipow und Gontscharow, *Pädagogik*, 7–24.

Ogorodnikow/Schimbiriew ergänzten dies wenig später durch die Aufgabe, „das pädagogische Erbe der Vergangenheit kritisch zu verarbeiten".[47]

Jessipow/Ogorodnikow zufolge leitet pädagogisches Wissen und Können die Kunst des Erziehens zum Erfolg, allerdings nicht unabhängig vom Talent, und der natürlichen Begabung des Erziehers und seiner „Liebe zu den Kindern" (Paragraf 2). Erziehung sei Bestandteil der Geschichte der menschlichen Gesellschaft und bereits „in der primitiven Gesellschaft" „kein bloßer Naturprozeß, sondern ein gesellschaftlicher, zielgerichteter, planmäßiger Vorgang".

Das „marxistisch-leninistische" Dogma wurde sodann in den Paragrafen 3 bis 7 explizit in der Deutung des Klassencharakters der Erziehung und Pädagogik entfaltet. Die Systematik folgt der „marxistisch-leninistisch" definierten Abfolge der zum Kommunismus aufsteigenden Gesellschaftsformationen.

Paragraf 8 widmet sich dem Verhältnis von Politik und Pädagogik. Während die Auffassung von der Unmöglichkeit einer politikfreien Schule mit Lenin autorisiert wird, zitieren die Autoren zur Rechtfertigung pädagogischer Politisierung Stalin, der Bildung als Waffe propagierte.

Paragraf 10 widmet sich den leitenden Begriffen, und zwar vorgeblich nicht im Allgemeinen, sondern in deren kommunistischer Ausrichtung. Die Differenz wird allein kenntlich durch das Attribut „kommunistisch", sodass die begriffliche Substanz unberührt bleibt. Typisch ist, dass neben Erziehung und Bildung mit dem Terminus Unterricht eine dritte paradigmatische Säule aufgerichtet wird. Sie leitet sich aus dem Diktum ab, dass Erziehung ausschließlich ein zielgerichteter, planmäßiger Vorgang sei und sich vorzugsweise in institutionalisierter Form vollziehe.

Dem Terminus Erziehung schreiben Jessipow/Gontscharow eine doppelte Bedeutung zu. Zum einen stelle er den „umfassendsten Begriff dar", der „Erziehung, Bildung und Unterricht" einschließe. Zum anderen, oder wie dann maßgeblich für die Pädagogik in der DDR Ogorodnikow und Schimbiriew erklären, in einem engeren Sinne,[48] sei Erziehung auf die „Erarbeitung" einer „Weltanschauung" und „Überzeugungen" sowie Charaktereigenschaften

---

[47] Ogorodnikow und Schimbiriew, *Lehrbuch der Pädagogik*, 24.

[48] Vgl. Ogorodnikow und Schimbiriew, *Lehrbuch der Pädagogik*, 10.

gerichtet. Unterricht bezeichnen die Autoren als planmäßig in der Schule zu leistende Arbeit, „durch welche die Schüler Kenntnisse, Fähigkeiten und Gewohnheiten … erwerben". Bildung wird als Ergebnis des Unterrichts definiert, „als System von Kenntnissen, Fähigkeiten und Gewohnheiten, die intellektuelle Reife und durchformte … Weltanschauung der Schüler". Alle drei Grundbegriffe seien „in einem einheitlichen Prozeß untrennbar miteinander verbunden".

Der Paragraf 13 bezieht Erziehung und „marxistisch-leninistische" Ideologie aufeinander. Der Text illustriert, wie weit Sowjetpädagogik „philosophisch" von Marx distanziert wurde bzw. wie weit die intellektuelle Aushöhlung und Deformation des Marxschen Materialismus[49] durch den stalinistischen „Marxismus-Leninismus" sowjetpädagogisch etwa bis zur Mitte der 1950er Jahre getrieben wurde. Im Mittelpunkt steht das Verhältnis von Erziehung, Veranlagung und Entwicklung sowie die Beziehung von Erziehung und Umwelt. Akzeptiert wurden zwar individuell unterschiedliche Anlagen der Menschen, wobei Erziehung jedoch „am ehesten imstande" sei, „die positiven Anlagen zu entwickeln und die negativen zu beseitigen". Auch die Umwelt wirke auf die Entwicklung ein. Sie sei aber selbst wiederum „erst das Ergebnis der revolutionären gesellschaftlichen Umbildung und der … Erziehung".

Mehr wussten Jessipow und Gontscharow Studierenden sowjetischer Lehranstalten diesbezüglich nicht zu bieten. Das aber stellte sich sogar noch als Vorzug zumindest gegenüber dem „stalinistischen" Biologismus von Ogorodnikow/Schimbiriew heraus. In ihrer Darstellung suchen sie nach einer Synthese Marxscher Soziologie und Mitschurin-Lyssenkoscher Vererbungslehre. Es gehe um „die konkrete Untersuchung und wissenschaftliche Analyse der Veränderung der Erbanlagen und um die entscheidende Rolle der gesellschaftlichen Bedingungen und der Erziehung bei der Entwicklung der Persönlichkeit".[50] Die bedrohliche These von der Verbindung von Biologismus und Pädagogik zur Schaffung des sozialistischen

---

49 Vgl. hierzu bes. Karl Marx und Friedrich Engels, „Thesen über Feuerbach," in *Werke*, ed. Karl Marx und Friedrich Engels (Berlin: Dietz Verlag, 1959), 5–7 u. Karl Marx, „Das Kapital," in *Werke*, ed. Karl Marx und Friedrich Engels (Berlin: Dietz Verlag, 1962), 192.

50 Ogorodnikow und Schimbiriew, *Lehrbuch der Pädagogik*, 16.

Menschen[51] oder – noch weniger missverständlich – von der „organisierte(n) Produktionsweise des Menschen" ist bei Ogorodnikow/Schimbiriew angelegt und wurde ein Jahr später in der „Pädagogik" ungezügelt entfaltet.[52] Von der Adaption derartiger biologistischer Irrlehren mochten ostdeutsche Erziehungswissenschaftler durch die noch zeitlich nahe Erfahrung des Nationalsozialismus weitgehend gefeit gewesen sein.

Einig waren sich die Autoren der beiden ersten sowjetpädagogischen Lehrbücher in der SBZ/DDR hinsichtlich der „Ziele und Aufgaben der kommunistischen Erziehung". Unterschieden wurden allgemeine Ziele von denen der Körpererziehung, der geistigen Erziehung, polytechnischen Bildung, sittlichen und schließlich ästhetischen Erziehung.[53]

In beiden Pädagogiklehrwerken wurde unter Rückgriff auf Makarenko dem Kollektiv zwar eine wichtige Bedeutung zugeschrieben. Im Zentrum der Darstellung steht die Kollektiverziehung in der Schulklasse unter Leitung des Lehrers[54] jedoch nicht. Die erst nach dem Tod Makarenkos 1939 in der Sowjetunion breit einsetzende Rezeption der (Kollektiv-) Pädagogik Makarenkos und seiner Erhebung zum pädagogisch begnadeten und

---

[51] Die These wird mit Hilfe eines von aus dem Russischen ins Deutsche rückübersetzten, wenn auch nicht vollständig richtig wiedergegebenen, aber sinngemäß im ersten und ab dem dritten Satz überwiegend zutreffenden Zitat von Engels autorisiert. Die nicht korrekt voneinander abgesetzten Zitatteile beginnen mit den Sätzen: „Die Arbeit schuf erst den Menschen. Sie verlieh ihm seine heutige Gestalt". Ausgewiesen als zit. nach Karl Marx und Friedrich Engels, *Werke*, Bd. XIV. O.O., 453 u. 454. Vgl. N. F. Posnanski, „Vererbung, Umwelt und Erziehung in der Entwicklung und Formung des Menschen nach der materialistischen Lehre," *Pädagogik*, Nr. 5 (1950): 5, 3. In der vom Dietz Verlag besorgten Ausgabe heißt es: „Die Arbeit [...] hat den Menschen selbst geschaffen". Friedrich Engels, „Dialektik der Natur," in *Werke*, ed. Karl Marx und Friedrich Engels, (Berlin: Dietz Verlag, 1962), 305–568, hier 444. Der folgende Satz des Zitats findet sich in dem Kapitel „Der Anteil der Arbeit an der Menschwerdung des Affen" nicht.

[52] Posnanski, „Vererbung, Umwelt und Erziehung in der Entwicklung," 8.

[53] Vgl. Jessipow und Gontscharow, *Pädagogik*, 25–37; Ogorodnikow und Schimbiriew, *Lehrbuch der Pädagogik*, 51–68. Irritierend wirkt die Reihung der Ziele, in der die körperliche Erziehung vor der geistigen oder intellektuellen Erziehung rangiert. Das hatte in Deutschland auch zwischen 1933 und 1945 Tradition.

[54] Vgl. Jessipow und Gontscharow, *Pädagogik*, 279; Ogorodnikow und Schimbiriew, *Lehrbuch der Pädagogik*, 353.

emphatischen Genius sowie die erst anlässlich des 10. Todestages von Makarenko beschlossene russische Werkausgabe bietet dafür eine Erklärung.

Die „Pädagogik" veröffentliche 1949 die erste Rezension zu einem Buch Makarenkos in deutscher Sprache.[55] In den 1950er Jahren wurde Makarenkos Kollektivpädagogik zum wichtigen Bestandteil des sowjetpädagogischen Paradigmas. Die „Pädagogik" publizierte allein in den Jahren 1950 bis 1954 gut ein Dutzend Beiträge über Makarenko. Der Jahrgang 1955 richtete für die Diskussion der Kollektivpädagogik eine eigene Rubrik ein. Zwischen 1956 und 1961 erschien schließlich die siebenbändige Werkausgabe sowie 1962 ein Ergänzungsband in deutscher Übersetzung. In der (pädagogischen) Psychologie löste seit 1950 die Pawlow-Rezeption sukzessive den sowjetpädagogischen Mitschurin-Lyssenko-Mythos ab. Nicht zuletzt beteiligte sich die „Pädagogik" mit mehreren Beiträgen am Personenkult um Stalin und würdigte dessen Bedeutung für die „marxistisch-leninistische" Pädagogik. Sowjetpädagogische Beiträge nahmen in den Jahrgängen 1950 und 1951 fast die Hälfte der Abhandlungen ein. 1951 erschien eine schmale Monografie über Stalins pädagogische Bedeutung.[56]

Die weithin durchlässige innerdeutsche Grenze erleichterte all jenen, die der pädagogischen Tendenzwende zur Sowjetpädagogik in der DDR zu entkommen suchten, in die Bundesrepublik auszuweichen. Andere Erziehungswissenschaftler arrangierten sich mit der der pädagogischen Wissenschaft bildungs- und wissenschaftspolitisch zugeschriebenen Dienstleisterrolle für die intentionale, institutionalisierte Erziehung und speziell für den erziehlichen Schulunterricht. Alt- und Neulehrern dürfte besonders das sowjetpädagogische Gebot nach größerer Praxisnähe entgegengekommen sein. Zumal die 1950 verordnete Abkehr von der didaktisch anspruchsvolleren Reformpädagogik und die damit einhergehende Rückkehr zum schematischen erziehlichen Lernschulkonzept die Ausübung des Lehrerberufes zweifellos vereinfachte. Wenn auch der „Marxismus-Leninismus" in der Breite einige Akzeptanzprobleme mit sich gebracht

---

55 Max Gustav Lange, „Hans Siebert und Anton Semjonowitsch Makarenko," in *Vorträge über Kindererziehung*, ed. Anton Semjonowitsch Makarenko, herausgegeben von Hans Siebert. (Berlin/Leipzig: Volk und Wissen Verlags, 1949).

56 Hans Brumme, *Stalin über Volksbildung und Erziehung* (Berlin u. Leipzig: Volk und Wissen Verlags, 1951).

haben mochte, so sollte die Übernahme des Lernschulmodells den einen vertraut, den anderen durch die Abkehr von der Reformpädagogik die Bewältigung des beruflichen Alltags erleichtert haben. Die Orientierung pädagogischer Forschung auf die sog. Verallgemeinerung gedeihlichen pädagogischen Handelns versprach immerhin begehrte Antworten auf Fragen nach dem Wie ergebnisorientierter, rationeller, und – so gesehen – erfolgreicher Unterrichtsführung.[57]

Wie reibungslos sich eine zentrale Kategorie des sowjetpädagogischen Paradigmas durchsetzen und nicht nur mit der eigenen lernschulpädagogischen Tradition, sondern sich mitunter auch mit einer versteinerten, ansonsten eher zurückgehaltenen Gesinnung vereinbaren ließ, belegt eindrucksvoll die Substituierung des Gemeinschafts- durch den Kollektivbegriff. Sie vollzog sich schlicht durch die Ersetzung des Fachausdrucks, d.h. lediglich sprachlich, nicht begrifflich, und zwar während der gesellschaftspolitischen Tendenzwende und zeitlich synchron zur Durchsetzung des allumfassenden Führungsanspruchs der zur Partei neuen Typs formierten SED.[58]

Im Todesjahr Stalins und dem Jahr der für den kleineren deutschen Staat ersten existenzbedrohlichen, mit Hilfe der sowjetischen Militärmacht bewältigten Gesellschaftskrise 1953 erschien das erste Pädagogikbuch der DDR auf „marxistisch-leninistischer“ Grundlage. Verfasst hatte es der Direktor des forschungsleitenden DPZI Werner Dorst. Das vergleichsweise schmale Werk dokumentiert die substanzielle Übernahme des sowjetpädagogischen Paradigmas, d.h. von deren „marxistisch-leninistischer“ oder stalinistischer Grundlage, der doktrinären Charakterisierung des „Klassencharakters“ der Erziehung und der Schule, des Stalinkults, der grundlegenden Begriffe Erziehung, Bildung und Unterricht, des Diktums der Parteilichkeit, der Einschränkung des Gegenstandes auf die intentionale, zielgerichtete

[57] Vgl. „Verordnung über die Unterrichtsstunde als Grundform der Schularbeit, die Vorbereitung, Organisation und Durchführung der Unterrichtsstunde und die Kontrolle der Kenntnisse der Schüler vom 4. Juli 1950,“ in *Dokumente zur Geschichte des Schulwesens in der Deutschen Demokratischen Republik 1945–1955*, ed. Gottfried Uhlig und Karl-Heinz Günther (Berlin: Volk und Wissen Verlag, 1970), 365–367.

[58] Vgl. Ulrich Wiegmann, „Die semantische Reform. Von der Gemeinschafts- zur Kollektivpädagogik in der SBZ/DDR,“ in *Sozialpädagogik und Gemeinschaft. Historische Beiträge zur Rekonstruktion eines konstitutiven Verhältnisses*, editiert von Joachim Henseler und Jürgen Reyer (Hohengehren: Schneider Verlag, 2000), 122–135.

Erziehung Heranwachsender und insbesondere auf den Schulunterricht[59] sowie der Verallgemeinerung erfolgreichen pädagogischen Handels als Funktion pädagogischer Forschung. Das im mehrjährigen Nachgang sowjetischer Übersetzungen verfasste Werk versetzte Dorst in den Stand, die vergleichsweise stärkere Einbindung der Kollektivpädagogik Makarenkos und die inzwischen parteiliniengemäße Würdigung Pawlows einzuarbeiten.

Dorsts Adaption der Sowjetpädagogik prägte nicht nur den Gehalt des Buches, sondern in einigen Passagen auch den devoten stalinistischen Stil der Darstellung.[60] Als Gutachter des Manuskripts nennt Dorst den ehemaligen Buchenwald-Häftling, 1946 Gründer des Instituts für dialektischen Materialismus in Jena sowie erziehungswissenschaftlich und philosophisch wenig begnadeten Walter Wolf, den entschiedenen Verfechter der Sowjetpädagogik Hans Siebert, das Mitglied der KPD seit 1922 und DDR-Nationalpreisträger Johannes Feuer[61] sowie den früheren Oberstudienrat, ehemaligen Wehrmachtsoffizier, nach seiner Kriegsgefangenschaft Mitbegründer des Nationalkomitees Freies Deutschland (NKFD) und 1945–1950 für Volksbildung im Land Brandenburg verantwortlichen Minister Fritz Rücker.[62] Deren vorgebliche „Kritik und wesentliche Hilfe" hat der sowjetpädagogischen Adaption im Grunde nichts anhaben können. Das Buch belegt auch im Autorenverständnis Dorsts die grundsätzliche Übernahme des

59 „Die Pädagogik ist die Wissenschaft vom einheitlichen Prozess der Erziehung und Bildung der heranwachsenden Generation und vom Unterricht, dem Hauptweg seiner Verwirklichung. *Die Pädagogik erforscht die Gesetzmäßigkeiten dieses Prozesses und leitet aus ihnen Grundsätze und Regeln für die praktische Arbeit des Lehrers und Erziehers ab*". Aus dem Entwurf eines Lehrbuchs der Pädagogik. *Pädagogik*, no. 10 (1954): 789–802, zit. 800.

60 Exemplarisch: „Wer also den jungen Menschen behutsam aufzieht, ihn behütet und pflegt wie ein Gärtner den jungen Obstbaum – Stalin hat den Pädagogen dieses schöne Gleichnis gesagt –, muß ein Humanist im Sinne des Marxismus-Leninismus sein." Werner Dorst, „Schlußwort zur ‚Theoretisch-praktischen Konferenz über Fragen der polytechnischen Bildung in der deutschen demokratischen Schule'," *Pädagogik*, no. 7 (1953): 114.

61 Vgl. Erika Mädicke, „Johannes Feuer 1898 bis 1977. Förderer des Erstleseunterrichts und der Didaktik der Unterstufe," in *Wegbereiter der neuen Schule*, ed. Gerd Hohendorf, Helmut König und Eberhard Meumann (Berlin: Volk und Wissen Verlag, 1989), 71–78.

62 Vgl. die Kurzbiografien von Rücker und Wolf in Geißler, *Schule und Erziehung in der DDR*, 319 u. 324.

sowjetpädagogischen Paradigmas.[63] Und dies zu einem Zeitpunkt, als Stalins Tod und der 17. Juni 1953 neue Akzente in der Entwicklung pädagogischer Wissenschaft in der DDR ankündigte.

Pädagogische Wissenschaft in der DDR und Sowjetpädagogik nach Stalins Tod und dem 17. Juni 1953 bis zum erziehungswissenschaftlichen Generationswechsel an der Wende von den 1950er zu den 1960er Jahren

Die Geschichte einer sich nach Jahren sowjetpädagogischer Dogmatisierung in der Folge des 17. Juni 1953 im engsten Kreis der pädagogischen Elite seit Ende 1954 entwickelnden pädagogischen Diskussion ist bekannt. Sie entfaltete sich im Spätwinter 1955 und wurde zum – zwar randständigen – Bestandteil der gesellschaftspolitischen Debatte in der DDR nach dem XX. Parteitag der KPdSU 1956 mit der Verurteilung des Stalinschen Personenkults. Im Jahr darauf kulminierte sie in der Auseinandersetzung um einen als revisionistisch verurteilten Vorschlag für die strukturelle Differenzierung obligatorischer Allgemeinbildung. 1958 mündete sie in die Kampagne der SED-Führung gegen vermeintliche oder tatsächliche gesellschaftskritische, „revisionistische" Gegner. Die nun einsetzende kaderpolitische Säuberungs- und Disziplinierungswelle erfasste einen Großteil bis dahin einflussreicher Erziehungswissenschaftler bis hin zum Direktor des DPZI Werner Dorst. Sie führte auch zur Neubesetzung der Leitung des Volksbildungsministeriums mit Margot Honecker als Stellvertretende Ministerin und ab 1963 zu ihrer Ernennung als Ministerin. In der Folge der Revisionismuskampagne gelangten überwiegend um die 30 Jahre junge, in der SBZ/DDR ausgebildete und „politisch-ideologisch" geschulte Pädagogen in führende Positionen von Bildungspolitik, Bildungsverwaltung und Erziehungswissenschaft. Einflussreiche Positionen behielten sie vielfach bis kurz vor ihrem anstehenden Ausscheiden aus dem Arbeitsleben am Ende der DDR inne. Durch den Personalaustausch an der Wende zu den 1960er Jahren wurden die Bindungen an die erziehungswissenschaftlichen Diskurse in der Weimarer Zeit, die Zusammenhänge zum Niedergang der Erziehungswissenschaft

[63] Vgl. z.B. Dorst, „Schlußwort zur ‚Theoretisch-praktischen Konferenz',“ 8.

während des Nationalsozialismus und zum sozialwissenschaftlich inspirierten pädagogischen Aufbruch der ersten Nachkriegsjahre nachhaltig und folgenreich gekappt.[64]

Bildungsgeschichtlich weit weniger präsent als diese „erziehungswissenschaftliche Diskussion" sind unmittelbare Auswirkungen der 1953er Gesellschaftskrise. Während beispielsweise in den Ausgaben der „Pädagogik" des 1. Halbjahrs 1953 noch die Hälfte aller Heftseiten entweder mit Texten sowjetischer Autor(inn)en oder mit Beiträgen gefüllt waren, die von Entwicklungen in der Sowjetunion handelten, verringerte sich im 2. Halbjahr 1953 der Anteil sowjetpädagogisch relevanter Beitragsseiten schlagartig und drastisch auf nur noch 11 Prozent. Der Anteil sowjetpädagogischer Beiträge sank von über 40 Prozent 1952 gleichzeitig auf etwa ein Viertel, ein Jahr später auf ein Fünftel, bevor er sich 1955 auf unter 10 Prozent verringerte.

Die statistisch präsente Einbremsung der Sowjetisierung nach dem 17. Juni 1953 ging anfangs ohne jede begleitende erziehungswissenschaftliche Debatte einher und war dennoch mit einer bemerkenswerten Tendenz von der bis dahin beherrschenden extensiven zu einer intensiven Ideologisierung verbunden.[65] Dieser Trend lässt sich ebenfalls statistisch belegen, und zwar anhand der Häufigkeit doktrinärer Schlüsselwörter in der Zeitschrift „Pädagogik". Er dokumentiert sich besonders in der Zahl der Nennungen von Marx und Engels, Stalin und Lenin sowie der gängigen Bezeichnungen für die herrschende Doktrin, d.h. durch den Gebrauch der Termini Marxismus, Marxismus-Leninismus, Leninismus, historischer und dialektischer Materialismus und Materialismus. Während für das 1. Halbjahr 1953 noch durchschnittlich 2,5 dieser marxistisch-leninistisch-stalinistischen „Klassiker"-Namen und Begriffe pro Heftseite ermittelt wurden, hatte sich deren Häufung bereits im 2. Halbjahr 1953 auf ca. 1,1 Nennungen pro Seite halbiert. Von 1954 an waren es in etwa kontinuierlich rund 0,2 pro Seite. Stalins Name kam ab dem 2. Halbjahr 1954 und im Jahrgang 1955 insgesamt nur noch auf rund 12,5, Marx auf etwas unter 30 Nennungen.

---

64 Vgl. Geißler, *Schule und Erziehung in der DDR*, bes, 100–104.

65 Vgl. zum Folg. Ulrich Wiegmann, „Der 17. Juni und die Pädagogische Wissenschaft in der DDR," in *„Am Rande des Bankrotts …": Intellektuelle und Pädagogik in Gesellschaftskrisen der Jahre 1953, 1956 und 1968 in der DDR, Ungarn und der CSSR*, ed. Sonja Häder und Ulrich Wiegmann (Baltmannsweiler: Schönstatt-Verlag, 2004), 17–37.

Der freie Fall in der Rubrik Marxismus-Leninismus wurde indessen auf einem vergleichsweise doppelten bis dreimal so hohen Restniveau von durchschnittlich über 50 Nennungen pro Halbjahr abgebremst. Zugleich vollzog sich die Ablösung der seit der Tendenzwende eingebürgerten, ebenso stilistisch befremdlichen wie einfallslosen und unverhohlenen Indoktrination durch eine gefälligere Wissenschaftssprache und einen wissenschaftlich angemesseneren wissenschaftspublizistischen Stil. Diese Entwicklung kennzeichnet den Wandel von der personifizierten Doktrin zur Weltanschauung mit wissenschaftlichem Anspruch, von der textlichen Übersättigung mit autoritativen, für exemplarisch genommenen Einzelaussagen zum Theorem und von hier zum ideologisch fundierten System. Der 17. Juni bewirkte daher nicht etwa nur eine parteidoktrinäre Entlastung pädagogischen Denkens, sondern leitete zur Entwicklung pädagogischer Wissenschaft auf einer allerdings stärker als bislang an Marx orientierten „marxistisch-leninistischen" Grundlegung über.

Begünstigt wurde die vergleichsweise intensivere Hinwendung zu Marx bei gleichzeitiger Abkehr von Stalin durch den Umstand, dass sich im Todesjahr Stalins der Todestag von Karl Marx zum 70. Male jährte. Das mit einigem Pomp begangene „Marx-Jahr" bot der pädagogischen Wissenschaft Anlass, sich auf Marx zurückzubesinnen. In den Blickpunkt gerieten insbesondere das Bildungsideal des vollseitig entwickelten Menschen und die Idee der „Verbindung von produktiver Arbeit mit Unterricht und Gymnastik"[66] als Beitrag von Marx zur Idee der Polytechnisierung[67] allgemeiner Bildung.

Die sowjetischen Pädagogiklehrwerke hatten diesbezüglich wenig zu bieten. Jessipow/Gontscharow deuten immerhin kurz das Problem der „Entfremdung" einseitig ausgebeuteter Arbeiter bei gleichzeitigem Bedarf an vielseitig ausgebildeten Produzenten im kapitalistischen Industriezeitalter an, das vor allem aus der „maschinellen Produktionsweise" und der

---

[66] Marx, „Das Kapital", 508. Vgl. z.B. zur Diskussion in der „Pädagogik" den Beitrag von Walter Wolf, in Walter Wolf und Wilfried Lange, „Erkenntnistheoretische und didaktische Probleme der Verbindung des Unterrichts mit der produktiven Arbeit," *Pädagogik* 15 (1960): 1107–1121, zit. 1119.

[67] Vgl. v.a. Gotthold Krapp, *Marx und Engels über die Verbindung des Unterrichts mit produktiver Arbeit und die polytechnische Bildung* (Berlin: Volk und Wissen Verlag, 1958).

„hochentwickelte(n) Technik“ resultiere.[68] Auch von polytechnischer Bildung ist die Rede. Nach „Marx und Engels“ gehe es „um das Kennenlernen der allgemeinen wissenschaftlichen Prinzipien aller Produktionsprozesse“. Doch schon im selben Absatz wird das Dilemma doktrinärer und politischer Beschränkung offenbar. Zunächst noch stellen die Autoren mit Lenin klar, „daß das Prinzip des polytechnischen Unterrichts nicht einen Unterricht in allem, sondern in den Grundlagen der modernen Industrie überhaupt verlangt“. Im nächsten Satz jedoch behaupten die Autoren, dass Lenin „deshalb“ gefordert habe, „die Schüler mit der Anwendung der Elektrizität in der mechanischen und chemischen Industrie sowie mit den Grundlagen der Agronomie vertraut zu machen“. Die Marxsche Idee eines Unterrichts in Technologie – und nicht etwa in Technik – verlor sich in der erziehungswissenschaftlichen Anerkennung ökonomischer und parteiideologischer Zwänge. Sie mündete schließlich in den für die Sowjetpädagogik charakteristischen Konflikt zwischen allgemeiner und beruflicher Bildung. Selbstredend fehlte auch der Hinweis auf einen Beschluss der KPdSU aus dem Jahre 1931 nicht. Darin wird davor gewarnt, die „Polytechnisierung der Schule“ vom naturwissenschaftlichen Fachunterricht zu trennen, weil dies „übereinstimmend mit der Lehre von Marx und Lenin“ eine „‚grobe Entstellung der Ideen des polytechnischen Unterrichts‘“ sei.[69] Die unbedingte Unterordnung der Sowjetpädagogik unter die anerkannte Allweisheit der herrschenden Partei ist denn auch der Grund dafür, dass der für einen erziehlichen Unterricht an und für sich schlüssige Zusammenhang von polytechnischem Prinzip, „produktiver Arbeit der Schüler“ und Arbeitserziehung bei Jessipow/Gontscharow durch rund 150 Buchseiten verstellt ist.[70]

Auf diese sowjetpädagogische Sinndeutung der Polytechnik ließ sich eine zunehmend selbstbewusstere pädagogische Forschung in der DDR nach Stalins Tod und dem 17. Juni 1953 nicht ein. Der Unterschied zwischen ideologiegeleiteter didaktischer Konstruktion und erziehungswissenschaftlicher Forschung ist in verdichteter Form eindrucksvoll in einem Autorreferat

[68] Vgl. Jessipow und Gontscharow, *Pädagogik*, 25.
[69] Vgl. Brumme, *Stalin über Volksbildung*, 60 f.
[70] Vgl. Brumme, *Stalin über Volksbildung*, 143 u. 285–298.

von Gotthold Krapp dokumentiert.[71] Die erziehungswissenschaftliche Marx-Rezeption wurde allerdings mit der Tatsache konfrontiert, dass die herrschende Bildungspolitik nach raschen theoretischen und praktischen Resultaten verlangte, wissenschaftliche Forschung solchem Zeitdruck freilich nicht standzuhalten vermochte. Aber die Differenz zur Sowjetpädagogik wurde trotzdem bereits anlässlich der Auswertung der im „Marx-Jahr" seitens des DPZI veranstalteten „theoretisch-praktischen Konferenz über Fragen der polytechnischen Bildung" offensichtlich. Wie Dorst in seinem Schlusswort hervorhob, gehe es um „eine *poly*technische und nicht eine technische Ausbildung". Primär ziele polytechnische Bildung auf einen polytechnischen „Gesichtskreis", auf das „Verständnis für die elementarsten Prinzipien der Produktionstätigkeit in den wichtigsten Produktionszweigen" sowie auf „genauere Kenntnisse über die Produktionsprozesse".[72] Die terminologischen Säulen des erziehungswissenschaftlichen Paradigmas wurden im Nachgang des 17. Juni 1953 durch die erziehungswissenschaftliche Marx-Rezeption allerdings nicht erschüttert. Die Hinwendung zu Marx avisierte jedoch relative pädagogisch-wissenschaftliche Souveränitätsansprüche.

Weitere Indizien einer Ersetzung der bis dahin üblichen Übernahme der Sowjetpädagogik durch deren mehr oder minder „kritische" Rezeption sind nachweisbar. Im Gegensatz zur rigorosen stalinistischen Zurückweisung des internationalen und sowjetrussischen reformpädagogischen Erbes seit den 1930er Jahren in der Sowjetunion und in der adaptierten Verordnung über die Unterrichtsstunde aus dem Jahr 1950 plädierte Robert Alt in einem viel beachteten Aufsatz 1956 dafür, durch eine „marxistische Betrachtung … die richtige Gewichtung" der Reformpädagogik vorzunehmen. Dies bedeute Theorien und praktische Vorschläge, „die pädagogische Einsicht und pädagogisches Können bereichert haben", von jenen zu unterscheiden, die wir nicht „bejahen und unkritisch übernehmen können".[73] Andere Diskussionen, die sich zu einer selbstbewussten, mitunter auch kritischen Rezeption der

---

71 Gotthold Krapp, „Autorreferat: Der Gedanke der Verbindung des Unterrichts mit der produktiven Arbeit und der Gedanke der polytechnischen Bildung bei Karl Marx und Friedrich Engels," *Pädagogik* 11 (1956): 701–707.

72 Werner Dorst, „Schlußwort zur ‚Theoretisch-praktischen Konferenz'," 715–720, zit. 716 u. 718.

73 Robert Alt, „Unsere Stellung zur Reformpädagogik," *Pädagogik* 11 (1956): 345–370, hier 346.

Sowjetpädagogik ermutigt sahen, rankten sich um den Gegenstand und die tragenden Begriffe der Pädagogik.[74]

Gelegenheit, erziehungswissenschaftliches Selbstbewusstsein zu wagen, ergab sich ebenfalls durch den Auftrag des Staatssekretariats für das Hochschulwesen, ein eigenes Pädagogiklehrbuch herauszugeben und dabei auf Autoren aus dem der Volksbildungsadministration unterstellten DPZI zu verzichten.[75] Die Arbeiten kamen im Vorfeld der Revisionismuskampagne zum Erliegen. Immerhin bieten ein Vorabdruck des allerdings stark am sowjetpadagogischen Vorbild orientierten 1. Kapitels[76] und archivalisch überlieferte Kapitelentwürfe sowie schriftliche Stellungnahmen zu den Manuskripten Einblicke in das Maß souveräner Selbstverständigung der damaligen pädagogischen Elite an den Universitäten und Hochschulen der DDR über die Grundlagen der Erziehungswissenschaft. Dafür eignen sich vorzugsweise zwei Kapitel.[77] Zum einen das von Heinrich Deiters verfasste Manuskript „Wesen der Erziehung und Bildung", zum anderen das Manuskript des 1. Kapitels „Grundlagen der Pädagogik", das zwieträchtig von den Koautoren Hans Herbert Becker, Direktor des Hallenser Instituts für Praktische Pädagogik und Auslöser der folgenschweren Debatte um die schulstrukturelle Differenzierung allgemeiner Bildung, und Walter Wolf verantwortet wurde.

Becker und Wolf vergewisserten sich in dem unveröffentlichten wie schon im veröffentlichten Entwurf über ihren Gegenstand vorzugsweise durch die Adaption des sowjetpädagogischen Standpunktes. Stalin belehrte sie

---

74 Vgl. z. B Günther Röblitz, „Zum Gegenstand der Pädagogik," *Pädagogik* 10 (1955): 111–118; Walter Wolf, „Zu den Begriffen Bildung und Erziehung," *Pädagogik* 10 (1955): 223–231; Heinrich Deiters, „Zu den Begriffen Bildung und Erziehung," *Pädagogik* 10 (1955): 231–233; Reinhold Kunze, „Zur Bestimmung des Gegenstandes der Pädagogik," *Pädagogik* 11 (1956): 869–873; Walter Wolf, „Der Erziehungsbegriff und die Pädagogik," *Pädagogik* 11 (1956): 191–194.

75 Vgl. zum Folg. Ulrich Wiegmann, „Allgemeinbildungstheorie anstatt Allgemeiner Pädagogik. Zum Verhältnis von bildungspolitisch-doktrinärer Selbstdisziplinierung und gesellschaftspolitischer Instrumentalisierung ‚pädagogischer Wissenschaften' in der SBZ und DDR," in *Kindheit, Jugend und Bildungsarbeit im Wandel. Ergebnisse der Transformationsforschung (Zeitschrift für Pädagogik, Beiheft, 37)*, ed. Heinz-Elmar Tenorth (Weinheim/Basel: Beltz, 1997), 433–454, bes. hier 443–449.

76 „Gegenstand und Aufgaben der Pädagogik," *Pädagogik*, no. 9 (1954): 790–802.

77 Vgl. zum Folg. DIPF/BBF-Archiv, Nachlass Deiters, Mappe 18.

über die richtige Anwendung der dialektischen Methode. Sowjetpädagogik autorisierte das fortgeschrittene Wissen über das Verhältnis von Vererbung und Entwicklung. Pawlow garantierte ihnen, das Verhältnis von Erziehung zur „Umwelt" begriffen zu haben. Die Termini Erziehung, Bildung und Unterricht, blieben der Sowjetpädagogik entlehnt. Auch hinsichtlich der „Quellen der pädagogischen Forschung" blieb das sowjetpädagogische Vorbild unangetastet. Genannt werden hier die Werke der „marxistisch-leninistischen" Klassiker, Parteibeschlüsse und administrative Verordnungen, das „klassische pädagogische Erbe", das „Schrifttum der Sowjetpädagogik" sowie die pädagogische Belletristik und Werke der „schönen Literatur". Aus der pädagogischen Wirklichkeit interessierten vorzugsweise „die Erfahrungen unserer besten Lehrer, Erzieher, Pionierleiter, Eltern u.a.".

In bemerkenswerter Weise übte vor allem Heinrich Deiters an dem Kapitelentwurf substanzielle Kritik, während andere Stellungnahmen sich eher im Detail verlieren. Deiters wandte sich in seiner unveröffentlichten Stellungnahme gegen die sowjetpädagogische Behauptung, pädagogische Wissenschaft würde „erst … auf der philosophischen Grundlage des dialektischen und historischen Materialismus (möglich)" sein. Außerdem beklagte er, dass der Gegenstand der Pädagogik auf „die Erziehung der heranwachsenden Generation" eingeengt wurde. Weiter ketzerte er mit der Frage, ob für die Klärung des Verhältnisses von Vererbung und Entwicklung eine sowjetische Autorisierung zwingend sei. Vor allem wehrte er das sowjetpädagogische Verständnis der Begriffe Erziehung und Bildung ab.[78] Vielmehr, so Deiters, handele es sich um historisch gewachsene „Synonyma", „die den gleichen Gegenstand in seiner Gänze bezeichnen" und an den pädagogischen Anspruch allseitiger Menschenbildung geknüpft sind.

Statt eines Pädagogiklehrwerks kam die als eine Vorabveröffentlichung zum Hochschullehrbuch gedachte „Didaktik" zustande.[79] Die Autoren meinten, mit ihrem Werk neue Wege zu gehen, die an „fortschrittliche Traditionen

---

78 Vgl. Deiters, „Zu den Begriffen Bildung," 231–233. Zum sowjetpädagogischen Verständnis vgl. Ogorodnikow und Schimbirew, *Lehrbuch der Pädagogik*.

79 Karlheinz Tomaschewsky, *Didaktik. Unter besonderer Berücksichtigung des Unterrichts in den Klassen 1 bis 4 der deutschen demokratischen Schule*, redigiert von Helmut Klein (Berlin: Volk und Wissen Verlag, 1956).

der deutschen Didaktik" anknüpfen. Von Sowjetpädagogik ist nicht ausdrücklich die Rede.

Das Buch verdient eine umfängliche Analyse und Interpretation. Hier kann lediglich der Eindruck von einer Gemengelage aus akzeptiertem „marxistisch-leninistisch" geleitetem sowjetpädagogischem Paradigma, d.h. auch von in ihm auf „stalinistische" Weise gespiegeltem lernschulpädagogischem, herbartianistischem Schematismus, und dem selbstbewussten Eingehen auf didaktische Bedürfnisse der „deutschen demokratischen Schule" hingewiesen werden. So fehlt zwar nicht der sowjetpädagogisch unvermeidliche Hinweis auf den Klassencharakter von Schule und Unterricht, aber die „führende Rolle" „der" Partei bleibt unerwähnt. Unterricht würde bestimmt durch gesellschaftliche Forderungen *und* Entwicklungsgesetzmäßigkeiten des Kindes. Charakterisiert sei er durch das Verhältnis von Führung durch den Lehrer und „gemeinsamer Tätigkeit von Lehrer und Schüler".[80] In und zwischen den Zeilen verweisen die Autoren damit auf Marx und dessen Auffassung über die Bedeutung der tätigen Auseinandersetzung des Menschen mit der Natur außer ihm. Der Begriff Tätigkeit fehlt in der Definition von Unterricht z.B. bei Ogorodnikow/Schimbiriew.[81] Und die Auffassung, „der Unterricht ist in der deutschen demokratischen Schule die wichtigste Form der Bildungs- und Erziehungsarbeit", akzentuiert zumindest den sowjetpädagogischen Standpunkt, der eine nahezu sich ausschließlich im Schulunterricht vollziehende erziehliche Bildung suggeriert.

Bemerkenswert ist auch die Reihung unterrichtlicher Ziele. In der „Didaktik" wird die intellektuelle Bildung und Erziehung zuerst dargestellt, die der körperlichen an vorletzter Stelle, vor der ästhetischen. Jessipow/Gontscharow und Ogorodnikow/Schimbiriew waren sich hingegen einig darin, die „Körpererziehung" vor der intellektuellen Erziehung abzuhandeln. Ob sich das Autorenkollektiv der „Didaktik" mit der Übernahme der sowjetpädagogischen Reihen- – und damit gleichsam unvermeidlich auch der Rangfolge – nicht der nationalsozialistischen Privilegierung des Körpers vor dem Geist beugen mochte, ist ungeklärt. Hinsichtlich der Erziehung

---

80 Tomaschewsky, *Didaktik. Unter besonderer Berücksichtigung*, 9, 11 u. 17.

81 Vgl. Ogorodnikow und Schimbiriew, *Lehrbuch der Pädagogik*, 11.

zum Patriotismus fehlt in der „Didaktik“ die Erziehung zum Hass.[82] Die pädagogisch relevanten psychologischen Inhalte werden hingegen sowjetpädagogisch überwiegend durch Pawlow autorisiert.

Eine Fortsetzung ähnlich gelagerter Beispiele für eine selbstbewusstere Akzentuierung der bis 1953 adaptierten Sowjetpädagogik würde eine eingehendere Analyse und Interpretation selbstredend nicht ersetzen. Diese müsste freilich auch berücksichtigen, dass sich pädagogisches Denken auch in der Sowjetunion nach Stalin veränderte und auch in der Unterrichtstheorie neue Akzente zuließ.[83]

Vom Mauerbau bis zur Mitte der 1980er Jahre

Der Personalaustausch in einflussreichen Positionen pädagogischer Wissenschaft Ende der 1950er Jahre hatte neue Bedingungen für die sowjetpädagogische Rezeption und Einflussnahme geschaffen. Die in leitende Stellungen aufgerückte jüngere Generation pädagogischer Wissenschaftler lebte fortan mit der Erfahrung rigider „parteilicher“ Disziplinierung ihrer Vorgänger. Die Gefahr, wie auch immer begründet als Abweichler, Renegat, Revisionist oder Sektierer beschuldigt zu werden und in der Konsequenz den eigenen akademischen Status aufs Spiel zu setzen, blieb latent. Eine Strategie der Anpassung und/oder der Kompromissfindung zwischen „marxistisch-leninistischem“ Diktat und Marxrezeption, Beobachtung internationaler Entwicklungen und Bindung an nationale Traditionen sowie in der Privatsphäre die Bewahrung eigener (Teil)-Identität durch die Flucht in staatlicherseits schwer kontrollierbare Nischen als Ausweg ergab sich nach dem Mauerbau 1961 gewissermaßen unausweichlich. In einigen Texten ist – sofern man will und mit einiger Erfahrung – „zwischen den Zeilen“ das Unbehagen gegenüber „marxistisch-leninistischer“ Parteiideologie im Allgemeinen und sowjetpädagogischen Vorgaben nicht zu übersehen, während sich andererseits

---

82 Vgl. Tomaschewsky, *Didaktik. Unter besonderer Berücksichtigung*, 21 f.

83 So fand etwa die Subjektposition des „Zöglings“ im Unterricht späterhin auch bei Jessipow stärkere Beachtung. Vgl. B. P. Jessipow, *Pädagogik. Lehrbuch für Einrichtungen zur Ausbildung von Lehrern der unteren Klassen* (Berlin: Volk und Wissen Volkseigener Verlag, 1971), 18.

und beispielhaft z.B. die Redaktion der Zeitschrift „Pädagogik“ jedweden „politisch-ideologischen“ Wendungen bereitwillig fügte.[84]

Wie schwierig es war, die Gratwanderung zwischen eigenem Wissenschaftsverständnis und Nötigung zur „marxistisch-leninistischen“ „Parteilichkeit“ und damit zur Akzeptanz des sowjetpädagogischen Paradigmas[85] zu bewerkstelligen, demonstriert der enzyklopädische Beitrag von Gotthold Krapp zum Stichwort „Bildung“. Sein historisch und materialistisch hergeleiteter, auf „Menschenbildung“ zielender sowie mit Marx angebahnter und autorisierter, an Deiters erinnernder, aber trotzdem keinen sowjetpädagogischen Argwohn provozierender Kompromiss mündet in das Fazit: Bilden und Erziehen ist als „einheitlicher Prozeß“ „zweierlei, … das Fähigmachen und das Bereitmachen.[…] Die terminologische Unterscheidung beruht auf gedanklicher Analyse, um die komplexe pädagogische Praxis besser zu fassen und zu überschauen“.[86] Im sowjetpädagogischen Verständnis handelte es sich hingegen um einen mit Unterricht und miteinander „untrennbar verbundenen einheitlichen“[87] „Prozeß der Ausrüstung der Schüler mit einem System wissenschaftlicher Kenntnisse, mit Fähigkeiten und Fertigkeiten und die Formung der kommunistischen Weltanschauung“ (Bildung) und dem „Prozeß der Herausbildung des kommunistischen Bewußtseins und kommunistischen Verhaltens bei den Schülern und der Entwicklung ihres Erkenntnisvermögens und ihrer schöpferischen Fähigkeiten und Talente“ (Erziehung)[88].

In der Zeit gesellschaftlicher Stabilisierung nach dem Mauerbau wurde pädagogische Wissenschaft im Auftrag des Ministeriums für Volksbildung

---

84 Vgl. Ulrich Wiegmann, „Zum Umgang mit dem Verhältnis von Theorie und Praxis in der wissenschaftlichen Pädagogik (1946–1989),“ in *Pädagogische Wissenschaft in der DDR. Ideologieproduktion, Systemreflexion und Erziehungsforschung. Studien zu einem vernachlässigten Thema der Disziplingeschichte deutscher Pädagogik*, editiert von Heinz-Elmar Tenorth u. Ulrich Wiegmann (Bad Heilbrunn: Verlag Julius Klinkhardt, 2022), 362–423.

85 Vgl. „Vorwort,“ in *Pädagogische Enzyklopädie*, editiert von Heinz Frankiewicz u.a. (Berlin: VEB Deutscher Verlag der Wissenschaften, 1963), V f.

86 Gotthold Krapp, „Bildung,“ in *Pädagogische Enzyklopädie*, editiert von Heinz Frankiewicz u.a. (Berlin: VEB Deutscher Verlag der Wissenschaften, 1963), 122–126, hier 126.

87 Jessipow und Gontscharow, *Pädagogik*, 16.

88 Ogorodnikow und Schimbiriew, *Lehrbuch der Pädagogik*, 11.

(MfV) zunächst auf Arbeiten zur Ausgestaltung des einheitlichen sozialistischen Bildungssystems konzentriert. Zwar waren mit dem sozialistischen Schulgesetz 1959[89] bereits dafür die Grundlagen geschaffen worden. Doch erhob die neue pädagogische Elite die im SED-Parteiprogramm von 1963 verlangte Optimierung des Bildungssystems[90] geradezu zur Initiationsleistung ihrer erziehungswissenschaftlichen Generation.[91] 1964 verständigte sie sich auf einer Veranstaltung anlässlich des 15jährigen Bestehens des DPZI über das eigene „parteiliche" resp. „marxistisch-leninistische" Wissenschaftsverständnis im Zeitalter des entwickelten Sozialismus.[92]

In seinem Hauptreferat verzichtete der mit seiner Ernennung als Nachfolger Dorsts zum führenden pädagogischen Wissenschaftler in der DDR aufgestiegene Gerhart Neuner[93] darauf, die Fundamente der Erziehungswissenschaft eigens zu definieren. Als Grundlage pädagogischer Wissenschaft bezeichnete er die „marxistische Entwicklungsauffassung".[94] Dieser wiederum ruhe das „marxistisch-leninistische" Menschenbild auf, welches „die Grundkonzeption der Erziehung und Entwicklung des Menschen" bestimme.

---

89 „Gesetz über die sozialistische Entwicklung des Schulwesens in der Deutschen Demokratischen Republik vom 2. Dezember 1959," in *Quellen zur Geschichte der Erziehung*, editiert von Karl-Heinz Günther, u.a. (Berlin:Volk und Wissen Verlag, 1978), 532–539.

90 „Gesetz über das einheitliche sozialistische Bildungssystem. Auszug," in *Quellen zur Geschichte der Erziehung*, ed. Karl-Heinz Günther, u.a. (Berlin: Volk und Wissen Verlag, 1978), 539–546.

91 Vgl. „Die Gestaltung des einheitlichen sozialistischen Bildungssystems der DDR in den sechziger und siebziger Jahren," in *Geschichte der Erziehung*, editiert von Karl-Heinz Günther, u.a. (Berlin: Volk und Wissen Verlag, 1987), 713–722.

92 Vgl. zum Folg Wiegmann, „Allgemeinbildungstheorie anstatt Allgemeiner Pädagogik," 449–451.

93 Vgl. die Autobiografie von Gerhart Neuner, *Zwischen Wissenschaft und Politik. Ein Rückblick aus lebensgeschichtlicher Perspektive* (Köln: Böhlau Köln, 1996). Zu den Autobiografien von Neuner und Karl-Heinz Günter vgl. auch Ulrich Wiegmann, „Selbstbiografien ranghöchster DDR-pädagogischer Wissenschaftler im Vergleich: Karl-Heinz Günther und Gerhart Neuner," in *Der Bildungsgang des Subjekts. Bildungstheoretische Analysen. Zeitschrift für Pädagogik, 48*, ed. Sonja Häder und Heinz-Elmar Tenorth (Weinheim/Basel: Beltz, 2004), 137–152.

94 Gerhart Neuner, „Die Theorie der allseitigen Entwicklung und der neue Charakter der Allgemeinbildung im einheitlichen sozialistischen Bildungssystem," *Pädagogische Wissenschaft und Schule. Wissenschaftliche Veranstaltung über Probleme des einheitlichen sozialistischen Bildungswesens anläßlich des 15jährigen Bestehens des DPZI zu Berlin. Konferenzbericht* 2 (1964): 27–54, hier 39.

Die Marxsche Charakterisierung des „vollseitig entwickelten Menschen“[95] als „Grundprinzip“ einer „höheren“, also kommunistischen „Gesellschaftsform“[96], wäre freilich hinreichend gewesen, um das im Bildungsgesetz 1965 ausgerufene Ziel „allseitig gebildeter, das heißt sozialistisch bewußter, hochqualifizierter, gesunder, geistig und körperlich leistungsfähiger, kulturvoller Menschen“[97], zu autorisieren. Die Texte von Marx enthalten allerdings auch Formulierungen, die das im Bildungsgesetz ausgewiesene Ziel in nicht gerade unwesentlichen Teilen in Frage stellen. So ist bei Marx im zitierten Zusammenhang von „volle(r) und freie(r) Entwicklung jedes Individuums“ als Resultat der Entwicklung der Produktivkräfte und der Produktionsverhältnisse sowie als Bedingung dieser höheren Gesellschaftsform die Rede. Die Attribuierung des für die pädagogische Wissenschaft geltenden Menschenbildes durch Neuner verweist mithin nicht originär auf Marx, sondern einmal mehr auf die unbedingte Autorität herrschender Parteiideologie ebenso wie mittelbar auf die Geltung des parteiideologischen Fundaments angeeigneter Sowjetpädagogik. Beides mündete in den Verzicht darauf, souverän über die Grundlagen der Pädagogik als Wissenschaft zu verfügen. Was in Abhängigkeit von der herrschenden Partei und Parteiideologie blieb, war nach sowjetpädagogischer Art die Ziele, Inhalte und Methoden institutionalisierter Erziehung und Bildung vorrangig in der allgemeinbildenden Schule zu formulieren resp. den neuen Charakter der Allgemeinbildung „abzuleiten“[98]. Die Forderung Karl-Heinz Günthers[99] an den wissenschaftlichen Nachwuchs, sich die Grundlagen der pädagogischen Wissenschaft, d.h. die „wesentlichen pädagogischen Gesetzmäßigkeiten

---

95 Marx, „Das Kapital,“ 508.

96 Marx, „Das Kapital,“ 618.

97 „Gesetz über das einheitliche sozialistische Bildungssystem,“ 541.

98 Neuner, „Die Theorie der allseitigen Entwicklung,“ 42. Edgar Drefenstedt, einer der führenden Unterrichts- und Lernplantheoretiker in der DDR und zeitweiliger Stellvertretender Direktor des DPZI, brachte das „marxistisch-leninistische“ Wissenschaftsverständnis in seinem Konferenzbeitrag auf den Punkt. Seine wissenschaftliche Frage lautete: „Wie gehen wir an diese Aufgabe heran?“ Edgar Drefenstedt, „Neubestimmung der Allgemeinbildung und Entwicklung der Lernplantheorie,“ *Pädagogische Wissenschaft und Schule. Wissenschaftliche Veranstaltung über Probleme des einheitlichen sozialistischen Bildungswesens anläßlich des 15jährigen Bestehens des DPZI zu Berlin. Konferenzbericht* 2 (1964): 80–102, hier 80.

99 Karl-Heinz Günther war maßgeblicher Erziehungshistoriker der neuen Generation pädagogischer Wissenschaftler ab der Wende zu den 1960er Jahren und ab 1970 bis 1989 Vizepräsident der Akademie der Pädagogischen Wissenschaften (APW).

und kausalen Zusammenhänge, ... Begriffe und Kategorien, Theorien und Hypothesen" anzueignen[100], hätte freilich die Frage nach sich ziehen müssen, welches Lehrwerk sich dafür eigne. Nach Dorsts Pädagogiklehrwerk von 1953 war kein Lehrbuch mehr zustande gekommen. Allenfalls konnte die Pädagogische Enzyklopädie aus dem Jahr 1963 dem Anspruch einer sowjetpädagogischen Rezeption mit Rücksicht auf das Erbe pädagogischer Klassik und die besonderen gesellschaftlichen Bedingungen in der DDR anstatt einer reinen sowjetpädagogischen Adaption hier und da genügen.

Dabei blieb es trotz einer stattlichen Zahl allgemeinbildungs- und unterrichtstheoretischer bzw. didaktischer, psychologischer oder bildungsgeschichtlicher und -soziologischer Monografien und Sammelwerke. Ein Grundlagenwerk zum Zwecke der selbstbewussten Bestimmung eines allgemein in der DDR geltenden pädagogischen Paradigmas beanspruchten und ersetzten sie allesamt nicht.[101]

Anstatt eines von Autoren aus dem Kreis pädagogischer Wissenschaftler in der DDR verantworteten (allgemein-) pädagogischen Grundlagen- und Standardwerks erschien 1978 als „Gemeinschaftsarbeit" der Akademien der Pädagogischen Wissenschaften der UdSSR und der DDR das Buch mit dem anspruchsvollen Titel „Pädagogik"[102]. Angesichts des Covers und des im sowjetpädagogischen Modus[103] präsentierten „marxistisch-leninistischen" Gehalts wurde es unter der Hand als „Schwarze Pädagogik" karikiert. Seinen Inhalt konzentrierten die Autoren zugegeben wie die frühen sowjetischen Übersetzungen auf „Fragen der Erziehung im Kindes- und Jugendalter". Das schloss nunmehr immerhin nicht mehr aus, dass der Gegenstand der

---

[100] Karl-Heinz Günther, „Probleme der Ausbildung pädagogischer Wissenschaftler. Zehn Jahre Aspirantur am Deutschen Pädagogischen Zentralinstitut," *Pädagogische Wissenschaft und Schule. Wissenschaftliche Veranstaltung über Probleme des einheitlichen sozialistischen Bildungswesens anläßlich des 15jährigen Bestehens des DPZI zu Berlin. Konferenzbericht* 2 (1964): 128–159, hier 131.

[101] Ein solches Buch war in der DDR ausschließlich als konkurrenzloses Standardwerk denkbar.

[102] Gerhart Neuner et al., *Pädagogik. Gemeinschaftsarbeit von Mitgliedern und Mitarbeitern der Akademie der Pädagogischen Wissenschaften der UdSSR und der Akademie der Pädagogischen Wissenschaften der DDR* (Berlin: Volk und Wissen Verlag, 1978).

[103] Der charakteristische sowjetpädagogische Modus manifestiert sich bereits in der inhaltlichen Gliederung des Buches.

Pädagogik – theoretisch – weiter gefasst werden kann, aber – praktisch bzw. de facto – in dem Buch auf die Erziehung und Bildung Heranwachsender konzentriert blieb.[104] Die Aufgaben pädagogischer Forschung wurden im Wesentlichen ebenso grundsätzlich nicht angetastet wie die „marxistisch-leninistischen" Grundlagen der Pädagogik. Und analog zur Sowjetpädagogik richtete die sowjetisch-deutsche Autorengemeinschaft die Aufmerksamkeit auf Fragen des erziehlichen Unterrichts. Schließlich betonten die Herausgeber, dass das Buch sich „auf die reichen Erfahrungen der Sowjetpädagogik" und die „halbhundertjährige Praxis der sowjetischen Schule (stützt)", aber auch in der DDR und anderen sozialistischen Ländern gewonnene Erkenntnisse und Erfahrungen verarbeitet.[105]

Da es aus einer Kooperation erwuchs, repräsentiert das Buch wie auch immer zustande gekommene Kompromisse zwischen einer seit den 1940er Jahren weiterentwickelten, in den Säulen des Paradigmas zwar unveränderten, aber neu akzentuierten und durch die APW der UdSSR vertretenen Sowjetpädagogik einerseits und den Ergebnissen einer fast drei Jahrzehnte währenden Geschichte sowjetpädagogischer Rezeption in der DDR, hier in Gestalt des in der DDR maßgeblichen Pädagogikverständnisses der „forschungsführenden" erziehungswissenschaftlichen „Leiteinrichtung" andererseits.

Dass das sowjetpädagogische Paradigma in seinem Fundament unangetastet blieb, belegen nachdrücklich die Definitionen der tragenden Begriffe Bildung und Erziehung (im Einzelnen wie in ihrem Zusammenspiel) ebenso wie die Konzentration auf die intentionale und institutionalisierte, speziell auf Unterricht konzentrierte Einheit von Bildung und Erziehung. Die Behauptung, dass sich „die Begriffe der Pädagogik … in einer ständigen Entwicklung und Veränderung (befinden)", entpuppt sich durch den Abgleich der historischen und der damals aktuellen Definitionen letztlich als Rhetorik. Dem Anspruch der Autoren auf „Vervollkommnung des begrifflich-terminologischen Apparats" diente es auch nicht, dass dem Paradigma weitere Grundbegriffe zugeordnet wurden. Dabei handelt es sich zum einen um den Terminus „Herausbildung der Persönlichkeit", der aber ideologiegesättigt auch wiederum nur als zielgerichteter und von der „marxistisch-

---

[104] Neuner et al., *Pädagogik. Gemeinschaftsarbeit von Mitgliedern*, 103 f.
[105] Neuner et al., *Pädagogik. Gemeinschaftsarbeit von Mitgliedern*, 11–13.

leninistischen Partei“ geführter gesellschaftlicher Erziehungsprozess erklärt wird. Zum anderen um den Begriff „Pädagogischer Prozeß“, der gewissermaßen als eine Art intentionale Sozialisation bzw. als zielgerichtete und geführte „Erziehung im weiten Sinne“ gefasst wurde.[106] Beide Termini dekorieren das Paradigma durch eine Prozessauffassung von Erziehung, ohne damit dessen Substanz zu verändern.

Am Ende der DDR: Sowjetpädagogik vs. Pädagogik in der Sowjetunion

Mit der parteiideologisch gegenüber der sowjetischen Führungsmacht 1975/76 eingeleiteten „politisch-ideologisch“ Wende vom sozialistischen zum kommunistischen Erziehungsauftrag wurde pädagogische Wissenschaft in der DDR bildungspolitisch an das sowjetpädagogische Bildungs- und Erziehungsziel angeschlossen. Das kommunistische Erziehungsziel hob Pädagogik in der DDR selbstbewusst, wenn auch nur perspektivisch, auf dieselbe gesellschaftliche Formationsstufe wie in der UdSSR. Für die erziehungswissenschaftliche Elite kam die Anweisung aus dem MfV ebenso überraschend, wie sie irritierte.[107]

Der sich zum Forschungsproblem auswachsende kommunistische Erziehungsauftrag berührte auch das Verhältnis zur Sowjetpädagogik. Die dort von Anfang an doktrinär nie problematisierte Etikettierung des Bildungs- und Erziehungsziels als kommunistisch wurde selbst durch die sowjetische Praxis institutionalisierter Erziehung und Bildung nicht verunsichert. In der DDR hingegen löste der ernst genommene kommunistische Erziehungsauftrag einen zunächst lediglich „marxistisch-leninistisch“, im engeren revolutions- oder formationstheoretisch veranlassten Konflikt mit dem administrativen Auftraggeber aus, der das Verhältnis von wissenschaftlichem und „parteilichem“ Selbstverständnis gegen Ende der DDR zugunsten

[106] Neuner et al., *Pädagogik. Gemeinschaftsarbeit von Mitgliedern*, 114.
[107] Neuner et al., *Pädagogik. Gemeinschaftsarbeit von Mitgliedern*, bes. 248.

eines wissenschaftlichen Selbstverständnisses zu verschieben drohte.[108] Bereits die Tatsache, dass die herrschende Parteidoktrin durch den ministeriell verordneten Erziehungsauftrag mit wissenschaftlichen Fragen konfrontiert wurde und Widersprüche zwischen Auftraggeber und Auftragnehmer und damit zwischen Ideologie und Wissenschaft heraufbeschwor, konnte seitens des MfV nicht anders als Häresie wahrgenommen werden. Selbst wenn es sich überwiegend um eine unbeabsichtigte, aber sachlich unvermeidliche und eigens durch den Auftraggeber herbeibeschworene Ketzerei gehandelt haben mochte.

Indessen wurde pädagogische Wissenschaft im letzten Jahrzehnt ihrer Existenz nicht nur durch den kommunistischen Erziehungsauftrag irritiert, sondern auch durch die pädagogischen und schulpolitischen Reformdiskussionen in der UdSSR besonders seit der Gorbatschow-Ära geradezu erschüttert. Den überlieferten geheimpolizeilichen Beobachtungen zufolge oszillierte die Haltung pädagogischer Wissenschaftler beispielsweise in der Berliner APW-Zentrale zwischen Sympathie und Ablehnung pädagogischer Reform(diskusion)en, während Perestroika und Glasnost als gesellschaftspolitischer Kurs sich allgemeiner Zustimmung erfreute. Auf dem 9. Pädagogischen Kongress im Juni 1989[109] wandte sich die pädagogisch-wissenschaftliche Führung „parteilich" devot, aber selbstbewusst wie nie zuvor gegenüber der Führungsmacht des Ostblocks gegen die Reformdebatten in der UdSSR, einschließlich der dortigen Besinnung auf sowjetrussische reformpädagogische Traditionen.

Gerhart Neuner feierte die eigenen bildungspolitischen und erziehungswissenschaftlichen Erfolge und würdigte den Umgang in der SBZ/DDR

---

108 Vgl. hierzu ausführlich Heinz-Elmar Tenorth, „Die ‚Erziehung gebildeter Kommunisten' als politische Aufgabe und theoretisches Problem. Erziehungsforschung in der DDR zwischen Theorie und Politik," in *Wissen machen. Beiträge zu einer Geschichte erziehungswissenschaftlichen Wissens in Deutschland zwischen 1945 und 1990. Zeitschrift für Pädagogik*, ed. Sabine Reh et al. (Weinheim/Basel: Beltz Juventa, 2017), 207–275.

109 Vgl. Rede Gerhart Neuners in *Bulletin. Pädagogischer Kongreß der Deutschen Demokratischen Republik*, Nr. 3. (Manuskriptdruck) (Berlin, 1989), 30–35. Auf das sich in der Rede auch spiegelnde Verhältnis zur Sowjetpädagogik ging Neuner im Gegensatz zum Verhältnis zur sowjetischen Reformdiskussion in der Gorbatschow-Ära rückblickend nicht ein. Vgl. Dietrich Hoffmann, Hans Döbert und Gert Geißler, *Die unterdrückte Bilanz. Zum Verhältnis von Erziehungswissenschaft und Bildungspolitik am Ende der DDR* (Weinheim: Deutscher Studien Verlag, 1999), 256–265.

mit dem deutschen reformpädagogischen Erbe geradezu als vorbildlich. Letztlich verteidigte Neuner damit das sowjetpädagogische Paradigma in einer Situation, als dieses in der UdSSR und „einigen sozialistischen Ländern" aus den Fugen zu geraten schien. Neuners Festhalten am sowjetpädagogischen Paradigma betraf ausdrücklich nicht nur die zur Formel erstarrte Einsicht über das Verhältnis von Schule und Gesellschaft oder die Haltung zur Reformpädagogik, sondern vor allem das sowjetpädagogische Theorie-Praxis-Verhältnis, den Gegenstand und Zweck pädagogischer Forschung, die erziehungswissenschaftliche Konzentration auf allgemeine Schulbildung und vor allem das Festhalten am „Marxismus-Leninismus" als wissenschaftlichem Fundament ebenso wie am Prinzip der „Parteilichkeit". Aus der Nötigung, im Zusammenhang mit dem kommunistischen Erziehungsauftrag zwischen Ideologie und Wissenschaft zu lavieren, und angesichts der Haltung zur Reformdebatte im sowjetischen Einflussbereich, ergab sich ein diskursives Amalgam, das bis zur Implosion der DDR im Herbst 1989 nicht auskühlte.

Die letzte Kodifizierung der tragenden Begriffe pädagogischer Wissenschaft in der DDR erfolgte 1987 mit der Veröffentlichung des Pädagogischen Wörterbuchs[110]. Anhand der Termini Bildung, Erziehung, Erziehung im engeren und weiten Sinne lässt sich eine Distanzierung vom sowjetpädagogischen Paradigma schwerlich belegen. Aufweichungstendenzen zeichnen sich am deutlichsten innerhalb der paradigmatischen Grenzen ab. Das betrifft insbesondere erziehungswissenschaftliche Schlussfolgerungen aus der eigenen Marxrezeption. So hatten sich durch die vorrangig psychologische Besinnung auf die Rolle der tätigen Auseinandersetzung des Menschen mit der ihn umgebenden „Natur" außer ihm und die Rezeption gleichgerichteter sowjetpädagogischer Psychologie und Didaktik modernere Lernstrategien entwickeln lassen. In diesen rückte die (individuelle zumindest aber die Selbst-) Tätigkeit lernender „Persönlichkeiten" in den unterrichtstheoretischen Mittelpunkt. Deutlich hoben sich zudem Idee und Konzept der Polytechnisierung allgemeiner Bildung vom sowjetischen Modell ab. Und auch in der wissenschaftlichen Methodendiskussion kündigte sich mit der allerdings zaghaften Rückbesinnung auf das Aufsteigen zum Konkreten eine Hinwendung zu Marx und damit eine Abwendung vom parteiideologischen

---

110 Hans-Joachim Laabs, u.a., *Pädagogisches Wörterbuch* (Berlin: Volk und Wissen Verlag, 1987).

„Marxismus-Leninismus“ an.[111] Nicht zuletzt ließen die Definitionen der Begriffe Bildung und Erziehung im letzten Wörterbuch der Pädagogik in der DDR im Gegensatz zu den doktrinären Begriffsbestimmungen konventioneller Sowjetpädagogik Deutungsspielräume und Auffassungsunterschiede zu.

Darüber, wohin solche Diskussionen und Prozesse in der pädagogischen Wissenschaft der DDR geführt hätten, lässt sich allenfalls spekulieren. Folgte man allerdings der Logik der für Sowjetpädagogik grundlegenden „marxistisch-leninistischen“ Dialektik mit dem „Gesetz vom umschlagen quantitativer in qualitative Veränderungen“, gäbe es immerhin Grund zu der Annahme, dass sich durch „evolutionäre[n] Veränderungen“ von „Teilsystem(n)“ des Paradigmas ein künftiger Qualitätssprung des „Gesamtsystems“ ankündigte …[112] Mit der Implosion der DDR hatte sich freilich auch das erledigt – abgesehen von den erst allmählich abklingenden Nachwirkungen der pädagogischen Sowjetisierung bzw. des sowjetpädagogischen Einflusses in den Erziehungsverhältnissen auf dem Gebiet der ehemaligen DDR.

Fazit

Anders als die anderen ehemaligen sog. volksdemokratischen Staaten im Machtbereich der UdSSR, die sich zu westlich orientierten Demokratien entwickelten, sowie jene Staaten, die sich nach 1990 aus dem sowjetischen Staatenbund lösten und sodann dieselbe Entwicklung nahmen, ist die DDR untergegangen und abgeschlossene Geschichte geworden. Der Beitritt der Länder der ehemaligen DDR zur Bundesrepublik Deutschland am 3. Oktober 1990 besiegelte das Ende der kleineren deutschen Republik, die mit der Bildung der SBZ als Vorgeschichte ihren Anfang nahm. Die Historiografie über die DDR seitdem hat nachdrücklich bestätigt, dass die DDR weder von ihrem Ende her noch von ihrem Anfang und schon gar nicht allein durch die Jahre der Stalinära angemessen historisch begriffen werden kann. Es ist geboten, deren Geschichte bis zu ihrem Ende zu erzählen.

---

[111] Vgl. Wiegmann, „Zum Umgang mit dem Verhältnis von Theorie und Praxis.“

[112] Georg Klaus und Manfred Buhr, *Philosophisches Wörterbuch* (Leipzig: VEB Bibliographisches Institut, 1975), 275 f.

Literatur

Archivalien und gedruckte Quellen

„Aus dem Entwurf eines Lehrbuchs der Pädagogik." *Pädagogik*, no. 10 (1954): 789–802.

DIPF/BBF-Archiv, Nachlass Deiters, Mappe 18.

„Gesetz über die sozialistische Entwicklung des Schulwesens in der Deutschen Demokratischen Republik." In *Quellen zur Geschichte der Erziehung*, editiert von Karl Heinz Günther, u.a., 532–539. Berlin: Volk und Wissen Verlag, 1978.

„Gesetz über das einheitliche sozialistische Bildungssystem. Auszug." In *Quellen zur Geschichte der Erziehung*, editiert von Karl-Heinz Günther, u.a., 539–546. Berlin: Volk und Wissen Verlag, 1978.

Mädicke, Erika. „Johannes Feuer 1898 bis 1977. Förderer des Erstleseunterrichts und der Didaktik der Unterstufe." In *Wegbereiter der neuen Schule*, editiert von Gerd Hohendorf, Helmut König und Eberhard Neumann, 71–78. Berlin: Volk und Wissen Verlag, 1989.

„Über die Grund- und Mittelschule. Beschluß des Zentralkomitees der KPdSU (B) vom 5. Sept. 1931." In *Die Sowjetische Bildungspolitik seit 1917. Dokumente und Texte*, editiert von Oskar Anweiler und Klaus Meyer, 178–186. Heidelberg: Quelle & Meyer, 1961.

„Über die Lehrpläne und die Schulordnung der Grund- und Mittelschule. Beschluß des Zentralkomitees der KPdSU (B) vom 25. August 1932." In *Die Sowjetische Bildungspolitik seit 1917. Dokumente und Texte*, editiert von Oskar Anweiler und Klaus Meyer, 188–194. Heidelberg: Quelle & Meyer, 1961.

„Verordnung über die Unterrichtsstunde als Grundform der Schularbeit, die Vorbereitung, Organisation und Durchführung der Unterrichtsstunde und die Kontrolle der Kenntnisse der Schüler vom 4. Juli 1950," In *Dokumente zur Geschichte des Schulwesens in der Deutschen Demokratischen Republik: 1945–1955*, editiert von Gottfried Uhlig und Karl-Heinz Günther, 365–367. Berlin: Volk und Wissen Verlag, 1970.

Primärliteratur

Alt, Robert. *Die Industrieschulen. Ein Beitrag zur Geschichte der Volksschule.* Berlin/Leipzig: Volk und Wissen Verlag, 1948.

Alt, Robert. „Unsere Stellung zur Reformpädagogik." *Pädagogik* 11 (1956): 345–370.

Alt, Robert. „Zur gesellschaftlichen Begründung der neuen Schule." *Pädagogik* 1, no. 1 (1946): 12–22. Nachdruck in Karl-Heinz Günther, Helmut König und Rudi Schulz. *Alt, Robert: Erziehung und Gesellschaft. Pädagogische Schriften*, 68–85. Berlin: Volk und Wissen Verlag, 1975.

Brumme, Hans. *Stalin über Volksbildung und Erziehung.* Berlin/Leipzig: Volk und Wissen Verlags, 1951.

Deiters, Heinrich. „Der deutsche Lehrer vor der Welt." In *Pädagogische Aufsätze und Reden*, editiert von Heinrich Deiters, 187–202. Berlin: Volk und Wissen Volkseigener Verlag, 1957.

Deiters, Heinrich. „Zu den Begriffen Bildung und Erziehung." *Pädagogik*, no. 10 (1955): 231–233.

„Die Entwicklung der Wissenschaft in der Sowjetunion seit der Oktoberrevolution." *Pädagogik*, no. 3 (1948): 44–46.

„Die gegenwärtige Situation der psychologischen Forschung. Bericht über eine von der Volk und Wissen GmbH veranstaltete Psychologen-Zusammenkunft." *Pädagogik*, no. 6 (1948): 267–272.

„Die Gestaltung des einheitlichen sozialistischen Bildungssystems der DDR in den sechziger und siebziger Jahren." In *Geschichte der Erziehung*, editiert von Karl-Heinz Günther, u.a. 713–722. Berlin: Volk und Wissen Verlag, 1987.

Die Redaktion der Zeitschrift Pädagogik. „Zum Geleit." *Pädagogik*, no. 1 (1946): 1–2.

Dorst, Werner. *Erziehung, Bildung und Unterricht in der deutschen demokratischen Schule. Grundlagen.* Berlin: Volk und Wissen Verlag, 1953.

Dorst, Werner. „Schlußwort zur ‚Theoretisch-praktischen Konferenz über Fragen der Polytechnischen Bildung in der deutschen demokratischen Schule'." *Pädagogik*, no. 7 (1953): 715–720.

Drefenstedt, Edgar. „Neubestimmung der Allgemeinbildung und Entwicklung der Lernplantheorie.“ *Pädagogische Wissenschaft und Schule. Wissenschaftliche Veranstaltung über Probleme des einheitlichen sozialistischen Bildungswesens anläßlich des 15jährigen Bestehens des DPZI zu Berlin. Konferenzbericht* 2 (1964): 80–102.

Engels, Friedrich. „Dialektik der Natur.“ In *Werke*, Band 20, editiert von Karl Marx und Friedrich Engels, 305–568. Berlin: Dietz Verlag, 1962.

„Gegenstand und Aufgaben der Pädagogik.“ *Pädagogik*, no. 9 (1954): 790–802.

Gerhard, Karl. „Diltheys Lebensphilosophie und die Pädagogik.“ *Pädagogik* 2, no. 8 (1947): 14–24.

Gerhard, Karl und A. M. Pankratowa. „Geschichte der UdSSR. Moskau 1947.“ *Pädagogik* 3, no. 8 (1948): 373–379.

Günther, Karl-Heinz. „Probleme der Ausbildung pädagogischer Wissenschaftler. Zehn Jahre Aspirantur am Deutschen Pädagogischen Zentralinstitut.“ *Pädagogische Wissenschaft und Schule. Wissenschaftliche Veranstaltung über Probleme des einheitlichen sozialistischen Bildungswesens anläßlich des 15jährigen Bestehens des DPZI zu Berlin. Konferenzbericht* 2 (1964): 128–159.

Günther Karl-Heinz, Helmut König und Rudi Schulz. „Vorbemerkungen.“ In *Alt, Robert: Erziehung und Gesellschaft. Pädagogische Schriften*, editiert von Karl-Heinz Günther, Helmut König und Rudi Schulz, 67–68. Berlin: Volk und Wissen Verlag, 1975.

Heimann, Paul. „Darwinismus und Schule. Naturkundliche Unterrichtsprobleme im Spiegel der Sowjetpädagogik.“ *Pädagogik* 2, no. 4 (1947): 18–22.

Heimann, Paul. „Mensch und Umwelt im Geographieunterricht. Probleme und Erfahrungen im Spiegel der Sowjetpädagogik.“ *Pädagogik* 2, no. 5 (1947): 10–14.

Jessipow, B. P. „A.S. Makarenko, sein Wirken und seine pädagogischen Lehren.“ *Pädagogik* 2, no. 8 (1947): 25–29.

Jessipow, B. P. *Pädagogik. Lehrbuch für Einrichtungen zur Ausbildung von Lehrern der unteren Klassen*. Berlin: Volk und Wissen Volkseigener Verlag, 1971.

Jessipow, B. P. und N. K. Gontscharow. *Pädagogik. Lehrbuch für pädagogische Lehranstalten*. Berlin/Leipzig: Volk und Wissen Verlags, 1948.

Kelbert, Heinz. "Die nächsten Aufgaben der „Pädagogik." *Pädagogik*, no. 5 (1949): 218–224.

Klaus, Georg und Manfred Buhr. *Philosophisches Wörterbuch, Band 1*. Leipzig: VEB Bibliographisches Institut, 1975.

Krapp, Gotthold. „Autorreferat: Der Gedanke der Verbindung des Unterrichts mit der produktiven Arbeit und der Gedanke der polytechnischen Bildung bei Karl Marx und Friedrich Engels." *Pädagogik*, no. 11 (1956): 701–707.

Krapp, Gotthold. „Bildung." In *Pädagogische Enzyklopädie*, editiert von Heinz Frankiewicz u.a., 122–126. Berlin: VEB Deutscher Verlag der Wissenschaften, 1963.

Krapp, Gotthold. *Marx und Engels über die Verbindung des Unterrichts mit produktiver Arbeit und die polytechnische Bildung*. Berlin: Volk und Wissen Verlag, 1958.

Kunze, Reinhold. „Zur Bestimmung des Gegenstandes der Pädagogik." *Pädagogik* 11 (1956): 869–873.

Laabs, Hans-Joachim u.a. *Pädagogisches Wörterbuch*. Berlin: Volk und Wissen Verlag, 1987.

Lange, Max Gustav. „Die Hauptrichtungen der modernen deutschen Gesellschaftswissenschaft (Teil II)." *Pädagogik* 2, no. 8 (1947): 29–37.

Lange, Max Gustav. „Hans Siebert und Anton Semjonowitsch Makarenko." In *Vorträge über Kindererziehung (Beiträge zur Marxistischen Pädagogik)*, editiert von Anton Semjonowitsch Makarenko, herausgegeben von Hans Siebert. Berlin/Leipzig: Volk und Wissen Verlags, 1949.

Lange, Max Gustav. *Totalitäre Erziehung. Das Erziehungssystem der Sowjetzone Deutschlands*. Band 3. Frankfurt am Main: Verl. d. Frankfurter Hefte, 1954.

Lange, Max Gustav. „Zur Grundlegung der Erziehungswissenschaft." *Pädagogik*, no. 3 (1946): 16–26.

Lehmbruck, Gustav Wilhelm. „Stalin und die Entwicklung des sowjetischen Bildungswesens." *Pädagogik*, no. 12 (1949): 1–9.

Mädicke, Erika. „Johannes Feuer 1898 bis 1977. Förderer des Erstleseunterrichts und der Didaktik der Unterstufe." In *Wegbereiter der neuen Schule*, editiert von Gerd Hohendorf, Helmut König und Eberhard Meumann, 71–78. Berlin: Volk und Wissen Verlag, 1989.

Marx, Karl. „Das Kapital." In *Werke*, Band 23, editiert von Karl Marx und Friedrich Engels. Berlin: Dietz Verlag, 1962.

Marx, Karl und Friedrich Engels. „Thesen über Feuerbach." In *Werke*, Band 3, editiert von Karl Marx und Friedrich Engels, 5–7. Berlin: Dietz Verlag, 1959.

„Nachwort der Redaktion." *Pädagogik*, no. 5 (1949): 224–226.

Neuner, Gerhart. *Bulletin. Pädagogischer Kongreß der Deutschen Demokratischen Republik, Nr.* 3. Manuskriptdruck, 30–35. Berlin, 1989.

Neuner Gerhart. „Die Theorie der allseitigen Entwicklung und der neue Charakter der Allgemeinbildung im einheitlichen sozialistischen Bildungssystem." *Pädagogische Wissenschaft und Schule. Wissenschaftliche Veranstaltung über Probleme des einheitlichen sozialistischen Bildungswesens anläßlich des 15jährigen Bestehens des DPZI zu Berlin. Konferenzbericht* 2 (1964): 27–54.

Neuner, Gerhart et. al. *Pädagogik. Gemeinschaftsarbeit von Mitgliedern und Mitarbeitern der Akademie der Pädagogischen Wissenschaften der UdSSR und der Akademie der Pädagogischen Wissenschaften der DDR*. Berlin: Volk und Wissen Verlag, 1978.

Ogorodnikow, I. T. und P. N. Schimbiriew. *Lehrbuch der Pädagogik*. Berlin: Volk und Wissen Volkseigener Verlag, 1953.

Posnanski, N. F. „Vererbung, Umwelt und Erziehung in der Entwicklung und Formung des Menschen nach der materialistischen Lehre." *Pädagogik*, no. 3 (1950).

Röblitz, Günther. „Zum Gegenstand der Pädagogik." *Pädagogik* 10 (1955): 111–118.

Rubinstein S. L. „Die Struktur des Psychischen (Teil I)." *Pädagogik*, no. 9 (1948): 399–409.

Schabalow, Sergej Maximowitsch. „Uschinskij, der Vater der russischen Pädagogik." *Pädagogik* 1, no. 1 (1946): 29–33.

Skatkin, M. N. „Wissenschaft und Lehrfach (Teil I)." *Pädagogik* 3, no. 6 (1948): 249–257.

Skatkin, M. N. „Wissenschaft und Lehrfach (Teil II)." *Pädagogik* 3, no. 7 (1948): 309–317.

Smirnow, A. A. „Die Entwicklung der sowjetischen Psychologie." *Pädagogik* 3, no. 8 (1948): 349–359.

Tomaschewsky, Karlheinz. *Didaktik. Unter besonderer Berücksichtigung des Unterrichts in den Klassen 1 bis 4 der deutschen demokratischen Schule.* Redigiert von Helmut Klein. Berlin: Volk und Wissen Verlag, 1956.

„Vorwort." In *Pädagogische Enzyklopädie*, editiert von Heinz Frankiewicz u.a. Berlin: VEB Deutscher Verlag der Wissenschaften, 1963.

Wolf, Walter. „Der Erziehungsbegriff und die Pädagogik." *Pädagogik* 11 (1956): 191–194.

Wolf, Walter und Wilfried Lange, „Erkenntnistheoretische und didaktische Probleme der Verbindung des Unterrichts mit der produktiven Arbeit." *Pädagogik* (1960): 1107–1121.

Wolf, Walter. „Zu den Begriffen Bildung und Erziehung." *Pädagogik*, no. 10 (1955): 223–231.

Sekundärliteratur

Anweiler, Oskar. *Schulpolitik und Schulsystem in der DDR*. Opladen: Leske & Budrich, 1988.

Froese, Leonhard. *Die Sowjetisierung der deutschen Schule. Entwicklung und Struktur des mitteldeutschen Bildungswesens. (Das Pädagogische Gespräch).* Freiburg/Basel/Wien: Herder, 1962.

Geißler, Gert. „Die bildungspolitische Tendenzwende 1947–1949." In *Schule und Erziehung in der DDR. Studien und Dokumente*, editiert von Gert Geißler und Ulrich Wiegmann, 41–68. Neuwied: Luchterhand, 1995.

Geißler, Gert. „Dokumente und Personen." In *Schule und Erziehung in der DDR. Studien und Dokumente*, editiert von Gert Geißler und Ulrich Wiegmann, 207–344. Neuwied: Luchterhand, 1995.

Geißler, Gert. „Hans Siebert – zur erziehungsgeschichtlichen Spur eines emigrierten politischen Pädagogen." *Zeitschrift für Pädagogik*, no. 5 (1994): 781–799.

Häder, Sonja. „Sozialporträt der Pädagogischen Fakultät der Universität Halle-Wittenberg von ihrer Gründung 1946/47 bis zu ihrer Auflösung 1955." In *Strukturwandel vs. bürgerliche Kontinuität. Eliten im Sozialismus. Beiträge zur Sozialgeschichte der DDR*, editiert von Peter Hübner, 381–403. Köln: Böhlau, 1999.

Hoffmann, Dietrich, Hans Döbert und Gert Geißler. *Die unterdrückte Bilanz. Zum Verhältnis von Erziehungswissenschaft und Bildungspolitik am Ende der DDR*. Weinheim: Deutscher Studien Verlag, 1999.

Krapp, Gotthold. „Bildung." In *Pädagogische Enzyklopädie*, editiert von Heinz Frankiewicz u.a., 122–126. Berlin: VEB Deutscher Verlag der Wissenschaften, 1963.

Laufer, Jochen. „Von den Demontagen zur Währungsreform – Besatzungspolitik und Sowjetisierung Ostdeutschlands 1945–1948." In *Sowjetisierung und Eigenständigkeit in der SBZ/DDR*, Zeithistorische Studien, Bd. 13), editiert von Michael Lemke, 163–186. Köln/Weimar/ Wien: Böhlau, 1999.

Lost, Christine. *Sowjetpädagogik. Wandlungen Wirkungen Wertungen in der Bildungsgeschichte der DDR*. Hohengehren: Schneider, 2000.

Lost, Christine. „Sowjetpädagogik. Zur Verabschiedung untauglicher Interpretationsmuster der Bildungs- und Pädagogikgeschichte der SBZ/DDR." *Jahrbuch für Historische Bildungsforschung*, no. 4 (1998): 299–341.

Medinskij, E. N. „Grundprinzipien einer Geschichte der Pädagogik." *Pädagogik* 3 (1948): 35–39.

Neuner, Gerhart et. al. *Pädagogik. Gemeinschaftsarbeit von Mitgliedern und Mitarbeitern der Akademie der Pädagogischen Wissenschaften der UdSSR und der Akademie der Pädagogischen Wissenschaften der DDR*. Berlin: Volk und Wissen Verlag, 1978.

Neuner, Gerhart. *Zwischen Wissenschaft und Politik. Ein Rückblick aus lebensgeschichtlicher Perspektive*. Köln: Böhlau Köln, 1996.

Tenorth, Heinz-Elmar. „Die ‚Erziehung gebildeter Kommunisten' als politische Aufgabe und theoretisches Problem. Erziehungsforschung in der DDR zwischen Theorie und Politik." In *Wissen machen. Beiträge zu einer Geschichte erziehungswissenschaftlichen Wissens in Deutschland zwischen*

1945 und 1990, editiert von Sabine Reh, Edith Glaser, Britta Behm und Tilman Drope, 207–275. Weinheim/Basel: Beltz Juventa, 2017.

Uhlig, Christa. *Rückkehr aus der Sowjetunion: Politische Erfahrungen und pädagogische Wirkungen. Emigranten und ehemalige Kriegsgefangene in der SBZ und frühen DDR*. Weinheim: Deutscher Studien Verlag, 1998.

Wiegmann, Ulrich. *Agenten – Patrioten – Westaufklärer. Staatssicherheit und Akademie der Pädagogischen Wissenschaften der DDR*. Berlin: Metropol, 2015.

Wiegmann, Ulrich. „Allgemeinbildungstheorie anstatt Allgemeiner Pädagogik. Zum Verhältnis von bildungspolitisch-doktrinärer Selbstdisziplinierung und gesellschaftspolitischer Instrumentalisierung ‚pädagogischer Wissenschaften' in der SBZ und DDR." In *Kindheit, Jugend und Bildungsarbeit im Wandel. Ergebnisse der Transformationsforschung (Zeitschrift für Pädagogik, Beiheft, 37)*, editiert von Heinz-Elmar Tenorth, 433–454. Weinheim/Basel: Beltz, 1997.

Wiegmann, Ulrich. „Der 17. Juni und die Pädagogische Wissenschaft in der DDR." In *„Am Rande des Bankrotts …": Intellektuelle und Pädagogik in Gesellschaftskrisen der Jahre 1953, 1956 und 1968 in der DDR, Ungarn und der CSSR*, editiert von Sonja Häder und Ulrich Wiegmann, 17–37. Baltmannsweiler: Schönstatt-Verlag, 2004.

Wiegmann, Ulrich. „Die semantische Reform. Von der Gemeinschafts- zur Kollektivpädagogik in der SBZ/DDR." In *Sozialpädagogik und Gemeinschaft. Historische Beiträge zur Rekonstruktion eines konstitutiven Verhältnisses*, editiert von Joachim Henseler und Jürgen Reyer, 122–135. Hohengehren: Schneider Verlag, 2000.

Wiegmann, Ulrich. „Heinrich Deiters – berufliche Ausgrenzung und ‚erziehungswissenschaftliche Remigration'." *Zeitschrift für Pädagogik* H 40, Nr. 5 (1994): 765–780.

Wiegmann, Ulrich. „Max Gustav Lange." In *Klinkhardt Lexikon Erziehungswissenschaft (KLE)*, editiert von Klaus-Peter Horn, Heidemarie Kemnitz, Winfried Marotzki und Uwe Sandfuchs, 268–269. Bad Heilbrunn: Klinkhardt, 2012.

Wiegmann, Ulrich. „Robert Alt". In *Klinkhardt Lexikon Erziehungswissenschaft (KLE)*, editiert von Klaus-Peter Horn, Heidemarie

Kemnitz, Winfried Marotzki und Uwe Sandfuchs, 36. Bad Heilbrunn: Klinkhardt, 2012.

Wiegmann, Ulrich. „Selbstbiografien ranghöchster DDR-pädagogischer Wissenschaftler im Vergleich: Karl-Heinz Günther und Gerhart Neuner." In *Der Bildungsgang des Subjekts. Bildungstheoretische Analysen. Zeitschrift für Pädagogik, 48*, editiert von Sonja Häder und Heinz-Elmar Tenorth, 137–152. Weinheim/Basel: Beltz, 2004.

Wiegmann, Ulrich. „Über vergessene, verschwiegene und verdrängte Ursprünge des marxistischen Erziehungsbegriffs bei Robert Alt." In *Jahrbuch für Historische Bildungsforschung*, Band 10, redigiert von Peter Dudek, Hanno Schmitt und Heinz Elmar Tenorth, 75–100. Bad Heilbrunn: Klinkhardt, 2004.

Wiegmann, Ulrich. „Zum Umgang mit dem Verhältnis von Theorie und Praxis in der wissenschaftlichen Pädagogik (1946–1989)." In *Pädagogische Wissenschaft in der DDR. Ideologieproduktion, Systemreflexion und Erziehungsforschung. Studien zu einem vernachlässigten Thema der Disziplingeschichte deutscher Pädagogik*, editiert von Heinz-Elmar Tenorth und Ulrich Wiegmann, 362–423. Bad Heilbrunn: Verlag Julius Klinkhardt, 2022.

Wiegmann, Ulrich. „Zur Geschichte des Lebensbildes von Robert Alt." In *Robert Alt (1905–1978)*, editiert von Bodo Friedrich, Dieter Kirchhöfer und Christa Uhlig, 143–157. Frankfurt am Main: Lang, Peter GmbH, Internationaler Verlag Der Wissenschaften, 2006.

PART THREE

Actors

The End of Free Educational Research and the Beginning of Sovietization of Educational Sciences in Slovakia[1]

Blanka Kudláčová

Abstract: The struggle for the character of educational sciences in Slovakia in the second half of the 20th century was already taking place during the Second World War. In this period, two ideological concepts were being formed in parallel: the first conception followed the traditions of the interwar educational sciences, developed by the first Slovak professor Juraj Čečetka, and the second conception copied the model of the Soviet educational sciences and it was developed by Ondrej Pavlík. Pavlík was a key figure in the field of educational sciences and school policy during socialism. The aim of the author's research is to seek answers to the following questions: What impacted his left-wing orientation? When and in what way did Pavlík achieve the position of the leader in the field of educational sciences and practice? What was his relationship to the interwar educational theory? In what way did he promote his proposals and reforms in the field of education? The research is based on the study of historical sources and journals as well as legislative documents.

Keywords: educational research, educational sciences, socialism, sovietization, Slovakia

Introduction

The establishment of Czechoslovakia in 1918 marked a new stage in the development of both nations, the Czechs and the Slovaks. Even though the coexistence of the Czechs and the Slovaks in one state does not need to be idealized, it was certainly a new impulse for their democratic development. In the interwar period, an important development of educational thinking took place in Slovakia, mainly thanks to the Pedagogical Seminar, which was established in 1923/24 at the Faculty of Arts, Comenius University (CU) in Bratislava.[2] Due to the lack of a Slovak intelligentsia caused by strong Magyarization at the end of the 19th century and the beginning of the

1 The paper is a part of the project VEGA No. 1/0190/24: Regime Engagement vs. Silent Resistance in Totalitarian Education in Slovakia.

2 Blanka Kudláčová, "Pedagogy as Part of University Education in Slovakia – Historical and Contemporary Perspective," *Historia Scholastica* 3, no. 1 (2017): 8.

20th century, the seminar was led by three Czech professors of educational sciences (O. Chlup, J. Hendrich and J. Uher) in the first two decades. They transmitted the high level of the Czech educational discussion also to Slovakia and significantly impacted orientation of educational sciences. According to Krankus, "the inclination toward empiricism and practice both in the Czech and the Slovak educational sciences may be regarded as a positive fact"[3] as well as the reform activity that brought many stimuli for the development of students' personalities. Before the fall of the Berlin Wall, the period of two decades in interwar Czechoslovakia was the only period of free development of sciences and research.

The Socio-Political Situation in Slovakia during the Second World War and Its Reflection in Educational Sciences

After twenty years of building of democracy in Czechoslovakia and the progressive development in many areas, several geopolitical changes caused by Hitler's foreign policy occurred in the Central-European region at the end of the 1930s. In March 1939, the independent Slovak State was announced and it was followed by the announcement of the Protectorate of Bohemia and Moravia. After the conference in Salzburg (July 1940), Slovakia was subjugated by Hitler's Germany. Hlinka's Slovak People's Party (HSPP) had a dominant position in the Slovak autonomous government. According to its main ideologist, Štefan Polakovič (1912–1999), Slovak national socialism was supposed to be built as a particular type of national socialism, adapted to Slovak conditions. He described it in his work *Slovenský národný socializmus. Ideové poznámky* [The Slovak National Socialism. Ideological Notes] (1941), where, in the third chapter *Princípy slovenskej národnosocialistickej výchovy* [The Principles of the Slovak National-Socialist Education], he dealt with the goals and methods of ideological education, the meaning of which was to educate "new youth" and a "new man".[4] Educational sciences adapted to new

---

3 Milan Krankus, "Recepcia svetového pedagogického myslenia v slovenskej pedagogike," in *Pedagogické myslenie, školstvo a vzdelávanie na Slovensku v rokoch 1918–1945*, ed. Blanka Kudláčová (Trnava: Typi Universitatis Tyrnaviensis, 2016), 113.

4 Štefan Polakovič, *Slovenský národný socializmus. Ideové poznámky* (Bratislava: Generálny sekretariát HSĽS, 1941), 57–88.

conditions and began to develop in the national-socialist variant, which was inspired by the German educational sciences and model of education. After the forced departure of the Czech professors from Slovakia (1938), the first Slovak, Juraj Čečetka[5] (1907–1983), became the director of the Pedagogical Seminar. In the autumn of 1939, he was appointed an associate professor and in 1940 a full professor. The period of the Second World War was very fruitful in Čečetka's scientific life. His research work shifted from the field of psychology and counselling to the field of educational sciences and history of education. He published several important works: *Slovenské evanjelické patronátne gymnázium v Turčianskom sv. Martine* [The Slovak Evangelical Patronal Grammar School in Turčiansky sv. Martin] (1939), *Zo slovenskej pedagogiky* [From the Slovak Education] (1940), *Príručný pedagogický lexikón I. and II.* [Handy Lexicon of Education, I. and II.] (1943), *Úvod do všeobecnej pedagogiky* [Introduction to General Pedagogy] (1944). The work *Zo slovenskej pedagogiky* [From the Slovak Education] may be considered a pioneer work, it is an important source of information on the Slovak educational past from the 17th century up to the beginning of the 20th century. Another pioneering work is his two-volume *Príručný pedagogický lexikón* [Handy Lexicon of Education], which contains 1250 entries. These works were analysed in regard to the then national-socialist ideology. The research showed that the first two above-mentioned Čečetka's works represent a purely professional text. Considering the lexicon, "some entries bear the stamp of its time, however, it mainly regards the aspect of informativeness, without a significant

5 Čečetka studied philosophy and the French language at Charles University in Prague, where he met several important Czech personalities in the field of educational sciences (e.g. O. Kádner) and psychology (e.g. F. Krejčí, V. Příhoda). It influenced him to deal with educational psychology as a synthesis of psychology and educational sciences. Already during his studies in Prague he volunteered in the Prague Pedological Institute and Psychotechnical Institute, which later opened the opportunity to work in the Psychotechnical Institute in Bratislava (from 1929). Here he met his lifelong friend, the founder of psychology in Slovakia, A. Jurovský. The focus on the issues of the youth, their diagnosing, counselling and career choice led Čečetka to cooperate with pedagogues who worked at the Pedagogical Seminar at the Faculty of Arts, CU at that time. Under the influence of J. Hendrich, he qualified in educational sciences with a work *Pedagogika a adlerovská individuálna psychológia* [Education and Adlerian Individual Psychology] (1936).

attempt to ideologize".[6] The same applies to *Úvod do všeobecnej pedagogiky* [Introduction to General Pedagogy], in which a description of the Italian and German education can be found.

However, regarding journal publications, it was different. In 1934, Čečetka founded the journal *Pedagogický sborník* [Pedagogical Proceedings], which was the most significant journal of its time.[7] Between 1938 and 1944, interconnection of the journal and the ideology of the era can be seen.[8] Čečetka published there articles on national education in Slovak schools (1938), reform of the Slovak education (1938, 1940), the German education (1940, 1941, 1942) as well as translations of German and Italian authors.

The situation in the Slovak educational sciences after the end of the Second World War was indefinite and there was no significant theoretical background that would determine its character in a form of directions or conceptions. The focus on national and Christian education was motivated politically, not by a professional discourse. In the state of war, the scientific contacts from the first Czechoslovak Republic were interrupted, there was a lack of information about educational thinking abroad and thus, discourse in educational sciences was impossible.

The Turn to Left-Wing Educational Sciences after the Second World War and the Role of Ondrej Pavlík

Towards the end of the Second World War, and especially after the outbreak of the Slovak National Uprising (SNU) in 1944, a new political orientation emerged. On September 6, 1944, the insurgent Slovak National Council (SNC), passed a regulation no. 5, which nationalised "schools of all categories and degrees from kindergartens to universities in Slovakia..."[9] Thus,

---

[6] Blanka Kudláčová, "Charakteristika vybraných reprezentatívnych diel slovenskej pedagogiky v rokoch 1939–1945 z hľadiska spoločensko-politického kontextu," in *Pedagogické myslenie a školstvo na Slovensku v rokoch 1939–1945*, ed. Blanka Kudláčová (Trnava: Typi Universitatis Tyrnaviensis, 2015), 46.

[7] Jozef Mátej, "Slovenská pedagogika v rokoch 1939–1945," in *Dejiny českej a slovenskej pedagogiky*, ed. Jozef Mátej (Bratislava: SPN, 1976), 397.

[8] Cf. Blanka Kudláčová and Lucia Valkovičová, "Tvorba Juraja Čečetku a ideológia Slovenského štátu v rokoch 1939–1945," *Historia scholastica* 1, no. 2 (2015): 38–51.

[9] *Nariadenie Slovenskej národnej rady o poštátnení školstva na Slovensku*, no. 5/1944, Coll. from September 6, 1944, §1.

all teachers and school staff became civil servants. It was the first act of domestic left-wing politics. Nationalisation of education in Slovakia was thus implemented three years before it was codified by the first socialist school act. Changes in political and cultural orientation as well as in school policy were declared already in March 1945 in the *Košice Government Program*. It meant establishment of a regime of limited democracy, euphemistically called "people's democracy" and orientation on the Soviet Union. According to Krankus, in the period from the end of the Second World War to the establishment of socialism in Czechoslovakia (1945–1948), "there was an ideological struggle, but at the same time, there was a certain degree of tolerance for different opinions",[10] however, he considers the years 1948–1953 "the period of definite establishment of the communist totalitarian power with a complete subordination of educational theory to the Marxist-Leninist ideology and politicisation of its scientific profile".[11]

The left-wing orientation of educational sciences and education in Slovakia is significantly connected with the name of Ondrej Pavlík (1916–1996). Pavlík established himself on the new political scene thanks to his good political intuition already during the SNU and found himself in the whirl of high politics after the war was over. From May 1945 to February 1948, he held the position of a deputy of the appointee of the SNC for education and edification (the appointee was L. Novomeský). In 1945, he was elected a member of the Central Committee of the Communist Party of the Slovakia (CPS) and a member of the Temporal National Assembly. In the CPS, he was considered the greatest expert on issues of educational sciences and education. In 1945, he prepared a proposal for a new education system and also became the head of the commission for elaboration of the national education act, which was established in 1946 in Prague. With his work in educational sciences and speeches at teacher conferences throughout Slovakia, he influenced a new form of educational theory and education. According to Hotár, he is

10 Milan Krankus, "Ideový zápas v slovenskej pedagogike v rokoch 1945–1953," in *Pedagogické myslenie a školstvo na Slovensku od konca 2. svetovej vojny po obdobie normalizácie*, ed. Blanka Kudláčová (Trnava: Typi Universitatis Tyrnaviensis, 2017), 36.

11 Krankus, "Ideový zápas," 36.

"the founding personality of the Czechoslovak socialist pedagogy".[12] What impacted Pavlík's left-wing orientation? When and in what way did he become the leader in the field of educational sciences and education?

Pavlík was born into a poor peasant family, which probably foreshadowed his left-wing orientation. From 1932, he studied at the State Czechoslovak Coeducational Teacher Training Institute in Lučenec. He worked here in a Marxist student circle and was known for communist thinking. After graduation, he worked for three years as a teacher in several folk schools in central Slovakia. In 1938, he joined the illegal Communist Party and became involved in the resistance. In the same year, he began to study philosophy and natural sciences at the Faculty of Natural Sciences and Faculty of Arts, CU in Bratislava, where he met left-wing students. They invited him to live in the Lafranconi student dormitory, where they formed an illegal communist cell. As he writes himself, his political maturity and enthusiasm for communist ideals was shaped both by the study of Marxist literature and also by close contacts "with important older comrades".[13] He was expelled from the dormitory because of his left-wing orientation. Asylum was granted to him in 1940 by G. Husák,[14] who provided a shelter for several left-wing students, writers and artists in a rented villa. In April 1943, Pavlík was imprisoned for half a year for his illegal activities.[15]

Pavlík`s educational writings were indicated by his dissertation *Vývin sovietskeho školstva a pedagogiky* [Development of Soviet Education and Educational Sciences], which he wrote between 1940 and 1942. Since Slovakia was at war with the Soviet Union at the time, it could be published only after the war (1945). Pavlík's second publication focused on the Soviet education

[12] Viliam Hotár, "Ondrej Pavlík – život a dielo," in *Náčrt personálnej bibliografie Ondreja Pavlíka, vydanej k jeho 70. narodeninám*, ed. Viliam Hotár (Martin: Matica slovenská, 1986), 7–8.

[13] Pavlík Ondrej, *Svedectvo dokumentov* (Bratislava: Vydavateľstvo politickej literatúry, 1968), 16.

[14] The most important Slovak communist politician in the second half of the 20th century.

[15] For more on Pavlík see: Blanka Kudláčová and Andrea Faktorová, "Ondrej Pavlík, tvorca socialistickej pedagogiky a reformátor školstva a vzdelávania po druhej svetovej vojne," in *Pedagogické myslenie, školstvo a vzdelávanie na Slovensku v rokoch 1945–1989*, ed. Blanka Kudláčová (Trnava: Typi Universitatis Tyrnaviensis, 2019), 113–151; also Vladimír Michalička and Miroslava Slezáková, eds., *Ondrej Pavlík [1916–1996]* (Bratislava: CVTI SR, 2016).

was a monograph *Vysoké školy v Sovietskom zväze [Higher Education in the Soviet Union]* (1947). Both publications are considered to be the first works in the Marxist educational sciences in Slovakia.

Pavlík was also significantly involved in the field of journals. After the resumption of the publication of the *Pedagogický sborník* [Pedagogical Proceedings] in 1948 (the publication of the journal was stopped between 1944 and 1947), he held the position of editor until 1950, when the journal ceased to exist. From the contents of individual issues during Pavlík's editorship it is evident that he edited articles on the Soviet educational sciences and education by Slovak authors, as well as translations of Soviet authors. From 1945, the journal *Jednotná škola* [Unified School], edited by Gustáv Pavlovič,[16] began to be published. In the first stage of its existence "it was focused on promotion and implementation of basic principles of the new school policy, especially the principle of a unified and state school".[17]

Between 1946 and 1948, Pavlík lectured on educational sciences based on Marxism-Leninism at the newly established Faculty of Education, CU. In the autumn of 1948 he was appointed an associate professor in the field Educational Sciences. He was only 32 years old in the time, a testament to his ambition. Pavlík was also active in founding institutions focused on the development of Marxist educational sciences and education. In 1947, he founded The National Institute for Education (later Research Institute for Education), which "together with the help of the journal Unified School contributed to elaboration of the new, state and unified school policy, to democratisation of education, promotion of the Marxist-Leninist theory and methodology in the Slovak educational sciences".[18] Pavlík's way of

---

16 Gustáv Pavlovič (1907–1990), a participant in the SNU; in 1945–1947, he led the reformatory department of the Commission for Education and Edification [orig. oddelenie Povereníctva školstva a osvety]; in 1947–1951, he was a director of the National Institute for Education in Bratislava [orig. Štátny pedagogický ústav], head of the Department of Higher Education of the Commission for Education, Sciences and Arts [orig. Odbor vysokých škôl Povereníctva školstva, vied a umení] (1951–1953); and in 1953–1959 he was a rector of the School of Higher Education in Bratislava. After 1945, he promoted and defended the unified state school and participated in the preparation of the school act (1948). He founded the journal *Jednotná škola*.

17 Ondrej Pavlík, ed., *Pedagogická encyklopédia Slovenska 1* (Bratislava: VEDA, 1984), 370.

18 Ondrej Pavlík, ed., *Pedagogická encyklopédia Slovenska 2* (Bratislava: VEDA, 1985), 579.

promotion of his proposals and reforms in the field of educational sciences and education could be observed already in his initiatives during the SNU. His political and professional career were closely interconnected, he fully used his political competences and directly interfered in the formation of school legislation, personnel policy, establishment of new institutions as well as training of prospective teachers.

Pavlík's influence on educational sciences and education was different to the way of Čečetka. Čečetka, after the dissolution of the first Slovak Republic, could not perform activities which he was entitled to by his full professorship, because in terms of outcomes of verification of professors he did not define himself sufficiently against the ideology (the restriction lasted until 1946). In this period, he could not lead the Pedagogical Seminar,[19] he led it again from 1947. He also continued in intensive publication activity: *Výber zo slovenských pedagógov* [Selection from the Slovak Pedagogues] (1947) and a two-volume university textbook *Pedagogika* [Educational Sciences] 1947 and 1948. Čečetka's work from the 1940s represents fundamentals of educational sciences in Slovakia and it is an extensive work,[20] however, it is difficult to assign it to a certain educational direction. According to Wiesenganger, Čečetka rather determines himself against individual authors and directions, "he was not a direct follower of any philosophical tradition", he formulated his own views and evaluations very cautiously.[21] It might be related to his experience with the regime of the first Slovak Republic.

The situation in the non-communist and democratic camp of pedagogues did not develop positively between 1945 and 1948, "they were gradually paralysed by political pressure and displaced from important positions, which made them stand at the margin of professional discussion".[22] Their platform

---

19 Between 1945–1947 the Pedagogical Seminar was led by professor A. Jurovský.

20 Čečetka's enormous diligence is testified by the data of his bibliography: he published 556 works, of which 24 books, see Mária Mihálechová, *Život a dielo Juraja Čečetku* (Bratislava: Infopress, 2007).

21 Marek Wiesenganger, "Filozoficko-pedagogické východiská v tvorbe Juraja Čečetku do r. 1945," in *Pedagogické myslenie, školstvo a vzdelávanie na Slovensku v rokoch 1918–1945*, ed. Blanka Kudláčová (Trnava: Typi Universitatis Tyrnaviensis, 2016), 131.

22 Milan Krankus, "Vývoj pedagogického myslenia a pedagogický diskurz," in *Pedagogické myslenie, školstvo a vzdelávanie na Slovensku v rokoch 1945–1989*, ed. Blanka Kudláčová (Trnava: Typi Universitatis Tyrnaviensis, 2019), 86.

was the journal *Nové prúdy* [New Currents]. They particularly criticised the model of the unified state school there, in which they saw the cessation of pluralism in education. The discussion on the form of educational sciences after the war was not their dominant topic, which opened up space for left-wing pedagogues. It also needs to be mentioned that the ideas of reform of educational sciences still persisted in this period, which is certified by articles in the journal *Jednotná škola* (e.g. Vrána carried out lectures around Slovakia and presupposed "opening of new experimental schools"[23], Berka even demanded inclusion of experimental schools to the system of unified school[24]). Naturally, reform-pedagogy was no longer the subject of wider discussion, it regarded only some partial topics such as global learning, differentiation of students, etc.

The Creation of Socialist Educational Sciences and Unified Education after the Communist Coup in 1948

The communist coup in 1948 resulted in the creation of the power monopoly of the Communist Party and dissemination of its ideology of Marxism-Leninism into all areas of society.[25] A fundamental step in the formation of the totalitarian regime was the adoption of the Constitution of the Czechoslovak Republic on May 9, 1948, which defined Czechoslovakia as a "people's democratic" state, which, thanks to the victory of the working class, embarked on the path of socialism.[26] Sovietization began in all areas in the sense of the motto "The Soviet Union our model". The 9th Congress of the Communist Party of Czechoslovakia (CPC) in 1949 declared "the general line of building socialism".[27] In the field of education, this meant a gradual reconstruction of the existing school system into a model of a unified socialist school, enacted

---

23 Stanislav Vrána, "O pedagogickom seminári bratislavských učiteľov," *Jednotná škola* 1, no. 8–10 (1945/46): 371.

24 Mikuláš Berka, "Potreba pokusnej školy," *Jednotná škola* 2, no. 3 (1946/47): 122–123.

25 Milan Olejník, *Implementácia marxisticko-leninskej ideológie vo sfére vzdelávania na Slovensku v kontexte politického vývoja v rokoch 1948–1953* (Košice: Universum, 2018).

26 *Ústava Československej republiky*, No. 150/1948, Coll. from May 9, 1948, Art. 1., Par. 2.

27 *Protokol řádného IX. sjezdu Komunistické strany Československa: v Praze 25.–29. května 1949* (Praha: ÚV KSČ, 1949).

by the Education Act no. 95/1948 of April 21st 1948. In its sense, schools were to educate "nationally and politically conscious citizens of the people's democratic state, brave protectors of the homeland and devoted supporters of the working people and socialism".[28] The key role in the preparation of the reform of the school system was played by two earlier documents written by Pavlík: *Návrh na reformu školského systému* [A Proposal for the Reform of School System] (1945) and *Školstvo – základ kultúrnej výstavby* [Education – The Foundation of Cultural Construction] (1946). Thanks to them, the CPS disposed of an elaborated, complex programme of educational and cultural policy in Slovakia.

In the field of educational sciences, the change of the regime brought diversion from all other concepts of educational sciences (labelled as bourgeois sciences or pseudo sciences) that were different to educational sciences established on the principles of Marxism-Leninism, which was the only one which had the attribute "scientific". The 9th congress of the CPS (1950) defined socialist education as "education in the spirit of the fight against reactionary influence and demonstrations of pseudo sciences and ideologies".[29] The highest party and governmental bodies advocated "the demand of a complete revision of orientation of educational sciences, even the entire national and international history of educational thinking and its precise interpretation in the spirit of the Marxist-Leninist schemes".[30] According to Pavlík,

> if we want to develop a new Czechoslovak educational theory following the model of Soviet educational sciences, we must first of all clear away the corpse that rots and poisons the air, clear the construction site and raise a brave building of the socialist Czechoslovak educational sciences based on solid ideological and methodological foundations.[31]

---

[28] *Zákon o základní úpravě jednotného školství (školský zákon)*, No. 95/1948, Coll. from April 21, 1948, §2.

[29] *Protokol IX. zjazdu Komunistickej strany Slovenska: v Bratislave dňa 24.–27. mája 1950* (Bratislava: Pravda, 1950), 224.

[30] Krankus, "Vývoj pedagogického myslenia," 87.

[31] Ondrej Pavlík, "Některé úkoly školy a pedagogiky po zasedání ÚV KSČ," *Pedagogika* 1, no. 1–2 (1951): 4–5.

Similar statements can be observed from other representatives of educational sciences, especially Ernest Sýkora[32], Ľudovít Bakoš[33] and the previously mentioned Gustáv Pavlovič. They all studied at the Faculty of Arts, CU in Bratislava, they were politically engaged and, together with Pavlík, shaped the left-wing form of educational sciences and school policy after the Second World War. Acquisition of the new Marxist-Leninist and Soviet educational sciences, however, according to the "educational elites", did not proceed sufficiently fast, which led to the search for reasons for this apparent lack of progress. According to Sýkora, "the socialist educational sciences do not find access to a great part of our schools even today, because the bourgeois educational sciences have the right of domicile there".[34] Pavlovič saw a mistake in the fact that we have not developed "criticism and self-criticism. We have been delayed in the study of opinions of the classics of Marxism-Leninism on educational sciences, in the study of the Soviet educational theory and practice and its great success".[35] According to Bakoš, it was necessary to "consistently eliminate the remains of bourgeois ideologies in school education and teaching".[36] Pavlík demanded "deepening of ideological education at schools".[37]

---

32 Ernest Sýkora (1914–2000), a participant of the SNU, member of the Central Committee of the CPC. Between 1945 and 1950 he worked at the Commission of the SNC for Education and Edification and was released in order to work with the youth in the Union of the Slovak Youth and the Czechoslovak Union of Youth. Between 1950 and 1958 he was a commissioner for education and culture, in 1953 he was a Minister of Education. From 1959, he was a professor of educational sciences at the Faculty of Arts, CU in Bratislava. He contributed particularly in establishing a unified socialist youth organisation and its educational conception.

33 Ľudovít Bakoš (1919–1974) worked at the Commission for Education and Edification, also at the Faculty of Arts, CU in Bratislava as an assistant (1946–1947), lectured at the University of Education (1953–1959) and later again at the Faculty of Arts, CU, where he obtained senior lecturership and subsequently, full professorship. He dealt particularly with in-service teacher education and theory of education.

34 Ernest Sýkora, "Výňatok z prejavu povereníka školstva E. Sýkoru povedaného na aktíve školských pracovníkov v Bratislave," *Pedagóg* 2, no. 4 (1949–50): 282–284.

35 Gustáv Pavlovič, "Uplatnenie zásad socialistickej pedagogiky v našej škole," *Jednotná škola* 6, no. 1 (1950/51): 30.

36 Ľudovít Bakoš, "Úlohy našej školy po X. zjazde KSS," *Jednotná škola* 8, no. 5 (1952/53): 395.

37 Ondrej Pavlík, "Některé úkoly školy," 2.

In February 1951, a weekly journal *Učiteľské noviny* [Teacher Magazine], which was meant to shape teachers toward socialist nationalism, began publication.

Pavlík continued in his rapidly developing political career. In 1948, he was elected a member of the SNC and appointed a commissioner for information and edification, which enabled him to participate in meetings of the Chair of the Central Committee of the CPS. At the end of 1949, he suggested the establishment of a committee for personnel and ideological control of science – the Scientific Board of the CPS. Within it, a programme of education of "socialist scientists" was adopted (to facilitate the study of Soviet literature, the Russian language and Marxism-Leninism).[38]

In 1950, Pavlík became a deputy Minister of Education, Science and Arts and chairman of the State Committee for Higher Education in Prague. The Committee was established in accordance with the new Act on Higher Education Institutions no. 58/1950 Coll. and its application in practice caused politicization of the university environment and complete subordination of universities to state power.[39] Between 1953 and 1955 he was a chair of the Slovak Academy of Sciences and in 1953, he established the Cabinet of Education at the Slovak Academy of Sciences, which he also led (its existence was terminated in 1957). Between 1952 and 1957 he was a full professor at the Faculty of Education, CU in Bratislava and from 1953, also at the the School of Higher Education [orig. Vysoká škola pedagogická] in Bratislava. He published the work *Didaktika* [Didactics] (in 1949 twice, and in 1950, a revised edition). His aim was to "purify didactics from pseudo-scientific principles"[40] and to represent a breakthrough work in the field of socialist didactics. The publication, however, does not offer a systematic didactics built upon the Marxist-Leninist principles. It represents rather a system of classical didactic knowledge which is criticized by the author. Pavlík promotes the Soviet educational sciences and polytechnic education there. The analysis of Pavlík's works clearly shows that he created educational sciences based on Marxist principles, close to the Soviet educational sciences, which was incompatible with the nature of the

---

38 Adam Hudek, "Slovenská akadémia vied a umení v rokoch 1945–1952," in *Dejiny Slovenskej akadémie vied*, edited by Dušan Kováč et al. (Bratislava: Veda, 2014), 80.

39 Soňa Gabzdilová, *Ako sme študovali v totalite. Vysokoškolské vzdelávanie na Slovensku pod ideologickým diktátom KSČ (1948–1953)* (Košice: Universum, 2018).

40 Ondrej Pavlík, *Didaktika* (Bratislava: Štátne nakladateľstvo, 1949), 4.

Slovak educational sciences, whose creator was Čečetka, who followed the tradition of the Czech interwar educational sciences.

In the period of Stalinism, Čečetka delivered lectures on educational sciences at the Pedagogical Seminar at the Faculty of Arts, CU in Bratislava. In 1950, in accordance with the Act on Higher Education Institutions no. 58/1950 Coll., seminars were replaced by departments and educational sciences were incorporated into the Department of History of Philosophy. In 1953, an independent Department of Educational Sciences and Psychology was established under the leadership of Čečetka. In 1950, Čečetka was forced to public self-criticism[41], however, he continued to work at the faculty after this purge.[42] In the 1950s, his work was oriented especially on historical-educational writings, likely due to tactical reasons. He covered several Slovak personalities from the field of educational sciences: *Učiteľ ľudu Samuel Tešedík* [Samuel Tešedík, the Teacher of People] (1952), *Vavrinca Benediktiho z Nedožier Vnútorná sústava školská a Reč nápravná* [Vavrinec Benedikti of Nedožery and His Internal System of School and Moral Communication] (1955), *Pedagogické dielo Jána* Seberíniho [Educational Work of Ján Seberíni] (1957), *Pedagogické dielo Samuela Tešedíka* [Educational Work of Samuel Tešedík] (1959). The influence of the pre-war educational thinking can be clearly observed in Čečetka's work after 1945, when he did not declare his support for the Soviet educational sciences.

The occasional discussions on education reform in the after-war period were completely extinguished in the period of Stalinism. Váňová also confirms that "the discussion on the so-called educational reformism was ended in 1953".[43] 1953 marked the period of the worst Stalinist terror, however, the essence of the totalitarian regime remained. Educational sciences and school policy were closely coordinated with the course of events in the Soviet Union, the resolutions of the Communist Party transferred to the resolutions of the congresses of the CPC and the CPS. The Education Act of 1953 brought the organisation of Slovak education closer to the Soviet model, which caused

---

41 Pavlovič "drew attention" to him in the journal *Jednotná škola*, where he stated that Čečetka's opinions are based on views of representatives of "reactionary" philosophical directions. See Pavlovič, "Uplatnenie zásad," 24–48.

42 He had to leave the Faculty of Arts in 1959.

43 Růžena Váňová, "Vědy o výchově na stránkách Pedagogiky. K 50. výročí vzniku časopisu," *Pedagogika* 50, no. 4 (2000): 316.

many problems. It was necessary to focus on the practical preparation of new curricula, plans, textbooks and methodologies associated with the reform of education. This resulted in such a state that educational theory lagged behind educational practice, which again became the subject of criticism.

Conclusion

Totalitarian practices and the environment of fear and mistrust do not favour any science, particularly the humanities and social sciences. The period of the 1940s and 1950s was one of dramatic change in Slovakia with many negative consequences caused by two totalitarian regimes: the period of the first Slovak Republic with national socialist ideology and the period of socialism with Marxist-Leninist ideology. Examination of educational sciences in the period of socialism is in its infancy. However, some conclusions emerge from my research. The first conclusion is that ideology in totalitarian regimes of any kind is usually "pre-prepared" by someone (Š. Polakovič, O. Pavlík) and thus, it can be quickly disseminated after a political coup. The second conclusion reveals similarities of practice in totalitarian regimes: in general, they consider it crucial to control "educational institutions, from families through youth organisations to schools" under their guardianship,[44] since they are an appropriate tool to spread ideology, which is also certified by my research. The third conclusion is the result of an examination of the career of Pavlík, the main protagonist of the socialist educational sciences and education in Slovakia. The analysis uncovers that his political and professional career are closely related. Political competences enabled him to promote his educational opinions and reforms quickly and successfully. It is also apparent that Pavlík defined himself against the interwar educational sciences, which he considered a bourgeois pseudo-science.

It is not possible to analyse the entire field of educational sciences in the period between 1945 and 1956 in the presented paper, rather than that, new questions arise. Besides analyses of source literature and legislation, it would be interesting to examine, for instance, relationships among pedagogues in

---

[44] Anja Giudici, Thomas Ruoss and Sarah van Ruyskensvelde, "Educating the Volksgemeinschaft: Authoritarian Ideals and School Reforms in Europe's Fascist Era," *Paedagogica Historica* 56, no. 5 (2020): 569.

the period of Stalinism, when the representatives of the interwar educational sciences and the shaping generation of the socialist educational sciences coexisted next to each other. However, this is difficult to be grasped methodologically. In my opinion, the relationship between Čečetka and Pavlík is thought-provoking, since Čečetka was the most influential pedagogue until the arrival of Pavlík. After the Second World War, both of them devoted maximal effort to their goals: Čečetka dealt with establishment of the Pedagogical Seminar, training of secondary school teachers and educational writing, as well as clearing his name of accusations of collaboration with the regime of the first Slovak Republic; and Pavlík dealt with preparation of documents and legislative measures to enforce the model of the socialist education and socialist educational sciences and establishment of his own political career. The research has come across several objective limits: the archive material of the Ministry of Education and also the extensive personal writings of O. Pavlík have not as yet been processed in a complex manner in the Slovak National Archives in Bratislava.

Sources

Bakoš, Ľudovít. "Úlohy našej školy po X. zjazde KSS." *Jednotná škola* 8, no. 5 (1952/53): 385–395.

Berka, Mikuláš. "Potreba pokusnej školy." *Jednotná škola* 2, no. 3 (1946/47): 122–123.

Hotár, Viliam. "Ondrej Pavlík – život a dielo." In *Náčrt personálnej bibliografie Ondreja Pavlíka, vydanej k jeho 70. narodeninám*, edited by Viliam, Hotár, 7–14. Martin: Matica slovenská, 1986.

Mátej, Jozef. "Slovenská pedagogika v rokoch 1939–1945." In *Dejiny českej a slovenskej pedagogiky*, edited by Jozef Mátej, 395–397. Bratislava: SPN, 1976.

Pavlík, Ondrej. *Didaktika*. Bratislava: Štátne nakladateľstvo, 1949.

Pavlík, Ondrej. "Některé úkoly školy a pedagogiky po zasedání ÚV KSČ." *Pedagogika* 1, no. 1–2 (1951): 1–5.

Pavlík, Ondrej. *Svedectvo dokumentov*. Bratislava: Vydavateľstvo politickej literatúry, 1968.

Pavlík, Ondrej, ed. *Pedagogická encyklopédia Slovenska 1*. Bratislava: VEDA, 1984.

Pavlík, Ondrej, ed. *Pedagogická encyklopédia Slovenska 2*. Bratislava: VEDA, 1985.

Pavlovič, Gustáv. "Uplatnenie zásad socialistickej pedagogiky v našej škole." *Jednotná škola* 6, no. 1 (1950/51): 24–48.

Polakovič, Štefan. *Slovenský národný socializmus. Ideové poznámky*. Bratislava: Generálny sekretariát HSĽS, 1941.

Sýkora, Ernest. "Výňatok z prejavu povereníka školstva E. Sýkoru povedaného na aktíve školských pracovníkov v Bratislave." *Pedagóg* 2, no. 4 (1949–50): 282–284.

Vrána, Stanislav. "O pedagogickom seminári bratislavských učiteľov." *Jednotná škola* 1, no. 8–10 (1945/46): 371–373.

Legislative regulations

Nariadenie Slovenskej národnej rady o poštátnení školstva na Slovensku, no. 5/1944, Coll. from September 6, 1944.

Protokol řádného IX. sjezdu Komunistické strany Československa: v Praze 25.–29. května 1949. Praha: ÚV KSČ, 1949.

Protokol IX. zjazdu Komunistickej strany Slovenska: v Bratislave dňa 24.–27. 5. 1950. Bratislava: Pravda, 1950.

Ústava Československej republiky, no. 150/1948, Coll. from May 9, 1948.

Zákon o základní úpravě jednotného školství (školský zákon), no. 95/1948, Coll. from April 21, 1948.

Literature

Gabzdilová, Soňa. *Ako sme študovali v totalite. Vysokoškolské vzdelávanie na Slovensku pod ideologickým diktátom KSČ (1948–1953)*. Košice: Universum, 2018.

Giudici, Anja, Ruoss, Thomas, and Sarah van Ruyskensvelde. "Educating the Volksgemeinschaft: Authoritarian Ideals and School Reforms in Europe's Fascist Era." *Paedagogica Historica* 56, no. 5 (2020): 569–571.

Hudek, Adam. "Slovenská akadémia vied a umení v rokoch 1945–1952." In *Dejiny Slovenskej akadémie vied*, edited by Dušan Kováč et al., 69–86. Bratislava: Veda, 2014.

Krankus, Milan. "Recepcia svetového pedagogického myslenia v slovenskej pedagogike." In *Pedagogické myslenie, školstvo a vzdelávanie na Slovensku v rokoch 1918–1945*, edited by Blanka Kudláčová, 86–116. Trnava: Typi Universitatis Tyrnaviensis, 2016.

Krankus, Milan. "Ideový zápas v slovenskej pedagogike v rokoch 1945–1953." In *Pedagogické myslenie a školstvo na Slovensku od konca 2. svetovej vojny po obdobie normalizácie*, edited by Blanka Kudláčová, 36–52. Trnava: Typi Universitatis Tyrnaviensis, 2017.

Krankus, Milan. "Vývoj pedagogického myslenia a pedagogický diskurz." In *Pedagogické myslenie, školstvo a vzdelávanie na Slovensku v rokoch 1945–1989*, edited by Blanka Kudláčová, 82–112. Trnava: Typi Universitatis Tyrnaviensis, 2019.

Kudláčová, Blanka. "Charakteristika vybraných reprezentatívnych diel slovenskej pedagogiky v rokoch 1939–1945 z hľadiska spoločensko-politického kontextu." In *Pedagogické myslenie a školstvo na Slovensku v rokoch 1939–1945*, edited by Blanka Kudláčová, 42–59. Trnava: Typi Universitatis Tyrnaviensis, 2015.

Kudláčová Blanka. "Pedagogy as Part of University Education in Slovakia – Historical and Contemporary Perspective." *Historia scholastica* 3, no. 1 (2017): 4–15.

Kudláčová, Blanka, and Lucia Valkovičová. "Tvorba Juraja Čečetku a ideológia Slovenského štátu v rokoch 1939–1945." *Historia scholastica* 1, no. 2 (2015): 38–51.

Mihálechová, Mária. *Život a dielo Juraja Čečetku*. Bratislava: Infopress, 2007.

Olejník, Milan. *Implementácia marxisticko-leninskej ideológie vo sfére vzdelávania na Slovensku v kontexte politického vývoja v rokoch 1948–1953*. Košice: Universum, 2018.

Váňová, Růžena. "Vědy o výchově na stránkách Pedagogiky (K 50. výročí vzniku časopisu)." *Pedagogika* 50, no. 4 (2000): 313–339.

Wiesenganger, Marek. "Filozoficko-pedagogické východiská v tvorbe Juraja Čečetku do r. 1945." In *Pedagogické myslenie, školstvo a vzdelávanie na Slovensku v rokoch 1918–1945*, edited by Blanka Kudláčová, 117–137. Trnava: Typi Universitatis Tyrnaviensis, 2016.

Sovietization of Pedagogy (Educational Sciences) in Latvia after World War II: Input of Soviet "Missionaries"

Iveta Kestere and Alida Zigmunde

Abstract: At the end of the Second World War, the special communist "task forces" were established in Moscow for the renewal of Soviet dictatorship in the Baltic States. Under the leadership of the "missionaries" sent by Moscow, the sovietization of pedagogy (or educational sciences) began in Soviet Latvia. In our study, the biographies of Soviet missionaries were analysed considering three research questions: (1) Why and how did these people undertake the duties of missionaries of Soviet power? (2) What were the available instruments and mechanisms that allowed for and contributed to their actions as Soviet agents in the field of pedagogy in Latvia? (3) What were the "new" imported educational sciences? Study of three biographies showcased missionaries as victims scared by the ruling Soviet power; but on the other hand, as pillars of the regime and winners of all the benefits the regime provided. The missionaries brought a new politicized education paradigm explaining the world in terms of socio-economic antagonism and struggle. This trivial approach resulted in a shoddy methodology or the absence of any defined methodology at all.

Keywords: biographical method, politicized pedagogy, Soviet missionaries, sovietization, Soviet Latvia, prosopography

Introduction

In the spring of 1944, when the victory of the Allies in World War II became obvious, preparations for the renewal of Soviet dictatorship in the Baltic States began. For this purpose, special communist 'task forces' were created in Moscow.[1] These groups followed on the heels of the Red Army with the purpose to import Soviet values, ideology and order to the territories freshly liberated from the Nazis and immediately annexed by communists including the Baltic States – Estonia, Latvia and Lithuania.

---

[1] Andrejs Plakans, *A Concise History of the Baltic States* (Cambridge University Press, 2011), 360.

Several researchers consider the concept 'colonialism'[2] or 'covert colonialism'[3] to be appropriate to explain the behaviour and actions of the Soviet Union towards smaller and/or militarily weaker states. Analysing Soviet policies in East German universities, Tsvetkova, for example, speaks of 'cultural transfer', 'expansion', 'Sovietisation', and 'cultural imperialism'.[4] Indeed, similarities with colonisation are obvious: being convinced of the supremacy of their culture and ideology, the Soviets undertook the mission of "civilizing" the "indigenous" population of the Baltic States. As Ashcroft et al. noted, "colonization could be (re)presented as a virtuous and necessary 'civilizing' task involving education and paternalistic nurture"[5].

Communist missionaries performed the 'civilizing' of Baltic people with a "patronizing pedagogical attitude," to borrow Depaepe's term for colonizers' of Belgian Congo.[6] The missionaries sent by the metropolis, i.e. Moscow, imported the Soviet order to every single part of Baltic people's lives: the totalitarian political system was propagated as 'democratisation'; the Communist party was the only political power; repressions and control over social movements and information were carried out; production, trade and banks were nationalized and incorporated in the centralised planned Soviet economy; the educational system and culture were unified according to Moscow standards.[7]

---

2 Violeta Kalertas, "Baltic Postcolonialism and Its Critics," in *Baltic Postcolonialism*, edited by Violeta Kalertas (Amsterdam: Rodopi, 2006), 1–9.

3 Thomas Lane, *Lithuania: Stepping Westward* (London: Routledge, 2001).

4 Natalia Tsvetkova, *Failure of American and Soviet Cultural Imperialism in German Universities, 1945–1990* (Leiden, Boston: Brill, 2013).

5 Bill Ashcroft, Gareth Griffiths and Helen Tiffin, *Post-Colonial Studies: The Key Concepts* (London: Routledge, 2000), 47.

6 Marc Depaepe, "Sometimes a Little Distance is Needed to See What Really Happened: The Study of the Belgian Educational Policy in Congo as an Example of the Critical Vigour of Colonial History of Education," in *Between Educationalization and Appropriation: Selected Writings on the History of Modern Educational Systems*, edited by Marc Depaepe (Leuven: Leuven University Press, 2012), 233–234.

7 Erwin Oberländer, "Instruments of Sovetization in 1939/1940 and after 1944/45," in *The Soviet Occupation Regime in the Baltic States 1944–1959: Policies and Their Consequences. Materials of an International Conference, 13–14 June, 2002, Riga*, edited by Andris Caune et al. (Rīga: Latvijas vēstures institūta apgāds, 2007), 50–58.

Pedagogy (or Educational Sciences)[8] did not escape the Soviet modification too. This field was of particular importance due to its close connection with teacher education. Accumulating different opinions, school becomes a strategic place in times of political transitions. Therefore, from the first days of the Soviet rule teachers had to turn into mediators of communist ideology. Communist party institutions organized teacher training, officials published articles in the press and delivered lectures and seminars for educators.[9] Communist ideology set teacher education and re-education among essential targets of the communist 'task forces,' hence pedagogy moved to the forefront.

However, current history books mostly present generalised information about the 'task forces', briefly introducing the reader with the arrival of Moscow missionaries in the territory of Latvia in July 1944. Texts about the "colonisation" of Eastern Europe neglect its actual people or actors, their ability (or inability) to influence events, their internal motivation and rationale behind their actions. We would like to emphasise that 'task forces' consisted of people with particular backgrounds and their own agendas. Therefore, we have chosen the biographical method for our study.

The biographies of Soviet missionaries were analysed considering three research questions: (1) Why and how did these people undertake the duties of missionaries of Soviet power? (2) What were the available instruments and mechanisms that allowed for and contributed to their actions as Soviet agents in the field of pedagogy in Latvia? (3) What were the 'new' imported pedagogical sciences?

Methodological Issues

The biographical method allows us to connect macro and micro levels of history and prompts the analysis of social history and individual personality, documenting processes and experiences of social changes. The biographical method (or approach) provides a means for accessing and understanding those

---

8 Hereafter, we use 'pedagogy sciences', 'pedagogy' and 'educational sciences' as synonyms due to the fact that since 1939, doctorates in Latvia have been awarded in pedagogy sciences and even today the name of the field is being under discussion.

9 Roberts Miķelsons, "Pedagoģiskās domas attīstība," in *Skolas un pedagoģiskās domas attīstība Padomju Latvijā*, edited by Roberts Miķelsons (Rīga: Zvaigzne, 1969), 51.

the community groups, in the present and the past, whose experiences could not be directly tapped through documentary or formal survey.[10] Scrutinizing life stories in a broader historical context and comparing biographies allow us to understand people and their era better. It is especially important in studies of dictatorships, where any reality is impregnated with censor-created misconceptions. Morgan noted, that "through the disaggregation of biography the diversity and complexity of the communist experience was more fully registered than perhaps any other method".[11]

Three biographies of Soviet missionaries related to research and teaching of pedagogy in Latvia have been analysed, and they are of Roberts Mikelsons (*Miķelsons*) (1889–1973), Milda Drizule (*Drīzule*) (1895–1992) and Vladimirs Usins (*Ūsiņš*) (1918–2001). These three case studies are used for revealing the common traits of the "group portrait" reconstructed with the method of prosopography.[12]

Although "biographical control" was typical of the communist regime[13] – autobiographies of Soviet citizens had to be regularly written and rewritten – collecting facts of missionaries' biographies is not an easy task due to the following reasons. First of all, as all information about 'good' communists, the biographies of missionaries were modified by Soviet censorship. Morgan notes that "prior to 1991 barely a handful prominent communist party leaders were provided with a satisfactory biography".[14] Secondly, true stories of Moscow envoys were carefully kept away by their relatives and peers, who cherished fond memories about them. Finally, missionaries themselves falsified data in fear of the Soviet authorities. For example, they never revealed the detail of their legation from Moscow to Latvia. Further, we will openly acknowledge facts that are still confusing.

---

[10] Tom Wengraf, Prue Chamberlayne and Joanna Bornat, "A Biographical Turn in the Social Sciences? A British-European View," *Cultural Studies-Critical Methodologies* 2, no. 2 (2002): 246–247.

[11] Kevin Morgan, "Comparative Communist History and the 'Biographical Turn'," *History Compass* 10, no. 6 (2012): 458.

[12] See Morgan, "Comparative Communist History," 455–466. Thomas F. Carney, "Prosopography: Payoffs and Pitfalls," *Phoenix* 27, no. 2 (1973): 156–179.

[13] Morgan, "Comparative Communist History," 462.

[14] Morgan, "Comparative Communist History," 458.

For the reconstruction of the biographies we used archival sources (Latvian State Archives, Archives of the University of Latvia and funds of the Museum of Pedagogy at the University of Latvia), as well as articles in the press and interviews with missionaries' contemporaries. Biographical analysis was supplemented with documents revealing the mechanisms and ways how certain individuals could influence and implement changes in the field of education in Latvia, and these documents are 1) educational institution documents (including those of educational research centres); 2) pedagogical press, textbooks, and the pedagogy curricula, which document new methodological approaches, space and time limitations in the field.

The Beginnings of Pedagogical Science in Latvia in the 1920s–1930s and the First Soviet Pedagogical Missionaries in 1940/41

The development of pedagogy as an academic field in Latvia is related to the establishment of the University of Latvia in 1919 after the liberation of Latvian territory from Russian control and the declaration of an independent state on November 18, 1918. On October 1, 1919, the head of the Department of Pedagogy of the University of Latvia, theologian Karlis Kundzins (*Kundziņš*) (1883–1967) gave the first lecture in pedagogy at the academic level.[15] This lecture initiated the development of a study course in pedagogy at the higher education establishments as well as systematic, academic research in the field.

In choosing their model of pedagogy, Latvian academia turned to Germany because of their long historical ties, their knowledge of the language, and also because of the leading role of German scholars in European philosophy, psychology and, consequently, pedagogy. Thus, pedagogy in Latvia in the inter-war period developed in the tradition of the German liberal arts pedagogy (*geisteswissenschaftliche Pädagogik*).[16] The task of pedagogy was to

---

[15] *Latvijas Universitātes piecgadu darbības pārskats. 1919–1924* (Rīga: Latvijas Universitāte, 1925), 290.

[16] Iveta Ozola, "Pedagoģijas zinātnes ģenēze Latvijā no 20.gs. 20.gadiem līdz 20.gs. 60.gadu sākumam" (PhD diss., University of Latvia, 2014). Iveta Ozola and Iveta Ķestere, "Pedagoģijas kā zinātnes ģenēze Eiropā (18. gs. – 20. gs. 20.-30. gadi): historiogrāfiskais aspekts," in *Pedagoģijas vēsture: 15 jautājumi. Zinātnisko rakstu krājums*, edited by Aīda Krūze and Iveta Ķestere (Rīga: RaKa, 2010), 78–105.

"introduce the youth to culture",[17] with the concept of culture being understood in its broadest sense – social culture, economic culture, aesthetic culture, etc. In line with the European tradition, Latvian academia built a model of pedagogical sciences from the history of education, didactics, and the study of school management.[18] The curriculum of the pedagogy was a reflection on the insights of past and modern thinkers of the Western world in pedagogy, psychology, and philosophy.[19]

In June 1940 the Soviet Union occupied the Baltic States and in August the reorganisation of the University of Latvia was initiated upon Moscow's instructions. In October 1940, the Department of Pedagogy, which had been the first institution in Latvia to train teachers at the academic level and had successfully performed this task for 21 years, was dissolved. The dissolution of the Department of Pedagogy was a manoeuvre of the new authorities to get rid of professors who were not wanted by the communists. In October 1940, the Department of Pedagogy and Psychology was established at the Faculty of History and Philology, with the staff approved by the Soviet authorities.[20]

Soviet officials adopted a variety of tactics to evaluate personnel: first, screening and retraining existing professionals; second, importing loyal people from the metropole, i.e Russia; third, dismissing or even destroying "old" staff. During the mass dismissals of teaching staff no one was accused of breaches of work discipline or poor quality of work, but of ideological incompatibility: political views hostile to the Soviet authorities, religious affiliation or inappropriate social background, i.e. belonging to "bourgeois families".[21] Professor Eduards Petersons (*Pētersons*) (1882–1958), who taught

---

[17] Aleksandrs Dauge, *Vispārīgā paidagoģija.* (*Latvijas Ūniversitātē lasāmo lekciju kurss*). *Rokraksta vietā*. (Rīga: 1932), 9.

[18] Pauls Jurevičs, "Paidagōģija," in *Latviešu konversācijas vārdnīca, 15.sēj.*, edited by Arveds Švābe (Rīga: Grāmatu apgādniecība A. Gulbis, 1937), 30349. column.

[19] Latvian State Historical Archive, Fund 7427, description 13, file 719, 28; Latvian State Historical Archive, Fund 7427, description 6, file 63; Latvian State Historical Archive, Fund 3297, description 1, file 131, 15.

[20] Latvian State Historical Archive, Fund 7427, description 7, file 9.

[21] Henrihs Strods, ed., *Latvijas Valsts Universitātes vēsture 1940–1990* (Rīga: Latvijas Universitāte, 1999).

courses in pedagogy and the history of education, was dismissed[22] "as a bearer of the manifestation of the oppressive old power".[23]

As reported in the communist-created Soviet Latvian press in 1941, the training of teachers at universities was discussed at the USSR Conference on Pedagogical Sciences, defining three main tasks: to be armed with Marxist-Leninist theory, to acquire Soviet pedagogy and knowledge of a certain branch of science (subject in the school curriculum).[24]

The psychologist Rudolfs Drillis (1893–1983) became the first head of the 'new' Department of Pedagogy and Psychology at the Latvian State University.[25] The grounds for his recruitment are traceable in the request of the Rector of the University addressed to the People's Commissar of Education of the Latvian SSR, which states that "Drillis comes from the circles of the socialist working intelligentsia, takes an active part in the reorganisation of the University, has managed to prove his excellent working ability and objectivity in the performance of the duties entrusted to him."[26] However, Drillis held this position only for a few months, from 1 October to 1 December 1940.[27] During the Nazi occupation he was reinstated at the University with the opinion that "he had not run with the Bolsheviks or done anything of the sort, but rather had helped imperilled academics and had been concerned about his own fate".[28]

Since the first days of Soviet rule, dedicated educational leaders and university teachers were imported to the Baltics from the 'center' or metropolis.[29] Hence, in December 1940, Izidors Meikshans (*Meikšāns*) (1900–1975),[30] born

---

22 "Jauni mācību spēki Latvijas Valsts Ūniversitātē," Padomju Latvija, October 28, 1940; Kārlis Straubergs, "Latvijas Universitāte," *Trimdas Skola* 16 (1959): 605–607.

23 Latvian State Historical Archive, Fund 7427, description 13, file 1309.

24 Roberts Miķelsons, "Vissavienības pedagoģisko zinātņu konference," *Padomju Latvijas Skola* 6 (1941): 8–10.

25 Indulis Zvirgzdiņš, "Rūdolfs Drillis un LU," *Zinātņu vēsture un muzejniecība* 684 (2005): 147–152.

26 Latvian State Historical Archive, Fund 7427, description 13, file 399.

27 Latvian State Historical Archive, Fund 7427, description 13, file 399.

28 Latvian State Historical Archive, Fund 7427, description 13, file 399.

29 Iveta Ķestere and Gunta Marihina, "Milda Drīzule (1895–1992) – pedagoģijas vēsturniece un LVU Pedagoģijas un psiholoģijas katedras vadītāja (1948–1960)," *Latvijas Universitātes raksti. Zinātņu vēsture un muzejniecība* 800 (2014): 99–109.

30 Latvian State Archive, Fund 1340, description 2. p., file 303.

in Latvia but raised and educated in Russia, a graduate of the Communist University of the National Minorities of the West in Moscow, a member of the Communist Party since 1929, was appointed as the head of the Department of Pedagogy and Psychology.[31] In the documents of the Nazi occupation authorities, he is especially noted as a reformer of Latvian higher education following the model of the Soviet Union, "a servant of the letter and indulger of Moscow".[32]

Meikshans was by no means the only 'missionary' sent from the USSR by the Soviet authorities. For example, the personal file of Roberts Jonas (*Jonāss*) (1889–1955), an assistant professor at the Marxism-Leninism Department of the Latvian State University, contains a certificate dated 15 January 1941 from the All-Union Committee for Higher Education of the USSR Council of People's Commissars that "Comrade Jonas Roberts son of Peteris is sent to the Latvian SSR to perform teaching work at higher education institutions".[33] In January 1941, the educator Robert Mikelsons also arrived in Latvia, but more about him will follow later.

In February 1941, the Latvian State University began examinations according to the rules of the new authorities and students had to take an exam in pedagogy.[34] The question arises as to who was entrusted to teach this course if the 'old' teaching staff was declared unfit. Since the documents are incomplete, it might be assumed that it was Izidors Meikshans and Janis Bunduls (1899–1981). It is known that the chair of the State Examination Board in Pedagogy was Augusts Blumfelds (*Blūmfelds*) (1894–1965), dean of the Faculty of History and Philology in the academic year 1940/41 and assistant professor in the chair of Marxism-Leninism. He came to Riga from Russia in 1940, where he had studied at the Communist and Red Professorate Institutes.[35] Blumfelds was assisted by the already mentioned Meikshans and Drillis, as well as Janis Bunduls.[36] Bunduls was recruited to the University in October 1940 as an assistant professor of pedagogy. He was born and educated in Latvia, had worked as a teacher in various Latvian schools, and knew

[31] Latvian State Archive, Fund 1340, description 2. p., file 303.
[32] Latvian State Historical Archive, Fund P-949, description 1, file 18.
[33] Latvian State Archive, Fund 1340, description 2. p., file 174, 1.
[34] See Latvian State Historical Archive, Fund 7427, description 1, file 12157, 44.
[35] Latvian State Historical Archive, Fund 7427, description 1, file 12157.
[36] Latvian State Historical Archive, Fund 7427, description 1, file 7771.

11 foreign languages. Bunduls graduated from the University of Latvia with a degree in philosophy, and then furthered his knowledge in Germany. His interests were mainly in psychology, and he wrote several papers analysing Latvian literature from the point of view of individual psychology.[37] It is hard to say why the Soviets considered Bunduls trustworthy enough. Perhaps it was because one of his workplaces (1925–1930) was the State Central Pedagogical Institute, which was considered an institution with a left-wing sentiment and which was closed in 1935, when Latvia was ruled by a national authoritarian regime. Bunduls did not enjoy the trust of the communists for long, but we will come back to that later. In July 1941, German troops entered Riga and established their own order at the University of Latvia. Soviet occupiers were replaced by Nazi occupiers.

Three Missionaries of Soviet Pedagogy: Up the Career Ladder in Soviet Latvia

The liberation of Latvia from the Nazis began in 1944. The German occupation was succeeded by the Soviet dictatorship, which returned with its communist missionaries from the metropolis. The role of missionaries was initially assigned to people of Latvian, Estonian, and Lithuanian origin who, for various reasons, had lived in the Soviet Union and had acquired the appropriate ideological 'hardening' and knew clearly that one should not joke with the Communists, and therefore, in Soviet terms, had the 'right' mindset. Russian Latvians were later followed by a wide stream of a Russian-speaking working force who, in the eyes of the local Latvians, hardly speaking Russian themselves, all became 'Russians' – aliens both culturally and linguistically.[38] The Moscow missionaries were witnesses to Stalin's Great Purge – a campaign of political repressions in the Soviet Union between 1936 and 1938. The Latvian community in Russia was persecuted due to two reasons, i.e. their nationality and long-standing membership in the Communist party, which meant faithfulness to Lenin's ideals of communism and possible dissatisfaction with Stalin's rule. Most Latvians who lived in Soviet Russia

---

37 Latvian State Archive, Fund 1340, description 2. p., file 70.

38 Plakans, *A Concise History*, 362.

were killed, but the survivors were greatly intimidated.[39] We will continue the story of three missionaries of Latvian origin, whose task was to reorganise the Latvian educational field in line with Moscow's prescriptions.

Robert Mikelsons was born in 1889 in the territory of Latvia into a peasant family, but in 1906 he was already studying in Russia at the Velikiye Luki Real School.[40] It is not known why the Mikelsons family left their homeland. It could have been related to the revolutionary events of 1905 when some of the participants fled from the repressive measures of the Russian tsarist government, or to the search for better economic conditions. Both of these reasons led many Latvian families to emigrate at the beginning of the 20th century. In 1913, Mikelsons graduated from the Department of Biology at St. Petersburg State University and began working as a teacher. Another biography of Mikelsons states that he graduated from the St. Petersburg Pedagogical Academy alongside his university studies.[41] In any case, Mikelsons received a very good education for a peasant son of his time.

After the Russian Bolshevik Revolution of 1917, Mikelsons was apparently recognised as a teacher loyal to the Soviet authorities. After working for a few years as a teacher of pedagogy and natural sciences at the Tobolsk Teachers' Institute, Mikelsons was "summoned" (this is the term used in his record of 1946) to Moscow in 1920.[42] In the capital, he was appointed as a school principal and lectured in pedagogy at various higher education institutions, such as the Nadezhda Krupskaya Academy of Communist Education. According to Mikelsons himself, he contributed to the first textbook in Soviet pedagogy.[43]

Apparently, Mikelsons was satisfied with his career in Soviet Russia, he found his safe place in the profession. This is evidenced by Mikelsons' reluctance to leave for his homeland, unlike many other Latvians who took the opportunity in the 1920s to return and pursue a professional career in independent Latvia.[44] The situation changed when Latvia was occupied by the Soviet Union. Mikelsons arrived in Riga in January 1941, established

39 Juris Goldmanis, ed., *Latvieši PSRS varas virsotnēs* (Rīga: Zvaigzne ABC, 2013).
40 Latvian State Archive, Fund 464, description 1, file 2578-y, 3.
41 The Museum of Pedagogy at the University of Latvia, Fund of Roberts Miķelsons, 6.
42 The Museum of Pedagogy at the University of Latvia, Fund of Roberts Miķelsons, 6.
43 The Museum of Pedagogy at the University of Latvia, Fund of Roberts Miķelsons, 6.
44 Many Latvians who later hold professorship at the University of Latvia repatriated from Russia in the 1920s.

and headed the Methodological Cabinet of the People's Commissariat of Education of the Latvian SSR and the Department of Pedagogy at the State Pedagogical Institute (the name of the institution was changed several times over the years).[45] Mikelsons can be considered the first proponent of the Soviet pedagogical paradigm in Latvia – many of his programmatic articles were published in the magazine 'Soviet Latvia School', founded by the communists in 1941. At this stage, Mikelsons' career in Latvia was short-lived: before the Nazi occupation in July 1941, Mikelsons evacuated to Russia together with other Soviet authorities, where he headed the Department of Pedagogy at the Chuvash State Pedagogical Institute.[46]

After the war, in 1944, Mikelsons returned to Riga and was appointed the Chief of School Division of the People's Commissariat of Education of Latvian SSR. From 1947 to 1956, Mikelsons was the Deputy Minister of Education of the Latvian SSR. Needless to say, this position was largely decorative, as the Soviet education system was centralised and all decisions were taken in Moscow. However, at the local level, the deputy minister was a highly privileged position. In 1948, Mikelsons joined the Communist Party of the Soviet Union.

Alongside his administrative duties, Mikelsons also worked as an academic: from 1944 to 1958 he was a lecturer at the Latvian State University and the State Pedagogical Institute, and from 1956 to 1968 he was the Director of the Institute of Pedagogical Research at the Ministry of Education of Latvian SSR (the name of the Institute was changed several times). In 1957 Mikelsons became a corresponding member of the Russian Academy of Pedagogy Sciences.[47] Mikelsons held all these positions related to academic research without a scientific degree – he defended his thesis as a candidate of pedagogic sciences only in 1965.[48]

---

45 Latvian State Archive, Fund 464, description 1, file 216.

46 Latvian State Archive, Fund 464, description 1, file 2578-y.

47 Latvian State Archive, Fund 464, description 1, file 216; Alfrēds Staris, "Roberts Miķelsons (1889–1973)," in *Pedagoģiskā doma Latvijā no 1940.gada līdz mūsu dienām*, edited by Alfrēds Staris (Rīga: Puse, 1998), 27–29.

48 During the Soviet era, Latvia introduced a two-tier scientific degree system: first, the candidate's degree in pedagogical sciences and, second, the doctoral degree in pedagogical sciences.

There is no record of Mikelsons being affected by the turbulent events in the Soviet Union – he lived through Stalin's Great Purge, the denunciation of Stalin's personality cult in 1956 and the persecution of Latvian communists in 1959. Mikelsons built a brilliant career and regularly received official honours, including a high Soviet government and Communist Party award, the Order of the Red Banner of Labour in 1950.[49]

Mikelsons' activities in Latvia was evaluated by his colleague at the research institute as follows: "R. Mikelsons denied the achievements of national education and pedagogical sciences of independent Latvia. During his career and with his direct participation, the school of [independent] Latvia was reorganised into a Soviet school. The promotion of Soviet pedagogical principles was *the credo* of his life. He often tried to implement the ideas of the Soviet school with voluntary methods. R. Mikelsons also supervised the research of school history. As a result new ideas in the life of Latvian schools, but especially in the research of the history, could appear only with R. Mikelsons' blessing."[50]

Johanna Milda Kristine Trauberg Drizule was born in a family of Latvian peasants in 1895. She was bright and diligent, and graduating gymnasium she also received a home teacher's licence. She was invited to work in Irkutsk, Siberia, where her duty was teaching German in a wealthy Russian family.[51] Irkutsk was the place for political exile in Tsarist Russia, and during World War I and the Russian Revolution of 1917 heated political debates sparked there. Milda became attracted to leftists in general and anarchists in particular.[52]

After World War I, Milda returned back to Latvia. Milda quietly worked as a teacher in a gymnasium until she fell in love.[53] Her beloved man was a communist. Even more, he was sent as a Soviet agent to Latvia and worked undercover there. A more romantic character is hard to imagine. Their love story rapidly unfolded: in 1919 Milda became a member of the Communist party[54] and followed her husband Arvids Drizulis (*Drīzulis*) (1890–1939)

---

49 Latvian State Archive, Fund 464, description 1, file 216.
50 Staris, "Roberts Miķelsons," 29.
51 University of Latvia Archive Fund, description 7, file 647, 5.
52 Anna Celmiņa, "Ar nedziestošu jaunības dzirksti," Oktobra Karogs, December 27, 1980.
53 Mirdza Gaile, "Vienmēr ierindā," Skolotāju Avīze, January 7, 1981.
54 University of Latvia Archive Fund, description 7, file 647, 5.

to Russia when he had to flee from Latvia. They both participated in the Russian civil war on the side of the Bolsheviks. Their son was born near the front line in 1920.

At the same time, Milda Drizule continued her education. She studied at the Moscow State Pedagogy Institute, but Drizule's studies lasted nine months only: from October 1 to August 1 of 1931. Moreover, during this period, she had to complete three courses of practical training, each one a month-long, and two of them were spent in a factory and kolkhoz.[55] It means that for Drizule theoretical studies lasted only six months.

After her studies at the Pedagogy Institute in 1931, Drizule was invited to continue her education in a doctoral programme (*aspirantura*), which she completed in three years.[56] Alongside her studies, Drizule worked together with Nadezda Krupskaya (1869–1939), the widow of the leader of the Bolsheviks Vladimir Lenin (1870–1924). As Drizule told later in her interviews, they both organized the Soviet school system and teacher training. In the Marxist Association led by Krupskaya, Drizule attended lectures delivered by the innovators - seen today as classics of Soviet pedagogy – Anton Makarenko and Peter Blonsky.[57] It is a moot question as to how important Drizule's role really was in all these activities. It is typical of communist biographies to showcase special relationships and closeness with communist leaders. In Soviet society, it was not only beneficial for developing one's career, but it was also good for personal safety reasons.

However, the Drizulis family failed to escape Stalin's Great Purge. Milda's husband was arrested in October 1938. Until the end of her life, she remembered the bang of the locking door of their apartment and shouting after her husband, who was sentenced to death by Stalin's KGB. Drizule never remarried again. In 1939 she was expelled from the Communist party as a wife of a political prisoner,[58] which meant a loss of work and bread during the Stalin's era. However, in this hopeless situation Drizule's Latvian origin saved her in a paradoxical way. In 1944, she was invited to the Commissariat of Education in Moscow and, together with other Latvians, became a member of

55 University of Latvia Archive Fund, description 7, file 647, 5.
56 University of Latvia Archive Fund, description 7, file 647, 5.
57 Celmiņa, "Ar nedziestošu jaunības dzirksti."
58 University of Latvia Archive Fund, description 7, file 647, 5.

the communist 'task force'. Drizule was sent to the Latvian State University for establishing the Soviet-style pedagogy. The appointment to Latvia coincided with Drizule's own wish, as in May 1944 she had submitted an application to the People's Commissar for Education requesting permission to work in her native land.[59]

On her arrival in Latvia, Drizule learnt about an unexpected development, namely, that at the end of World War II both of her brothers escaped from the upcoming communist dictatorship to the United States. Relatives abroad put any Soviet citizen during the Stalin era under suspicion. After the imprisoned husband, the brothers living abroad were another factor enabling Moscow keep Drizule on a short leash.

Drizule started her career at the Latvian State University in December 1944, and in 1948 she became the Head of the Department of Pedagogy and Psychology,[60] as well as one of the first Soviet historians of education in Latvia. Drizule got her degree 'candidate of pedagogical sciences' in 1947. She was the first, and until 1957 the only, person to obtain a candidate's degree in pedagogy in Soviet Latvia. From 1949 Drizule also worked as the dean and deputy dean of the Faculty of Philology at the Latvian State University,[61] was the secretary of the Communist Party Organisation of the faculty,[62] and was elected to the faculty's party committee several times.[63] Like Mikelsons, she also received public recognition from the Soviet government and the Communist Party – in 1965 Drizule was awarded the USSR Order "Sign of Honour".[64]

Drizule retired from the University in 1960. After retirement, she lived an active life with her son's family and saw the ideals of her youth collapse together with the collapse of the Soviet Union in 1991. During the interview, her granddaughter was asked about Drizule's reaction to anti-communist demonstrations and restoration of Latvian independence. She remembered

59 University of Latvia Archive Fund, description 7, file 647, 6, 21, 148.
60 University of Latvia Archive Fund, description 7, file 647, 21, 26.
61 University of Latvia Archive Fund, description 7, file 647, 45.
62 University of Latvia Archive Fund, description 7, file 647, 61.
63 University of Latvia Archive Fund, description 7, file 647, 82.
64 University of Latvia Archive Fund, description 7, file 647, 122.

how sitting at the window and looking at the protesters, 95-year-old Drizule commented: "Well, it goes the same way as in Irkutsk in 1917!"[65]

Vladimirs Usins was born in 1918 into a family of Latvian peasants in Smolensk Oblast, Russia. The time and reason for his parents' emigration from Latvia are unknown. Vladimir's parents died early, and the boy ended up in an orphanage in Smolensk.[66] Knowing the history of post-revolutionary Russia, this is an important fact: after the tragedies of World War I and the Russian Revolution, overcrowded orphanages were a special focus of communist interests. They were institutions where collective discipline was purposefully taught and communist ideology indoctrinated.[67]

In 1939 Usins graduated from the Pedagogical School in Leningrad (now St. Petersburg),[68] but the newspaper article dedicated to Usins' 50th birthday says that he studied at the Leningrad Latvian Pedagogical Technical School.[69] During World War II, after part-time studies, he graduated from the Stalin's Institute of Teacher Training.[70] Before coming to Latvia, Usins worked as a teacher in various schools in Russia. During World War II, he served in the Soviet army but was retired as an irreplaceable pedagogical specialist[71] or because of ill health.[72] In any case, in 1943 Usins returned to teaching.

In 1945, citing Usins' file in the archives, he arrived in Latvia at the summons of the Council of People's Commissars of the Latvian SSR and was placed at the "disposal" of the People's Commissariat of Education.[73] His modest education was no obstacle to becoming a school inspector in the People's Education Department of a large Latvia district – that is, to inspect and evaluate the work of schools and teachers. It seems that Usins' education also raised questions for his employers, hence, according to his personal file, Usins graduated from the Riga Pedagogical Institute in 1947.[74] However,

---

65 Viktorya in interview with Iveta Kestere, February 15, 2014.
66 The Museum of Pedagogy at the University of Latvia, Fund of Vladimirs Ūsiņš.
67 See Catriona Kelly, *Children's World: Growing Up in Russia, 1890–1991* (New Haven: Yale UP, 2007).
68 Latvian State Archive, Fund 464, description 2, file 34.
69 Valdis Vanags, "Loks ved augšup," Skolotāju Avīze, January 1, 1969.
70 The Museum of Pedagogy at the University of Latvia, Fund of Vladimirs Ūsiņš.
71 The Museum of Pedagogy at the University of Latvia, Fund of Vladimirs Ūsiņš.
72 Latvian State Archive, Fund 464, description 2, file 34, 2.
73 Latvian State Archive, Fund 464, description 2, file 34, 2.
74 The Museum of Pedagogy at the University of Latvia, Fund of Vladimirs Ūsiņš.

other documents indicate that he graduated from the Riga Pedagogical Institute only in 1952.[75] In 1952 Usins became a senior research fellow at the Institute of Pedagogical Research at the Ministry of Education of Latvian SSR and in 1954 – the deputy director for scientific work.[76] Neither the lack of an academic education nor of a scientific degree hindered conducting the research work of others. Usins defended his candidate of pedagogical sciences thesis only in 1962.

The turbulent political changes in the Soviet Union did not hinder Usins' career either. Like Mikelsons and Drizule, he received state and Communist Party awards, including the Order of the Red Banner of Labour in 1960. After the restoration of Latvia's independence in 1991, Usins continued to work at the research institute, exploring the history of education and publishing several books that are still respected.

In the memories of his contemporaries and colleagues, words of praise are dedicated to Usins. The account of a professor with an 'unacceptable biography' testifies to the trend: Leonards Zukovs (*Žukovs*) (1922–2019) experienced Soviet repressions and was banned from working. Having arrived at the Institute of Pedagogy Research in Riga he was welcomed by Vladimirs Usins, who told him that he knew and understood the professor's situation. "Surely, Usins was a communist, but he was a Latvian first of all," Zukovs kept repeating during our conversation.[77]

Introduction of Soviet Pedagogy in Latvia

Immediately after the Soviet occupation pedagogy was isolated from Western influences and cut off from the national past. The pedagogical press published during Latvia's independence were closed down, Latvian educators' books were placed in 'specialised funds' of libraries, access to which was subject to special permission by Soviet authorities. Hence, similarly to the entire Soviet society, scholars were divided by their access to information.

75 The Museum of Pedagogy at the University of Latvia, Fund of Vladimirs Ūsiņš; Latvian State Archive, Fund 464, description 2, file 34, 2.
76 Latvian State Archive, Fund 464, description 2, file 34, 2.
77 Leonids Zukovs in interview with Iveta Kestere, September 23, 2011.

As Musolff notes, in totalitarianism, only small circles of insiders are provided with true knowledge.[78]

Soviet officials set up new press publications, working under the strict control of Communist censorship. The main 'source of truth' was now located in Moscow, in the USSR Academy of Pedagogy Sciences. The textbooks included in pedagogical curriculum were written by Russian scholars, and all the teaching materials underwent rigorous testing in Moscow.

Researchers from Soviet republics went to the metropolis for advice as well as to attend meetings and conferences. For example, in December 1945 the Rector of the Latvian State University wrote a request to the Council of People's Commissars of the Latvian SSR to grant an academic trip to Milda Drizule "for her dissertation work, since she can receive the necessary advice only in Moscow".[79] Even though trips like this were referred to as the all-union inter-institutional cooperation in reports on research activity,[80] their purpose was to receive instructions and get 'blessings' for further research in the 'provinces'. On the other hand, such trips were not done for show only. It has to be admitted that scholars working in Moscow were outstanding personalities considering the limitations of the epoch, for mediocrities were never invited to work in the institutions in the capital. Metropolitan scholars had access to a wider range of literature and broader international experience. Therefore, cooperation with colleagues from the metropolis really enriched pedagogy research in the Baltic States.[81] Of course, none of the researchers dared to question the fundamental principles of Soviet ideology.

Almost all Western educators starting from the end of the 19th century were considered bourgeois and therefore 'bad ones'. In 1948, at the meeting of the Department of Pedagogy and Psychology, Milda Drizule criticized

---

78 Andreas Musolff, "Language under Totalitarian Regimes: the Example of Political Discourse in Nazi Germany," in *The Routledge Handbook of Language and Politics (Routledge Handbooks in Linguistics)*, edited by Ruth Wodak and Bernhard Forchtner (New York: Routledge, 2017), 9.

79 University of Latvia Archive Fund, description 7, file 647, 139.

80 The Museum of Pedagogy at the University of Latvia, Index 02-3, 122.

81 See Iveta Kestere, Zanda Rubene and Iveta Ozola, "Educational Sciences Between "Real" Moscow and the "Imaginary" West: The Case of Latvia (1989–1999)," in *Folds of Past, Present and Future*, edited by Sarah Van Ruyskensvelde, Geert Thyssen, Frederik Herman, Angelo Van Gorp and Pieter Verstraete (Oldenburg: De Gruyiter, 2021), 249–267.

"cosmopolitism." She spoke against "bourgeois ideas in history" and claimed that Soviet pedagogy was completely new and qualitatively different from all past and present bourgeois pedagogies. She said that too much attention was devoted to John Dewey and Johann Friedrich Herbart in Soviet textbooks whereas Krupskaya was undervalued there.[82] Almost 10 year later, in 1956, Drizule criticised the lecture delivered by her colleague arguing that "it is not necessary to discuss trends in bourgeois pedagogy, Herbart would suffice". She also considered it redundant to inform students about self-government in American schools. She believed that "the theory of upbringing should be better in line with Makarenko than with representatives of bourgeois pedagogy because our circumstances are special".[83]

Drizule's ungrounded claims as to the supremacy of the Soviet pedagogy are typical of propaganda under dictatorships.[84] For Latvian scholars, who had long-standing ties with Western culture, these statements were astonishing. Nevertheless, they kept silent because many of their colleagues had already been dismissed and even sent to Siberia by communists.

The content of Soviet pedagogy consisted of a politicised and ideologised theory of education (*vospitanye*), which dealt with various strands of communist education (intellectual, patriotic and international, labour, ethical, etc. education), the theory of school organisation and management (including work with Young Pioneer and Komsomol organisations), didactics and the history of education.

The dialectical materialism was proclaimed in the Soviet Union as the only correct and scientific view of the world. 'Idealism' became an unforgivable sin. The pedagogy of liberal arts was replaced by trivialized Marxism based on social theories, imported from the Soviet Union.[85] Pedagogy was translated into a science that emerged out of society's need to prepare future generations more effectively for the preservation and improvement of social

---

[82] Latvian State Archive, Fund 1340, description 23, file 2, 19.

[83] Latvian State Archive, Fund 1340, description 23, file 9.

[84] Garth S. Jowett and Victoria J. O'Donnell, *Propaganda and Persuasion* (SAGE, 2012), 293, 300.

[85] On the development of pedagogical science in Latvia during the Soviet occupation, see Aīda Krūze and Iveta Ozola, "Pedagogy as a Science in Latvia," in *History of Pedagogy and Educational Sciences in the Baltic Countries from 1940 to 1990: an Overview*, edited by Iveta Ķestere and Aīda Krūze (Rīga: RaKa, 2013), 234–242.

production.[86] The end result of Soviet pedagogy was to be a comprehensively developed citizen, the New Soviet Man, who would devote his strength, skills, and knowledge to building a utopian social system – communism.[87]

In the history of education, social processes were viewed through the prism of Marxist-Leninist social theories, where the world was explained as an antagonism of different forces (exploited *versus* exploiters, workers *versus* bourgeoisie, peasants *versus* kulaks, revolution *versus* counter-revolution, socialism *versus* capitalism, etc.). This formula, which explained the world in a very simplistic way,[88] was reduced to a trivial and ideologised scheme.[89] At the University, in the course of History of Education Milda Drizule and Roberts Mikelsons lectured on such topics as 'Marx and Engels as founders of the proletarian pedagogy',[90] 'Marx, Engels, Lenin and Stalin on communist upbringing',[91] 'The history of Marxist scientific pedagogy', 'Revolution in science – the rise of Marxism'.[92]

The departure from the Marxist-Leninist view of the world as a totality of matter was labelled by Soviet scholars as "reactionary views", that is, a rejection of the "new and progressive" Soviet methodology, a return to the "old and bourgeois" philosophy. In 1948, Milda Drizule initiated and voted 'for' the dismissal of her colleague, the famous psychologist Janis Bunduls from the Latvian State University. Bunduls was accused of disseminating "reactionary ideas".[93] Drizule's action, in this case, was very typical, i.e. she did what she had to do, and otherwise, she could be fired together with her colleague Bunduls. It was the time of Stalinism and Drizule knew what

86 On the philosophical basis of Soviet pedagogy, see Zanda Rubene, "Geisteswissenschaften und akademische Bildung in Lettland," *Theodor-Litt-Jahrbuch* 7 (2010): 57–73.

87 Iveta Kestere and Manuel Fernández González, "Educating the New Soviet Man: Propagated Image and Hidden Resistance in Soviet Latvia," *Historia scholastica* 7, no. 1 (2021): 11–33.

88 Bertrand Russel, *Education and the Social Order* (London, New York: Routledge, 1932/1993), 112–122.

89 Iveta Kestere, "History of Education and the Struggle for Intellectual Liberation in Post-Soviet Baltic Space After the Fall of the Berlin Wall," *Paedagogica Historica*, 50, no. 6 (2014): 744–851.

90 Latvian State Archive, Fund 464, description 1, file 128, 10.

91 Latvian State Archive, Fund 464, description 1, file 108, 2.

92 Latvian State Archive, Fund 464, description 1, file 194, 2, 13.

93 Latvian State Archive, Fund 1340, description 23, file 1, 22.

Stalin's repression meant. In the report of the Rector of the Latvian State University to the Central Committee of the Communist Party, the following justification was given for the dismissal of Bunduls: "In his lectures he introduced Menshevik and idealistic views. A typical bourgeois nationalist."[94]

Alongside the textbooks in Russian sent from the Soviet Union, the new understanding of pedagogy was propagated through the pedagogical press. The most active authors were Robert Mikelsons and Vladimir Usins – between the late 1940s and the early 1960s each of them published about 50 articles in the Latvian press.[95] The subjects of these articles were broad and very similar, namely, issues of communist education, with particular emphasis on education for work and Soviet patriotism, problems of school organisation, compulsory teaching of the Russian language, teacher training and the introduction of teachers to the experience of pedagogy in Soviet Russia.

The training of new scholars from local 'material' was slow. From 1944 to 1960, only two people studied at the postgraduate programme of pedagogy: Anna Laure (1923–1981) was born and educated in Latvia, while Galina Rumyantseva (1922–?) arrived in Riga in 1948 with education and work experience acquired in Simferopol (then a city in Russia).[96] The situation changed in the 1960s when the rigid personnel selection procedures of the Stalin era were relaxed and researchers educated in Soviet Latvia entered the field of pedagogical science.

Conclusions

Several features can be identified and generalized from the biographies of the Soviet missionaries, who were sent to reorganise education and pedagogical science in Soviet Latvia after World War II.

---

94 "Latvijas Valsts Universitātes rektora J. Jurgena izziņa Latvijas Komunististiskās (boļševiku) partijas CK par kadru tīrīšanu universitātē 1949. gada 29. jūlijā, Rīgā," *Latvijas Vēsture* 29, no. 1 (1998): 124–132.

95 Latvian State Archive, Fund 464, description 1, file 2578-y; Latvian National Digital Library. "Periodika." Accessed November 28, 2022. http://periodika.lv/.

96 Vija Medne, ed., *Latvijas Universitātes aspiranti un doktoranti. I daļa. Aspirantūras un doktorantūras personāliju, aizstāvēto disertāciju un iegūto zinātnisko grādu apkopojums. 1945–2005* (Rīga: LU Akadēmiskais apgāds, 2009).

First, the biographies of all three missionaries confirm that they had established good professional careers in Soviet Russia, which means that their loyalty to the communist regime has been tested and recognised as safe to continue their careers in Soviet Latvia. Moreover, although both Vladimirs Usins and Roberts Mikelsons survived Stalin's Purges without obvious losses, all Latvians in Russia felt intimidated. Communist authorities found it quite useful, for scared people were submissive to the authoritarian rule and the Latvians' fear could be exploited.

The second essential point in common for all Soviet missionaries is their real level of education. All three missionaries defended their dissertations and became 'candidates of pedagogical sciences' after they had been appointed by Moscow to the leading positions in the institutions of pedagogy research of Latvia. From the perspective of Moscow, the scientific degree was not a prerequisite for leading the local academia, and the ideological conviction and obedience to the Soviet power were ranked higher than researcher's competencies.

Third, the metropolis scheming proved accurate: communist authorities believed that indigenous communities would trust their own people more than Russians. Missionaries were gradually accepted by Latvian scholars where Baltic family names and knowledge of local language played an important role. It was not a high rank as much as the ethnicity that served as an entry ticket to the local Latvian academic community.

Fourth, Soviet missionaries seem to have truly believed in their mission as enlighteners. Although they were sent to their homeland by order of the Soviet authorities, coming to Latvia was also their voluntary decision. They might have looked for new career opportunities or longed for a more prosperous life, but the main desire was to 'help', 'enlighten', and 'educate' the local population, a trait typical of missionaries vividly described by Depaepe et al.[97]

---

[97] Marc Depaepe, Frank Debaere and Lies Van Rompaey, "Missionary Education in the Belgian Congo during the Colonial Period (1908–1960)," *Neue Zeitschrift für Missionswissenschaft. Nouvelle Revue de science missionaire* 48, no. 4 (1992): 265–280; Marc Depaepe, "'Rien ne va Plus…' The Collapse of the Colonial Educational Structures in Zaire (1960–1995)," *Education and Society* 16, no. 1 (1998): 37–53; Marc Depaepe, "An Agenda for the History of Colonial Education," in *The Colonial Experience in Education. Historical Issues and Perspectives*, edited by Antonio Novoa, Marc Depaepe and Erwin V. Johanningmeier (Gent: C.S.H.P., 1995), 15–21.

Before the Soviets occupied Latvia in 1940, pedagogy at the University of Latvia had been taught by professors educated in France, Germany and the outstanding University of Tartu in Estonia. Now, professorships were taken by Moscow envoys, who were poorly educated and intimidated by the totalitarian power. At the same time, they looked enthusiastic, interested, diligent and happy to come back to their motherland and to bring communist values to local people. They restlessly delivered lectures and wrote articles to educate new Soviet citizens in Latvia about supremacy of the Soviet education system, necessity to acquire the Russian language, positive role of productive labour in education and introduction of strict discipline at school. The missionaries brought a new politicized pedagogy paradigm based on Marxism, the paradigm explaining the world in terms of socio-economic antagonism and struggle. This trivial approach resulted in a shoddy methodology or the absence of any defined methodology at all. The lack of research methodology is the most painful Soviet legacy in the field of pedagogy, the consequences of which were felt in post-Soviet academic research for a long time.

The Soviet missionaries completed their mission using the privileges granted by Moscow and this backing together with their high rank were their main active tools. On the one hand, missionaries were victims scared by the ruling power; on the other hand, they became pillars of the regime and enjoyed all the benefits the regime provided. Everybody adapted, which, according to Grüttner, is a situation characteristic of totalitarian regimes that exist for a long time.[98]

Bibliography

Ashcroft, Bill, Gareth Griffiths, and Helen Tiffin. *Post-Colonial Studies: The Key Concepts*. London: Routledge, 2000.

Carney, Thomas F. "Prosopography: Payoffs and Pitfalls." *Phoenix* 27, no. 2 (1973): 156–179.

Celmiņa, Anna. "Ar nedziestošu jaunības dzirksti." Oktobra Karogs, December 27, 1980.

[98] Michael Grüttner, "Concluding Reflections: Universities and Dictatorships," in *Universities under Dictatorship*, edited by John Connelly, and Micahel Grüttner (University Park: The Pennsylvania State University Press, 2005), 295.

Dauge, Aleksandrs. *Vispārīgā paidagoģija. (Latvijas Ūniversitātē lasāmo lekciju kurss). Rokraksta vietā.* Rīga: 1932.

Depaepe, Marc, Frank Debaere, and Lies Van Rompaey. "Missionary Education in the Belgian Congo during the Colonial Period (1908–1960)." *Neue Zeitschrift für Missionswissenschaft. Nouvelle Revue de science missionaire* 48, no. 4 (1992): 265–280.

Depaepe, Marc. "'Rien ne va Plus...' The Collapse of the Colonial Educational Structures in Zaire (1960–1995)." *Education and Society* 16, no. 1 (1998): 37–53.

Depaepe, Marc. "An Agenda for the History of Colonial Education." In *The Colonial Experience in Education. Historical Issues and Perspectives*, edited by Antonio Novoa, Marc Depaepe, and Erwin V. Johanningmeier, 15–21. Gent: C.S.H.P., 1995.

Depaepe, Marc. "Sometimes a Little Distance is Needed to See What Really Happened: The Study of the Belgian Educational Policy in Congo as an Example of the Critical Vigour of Colonial History of Education." In *Between Educationalization and Appropriation: Selected Writings on the History of Modern Educational Systems*, edited by Marc Depaepe, 223–24. Leuven: Leuven University Press, 2012.

Gaile, Mirdza. "Vienmēr ierindā." Skolotāju Avīze, January, 7, 1981.

Goldmanis, Juris, ed. *Latvieši PSRS varas virsotnēs*. Rīga: Zvaigzne ABC, 2013.

Grüttner, Michael. "Concluding Reflections: Universities and Dictatorships." In *Universities under Dictatorship*, edited by John Connelly, and Micahel Grüttner, 283–295. University Park: The Pennsylvania State University Press, 2005.

"Jauni mācību spēki Latvijas Valsts Ūniversitātē." Padomju Latvija, October 28, 1940.

Jowett, Garth S., and Victoria J. O'Donnell. *Propaganda and Persuasion*. SAGE, 2012.

Jurevičs, Pauls. "Paidagōģija." In *Latviešu konversācijas vārdnīca, 15.sēj*, edited by Arveds Švābe, 30349. column. Rīga: Grāmatu apgādniecība A. Gulbis, 1937.

Kalertas, Violeta. "Baltic Postcolonialism and Its Critics." In *Baltic Postcolonialism*, edited by Violeta Kalertas, 1–9. Amsterdam: Rodopi, 2006.

Kelly, Catriona. *Children's World: Growing Up in Russia, 1890–1991.* New Haven: Yale UP, 2007.

Ķestere, Iveta, and Gunta Marihina. "Milda Drīzule (1895–1992) – pedagoģijas vēsturniece un LVU Pedagoģijas un psiholoģijas katedras vadītāja (1948–1960)." *Latvijas Universitātes raksti. Zinātņu vēsture un muzejniecība* 800 (2014): 99–109.

Kestere, Iveta, and Manuel Fernández González. "Educating the New Soviet Man: Propagated Image and Hidden Resistance in Soviet Latvia." *Historia scholastica* 7, no. 1 (2021): 11–33.

Kestere, Iveta, Zanda Rubene, and Iveta Ozola. "Educational Sciences Between "Real" Moscow and the "Imaginary" West: The Case of Latvia (1989–1999)." In *Folds of Past, Present and Future*, edited by Sarah Van Ruyskensvelde, Geert Thyssen, Frederik Herman, Angelo Van Gorp and Pieter Verstraete, 249–267. Oldenburg: De Gruyiter, 2021.

Kestere, Iveta. "History of Education and the Struggle for Intellectual Liberation in Post-Soviet Baltic Space After the Fall of the Berlin Wall." *Paedagogica Historica* 50, no. 6 (2014): 744–851.

Krūze, Aīda, and Iveta Ozola, "Pedagogy as a Science in Latvia." In *History of Pedagogy and Educational Sciences in the Baltic Countries from 1940 to 1990: an Overview*, edited by Iveta Ķestere and Aīda Krūze, 234–242. Rīga: RaKa, 2013.

Lane, Thomas. *Lithuania: Stepping Westward.* London: Routledge, 2001.

Latvian National Digital Library. "Periodika [Periodicals]." Accessed November 28, 2022. http://periodika.lv/.

Latvian State Archive, Fund 1340, description 2. p., file 174.

Latvian State Archive, Fund 1340, description 2. p., file 303.

Latvian State Archive, Fund 1340, description 2. p., file 70.

Latvian State Archive, Fund 1340, description 23, file 2.

Latvian State Archive, Fund 1340, description 23, file 9.

Latvian State Archive, Fund 464, description 1, file 108.

Latvian State Archive, Fund 464, description 1, file 128.

Latvian State Archive, Fund 464, description 1, file 194.

Latvian State Archive, Fund 464, description 1, file 216.

Latvian State Archive, Fund 464, description 1, file 2578-y.

Latvian State Archive, Fund 464, description 2, file 34.

Latvian State Historical Archive, Fund 3297, description 1, file 131.

Latvian State Historical Archive, Fund 7427, description 1, file 12157.

Latvian State Historical Archive, Fund 7427, description 1, file 7771.

Latvian State Historical Archive, Fund 7427, description 1, file 21514.

Latvian State Historical Archive, Fund 7427, description 13, file 1309.

Latvian State Historical Archive, Fund 7427, description 13, file 399.

Latvian State Historical Archive, Fund 7427, description 13, file 719.

Latvian State Historical Archive, Fund 7427, description 6, file 63.

Latvian State Historical Archive, Fund 7427, description 7, file 9.

Latvian State Historical Archive, Fund P-949, description 1, file 18.

"Latvijas Valsts Universitātes rektora J. Jurgena izziņa Latvijas Komunististiskās (boļševiku) partijas CK par kadru tīrīšanu universitātē 1949. gada 29. jūlijā, Rīgā." *Latvijas Vēsture* 29, no. 1 (1998): 124–132.

Latvijas Universitātes piecgadu darbības pārskats. 1919–1924. Rīga: Latvijas Universitāte, 1925.

Medne, Vija, ed. *Latvijas Universitātes aspiranti un doktoranti. I daļa. Aspirantūras un doktorantūras personāliju, aizstāvēto disertāciju un iegūto zinātnisko grādu apkopojums. l945–2005*. Rīga: LU Akadēmiskais apgāds, 2009.

Miķelsons, Roberts. "Pedagoģiskās domas attīstība." In *Skolas un pedagoģiskās domas attīstība Padomju Latvijā*, edited by Roberts Miķelsons, 48–76. Rīga: Zvaigzne, 1969.

Miķelsons, Roberts. "Vissavienības pedagoģisko zinātņu konference." *Padomju Latvijas Skola* 6 (1941): 8–10.

Morgan, Kevin. "Comparative Communist History and the 'Biographical Turn.'" *History Compass* 10, no. 6 (2012): 455–466.

Musolff, Andreas. "Language under Totalitarian Regimes: the Example of Political Discourse in Nazi Germany." In *The Routledge Handbook of Language and Politics (Routledge Handbooks in Linguistics)*, edited by Ruth Wodak and Bernhard Forchtner, 660–672. New York: Routledge, 2017.

Oberländer, Erwin. "Instruments of Sovetization in 1939/1940 and after 1944/45." In *The Soviet Occupation Regime in the Baltic States 1944–1959: Policies and Their Consequences. Materials of an International Conference, 13–14 June, 2002, Riga*, edited by Andris Caune et al., 50–58. Rīga: Latvijas vēstures institūta apgāds, 2007.

Ozola, Iveta, and Iveta Ķestere. "Pedagoģijas kā zinātnes ģenēze Eiropā (18. gs. – 20. gs. 20.–30. gadi): historiogrāfiskais aspekts." In *Pedagoģijas vēsture: 15 jautājumi. Zinātnisko rakstu krājums*, edited by Aīda Krūze, and Iveta Ķestere, 78–105. Rīga: RaKa, 2010.

Ozola, Iveta. "Pedagoģijas zinātnes ģenēze Latvijā no 20.gs. 20.gadiem līdz 20.gs. 60.gadu sākumam." PhD diss., University of Latvia, 2014.

Plakans, Andrejs. *A Concise History of the Baltic States*. Cambridge University Press, 2011.

Roberts, Brian. *Biographical Research*. Buckingham, Philadelphia: Open University Press, 2002.

Rubene, Zanda. "Geisteswissenschaften und akademische Bildung in Lettland." *Theodor-Litt-Jahrbuch* 7 (2010): 57–73.

Russel, Bertrand. *Education and the Social Order*. London, New York: Routledge, 1932/1993.

Staris, Alfrēds. "Roberts Miķelsons (1889–1973)." In *Pedagoģiskā doma Latvijā no 1940.gada līdz mūsu dienām*, edited by Alfrēds Staris, 27–29. Rīga: Puse, 1998.

Straubergs, Kārlis. "Latvijas Universitāte. *Trimdas Skola* 16 (1959): 605–607.

Strods, Henrihs, ed. *Latvijas Valsts Universitātes vēsture 1940–1990*. Rīga: Latvijas Universitāte, 1999.

The Museum of Pedagogy at the University of Latvia, Fund of Roberts Miķelsons.

The Museum of Pedagogy at the University of Latvia, Fund of Vladimirs Ūsiņš.

The Museum of Pedagogy at the University of Latvia, Index 02-3.

Tsvetkova, Natalia. *Failure of American and Soviet Cultural Imperialism in German Universities, 1945–1990*. Leiden, Boston: Brill, 2013.

University of Latvia Archive Fund, description 7, file 647.

Vanags, Valdis. "Loks ved augšup." Skolotāju Avīze, January 1, 1969.

Viktorya in interview with Iveta Kestere, February 15, 2014.

Wengraf, Tom, Prue Chamberlayne, and Joanna Bornat. "A Biographical Turn in the Social Sciences? A British-European View." *Cultural Studies-Critical Methodologies* 2, no. 2 (2002): 245–269.

Zukovs, Leonids in interview with Iveta Kestere, September 23, 2011.

Zvirgzdiņš, Indulis. "Rūdolfs Drillis un LU." *Zinātņu vēsture un muzejniecība* 684 (2005): 147–152.

Abbruch oder Wende? Polnische Allgemein-Pädagogen und Sowjetisierung (drei Beispiele)

Dariusz Stępkowski

Abstrakt: Sowjetisierung der akademischen Erziehungswissenschaften (Pädagogik) in Polen nach dem Zweiten Weltkrieg bleibt immer noch ungeklärt. In diesem Beitrag werden wissenschaftliche Publikationen aus den Jahren 1948–1950 dreier prominenter Vertreter der polnischen allgemeinen Pädagogik: Zygmunt Mysłakowski (1890–1971), Kazimierz Sośnicki (1883–1976) i Bogdan Suchodolski (1903–1992) mittels des Konzeptes der Nichtaffirmativität untersucht. In dem ersten Kapitel werden zwei Denkformen und Modelle pädagogischen Denkens – eines affirmativ unkritischen und nichtaffirmativ reflexiven – skizzenhaft erläutert. Der zweite wendet sich ausgewählten Texten von den drei genannten Autoren zu, die nach ihrer Stellungnahme gegenüber der Sowjetisierung der schulischen Erziehungspraxis und der erziehungswissenschaftlichen Theoriebildung (Pädagogik) gefragt werden. Der dritte entwickelt eine synthetisierende Gesamtschau auf die Thematik, die im zeitgenössischen pädagogischen Diskurs in Polen bis heute von Bedeutung ist.

Schlagworte: Sowjetisierung, Stalinismus, Union der Sozialistischen Sowjetrepubliken, (Volks)Republik Polen, Nichtaffirmativität, Affirmativität, Bildung, Erziehung, Arbeiterpädagogik, Zweiter Weltkrieg, Marxismus-Leninismus

Vorüberlegungen

Noch vor Ende des Zweiten Weltkriegs begann man in der Republik Polen, die 1952 in Volksrepublik Polen umbenannt wurde, mit der programmierten und von außen her kontrollierten Implementation sozialer, wirtschaftlicher und kultureller Modelle aus der Union der Sozialistischen Sowjetrepubliken (UdSSR). Das Ziel der Sowjetisierung war nicht nur die Anpassung aller Lebensbereiche, einschließlich der Wissenschaft, an sowjetische Standards, sondern auch eine dauerhafte Unterwerfung des polnischen Volkes und Gemeinwesens unter das Herrschaftssystem der UdSSR.

In der schulischen Erziehungspraxis und der erziehungswissenschaftlichen Theoriebildung (Pädagogik) vollzog sich die Sowjetisierung noch dramatischer als in anderen Gesellschaftssphären. Ursächlich hierfür war, dass das polnische Erziehungssystem mit der Aufgabe betraut wurde, das kommunistische ideal des „neuen Menschen" in Polen zu verwirklichen.

In den Folgejahren wurde die Erziehung in Polen allmählich zu einer Front im Kampf gegen die Vergangenheit und für eine utopische Zukunft, die außerhalb von Polen zum Zwecke der Etablierung eines umfassenden sowjetischen Herrschaftssystems entwickelt wurde. In den Jahren 1948–1950 kam es zu einem grundlegenden Wandel in der Art und Weise, wie dieser Kampf geführt wurde. Mit der Ankündigung der „ideologischen Offensive" nahm die Sowjetisierung die Form einer radikalen Stalinisierung an,[1] die bis zur ersten Krise des sozialistischen Machtsystems in Mittel- und Osteuropa im Jahr 1956 und dem daraus resultierenden sog. Oktobertauwetter andauerte.

Im Folgenden soll die erste Phase der Stalinisierung als die der Durchsetzung des dogmatischen (affirmativen) Denkmodells der sowjetischen Pädagogik anhand ausgewählter Zeitschriftbeiträge von polnischen Pädagogikwissenschaftlern nachgezeichnet werden. Bislang wurde der Sowjetisierungsprozess vor allem unter dem Gesichtspunkt der von den sozialistischen Machthabern eingeführten „Reformen" des Erziehungs- und Bildungssystems analysiert.[2] Auch die Geschichte der Pädagogik als wissenschaftliche Disziplin war Gegenstand solcher historischer Untersuchungen.[3] Eine besondere Aufmerksamkeit verdienen in diesem Zusammenhang Studien, die nach dem Fall des Eisernen Vorhangs in 1989 das sozialistische

---

1 Teresa Hejnicka-Bezwińska, *Praktyka edukacyjna w warunkach zmiany kulturowej* (Warszawa: Wydawnictwo Naukowe PWN, 2015), 224–290.

2 Hejnicka-Bezwińska, *Praktyka edukacyjna*, 168–362; Eugeniusz C. Król und Marian Walczak, *Na przełomie: antologia relacji nauczycieli i uczniów z lat 1944–1956. Część 1* (Warszawa: Instytut Badań Edukacyjnych, 1994); Stanisław Mauersberg und Marian Walczak, *Na przełomie: antologia relacji nauczycieli i uczniów z lat 1944–1956. Części 2–3* (Warszawa: Polskie Towarzystwo Pedagogiczne Zarząd Główny – Radom: Instytut Technologii Eksploatacji, 1994); Stanisław Mauersberg und Marian Walczak, *Oświata polska 1944–1956: wybór źródeł. Części 1–2* (Warszawa: Polskie Towarzystwo Pedagogiczne Zarząd Główny – Radom: Instytut Technologii Eksploatacji, 2000); Stanisław Mauersberg und Marian Walczak, *Szkolnictwo polskie po drugiej wojnie światowej: 1944–1956* (Warszawa: Polskie Towarzystwo Pedagogiczne Zarząd Główny – Radom: Instytut Technologii Eksploatacji, 2005).

3 Władysława Szulakiewicz, *Historia oświaty i wychowania w Polsce 1944–1956* (Kraków: Wydawnictwo WAM, 2006).

Pädagogikmodell und seinen Einfluss auf das pädagogische Denken in Nachkriegspolen rekonstruiert haben.[4]

Zur Verbreitung des sowjetischen Modells pädagogischen Denkens finden sich zwar verstreute Bemerkungen in vielen Veröffentlichungen, doch wurde dieser Vorgang bisher nicht als eigenständiges Problem behandelt. Einer der Gründe hierfür mag darin liegen, dass sich das Phänomen der Sowjetisierung in der Pädagogik einer klaren Definition, auf welche Kritik Bezug nehmen könnte, entzieht.[5] Das Fehlen von Auseinandersetzungen mit diesem Thema mag auch ein Grund dafür sein, dass das affirmative Denken durch die sog. Hintertür in die gegenwärtigen pädagogischen Diskurse in Polen neuerlich eindringt. Der Unterschied ist aber der, dass dieses Denken früher mit Verweisen auf die kommunistische Ideologie und diese unterstützenden administrativen Machtinstrumente vorangetrieben wurde, während Affirmationen heute verstärkt als ein postmodernes Phänomen auftreten und legitimiert werden.

Der hier vorgelegte Beitrag ist eine Pilotstudie. Sie konzentriert sich auf drei bedeutende Vertreter der polnischen allgemeinen Pädagogik: Zygmunt Mysłakowski (1890–1971), Kazimierz Sośnicki (1883–1976) i Bogdan Suchodolski (1903–1992), und ihre wissenschaftlichen Publikationen. Als Forschungsmaterial wurden Artikel aus pädagogischen Fachzeitschriften aus den Jahren 1948–1950 ausgewählt, in denen diese zentrale pädagogische Probleme erörtert und sich *expressis verbis* auf Quellentexte sowjetischer bzw. marxistischer Provenienz bezogen haben. Im ihrem Zentrum stehen zwei antinomische Themen oder Oppositionen: (1) Pädagogik *versus* Politik und (2) Vergangenheit *versus* Gegenwart. Bei der Auswertung von zu diesen Themen von den drei Wissenschaftlern vertretenen Positionen wird ein Konzept der Nichtaffirmativität zu Rate gezogen, mit dem Dietrich Benner zwischen zwei heterogenen Modellen pädagogischen Denkens unterschieden hat: einem

---

[4] Teresa Hejnicka-Bezwińska, *W poszukiwaniu tożsamości pedagogiki. Świadomość teoretyczno-metodologiczna współczesnej pedagogiki polskiej (geneza i stan)* (Bydgoszcz: Wydawnictwo Uczelniane Wyższej Szkoły Pedagogicznej, 1989); Andrea Folkierska, *Pytanie o pedagogikę* (Warszawa: Wydawnictwa Uniwersytetu Warszawskiego, 1990); Bogusław Śliwerski, "Main Development Lines of Polish Pedagogy from Socialist Orthodoxy to Postmodern Heterogeneity," *Polska Myśl Pedagogiczna* 5, no. 1 (2019): 17–51.

[5] Hejnicka-Bezwińska, *Praktyka edukacyjna*, 182–184.

affirmativen und einem nichtaffirmativen.[6] Mit Hilfe dieser Unterscheidung wird der Versuch unternommen, die Denkmodelle der genannten polnischen Allgemeinpädagogen zu identifizieren und auf ihre Wandlungen unter dem Einfluss von Sowjetisierung zu befragen.

Das Kapitel besteht aus drei Teilen. In dem ersten wird das Konzept der Nichtaffirmativität und seine Gegenüberstellung zweier Denkformen und Modelle pädagogischen Denkens skizzenhaft erläutert. Der zweite wendet sich ausgewählten Texten zu, in denen die zwei genannten Problemstellungen behandelt werden. Der dritte entwickelt eine synthetisierende Gesamtschau auf die analysierte Thematik und Problematik.

Über Nichtaffirmativität im pädagogischen Denken

Affirmative Reflexionsformen und Analysen sind nicht erst im Zusammenhang mit der sowjetischen Pädagogik entstanden, sondern können auf eine lange Problemgeschichte zurückblicken, in der u. a. Rousseau eine wichtige Rolle spielt. In Auseinandersetzung mit der sich u. a. auf Marx berufenden emanzipatorischen Pädagogik der 1970er Jahre in Deutschland hat Dietrich Benner gezeigt, dass diese weithin einem affirmativen Verständnis von Emanzipation verpflichtet war, das hinter klassische Positionen moderner Pädagogik zurückfiel.[7] Dies gilt insbesondere für das von Rousseau entwickelte Verständnis moderner Pädagogik, das Erziehung vom Begriff der Bildsamkeit des Menschen (*perfectibilité*) her zu begründen sucht. Bildsam nennt Rousseau die menschliche Natur, die nicht nur unbestimmt und offen ist, sondern durch Wechselwirkungen des heranwachsenden Menschen mit der Natur, mit den Dingen und mit anderen Menschen auch gebildet werden kann und muss. Rousseau's Begriff der perfektiblen menschlichen Natur weist der Eigentätigkeit des zu erziehenden Kindes und Heranwachsenden die Bedeutung einer unabdingbaren Voraussetzung für pädagogisches Denkens und Handeln im modernen Sinne zu.

Ein sichtbarer Ausdruck des neuen Pädagogik-Verständnisses der Moderne war das Aufkommen des Begriffs „Bildung", der in vielen Nationalsprachen

---

[6] Dietrich Benner, "On Affirmativity and Non-affirmativity in the Context of Theories of Education and Bildung," in *Non-affirmative Theory of Education and Bildung*, ed. Michael Uljens (Cham: Springer, 2023), 29–39.

[7] Dietrich Benner, *Hauptströmungen der Erziehungswissenschaft* (Weinheim und Basel: Beltz, 2001), 273–318.

Europas an der Schwelle vom 18. zum 19. Jahrhundert Eingang in die pädagogische Terminologie fand. Im Polnischen geschah dies durch den Einbau des Begriff *kształcenie* in die Sprache der Pädagogik. Zwar entstand der polnische Begriff später als der deutsche, er ist gleichwohl mehr als nur eine semantische Nachbildung des Deutschen Wortes „Bildung“ und markiert eine eigenständige Leistung in der Entwicklung der polnischen pädagogischen Fachsprache.[8]

Die Begriffe „Bildung“ und „kształcenie“ sind unabhängig voneinander entstandene sprachliche Neuschöpfungen und Neuinterpretationen pädagogischer Sachverhalte und Zusammenhänge zu würdigen. Sie haben einen ähnlichen Inhalt, der sich in einer durch sie sich artikulierenden Wiederbelebung des paideutischen Denkens in der zweiten Hälfte des 18. Jahrhundert zeigt, die in Polen wie in Deutschland an den griechischen Begriff der *paideia* anknüpfte, der schon bei Platon eine nicht-affirmative Bedeutung hatte, an der auch die Begriffe „Bildung“ und „kształcenie“ partizipieren. In der Höhlenerzählung im 7. Buch seiner Abhandlung über den Staat deutete Platon die *paideia* als eine doppelte „Kunst der Umlenkung des Blicks“, einmal als Kunst, den eigenen Blick von schon Bekanntem auf Unbekanntes und von schon Verstandenen auf Nicht-Verstandenes zu wenden, dann aber auch als Kunst, andere zu solchen Wendungen des Blicks zu veranlassen und in den hierfür erforderlichen Anstrengungen zu unterstützen. Das Besondere an dieser Definition war, dass die erziehende Umwendung des Blicks vorbereiten, aber nicht festlegen, sondern für neue bildende Erfahrungen offen halten sollte.[9]

Auf einer oberflächlichen Ebene sind die Substantive *Affirmativität* und *Nichtaffirmativität* sowie die von ihnen abgeleiteten Adjektive *affirmativ* und *nichtaffirmativ* mit Bejahung und Verneinung bzw. als bejahend und verneinend zu übersetzen. Im pädagogischen Sinne geht die sich in diesen Begriffen artikulierende Unterscheidung jedoch viel tiefer und verweist dann auf Zusammenhänge, die ein wesentliches Moment pädagogischen Denkens und Handelns ausmachen. Um erzieherisch richtig zu handeln, müssen

---

8 Krzysztof Maliszewski et al., *Istota, sens i uwarunkowania (wy)kształcenia* (Kraków: Oficyna Wydawnicza „Impuls“, 2019), 31–35.

9 Dietrich Benner et al., *Bildung – Moral – Demokratie. Theorien und Konzepte moralischer Erziehung und Bildung und ihre Beziehungen zu Ethik und Politik* (Paderborn: Schöningh Verlag), 32–39.

pädagogische Akteure Blickwendungen von Bekanntem auf Unbekanntes unterstützen, durch die sich Heranwachsende etwas aneignen, das sie sich durch eine bloß bejahende Übernahme von Nicht-Verstandenem nicht erlernen könnten.[10] Dieser Bestimmung zufolge basiert die Eigenlogik des Pädagogischen darauf, dass es einen eigenen Bereich menschlichen Handelns und menschlicher Reflexivität ausmacht, der durch bloße Indienstnahmen der Erziehung für außerpädagogische Zwecke, die ökonomisch oder politisch definiert werden, verfehlt wird.

Fasst man Nichtaffirmativität als Merkmal pädagogischen Denkens und Handelns, so lässt sich Erziehung nicht länger als eine Beeinflussungspraxis im Dienste außerpädagogischer Instanzen begreifen und verändern sich zugleich die Ziele selbst, an denen das pädagogische Handeln auszurichten ist. Das hat weitreichende Folgen für die Beziehungen des Pädagogischen zu außerpädagogischen Praxisbereichen. Der oben schon erwähnte Begriff der Bildsamkeit stellt nach Dietrich Benner ein grundlegendes, wenn auch nicht das einzige und hinreichende, Prinzip pädagogischen Denkens und Handels dar.[11] Dieses Prinzip bezieht sich auf die individuelle Seite der pädagogischen Interaktion. Sein Gegenpart ist das Prinzip der Nichthierarchizität, das auf die gesellschaftliche Seite der pädagogischen Praxis verweist. Es besagt, dass unter pädagogischen Gesichtspunkten alle Praxisbereiche in ein nichthierarchisches Verhältnis gebracht und als gleichwertig interpretiert werden müssen.[12] Betrachtet man diese beiden Prinzipien in gegenseitiger Verbindung, erhält man einen entscheidenden Hinweis darauf, wodurch sich nicht-affirmative von affirmativer Pädagogik unterscheidet. Nicht-Affirmativer Pädagogik geht es nicht nur darum, die oben beschriebene affirmative Haltung, wonach die Pädagogik der Ergänzung vonseiten anderen Praxisbereichen menschlichen Denkens und Handelns vonnöten hat, zu verneinen, sondern auch den positiven Aspekt eines solchen Zustandes einzusehen. Dieser Aspekt ergibt sich aus der durch Nichtaffirmativität eröffneten Möglichkeit, kritisch auf die Forderungen außerpädagogischen Instanzen zu reagieren, indem sie auf ihre pädagogische Relevanz befragt werden können. Der sog. dritte Weg kann

---

[10] Benner, "On Affirmativity," 43–45.

[11] Dietrich Benner, *Allgemeine Pädagogik. Eine systematisch-problemgeschichtliche Einführung in die Grundstruktur pädagogischen Denkens und Handelns* (Weinheim und Basel: Beltz Juventa, 2015), 74–81.

[12] Benner, *Allgemeine Pädagogik*, 118–127.

nicht durch eine Wahl zwischen vorgegebenen Problemlösungsvarianten aufgefunden werden, sondern allein durch ein nichtaffirmatives Fragen und Suchen nach neuen Betrachtungs- und Handlungsweisen beschritten werden.[13]

Affirmativität und Nichtaffirmativität sollen im Folgenden daher nicht als Bejahung bzw. Verneinung verstanden werden, sondern als zwei radikal entgegengesetzte Haltungen gegenüber Reflexion und Handeln in pädagogischen Kontexten. Die Nichtaffirmativität als Merkmal kritischen (reflexiven) pädagogischen Denkens und Handelns und zugleich als Kriterium der Differenzierung zwischen affirmativen und nichtaffirmativen Modellen wird im nächsten Punkt herangezogen, um die Spuren der Sowjetisierung in den Texten prominenter polnischer Allgemeinpädagogen ans Licht zu bringen und zu interpretieren zu helfen.

Spuren der Sowjetisierung bei polnischen Allgemeinen Pädagogen

Ein jeder der zu analysierenden Allgemeinpädagogen hatte einen anderen Lebensweg und eine andere wissenschaftliche Vergangenheit hinter sich. Was sie gemein hatten, war aktive Beteiligung an dem polnischen pädagogischen Denken in der Zwischenkriegszeit. In einer seinen Veröffentlichungen, die kurz vor dem Ausbruch des Zweiten Weltkriegs herausgebracht wurde, gab Bogdan Nawroczyński eine folgende Charakteristik dieses Denkens: „Die polnische Pädagogik strebt danach, Antinomien zu überwinden und Gegensätze nicht zu verschärfen. Sie zielte eindeutig auf eine Synthese ab.“[14] Aus der Perspektive der Nichtaffirmativität beweist diese Bewertung, dass sich das polnische pädagogische Denken vor dem Zweiten Weltkrieg auf die Ebene des nichtaffirmativen Modells gefunden hat. Dies besagt, dass es Pluralismus der Positionen zu respektieren und Differenzen mit Hilfe von argumentativen Beweisen auszudiskutieren wusste.

Um den Einfluss der Sowjetisierung auf die polnische pädagogische Wissenschaftskultur in der Nachkriegszeit zu rekonstruieren, wird im

---

13 Benner, “On affirmativity,” 46–48.

14 Bogdan Nawroczyński, *Polska myśl pedagogiczna. Jej główne linie rozwojowe i cechy charakterystyczne* (Siedlce: Wydawnictwo Naukowe Uniwersytetu Przyrodniczo-Humanistycznego, 2018), 287.

Folgenden das Augenmerk auf zwei Problemstellungen gerichtet, die anhand von Artikeln aus pädagogischen Fachzeitschriften auf das Vorhandensein von ausdrücklichen Bezügen und Zitaten aus sowjetischen bzw. marxistischen Publikationen hin untersucht und beurteilt werden sollen.

Pädagogik versus Politik

In seinem Artikel *Spór kompetencyjny o wychowanie* [Kompetenzstreit um Erziehung] entwickelt Zygmunt Mysłakowski eine Rechtfertigung für den Vorrang der staatlichen Politik vor der Pädagogik.[15] Er verliert kein Wort über mögliche alternative Wege, die diese beiden Praxissphären miteinander verbinden könnten. Ganz im Gegenteil versucht er den Leser zu überzeugen, dass seine Sichtweise und die daraus resultierenden Schlüsse vorbehaltlos anzunehmen sind. Diese Perspektive kommt in der folgenden Aussage deutlich zum Ausdruck: „Der Vorrang der Politik [...] ist im Leben der Gesellschaften nichts Neues; er war immer da und wird immer da sein, nur die Erkenntnis dessen kann in bestimmten Perioden der Geschichte mehr oder weniger klar und bewusst gewesen sein."[16]

In seiner einseitigen Argumentation bedient sich Mysłakowski ausgiebig der für die marxistisch-leninistische Position charakteristischen Terminologie, wie z.B. „Unterdrückung des Proletariats", „Gleichheit der Bildungschancen", „Erziehung des neuen Menschen", „auf dem Weg der Revolution" usw. Er stützt auf sie seine Überredungskunst. An zwei Stellen beruft er sich auf Aussagen von Lenin. Beim ersten Mal zitiert er eine Passage aus dem *Projekt der Revolution*. Mit ihrer Hilfe wird die Unvermeidbarkeit des revolutionären Umsturzes verdeutlicht, der das radikale Ende der bisherigen Klassenordnung bedeutet. In diesem Zusammenhang entwickelt Mysłakowski eine Rechtfertigung des Kommunismus und schreibt: „weder Lenin, noch irgendein anderer Marxist [hat] das kulturelle Erbe der Menschheit auslöschen, sondern es im Einklang mit den Interessen des um die Neugestaltung der Welt kämpfenden Proletariats bearbeiten wollen."[17]

---

[15] Zygmunt Mysłakowski, „Spór kompetencyjny o wychowanie," *Nowa Szkoła* 31–32, no. 5–6 (1948/1949): 1–20.

[16] Mysłakowski, „Spór kompetencyjny," 20.

[17] Mysłakowski, „Spór kompetencyjny," 15.

Der zweite Verweis auf Lenin steht im Zusammenhang mit der Rede von einer „klassenlosen Bildung", die sich das kommunistische Machtsystem als sein Ziel gesetzt hat. Das ausführliche Zitat soll den Leser dafür ermutigen, der „revolutionären Regierung" in allen Lebensbereichen, insbesondere in der Bildungspolitik, volles Vertrauen entgegenzubringen. In diesem Zusammenhang besteht die Rolle der Pädagogik laut Mysłakowski darin, die politischen Ziele mit erziehungstheoretischem Wissen in die Praxis wirkungsvoll umsetzen zu helfen.[18]

Mysłakowski's Text kann als Apologie des Marxismus-Leninismus und dessen Anspruch auf die autoritäre Entscheidungsvollmacht in Erziehungs- und Bildungsfragen betrachtet werden. So wurde es auch von den anderen polnischen Pädagogen dieser Zeit aufgenommen. Aus der Sicht der Nichtaffirmativität kann er zudem als eine bewusste Manipulation des Lesers gelesen werden. Ihm wird weder ein tiefergehendes Wissen um Zusammenhänge zwischen nicht-affirmativer Erziehung und demokratischer Politik zugetraut, noch die Chance gegeben, sich eigene Meinung zu bilden. Stattdessen sucht Mysłakowski den Eindruck zu erwecken, als ob nur eine Lösung möglich wäre und eben diese die von ihm dargestellte sei.

Einen anderen Ansatz verfolgt Kazimierz Sośnicki in seinem Artikel *Kierunki pedagogiczne w początkach XX wieku i ich aspekt polityczny* [Pädagogische Theorierichtungen im frühen 20. Jahrhundert und ihr politischer Aspekt].[19] Zu Beginn umfasst er ein durch zwei Haltungen definiertes Problemfeld, in dem er zwei gegensätzliche Stellungen hinsichtlich der Beziehung zwischen Politik und Pädagogik unterscheiden will. Die eine setzt auf eine „politische Neutralität" und „Uneigennützigkeit" der Erziehung, während die andere offen für eine „ideologische Erziehung" wirbt. Beiden Ansätzen fehlt nach Sośnicki das Verständnis dafür, dass in jedem pädagogischen System „politische Momente [...] mehr oder weniger offen auftreten."[20] Dies rührt seiner Meinung nach von daher, dass Erziehung immer auf der Beantwortung „zweier grundlegender Fragen [basiert]: 1. Was der Mensch eigentlich ist

18 Mysłakowski, „Spór kompetencyjny," 16.

19 Kazimierz Sośnicki, „Kierunki pedagogiczne w początkach XX wieku i ich aspekt polityczny," *Nowa Szkoła* 30, no. 4 (1947/1948): 1–21.

20 Sośnicki, „Kierunki pedagogiczne," 2.

und was sein Wesen ausmacht, und 2. Was die Welt ist, in der er lebt, und was ihr Wesen ist."[21]

Bei der Analyse der neutralen und ideologischen Antworten zeigt Sośnicki nicht nur den Reichtum der möglichen Ansätze verschiedener pädagogischer Systeme auf, sondern geht er auch auf ihre Argumentationsfiguren ein. Einer der diskutierten Ansätze ist der der sowjetischen Pädagogik.[22] Ohne sich auf einen bestimmten Autor zu beziehen, beschreibt Sośnicki die sowjetische Stellung zur Ideologisierung der Erziehung und stellt dann kritisch fest, dass die sowjetische Pädagogik eine „unbegrenzte Erziehbarkeit" des Zöglings annehme und die Aufgabe der Politik in einem kommunistischen Staat darin erblicke, „die gleichen, höchstmöglichen Ausbildungschancen für alle"[23] sicherzustellen.

Offensichtlich war diese Art der Behandlung der sowjetischen Pädagogik als eines der vielen möglichen pädagogischen Systeme nicht zufriedenstellend. So wurde Sośnicki's Artikel eine redaktionelle Einleitung vorangestellt. Darin wird der Leser über den Wert und gleichzeitig die Grenzen der Betrachtungsweise des Verfassersbelehrt. Die Redaktion hebt beim Verfasser seine „Gelehrsamkeit", „unabhängige Sichtweise" und „subjektiv bedingte kompromisslose Bewertung" hervor. Als symptomatisch für die gesamte polnische Pädagogik jener Zeit aber wird Sośnicki zugleich „Einseitigkeit" und „völlige Unkenntnis nicht nur der theoretischen Errungenschaften, sondern vor allem der enormen konkreten Leistungen der sowjetischen Pädagogik und der sowjetischen Schule" vorgeworfen.[24]

Betrachtet man Sośnicki's Artikel aus der Perspektive der Nichtaffirmativität, so verdient gerade seine pluralistische Ausrichtung eine besondere Würdigung. Dies ermöglicht es dem Leser, tief in die Problematik der politischen Bedingungen der Erziehung und Bildung sowie des Verhältnisses zwischen Pädagogik und Politik einzudringen und sich eigene Meinung zu bilden.

Die Bemühungen von Bogdan Suchodolski, dem dritten genannten Allgemeinen Pädagogen in Polen, gingen darauf, seine Leser mit aktuellen pädagogischen und psychologischen Veröffentlichungen sowjetischer

---

21 Sośnicki, „Kierunki pedagogiczne," 2.
22 Sośnicki, „Kierunki pedagogiczne," 19–20.
23 Sośnicki, „Kierunki pedagogiczne," 20.
24 Sośnicki, „Kierunki pedagogiczne," 1.

Autoren vertraut zu machen. Aus der Position eines Experten und Verfechter des sowjetischen Gedankenguts brachte er im Jahre 1949 einen Artikel mit dem Titel *Nowa pedagogika w nowych programach liceum pedagogicznego* [Neue Pädagogik in den neuen Programmen des pädagogischen Lizeums] heraus.[25] Dies war ein Kommentar zu dem kürzlich eingeführten sog. pädagogischen Lizeum, einer Sekundarschule, die anstelle der pädagogischen Fakultäten die Aufgabe der Ausbildung der Grundschullehrer zu übernehmen hatte.

Suchodolski beginnt seine Ausführungen mit einem Hinweis auf die Bedeutung des kommunistischen Axioms der völligen Unterordnung der Pädagogik unter die Politik. Charakteristisch für die „neue Pädagogik" ist seiner Ansicht nach das Bewusstsein, dass „Bildungsprozesse immer durch historische und klassenabhängige Faktoren bedingt waren und sind. Die heutigen Bildungsaufgaben laufen [...] darauf hinaus, die junge Generation so zu formen, dass sie zu harter und fruchtbarer Arbeit am Aufbau und der Verteidigung sozialistischer Lebensordnung fähig wird."[26]

Diese Annahme zu akzeptieren bedeutet, mit „allen Konzepten der angeblichen Autonomie der Erziehung"[27] endgültig zu brechen.

Um von der Gültigkeit einer solchen Vision der „neuen Pädagogik" zu überzeugen, verweist Suchodolski auf Beispiele von der UdSSR. Diese Beispiele erfüllen in seinem Text zwei Funktionen: erstens, verweisen sie auf Autoritäten, z.B. Akademie der Pädagogischen Wissenschaften in Moskau, die seine Ansicht bestätigen, und zweitens, stellen sie einen Bezugspunkt für theoretische Analysen her, z. B. Stalins Abhandlung *Über den dialektischen und historischen Materialismus*. Zwischen Suchodolski's Konzepten und den zitierten oder nur erwähnten Autoren/Autoritäten besteht keine Divergenz. Ganz im Gegenteil sie befinden sich in voller Übereinstimmung, deren Grund das bereits hingewiesene Axiom des Vorrangs der Politik vor der Pädagogik abgibt.

Ähnlich wie in Mysłakowski's Artikel, haben Suchodolski's Überlegungen einen im voraus bestimmten Charakter: der Leser soll von der „einzigen

---

25 Bogdan Suchodolski, „Nowa pedagogika w nowych programach liceum ogólnokształcącego," *Nowa Szkoła* 47–48, no. 1 (1949): 64–80.

26 Suchodolski, „Nowa pedagogika," 64.

27 Suchodolski, „Nowa pedagogika," 65.

Richtigkeit“ der dargelegten Sichtweise überzeugt werden und diese widerspruchslos und ohne Reflexion annehmen.

Vergangenheit versus Gegenwart

Die zweite thematische Opposition bezieht sich auf die Haltung der polnischen Allgemeinen Pädagogen gegenüber der Vergangenheit, genauer gesagt: gegenüber der Tradition des polnischen pädagogischen Denkens. In dieser Hinsicht war die Anfangszeit der Stalinisierung reich an Veröffentlichungen, die als sog. „Kritik“ und „Selbstkritik“ bezeichnet werden können. In ihnen nahmen Autoren Stellung sowohl zu fremden als auch zu eigenen Publikationen aus der Vorkriegszeit und warfen sich gegenseitig den bürgerlichen Charakter ihrer Überlegungen vor oder äußerten sich zu Rückständigkeit und Mangel ihres Verständnis für das Schicksal des Proletariats.

Einen in diesem Sinne „kritischen“ Charakter hat der Artikel von Zygmunt Mysłakowski und Ignacy Szaniawski *Pedagogika i oświata w Polsce w latach 1918–1939* [Pädagogik und Bildungswesen in Polen zwischen 1918 und 1939] aus dem Jahr 1950.[28] Er wurde, wie Autoren einleitend erklären, „aus der Notwendigkeit unserer Kulturrevolution heraus“[29] verfasst. Darüber hinaus stellen sie Vermutung, dass viele polnische Lehrer – „Soldaten unserer pädagogischen Front“[30] – veranlasst werden, unter dem Einfluss dieser Überlegungen ihre bisherige Meinung bezüglich der Zwischenkriegszeit zu ändern. Mysłakowski und Szaniawski gestehen, dass für sie „die Haltung zum revolutionären Flügel der Arbeiterklasse [...] das Kriterium der Bewertung von Strömungen, Richtungen und führenden Persönlichkeiten der polnischen Pädagogik dieser Zeit sein wird“.[31]

Gemäß dieser Erklärung teilen sie die Vertreter der polnischen Pädagogik in zwei verfeindete Lager – die Linken, die fortschrittlich und demokratisch seien, und die Rechten, die sich reaktionär und antidemokratisch verhielten.

Zweifelslos handelt es sich bei diesem Artikel um einen Versuch zur Neuschreibung der Geschichte der polnischen Pädagogik. Mysłakowski und Szaniawski richteten ihre ganze Aufmerksamkeit auf die „Fakten“, die sich

---

[28] Zygmunt Mysłakowski und Szaniawski Ignacy, „Pedagogika i oświata w Polsce w latach 1918–1939,“ *Nowa Szkoła* 1, no. 5 (1950): 251–287.

[29] Mysłakowski und Szaniawski, „Pedagogika i oświata,“ 251.

[30] Mysłakowski und Szaniawski, „Pedagogika i oświata,“ 251.

[31] Mysłakowski und Szaniawski, „Pedagogika i oświata,“ 253.

unter dem von ihnen angenommenen Kriterium als offensichtlich erwiesen. Hierbei ließen sie methodologische Prinzipien wie z. B. das der Objektivität der Forschung weit hinter sich.

Im Hinblick auf die Spuren der sowjetischen Pädagogik bzw. marxistischen Philosophie wird in Mysłakowski's und Szaniawski's Artikel eine Passage aus der Marx'schen *Deutschen Ideologie* zitiert, wonach die Verfügung über Produktionsmittel zugleich das Recht auf „geistige Produktion", in diesem Fall auf Kontrolle über Erziehung einschließe. In dem Kapitel, das den Personalismus kritisiert, findet sich ein Verweis auf Lenin's Gedanken zu *Materialismus und Empirie* sowie ein Satz aus dem *Kommunistischen Manifest*.[32] Der Artikel schließt mit einer Darstellung von Vorläufern der „marxistischen Pädagogik" in Vorkriegspolen ab. Władysław Spasowski (1877–1941) war laut Autoren einer der wichtigsten von ihnen. In einer besonderen Weise zeichnete er sich durch die „Begeisterung für die UdSSR"[33] aus.

Um den wahren Wert dieser Studie aus der Perspektive der nicht-affirmativer Reflexivität zu erkennen, genügt es, den ersten Satz des Abschlusskapitels zu prüfen. Er lautet: „So sieht die Gesamtheit der Erziehungs- und Bildungsprobleme in Polen 1918–1939 in einer synthetischen Zusammenfassung aus"[34]. Ist es wirklich die Gesamtheit, die von Mysłakowski und Szaniawski untersucht wurde? Aus der Sicht der Verfasser vielleicht schon, aber deren Denken stand unter der Voraussetzung, dass

> „alte pädagogische Ideen und alte Erziehungstheorien [...] unter den Bedingungen der politischen, industriellen und kulturellen Revolution in unserem Land sterben und aus dem jungen Organismus der Volksdemokratie in Polen verschwinden [müssen]"[35].

Nach diesen Worten kann aus der Vergangenheit nur das zählen, was eine Vorwegnahme der Gegenwart war. Alles andere fällt dem Nichts anheim. Spielen sich Mysłakowski und Szaniawski hiermit nicht als Herren der Geschichte auf?

Einem solchen Verschwinden wurden die Arbeiten des zweiten Autors empfohlen bzw. zugeführt. Nach kurzer Probezeit wurde Kazimierz Sośnicki

---

32 Mysłakowski und Szaniawski, „Pedagogika i oświata," 274.
33 Mysłakowski und Szaniawski, „Pedagogika i oświata," 285.
34 Mysłakowski und Szaniawski, „Pedagogika i oświata," 286.
35 Mysłakowski und Szaniawski, „Pedagogika i oświata," 287.

bis 1956 jede Möglichkeit entzogen, wissenschaftliche Arbeiten zu veröffentlichen. Man darf annehmen, dass er nicht nur der von Mysłakowski und Szaniawski neugeschriebene Pädagogikgeschichte zum Opfer fiel, sondern diese auch abgelehnt hat. Ganz anders verhielt sich Bogdan Suchodolski, der die Vision von einer neuen Geschichte nicht nur teilte, sondern diese in seinen historisch-pädagogischen Arbeiten noch weiter zuspitzte, so in dem Artikel *Pedagogika robotnicza* [Arbeiterpädagogik] aus dem Jahre 1950.[36] Der Titel der Abhandlung verspricht, die Erziehungserfahrungen der Arbeiter und die damit verbundenen Überlegungen zu Erziehung, ihren Zielen und Methoden zu thematisieren. Nach Suchodolski darf die wahre Kenntnis der tatsächlichen Erziehung des Proletariats, die die Grundlage für Arbeiterpädagogik abgibt, nicht aus den traditionell verstandenen Schulerfahrungen geschöpft werden, sondern aus der Arbeit als jenem Medium, das Arbeiter bildet. Im Leben des Proletariats war und sei die Arbeit „keineswegs ein autonomer Bereich“[37], sondern ein Handeln, das mit der Bildung auf innigste verbunden bleibe. Die Verschmelzung von Arbeit und Bildung soll das neue Merkmal der Arbeiterpädagogik sein. Das zweite ist die „Kampflust“, denn für Arbeiter ist Bildung „ein Instrument des Klassenkampfes für die Befreiung des Menschen“[38]. Man darf nicht überrascht sein, dass es zwischen der so verstandenen „neuen“ Pädagogik und der alten, „bürgerlichen“ weder eine Verwandschaft noch ein Übergang gibt. Der Beweis dafür ist „der Sieg des Sozialismus in der UdSSR“[39]. Im Zusammenhang mit diesem Beispiel weist Suchodolski auf das dritte Merkmal der Arbeiterpädagogik hin. Es ist der Kollektivismus. Alle drei Merkmale bestimmen die völlig neue Qualität im pädagogischen Denken, das nun Sozialismus verwirklichen helfen soll.

Obwohl sich Suchodolski nur ein Mal auf die sowjetische Pädagogik bezieht und auch nur ein Mal Marx und Engels nennt, besteht kein Zweifel, dass sich sein Artikel auf Begriffskategorien stützt, die zum Gedankenkreis des Marxismus-Leninismus gehören. Anhand dieser Kategorien bestimmt Suchodolski das Wesen der Arbeiterpädagogik, das ihn dazu verleitet hat, die pädagogische Tradition voll und ganz abzulehnen und für ein neues

---

[36] Bogdan Suchodolski, „Pedagogika robotnicza,“ *Życie Szkoły* 51, no. 4 (1950): 179–189.
[37] Suchodolski, „Pedagogika robotnicza,“ 183.
[38] Suchodolski, „Pedagogika robotnicza,“ 183.
[39] Suchodolski, „Pedagogika robotnicza,“ 184.

Erziehungsdenken einzutreten.[40] Betrachtet man dies durch das Prisma der Nichtaffirmativität, fällt gleich ins Auge, dass wie in dem ersten Themenbereich der Politik eine pädagogikbestimmende Funktion zugesprochen wurde, so hier das Gleiche für marxistische Philosophie gilt. In beiden Fällen wird Pädagogik ihrer Autonomie beraubt und zum Instrument einer politischen Utopie abgewertet.

Versuch einer Synthese

Mitte der 1950er Jahre wurden zwei Berichte herausgebracht, die die Entwicklung der polnischen Pädagogik in dem ersten Jahrzehnt der (Volks) Republik Polen zum Gegenstand hatten. Beide wurden von Vertretern der damaligen Mainstreamorientierung verfasst – Bogdan Suchodolski und Wincenty Okoń. Dieser (der zweite) zeichnete ein Bild der polnischen Pädagogik nach, in dem „Marasmus" vorherrschte.[41] Dabei verschwieg er nicht einmal, dass sich nur wenige der polnischen Allgemeinpädagogen aus der Vorkriegszeit an der Entwicklung eines auf marxistisch-leninistischen Ideen stützenden pädagogischen Denkens bisher beteiligten. Zwar erwähnt er die Gruppe der völlig Ausgegrenzten gar nicht, aber wirft den Loyalen vor, dass sie vorziehen, sich „mit Studium pädagogischen Denkens in der Vergangenheit" zu befassen und somit „der Gegenwart zu entfliehen", anstatt zur Bewältigung der vielfältigen Aufgaben beizutragen.[42]

Bei weitem schlechter wurde der Zustand der polnischen Pädagogik durch Suchodolski in seinem Artikel aus dem Jahr 1955 bewertet. Er meinte, dass die von ihm ausgearbeiteten Kategorien und Probleme der marxistischen Arbeiterpädagogik größtenteils auf Unverständnis und Missachtung gestoßen

---

40 Das Ergebnis langjähriger Arbeit von Suchodolski an „Elementen der Pädagogik" von Marx war eine umfassende Studie *Die Grundlagen der materialistischen Erziehungslehre*, die im Original auf Polnisch geschrieben und 1957 herausgebracht wurde. Sie wurde u.a. ins Spanische übersetzt und von Paulo Freire beim Verfassen der *Pädagogik der Unterdrückten* als Inspirationsquelle verwendet. Vgl. Piotr Stańczyk, „Freirego Suchodolskim – Suchodolskiego Freirem: pedagogika materialistyczna i krytyka ideologii," *Teraźniejszość – Człowiek – Edukacja* 82, no. 2 (2018): 7–30.

41 Wincenty Okoń, „O warunkach rozwoju polskiej pedagogiki," *Nowa Szkoła* 7, no. 6 (1956): 593.

42 Okoń, „O warunkach," 599.

seien. Aus diesem Grund sind in den pädagogischen Wissenschaften zahlreiche „Verwüstungen" zu beobachten.[43] Hoffnung auf ihre Überwindung erblickt er in der nachkommenden Generation, die den Marxismus nicht nur deklaratorisch, sondern ernsthaft annehmen und seine Konzepte in das pädagogische Forschungsprogramm umsetzen wird.[44]

Vor diesem Hintergrund erhalten die im vorangegangenen Abschnitt durchgeführten Analysen eine neue Bedeutung. Zu diesen Analysen wurden drei prominente Vertreter der Generation ausgewählt, die „die durch den Zweiten Weltkrieg verursachte Kriese bewältigen und am Prozess des großen kulturellen Wandels teilnehmen mussten"[45]. Diese Generation war vor der dramatischen Wahl gestanden, „eine polnische sozialistische Pädagogik mit hervorzubringen oder sich einen Platz an ihrem Rande auszusuchen."[46] Das Kriterium, das darüber entschied, in welcher der zwei möglichen Strömungen der polnischen Nachkriegspädagogik sich jemand eingefunden hat, war seine Stellung zur Sowjetisierung bzw. Stalinisierung. Es sollte betont werden, dass manche polnische Allgemeinpädagogen nicht einmal diese Wahl gehabt hatten, da sie durch politische Systementscheidungen von vornherein zum Ausschluss aus dem wissenschaftlichen Nachkriegsleben verurteilt wurden.[47]

Die Sowjetisierung war nicht nur mit einer Präferenz für gewisse Ideen verbunden, sondern auch mit dem Ausschluss aller anderen. Nur Konzepte, die das Merkmal der marxistisch-leninistischen Ideologie aufwiesen, waren als „wissenschaftlich" anzusehen. Zweifelsohne zeugt dies von Verschlossenheit und Dogmatismus, die man versucht hat, mittels der politischen und ökonomischen Instrumente einzuführen. In der Pädagogik hieß es Ausrottung der Nichtaffirmativität und Etablieren affirmativen Denkungsmodells.

Das affirmative Modell pädagogischen Denkens findet man in allen zwei untersuchten Themenbereichen vor als dominierend. Verfasser, die sich mit der marxistisch-leninistischen Position identifizierten, beriefen sich auf

---

43 Bogdan Suchodolski, „Perspektywy pedagogiki," *Myśl Filozoficzna* 19–20, no. 5–6 (1955): 28.

44 Suchodolski, „Perspektywy pedagogiki," 29.

45 Teresa Hejnicka-Bezwińska, *Tradycja: pomiędzy historią a pamięcią*. Unpubliziertes Manuskript, 3.

46 Hejnicka-Bezwińska, *Tradycja*, 3.

47 Marian Nowak, „Pedagogika i pedagodzy z marginesu wobec głównego nurtu pedagogiki socjalistycznej," *Polska Myśl Pedagogiczna* 4, no. 1 (2018): 277–295.

philosophische Prämissen, die ihnen zum Vorwand dienten, den Vorrang der Politik und Ökonomie vor Pädagogik und die Höherstellung der Gegenwart vor der Vergangenheit als unbestritten auszugeben. In Übereinstimmung mit dem affirmativen Denkungsmodell diese Autoren ließen andere pädagogische Positionen und Systeme völlig außer acht oder diskutierten sie unter Vorwegnahme des eigenen Rechthabens. Inwieweit ist dies der Sowjetisierung zu Last zu legen, ist heute kaum möglich zu bestimmen. Es scheint jedoch unbestreitbar, dass das affirmative Denkungsmodell, das damals in das polnische pädagogische Denken mit Hilfe der Sowjetisierung eingedrungen ist, bald eine neue Gestalt angenommen hat – die sozialistische Pädagogik. Ihr Erbe wirkt bis heute noch nach.

Schlussgedanke

„In Polen wehen die Winde meist aus dem Westen"[48], schrieb Bogdan Nawroczyński als metaphorische Zusammenfassung seiner Studie über die Identität polnischen pädagogischen Denkens. Auf diese Weise unterstrich er die Prädominanz der abendländischen Orientierung der polnischen Kultur, einschließlich der Pädagogik. Diese Orientierung änderte sich radikal nach dem Ende des Zweiten Weltkriegs, in dessen Folge Polen und viele andere Staaten Mittel- und Osteuropas in den Einflussbereich der UdSSR gerieten und der Sowjetisierung unterworfen wurden.

In Abwandlung der obigen Metapher kann gesagt werden, dass seit 1944 in Polen ein Wind aus dem Osten zu wehen begann. Welche Auswirkungen dies auf das polnische pädagogische Denken hatte, ist weiterhin wert zu klären und zwar sowohl mit Hilfe von dem philosophischen Paradigma der Ideologie, wie auch eigenen Kategorien der modernen Pädagogik. Mit dieser kleinen Studie soll ein Beitrag dazu geleistet werden, dieses Problem mehr plausibel zu machen. Die durchgeführten Analysen deuten darauf hin, dass die für die Jahre 1948–1950 nachgezeichnete Ostausrichtung polnischen pädagogischen Denkens tiefgreifende Transformationen zur Folge hatte, als heute angenommen wird. Dieser Wandel bestand in Wiederherstellung

---

[48] Nawroczyński, *Polska myśl pedagogiczna*, 273.

der Affirmativität und des darauf basierenden affirmativen Modells pädagogischen Denkens, das in der Folgezeit zur Grundlage der sozialistischen Pädagogik wurde.

Der Fall des Eisernen Vorhangs schien dazu geführt zu haben, dass der Ostwind in Polen nicht mehr weht. Wenn man dieses Problem aus der Perspektive der Nichtaffirmativität betrachtet, ist es nicht so sicher. Der Pluralismus der Positionen und die sachliche Diskussion werden durch Gesichtspunkte ersetzt, die überzeugt von ihrem Rechthaben zum Kampf um die Befreiung des postmodernen Menschen aufrufen. Kennen wir das nicht schon?!

Quellentexte

Mysłakowski, Zygmunt. „Spór kompetencyjny o wychowanie.“ *Nowa Szkoła* 31–32, no. 5–6 (1947/1948): 1–20.

Mysłakowski, Zygmunt und Ignacy Szaniawski. „Pedagogika i oświata w Polsce w latach 1918–1939.“ *Nowa Szkoła* 1, no. 5 (1950): 251–287.

Nawroczyński, Bogdan. *Polska myśl pedagogiczna. Jej główne linie rozwojowe i cechy charakterystyczne*. Siedlce: Wydawnictwo Naukowe Uniwersytetu Przyrodniczo-Humanistycznego, 2018.

Okoń, Wincenty. „O warunkach rozwoju polskiej pedagogiki.“ *Nowa Szkoła* 7, no. 6 (1956): 592–606.

Sośnicki, Kazimierz. „Kierunki pedagogiczne w początkach XX wieku i ich aspekt polityczny.“ *Nowa Szkoła* 30, no. 4 (1947/1948): 1–21.

Suchodolski, Bogdan. „Nowa pedagogika w nowych programach liceum ogólnokształcącego.“ *Nowa Szkoła* 47–48, no. 1 (1949): 64–80.

Suchodolski, Bogdan „Pedagogika robotnicza.“ *Życie Szkoły* 51, no. 4 (1950): 179–189.

Suchodolski, Bogdan. „Perspektywy pedagogiki.“ *Myśl Filozoficzna* 19–20, no. 5–6 (1955): 3–31.

Sekundärliteratur

Benner, Dietrich. “On Affirmativity and Non-affirmativity in the Context of Theories of Education and Bildung.” In *Non-affirmative Theory of*

Education and Bildung, editiert von Michael Uljens, 21–59. Cham: Springer, 2023.

Benner, Dietrich, Alexander von Oettingen, Zhengmei Peng und Dariusz Stępkowski. *Bildung – Moral – Demokratie. Theorien und Konzepte moralischer Erziehung und Bildung und ihre Beziehungen zu Ethik und Politik*. Paderborn: Schöningh Verlag, 2015.

Benner, Dietrich. *Allgemeine Pädagogik. Eine systematisch-problemgeschichtliche Einführung in die Grundstruktur pädagogischen Denkens und Handelns*. Weinheim und Basel: Beltz Juventa, 2015.

Benner, Dietrich. *Hauptströmungen der Erziehungswissenschaft*. Weinheim und Basel: Beltz, 2001.

Folkierska, Andrea. *Pytanie o pedagogikę*. Warszawa: Wydawnictwa Uniwersytetu Warszawskiego, 1990.

Hejnicka-Bezwińska, Teresa. *Tradycja: pomiędzy historią a pamięcią*. Unpubliziertes Manuskript.

Hejnicka-Bezwińska, Teresa. *W poszukiwaniu tożsamości pedagogiki. Świadomość teoretyczno-metodologiczna współczesnej pedagogiki polskiej (geneza i stan)*. Bydgoszcz: Wydawnictwo Uczelniane Wyższej Szkoły Pedagogicznej, 1989.

Hejnicka-Bezwińska, Teresa. *Praktyka edukacyjna w warunkach zmiany kulturowej*. Warszawa: Wydawnictwo Naukowe PWN, 2015.

Król, Eugeniusz C. und Marian Walczak. *Na przełomie: antologia relacji nauczycieli i uczniów z lat 1944–1956. Część 1*. Warszawa: Instytut Badań Edukacyjnych, 1994.

Maliszewski, Krzysztof, Dariusz Stępkowski und Bogusław Śliwerski. *Istota, sens i uwarunkowania (wy)kształcenia*. Kraków: Oficyna Wydawnicza „Impuls", 2019.

Mauersberg, Stanisław und Marian Walczak. *Na przełomie: antologia relacji nauczycieli i uczniów z lat 1944–1956. Części 2–3*. Warszawa: Polskie Towarzystwo Pedagogiczne Zarząd Główny – Radom: Instytut Technologii Eksploatacji, 1994.

Mauersberg, Stanisław und Marian Walczak. *Oświata polska 1944–1956: wybór źródeł. Części 1–2*. Warszawa: Polskie Towarzystwo Pedagogiczne Zarząd Główny – Radom: Instytut Technologii Eksploatacji, 2000.

Mauersberg, Stanisław und Marian Walczak. *Szkolnictwo polskie po drugiej wojnie światowej: 1944–1956*. Warszawa: Polskie Towarzystwo Pedagogiczne Zarząd Główny – Radom: Instytut Technologii Eksploatacji, 2005.

Nowak, Marian. „Pedagogika i pedagodzy z marginesu wobec głównego nurtu pedagogiki socjalistycznej." *Polska Myśl Pedagogiczna* 4, no. 1 (2018): 277–295.

Stańczyk, Piotr. „Freirego Suchodolskim – Suchodolskiego Freirem: pedagogika materialistyczna i krytyka ideologii." *Teraźniejszość – Człowiek – Edukacja* 82, no. 2 (2018): 7–30.

Szulakiewicz, Władysława. *Historia oświaty i wychowania w Polsce 1944–1956*. Kraków: Wydawnictwo WAM, 2006.

Śliwerski, Bogusław. "Main Development Lines of Polish Pedagogy from Socialist Orthodoxy to Postmodern Heterogeneity." *Polska Myśl Pedagogiczna* 5, no. 1 (2019): 17–51.

PART FOUR

Practices of Sovietization

Sovietising Higher Education and Scientific Research in East-Central Europe: Techniques and Attempts of Establishing a Total Control in the Region with a Special Focus on Hungary after 1945[1]

Imre Garai, Carla Liege Rodrigues Pimienta and András Németh

Abstract: The paper seeks to reveal the techniques of Sovietisation in higher education in certain Eastern-Central European countries. More precisely, the Czech, Polish and Hungarian cases are investigated as countries which followed a rather similar development in the modernisation of higher education.

This comparative study employed the document analysis of archival sources and secondary literature review as primary methods. A substantial amount of archival sources were involved in the investigation of the Hungarian case by revealing the documents preserved in the Mednyánszky Dénes Archive and Library and the National Archives of Hungary. Extended literature research related to the Czech and Polish cases was also carried out during the investigation.

Results suggest that despite the similar development curve of the higher education systems of the three countries, Zero Hour reached and found different conditions in the academic sectors of each region. Probably, that is the reason why Sovietisation began in different time periods and lasted for various terms. Nevertheless, the implemented techniques show remarkable similarities, e.g. the social transformation of students and the personnel of the higher education institutions, the transformation of the role of Scientific Academies in each country and the installation of blatant political propaganda in the training programmes. That resulted in a similar outcome, namely the abolition of the Humboldtian training idea of universities.

Keywords: abolition of Humboldtian training, Sovietisation, Czech higher education, Polish higher education, Hungarian higher education, Scientific Academies, political propaganda

Introduction

This study aims to approach the international context endeavours across the post-soviet part of Europe, with a particular focus on East-Central Europe countries, namely Poland, Czechoslovakia and Hungary, in the years

[1] The paper has been supported by the National Research, Development and Innovation Office (NKFIH) [grant number 127937].

following the II World War. It was a period of unique developments regarding the Soviet type of modernisation of higher education systems.

Hence, the focus in the first half would be put on national developments that maintain the continuity and discontinuity processes that, across East-Central Europe, have led to higher education frameworks, with Poland and Czechoslovakia to be our main focal countries. In the second half, a synopsis of Hungarian developments under the socialist influence on higher education contextualization and organizational variations of higher education institutions are involved. We are comparing higher education in Hungary through historical and geographical factors in an extensive aspect.

International Context about the Modernization Endeavors of the Higher Education Systems after the II World War

East-Central Europe is one of the geographical regions of Central Europe, which consists of Poland, Hungary, Slovakia, and the Czech Republic. The nations under Soviet rule are depicted by 'East', and the geographic context is assigned by 'Central'. Nevertheless, these terms have more than a geographic localization context and still have a homogenous history.[2] Eastern Europe is a region that has common interrelations and historical features with its counterparts; the countries in this region are, however, unique.[3]

The evolvement of modern education in the East-Central European states was closely linked to the political developments of the Prussian-German and the Habsburg empires (Austrian-Hungarian Monarchy after the Compromise in 1867) throughout the 18th and 19th centuries. Institutionalization processes of educational policy and pedagogy shared numerous common elements, e.g. the hegemony of educational philosophy oriented by theoretical

---

2 Adam Redzik, "Polish Universities During the Second World War," *Encuentros de Historia Comparada Hispano-Polaca/Spotkania poświęcone historii porównawczej hiszpańsko-polskiej conference*, no. 1 (2004): 1–20.

3 András Németh and Béla Pukánszky, "Herbartianism as an Eastern Central European and Its Reception in Hungary," *History Of Education & Children's Literature* 16, no. 1 (2021): 65–86.

pedagogy and the triumph of Herbartianism later the prevalence of the so-called Geisteswisschenschftliche Pädagogik. Additionally, common features of professionalization processes of various pedagogical professional groups and standardization of different types of schools could be identified.[4]

Following World War II, the Soviet Union suffered overwhelming losses in the form of human fatalities and infrastructure damage; consequently, the political developments and economic re-establishment were colossal tasks that required great efforts and investment to uplift the industries.[5]

In European history, the year 1945 is considered as nil or a zero year. Under Stalin's leadership, a new era began with fundamental changes in the economy, education, and society and was a result of the ending of World War II. To determine coherency and misalignment in the working of state-society relations, recommending improvements and reforms in the society as a whole and communism gaining power, everyone considered education as a critical instrument for achieving their purpose.

Higher education, particularly during the socialist era, was vital to spread countrywide principles and beliefs among states. They considered that men and women were a social outcome of the interaction, which gave a set of opportunities to the higher education to "uniform" people's democracies to teach the new *homo sovieticus.*

The Soviet model reformed the advances in higher education, supporting the preparation of a communist intellectual elite, awarding admissions for advanced education to the worker, concentrating on those who had incomplete secondary education, viz. "worker courses" (*dělnické kurzy*) in the Czech

---

4 See these trends in detail András Németh, "Die Entwicklungsperioden der ungarischen Erziehungswissenschaft im 19. und 20. Jahrhundert", in *University and Universality. The Place and Role of the University of Pécs in Europe from the Middle Ages to Present Day*, eds. Ágnes Fischer-Dárdai, István Lengvári and Éva Schmelczer-Pohánka (Pécs: University Library of Pécs and Centre for Learning, 2017), 309–328.

András Németh and Imre Garai, "Disciplinary Changes in the Hungarian 'Pädagogik' from the Second Half of the 19th Century to the Collapse of Stalinist-type Dictatorship", in *Education and "Pädagogik" – Philosophical and Historical Reflections: Central, Southern and South-Eastern Europe*, eds. Blanka Kudláčová and Andrej Rajský (Berlin: Peter Lang Verlag, Bratislava: VEDA, 2019), 214–217.

5 Mervyn Matthews, *Education in the Soviet Union: Policies and Institutions since Stalin* (London: Routledge, 2011).

regions, and the "preparation courses" (*kursy przygotowawcze*) in Poland, so they could pursue higher-level studies.[6]

The structure of institutes and curriculum were amended to dismiss the Western type of logical standards in favor of the socialist scholar of sciences. From this viewpoint, it succeeded in changing the communication plans, researcher worldview, and rational work judgment.[7]

The differences in the democracies of Soviet-type democracy and Western Europe were also depicted in the educational system reforms. Education has been centralized in Eastern Europe. In the relation between dynamics of nationalization and education, non-public universities, and the church, there were complete control over the schools, i.e., organizational conditions of emerging technology were developed.[8]

In both countries, the group accountable for higher education and establishing policies was under the management of central ministers linked with communist parties.

In this time-period, interestingly, the Humboldt model acted as teaching and research centers were thereby reformed as such that the state regulated the curriculum and study plans. The centers for academic and professional liberty and independence were exterminated completely.[9] It is important to point out that in Czechoslovakia, Poland, and Hungary, the Humboldtian idea that originated from Germany, was dominant until 1945.[10]

In the Humboldtian model, Czechoslovakia's prewar higher education was unwaveringly developed, while a reform called "de-Humboldtization" followed when the communists took the political leadership.

Efforts to implement the model of state control and obstinate ideology-based policy were involved. The Czech higher education system, between

---

6 John Connelly, *Captive University: The Sovietization of East German, Czech, and Polish Higher Education, 1945–1956* (Chapel Hill and London: UNC Press Books, 2014).

7 Imre Garai and András Németh, "Disciplinary Changes in Science Education in Hungary in the Era of the Stalinist Dictatorship," *Pedagogika* 67, no. 4 (2017): 431–442.

8 Marcelo Caruso, "Within, between, above, and beyond: (Pre) Positions for a History of the Internationalisation of Educational Practices and Knowledge," *Paedagogica Historica* 50, no. 1–2 (2014): 10–26.

9 Indra Dedze and Rubene Zanda, "Universities in Latvia – from the Soviet to European Higher Education Area," *Foro de Educación*, no. 14 (2016): 13–38.

10 Michael Dobbins, "Explaining Different Pathways in Higher Education Policy in Romania and the Czech Republic," *Comparative Education*, no. 2 (2011): 223–45.

1950 and 1989, was built on strong national control over curriculum, operations, procedures, and personal. The institutions were completely reliant on funds from the state, and decision-making was limited, which as a result influenced the higher education institutions' freedom.

In contrast to the Czech Republic, the Humboldt traditions were maintained in Poland. The connection between research and teaching was sustained. Between 1950 and 1980, in Polish higher education, there was a substantial increase in the tertiary sector regarding the number of teachers/students and institutes.[11]

Polish universities were the most resilient to dominant state control, yet open to scientists and to some degree, instigating various bilateral agreements via foreign professional networks.

Postwar Polish universities, on the other hand, acclimated to the Soviet model and planned obligatory coursework, resulting in a unified educational system. The management also announced its goal to partake extensively with the body of professors, irrespective of the fields they were in. Even in the humanities, the task of rebuilding Poland seemed too massive to consider allowing specialists' expiation. The higher education of Poland was reorganized and restructured, and many schools were built. Several faculties were split from the universities and were established as separate institutions like medical schools were converted to autonomous faculties known as academies of medicine.[12]

In May 1946 the Communist Party in Czechoslovakia achieved a major political victory. The intellectual strategy of the Czechoslovak Communist Party (Komunistická Strana Československa – KSČ) was overlooked, frequently falling behind the strategies of friendly meetings in such regions as labor education classes or political in doctrinarian; and, despite the inevitable hierarchical existence, the KSČ never achieved anything towards the development of loyal elites.[13]

---

[11] Michael Dobbins, "Exploring the Governance of Polish Public Higher Education: Balancing Restored Historical Legacies with Europeanization and Market Pressures," *European Journal of Higher Education*, no. 1 (2015): 18–33.

[12] Nellie Apanasewicz, *The Educational System of Poland. Education around the World* (Washington, D.C.: Office of Education [DHEW], 1976).

[13] Mary Heimann, *Czechoslovakia: The State That Failed* (New Haven: Yale University Press, 2011).

February 1948 was the unambiguous month of Czech postwar history. A usually altruistic administration which highly regarded the rights of Slovaks and Czechs was replaced by Communist management in that month.

The party *apparatchiks* played a key role in Czech University Law of 1950 in teacher nominations and providing consultation in student admissions. Between 1948 and 1950 the communist students took control over the universities. This period was known as the "studentocracy". In Prague and Olomouc, the theological faculties were detached from their universities.

However, there was less facilitated state arrangement during the initial years of the Communist rule, as the central Party management was less involved with the work of student committees, somewhat trusting them through intergenerational animosity. Radicalism was used as popular currency, for the evacuation and intimidation of teachers, for the expulsions and interrogation of students, and within the penetration of the higher education curriculum with Stalinist perspectives. It wasn't until 1953 that the Party seized control of higher education from Communist students and adopted more organized, if not liberal, policies for higher education.

Czech universities, during the 1950s (except for the year 1956), explicitly admitted "peasant and middle class" students and restricted the admission of *bourgeois* students i.e., students with intellectual backgrounds. In parallel to this, "one-year courses" were planned so that students could be prepared for universities. In Poland, the same situation took place where the communist minister of education Stanislaw Skrzeszewski, ordered universities to be established for students with underprivileged backgrounds.[14]

The major reform in the Czech Republic was the introduction of educational faculties of higher education in Prague, Brno, and Bratislava. Through Act No. 52/1952, the Czechoslovak Academy of Sciences was established, which consisted of an educated and learned society along with sophisticated research institutes.

The resulting transition also stressed those concerned about academic standards. Three additional chairs were added to the curriculum at Charles University, namely in Soviet history, Soviet literature, and Soviet law, and then staffed by individuals without habilitation.

---

14 John Connelly and Michael Grüttner, *Universities under Dictatorship* (University Park: Pennsylvania State University Press, 2010).

The Communist Polish Workers' Party (PPR) in Poland, through Wladyslaw Bienkowski who was a dissenter, managed to maintain their hold on the Higher Education Department of the ministry. Through these early stages, the PPR had their concentration on one issue of higher education only, that is, student admissions. The implantation pressures to the soviet model were resisted and refused by the Polish professoriate.[15]

Throughout Polish history, the enactment of underground education and the power of informal networks, known as the *srodowisko* was prevalent. The "TON" (*Tajna Organizacja Nauczycielska*) was the Secret Teaching Organization led by Kazimierz Maj, Zygmunt Nowicki, and Czeslaw Wycech, and founded by representatives of the prewar Polish Teachers Union (*Związek Nauczycielstwa Polskiego*) was the most popular one.[16]

The year 1956 was a notable educational occurrence, in which Poles protested against Stalinism's education reforms. Under Władyslaw Gomułka, who was the new communist first secretary, the projects of Stalinism were turned down and, this was the crucial time when postwar education reforms started[17]. The vocational program included technical preparation schools, along with the modification of specialized courses so that the cost of contact with genuine modern activities could be managed.[18]

Sovietisation of the Hungarian Higher Education[19]

Developments in the Hungarian higher education showed some similarities with other countries in the Eastern-Central European region, however a few differences also occurred. The most remarkable characteristic feature of the

---

[15] Connelly, *Captive's University*, 283.

[16] Redzik, "Polish Universities," 13.

[17] Andrzej Werblan, "Wladyslaw Gomulka and the Dilemma of Polish Communism," *International Political Science Review* 9, no. 2 (1988): 143–58.

[18] Katarzyna Charzynska, Marta Anczewska and Piotr Switaj, "A Brief Overview of the History of Education in Poland," *Bulgarian Comparative Education Society*, (2012): 92–98.

[19] This part of the paper follows the guideline of a previous overview, see: Imre Garai, "A magyar felsőoktatás strukturális átalakítási és államosítási kísérletei az 1949–1953 közötti időszakban," in *Neveléstudomány és pedagógiai kommunikáció a szocializmus időszakában*, ed. András Németh, Imre Garai and Zoltán András Szabó (Budapest: Gondolat Kiadó, 2016), 119–160.

Hungarian case was its extended pace of the transformation in time. Since the democratic period after the war lasted until 1949,[20] the Sovietisation of the higher education and the Academy of Sciences had just begun and accelerated after the communists succeeded in their effort to size the power.

New legislations were introduced that affected directly the operation of universities and provided equal accessibility for all citizens to higher education. As the outcome of this initiative, the ratio of admitted university students was more than double compared to the enrollment rates in the academic year of 1931–1932.[21]

Newly admitted students were supported by faculty organisations of the Hungarian Alliance of University and High School Students [*Magyar Egyetemsiták és Főiskolások Szövegsége*] (HAUHS) as an association to provide advocacy support, learning materials and even extracurricular activities for students.[22] Moreover, special colleges also emerged as special institutions which offered supportive seminars for their members.[23] However, communist influence was increasingly prevalent in both HAUHS organisations and special colleges that later helped in accelerating the Sovietisation process.[24]

Staff of higher education institutions also changed after the war. The Ministry of Religion and Public Education (MRPE) declared in June 1945 that the activity of university teachers has to be examined by National Interrogation Committees.[25] The Committee that investigated the teachers' behavior was set up in the National Museum and led by Gyula Ortutay. Nevertheless, those teachers were removed from their position who openly

---

20 Ignác Romsics, *Magyarország története a XX. században* (Budapest: Osiris Kiadó, 2004), 338.

21 Andor Ladányi, *Felsőoktatási politika 1949–1958* (Budapest: Kossuth Könyvkiadó, 1986), 7–10.

22 Andor Ladányi, "A felsőoktatás szocialista átszervezésének kezdete: az 1948. évi egyetemi reform," *Magyar Pedagógia* 70, no. 2 (1970): 171–173.

23 Imre Garai, Zoltán András Szabó, and András Németh, "Movement of Special Colleges for Advanced Studies and its Current Challenges in Hungary," *Historia scholastica* 6, no. 1 (2020): 131–132.

24 Ladányi, "A felsőoktatás szocialista," 172–173.

25 21.063/1945. Letter of Géza Teleki MRPE to the directiorat of the Eötvös Collegium. Budapest 7th June, 1945. MDLA 50th box, 96/a dossier. The Committees run by the the Hungarian National Independece Front. This organization is comprised of the parties of the coalition government. Romsics, "Magyarország története," 279–286.

supported the instructions of the far-right dictatorship. The vacant positions were often occupied by individuals who belonged to the younger generations and were now able to be promoted. Their blatant sympathy towards democratic or even communist ideas earlier prevented them from being appointed as full professors, but the democratic turn helped them to surpass political barriers.[26]

The Initial Phase of Sovietisation

After Dezső Keresztury resigned on 14th March 1947, Ortutay Gyula became the new MRPE minister who did not contradict to the communist endeavours in the field of school affairs. During 1948, HAUHS organistations began to play an increasing role in the operation of faculties. Additionally, local political organisations of Hungarian Workers' Party (HWP) also emerged thanks to the active support of communist members of the HAUHS. Furthermore, the ministry introduced a special secondary training form for students who did not have school qualifications in late 1948. The "*szakérettségi*" provided a few weeks long preparation for the final exam of secondary schools in two subjects. Passing the final exams resulted in being eligible to be admitted to universities or high schools in the appropriate subjects, from which the candidate graduated. This new type of training was an outright declaration of transforming the social background of university students and thus abolishing the old admission system that followed the principle of excellence. Introducing corresponding and evening training also contributed to increase the ratio of freshers with agriculture and labor background among students.[27]

The Committee of Agitation and Propaganda (CAP) of the HWP prepared the reforms and it was accepted in January 1949.[28] The 260/1949 decree of the Ministerial Council separated the training of humanities and nature sciences splitting them into two faculties at all universities. Moreover, it dissolved teacher training institutions that organized the theoretical training

26 Andor Ladányi, *A magyar felsőoktatás a 20. században* (Budapest: Akadémiai Kiadó, 1999), 75.

27 Géza Sáska, "A társadalmi egyenlőség megteremtésének kísérlete az ötvenes évek felsőoktatásában," *Educatio* 15, no. 3 (2006): 601–603.

28 Minute of the session of the CAP of HWP held on 4th January 1949. NA 276.f. 86. cs. 12. unit.

of secondary teacher candidates. Additionally, practicing secondary schools were also disbanded, in which secondary teacher candidates could spend their one-year training after finishing the theoretical part of their studies. Faculties became responsible for the organization of the scientific training and the teacher training for all students. These developments along with the emergence of new university-like institutions with narrow profiles[29] could be regarded as the end of the training concept followed by the Humboldt-idea of universities that had determined the development of the whole Hungarian higher education since the middle of the 19th century.

The reform did not meet with the expectations of the communist party. In fact, it resulted in more new challenges that had to be solved. One challenge arose from the fact that the implemented measures disintegrated the organisations of the faculties of full universities in a period, in which hundreds of students with insufficient preparation were admitted and both of the teacher training and the scientific training were in the middle of a transformation process.

Another challenge affected the administration of the faculties. From the local organisations of the HWP departments were formed with personnel and economics subdivisions. These new organisations tried to sort out the personnel, economics and study-related affairs of faculties. Consequently, these new organisations interfered with the authority of deans. As a result, even the party came to the conclusion that the direction of faculties shows symptoms of anarchy.[30]

Moreover, the reform also affected the curriculum of the subjects. The curricular regulations became prescriptive and tightened the students' possibilities to follow their own path among different subjects. The curricular reform resulted in sharp increase in number of study hours.[31] Even though the party admitted in documents for internal use that the high drop-out rate was the result of the reform and the high number of barely trained admitted

---

29 Between 1948 and 1949 several new type of "universities" emerged in Hungary, which differed from full universities in the fact that they offered a special training. Andor Ladányi, *Felsőoktatási politika 1949–1958*, (Budapest: Kossuth Könyvkiadó, 1986), 12–13.

30 Decrees of the CAP of HWP on the session of 29th September 1949. NA 276.f. 86. cs. 34. unit. Ladányi, "A felsőoktatás szocialista," 181.

31 Report and suggestions against high dropping-out rates of Hungarian Universities (Budapest, 20th December 1949), 31–32. NA 276. f. 54. cs. 78. unit.

freshers, the HWP claimed in news outlets that the Rajk-group[32] was responsible for the unsatisfactory performance of students. Therefore, it announced that the MRPE had to contradict and fight against the "secret conspiracy" of the group. Basically, this claim served as an ideological foundation of the new university reform that began in 1950.

It has to be also outlined that parallel to the initial phase of the Sovietisation of higher education the Hungarian Academy of Sciences was also transformed. The 38th Act of the Parliament established the Hungarian Scientific Council (*Magyar Tudományos Tanács*). According to its operation plan for the year of 1949, the main aim of the Council was to plan the main directions of the Hungarian scientific research activities. This planning, however, had to take into account the needs of the 3-year and the first 5-year economic plans.[33]

In the autumn of 1949, the Hungarian Scientific Council was integrated into the Academy by the 27th Act of the Parliament. The Academy gained the previous task of the Scientific Council in determining scientific research activities in Hungary. Membership of the Academy was revised, and those who were not considered as "productive" scholars were excluded.[34] The "reformed" Academy was empowered not only to rule over the main directions of the scientific research, but it also entailed the scientific preparation of young scholars. In late 1949, the Presidental Department of MRPE accepted the introduction of a new Soviet-style scientific training programme called doctoral aspirancy.[35] In essence, almost all kind of scientific research activities, including the scientific preparation above post gradual training was

---

32 László Rajk led the Ministry of Interior and Foreign Affairs between 1946–1949. Mátyás Rákosi chose Rajk as a subject of a show trial, in which Rajk was indicted with conspiracy against the party and treason. He was found guilty and executed in October 1949. Béla Szász, "Bevezető a Rajk perhez," in *Rajk László és társai a népbíróság előtt*, ed. Béla Szász (Budapest: IUS, 1984), 7–39.

33 Principles of the Hungarian Scientific Committee for the year of 1949. Session of the CAP of HWP 24th February 1949. NA 276. f. 54. cs. 31. unit.

34 György Alexits, Proposal for the Secretariat concerning the reorganization of the Hungarian Academy of Sciences and the Hungarian Scientific Council (Budapest, 1949), 14–21. Session of the Secretariat of HWS on 14th September 1949. NA 276.f. 86. cs. 34. unit.

35 Elaboration of the Presidental Department of MRPE concerning the introduction of doctoral aspirancy and candidacy (Budapest, 8th November 1949). NA XIX-I-1-s 213rd box.

centralized under the Academy. Universities were stripped of their right to provide scientific titles for doctoral candidates.

Acceleration of Sovietisation

In December 1949, contours of a new higher education reform became obvious. The Secretariat of HWP declared that study hours have to be limited. It also called for revising curricula and the possibility of reorganizing the MRPE's 6th Department, which was responsible for directing higher education institutions.[36]

The new reform resulted in a more centralized curricular environment with obligatory Russian language learning for 3 years and Marxism-Leninism courses in all training programs. Courses related to the military education were also implemented. Besides curricular changes, the ministry also implemented measures that affected the well-being of students. All dormitories were nationalized and placed under the directorate of National Company of Training Supplies (*Tanfolyamellátó Nemzeti Vállalat*). Moreover, the availability of state scholarships and social funding was extended.[37]

The reform measures also affected the organization of universities since faculty and university councils degraded as advisory boards. The ministry outlined that the principle of the leadership of one person had to be introduced.[38] This development can be regarded as the *de facto* end of the autonomy of universities.[39] Moreover, the loss of autonomy was made even more obvious by the fact that the 44th legal degree of the Presidental Council in 1950 introduced the doctoral aspirancy and candidacy training supervised by the Academy. In 1951, the 26th legal degree of the Presidental Council made it possible to revise the scientific degrees of scholars and reorder the inner hierarchy of scientific institutions following the Soviet model. The revision was made by the Scientific Ranking Committee (*Tudományos Minősítő Bizottság*)

---

36 Report and proposal for tackling against dropping-out mechanisms at universities (Budapest, 20th December 1949), 10–17. NA 276. f. 54. cs. 78. unit.

37 Ladányi, "Felsőoktatási politika," 23–26.

38 Minute of the CAP of HWP on the session of 15th August 1950. NA 276.f. 86. cs. 54. unit.

39 Ladányi, *Felsőoktatási politika*, 67.

of the Academy. Old scientific ranking drove out until March 1952.[40] Those scholars could be appointed as leaders of their faculty or university whom scientific ranks and political views met with the expectations of the party.

Since the party declared that the enemy infiltrated the MRPE, the ministry was split into two parts, and Ortutay was dismissed in February 1950.[41] Even its name was altered to Education Ministry after May 1951. These developments also affected the governance of higher education institutions. Until early 1953, 32 state-financed higher education existed that belonged under the supervision of 11 ministries.[42] The Education ministry preserved the supervision basically the full universities. In order to ensure a general overview of the institutions, Higher Education Council (*Felsőoktatási Tanács*) was set up under the presidency of the Education minister.[43]

Until 1952, the whole institutional background and governance were transformed of the Hungarian higher education. Newly emerged universities with narrow profiles were scrutinized by appropriate ministries and the Higher Education Council. Inner organizations of faculties were also altered completely.

Nonetheless, reports made for the Committee of Agitation and Propaganda of HWP suggest that the party considered the implemented reforms not entirely successful. The HWP labelled the performance of local party organisations at faculties[44] and institutions of the Academy unsatisfactory.[45] There were not enough trustworthy personal by whom the total control over the higher education and scientific research could have been exercised. In 1951, the party had to withdraw the proposal of appointing vice-rectors and

---

40 Garai, "A magyar felsőoktatás," 127–128.

41 Decree of the Central Directoriat of HWP concerning the operation of MRPE (Budapest, 29th March 1950) 29–30. Session of the Secretariat of HWP on 29th March 1950. NA 276. f. 54. cs. 92. unit.

42 Ladányi, "A felsőoktatás szocialista," 83.

43 Proposal of setting up Higher Education Council (Budapest, August 1950). Session of the CAP of HWP on 15th August 1950. NA 276.f. 86. cs. 54. unit.

44 Márton Horváth, Proposal for the Unification of Pary Organisations at Universities (Budapest, 2nd April 1952.), 10–13. Session of Secretariat of HWP on 4th June 1952. NA 276. f. 54. cs. 196. unit.

45 Márton Horváth, Report about Performance of Party Organisations in Scientific Institutions and the Academy, (Budapest, 1952), 49–53. Session of the Secretariat of HWP on 28th May 1952. NA 276. f. 54. cs. 195. unit.

vice-deans to universities since the political views most of the appointees were not "developed" enough.[46]

These circumstances incited the party to change methods in exercising unconditional control over the academic sphere. Following the Soviet example, a Higher Education Ministry was established in December 1952. The newly created ministry supervised most of the universities replacing the Higher Education Council. Nevertheless, its main aim was not just to renew the governance of universities but also to intrude into the teaching methods of subjects and the scientific research activities. The party was convinced that regulating the teaching methods and methodology of scientific research could depersonalize the control mechanisms, and thus scrutiny would become not a personal reliant question anymore.

The Higher Education Ministry could not fulfil its function since it was disbanded after the fall of Mátyás Rákosi in 1953. However, the structure created between 1950 and 1952 in higher education remain intact apart from a few integrations of institutions. Even though reform propositions were assigned, significant measures were not implemented.[47] The absence of reforms was one of the reasons why university students planned to hold a rally on 23rd October 1956, in which they merged their demands concerning the university reforms with the interest of other social strata.

Conclusion

In our paper, we gave an overview about the Sovietisation processes in East-Central Europe with a special focus on the Hungarian developments. From the overview, it might be obvious that some of the techniques were similar in the examined countries.

Admitting thousands of students with agriculture and labor background could be regarded as a similar technique in this process since a considerable amount of them helped the transformation within the institutions. "Reformed" Scientific Academies also played a vital role in the Sovietisation process through their regulator role in directions of scientific research activities.

46 Record related to the proposal of appointing vice-rectors and vice-deans (9th March 1951), 89. Session of the Secretariat of HWP on 14th March 1951. NA 276. f. 54. cs. 134. unit.

47 Ladányi, "A felsőoktatás szocialista", 89–91.

Even the final goal could be regarded as common in the examined countries. Creating unconditional control over scientific research to help in accelerating industrialization. Serving pure economic interests was an outright aim of the transformation in each country.

Nevertheless, common techniques and goals did not mean that the Sovietisation process followed exactly the same pattern. It reached the higher education of each country in a different development stance, in terms of governance, curriculum and policies enacted. This fact required a certain ingenuity from communist parties in using techniques previously implemented in the USSR. This fact might be the reason why Sovietisation did not follow the very same scenario in the examined countries.

Sources

Mednyánszky Dénes Library and Archive (MDLA)

50th Box, 96/a dossier Documents related to interrogation procedures in Baron Eötvös József Collegium after 1945.

National Archives of Hungary (NA)

XIX-I-1-s Presidental Department of the MRPE, legal elaborations 213rd box.

Minutes of the sessions of CAP of HWP

276.f. 86. cs. 12. unit. Session of 4 January 1949.

276.f. 86. cs. 34. unit. Session of 29 September 1949.

276.f. 86. cs. 54. unit. Session of 15 August 1950.

Minutes of the sessions of the Secretariat of the HWP

276. f. 54. cs. 31. unit. Session of 24 February 1949.

276.f. 86. cs. 34. unit. Session of 14 September 1949.

276. f. 54. cs. 78. unit. Session of 21 December 1949.

276. f. 54. cs. 92. unit. Session of 29 March 1950.

276. f. 54. cs. 100. unit. Session of 16 May 1950.

276. f. 54. cs. 134. unit. Session of 14 March 1951.

276. f. 54. cs. 195. unit. Session of 28 May 1952.

276. f. 54. cs. 196. unit. Session of 4 June 1952.

Bibliography

Apanasewicz, Nellie. *The Educational System of Poland. Education around the World*. Washington, D.C.: Office of Education (DHEW), 1976.

Applebaum, Anne. *Iron Curtain: The Crushing of Eastern Europe 1944–56*. London: Penguin UK, 2012.

Caruso, Marcelo. "Within, between, above, and beyond: (Pre) Positions for a History of the Internationalisation of Educational Practices and Knowledge." *Paedagogica Historica* 50, no. 1–2 (2014): 10–26.

Charzynska, Katarzyna, Marta Anczewska and Piotr Switaj. "A Brief Overview of the History of Education in Poland." *Bulgarian Comparative Education Society*, (2012): 92–98.

Connelly, John. *Captive University: The Sovietization of East German, Czech, and Polish Higher Education, 1945–1956*. Chapel Hill and London: UNC Press Books, 2014.

Connelly, John and Michael Grüttner. *Universities under Dictatorship*. University Park: Pennsylvania State University Press, 2010.

Dedze, Indra and Zanda Rubene. "Universities in Latvia – from the Soviet to European Higher Education Area." *Foro de Educación*, no. 14 (2016): 13–38.

Dobbins, Michael. "Explaining Different Pathways in Higher Education Policy in Romania and the Czech Republic." *Comparative Education*, no. 2 (2011): 223–45.

Dobbins, Michael. "Exploring the Governance of Polish Public Higher Education: Balancing Restored Historical Legacies with Europeanization and Market Pressures." *European Journal of Higher Education*, no. 1 (2015): 18–33.

Dobbins, Michael and Christoph Knill. "Higher Education Policies in Central and Eastern Europe: Convergence toward a Common Model?" *Governance* 22, no. 3 (2009): 397–430.

Garai, Imre. "A magyar felsőoktatás strukturális átalakítási és államosítási kísérletei az 1949–1953 közötti időszakban." In *Neveléstudomány és pedagógiai kommunikáció a szocializmus időszakában*, edited by Németh, András, Garai, Imre and Szabó Zoltán András, 119–160. Budapest: Gondolat Kiadó, 2016.

Garai, Imre, and András Németh. "Disciplinary Changes in Science Education in Hungary in the Era of the Stalinist Dictatorship." *Pedagogika* 67, no. 4 (2017): 431–442.

Garai, Imre, Szabó, Zoltán András and András Németh. "Movement of Special Colleges for Advanced Studies and its Current Challenges in Hungary." *Historia scholastica* 6, no. 1 (2020): 124–145.

Heimann, Mary. *Czechoslovakia: The State That Failed*. New Haven: Yale University Press, 2011.

Ladányi, Andor. *A magyar felsőoktatás a 20. században*. Budapest: Akadémiai Kiadó, 1999.

Ladányi, Andor. "A felsőoktatás szocialista átszervezésének kezdete: az 1948. évi egyetemi reform." *Magyar Pedagógia* 70, no. 2 (1970): 170–184.

Ladányi, Andor. *Felsőoktatási politika 1949–1958*. Budapest: Kossuth Könyvkiadó, 1986.

Matthews, Mervyn. *Education in the Soviet Union: Policies and Institutions since Stalin*. London: Routledge, 2011.

Németh, András. "Die Entwicklungsperioden der ungarischen Erziehungswissenschaft im 19. und 20. Jahrhundert." In *University and Universality. The Place and Role of the University of Pécs in Europe from the Middle Ages to Present Day*, edited by Ágnes Fischer-Dárdai, István Lengvári and Éva Schmelczer-Pohánka, 309–328. Pécs: University Library of Pécs and Centre for Learning, 2017.

Németh, András and Garai, Imre. "Disciplinary Changes in the Hungarian 'Pädagogik' from the Second Half of the 19th Century to the Collapse of Stalinist-type Dictatorship." In *Education and "Pädagogik" Philosophical and Historical Reflections: Central and South-Eastern Europe*, edited by Blanka Kudláčová and Andrej Rajský, 214–217. Berlin: Peter Lang, Bratislava: VEDA, 2019.

Németh, András and Béla Pukánszky. "Herbartianism as an Eastern Central European Phenomenon and Its Reception in Hungary." *History of Education & Children's Literature* 16, no. 1 (2021): 65–86.

Redzik, Adam. "Polish Universities During the Second World War." *Encuentros de Historia Comparada Hispano-Polaca/Spotkania poświęcone historii porównawczej hiszpańsko-polskiej conference*, no. 1 (2004): 1–20.

Romsics, Ignác. *Magyarország története a XX. században*. Budapest: Osiris Kiadó, 2004.

Sáska, Géza. "A társadalmi egyenlőség megteremtésének kísérlete az ötvenes évek felsőoktatásában." *Educatio* 15, no. 3 (2006): 593–608.

Szász, Béla. "Bevezető a Rajk perhez." In *Rajk László és társai a népbíróság előtt*, edited by Béla Szász, 7–39. Budapest: IUS, 1984.

Werblan, Andrzej. "Wladyslaw Gomulka and the Dilemma of Polish Communism." *International Political Science Review* 9, no. 2 (1988): 143–58.

Das Verhältnis zwischen jugoslawischer und sowjetischer Pädagogik in der Nachkriegszeit jenseits von Diktat und Politik – eine slowenische Perspektive

Zdenko Medveš

Zusammenfassung: Die Nachkriegsentwicklung der jugoslawischen Pädagogik in der „Stunde Null“ (im Jahre 1945) bedeutet eine Neuorientierung, und zwar weg von der Bindung an die Pädagogik Mitteleuropas hin zur sowjetischen bzw. russischen Pädagogik. Die Neuorientierung war keineswegs nur das Ergebnis externer Diktate oder diesem entgegenkommender eigener *politischer* Orientierungen, sondern die Folge einer auch selbst gewählten *pädagogischen* Sicht jugoslawischer Persönlichkeiten bei der Gestaltung einer marxistischen Pädagogik. Dieser Prozess war im ehemaligen Jugoslawien sehr komplex und vielfältig, auch aufgrund der historisch bedingten besonderen Verbindung verschiedener Regionen mit der Sowjetunion sowie dem zaristischen Russland einerseits und dem Nachwirken der historischen Verbindungen zu Österreich respektive dem deutschsprachigen Raum andererseits. Die Entwicklung der marxistischen Pädagogik war zwar das dominierende Ziel in der Arbeit pädagogischer Theoretiker im ganzen Land, begleitet von Intoleranz gegenüber abweichenden theoretischen Diskursen – mit der Folge eines oft radikalen Bruchs mit pädagogischen Traditionen der Vor- und Zwischenkriegszeit. Doch in Slowenien werden trotz der Dominanz der marxistischen Pädagogik während der gesamten Nachkriegszeit gleichwohl Diskurse erhalten, die die humanistische Tradition der pädagogischen Strömungen der Vorkriegszeit fortführen oder daran anknüpfen.

Schlüsselwörter: Pädagogisches Paradigma, Sozialkritische Pädagogik, Geisteswissenschaftliche Pädagogik, Reformpädagogik, Pädologie, Marxistische Pädagogik, Diskurs, Weltanschauungskritik, Diamat

Einführung

Bevor wir mit der Analyse der Sowjetisierungsprozesse der jugoslawischen Pädagogik nach 1945 beginnen, müssen wir definieren, was ein formales und was ein inhaltliches Kriterium für dieses Phänomen ist. Nach 1945 kam es zu einer Interferenz zweier unterschiedlicher Phänomene, die als zwei Formen der Sowjetisierung angesehen werden können. Einerseits handelt es sich um eine direkte, bisweilen sogar gewaltsame Sowjetisierung durch Auferlegung des sowjetischen Schulsystems sowie der zugehörigen Ideologie und Theorie, andererseits wird die Sowjetisierung durch autonome Übernahme sowjetischer pädagogischer und philosophischer Ideen, politischer Ansichten und

Ideologien in der Entwicklung der marxistischen Pädagogik forciert. Dies ermöglicht eine Analyse des Phänomens der Sowjetisierung auch in der Zeit nach der Informbiro-Resolution (1955), die einen zwischenstaatlichen Konflikt zwischen Jugoslawien und der Sowjetunion auslöste und innerhalb Jugoslawiens Vergeltungsmaßnahmen gegen Bürger, die tatsächliche oder vermeintliche Sympathisanten der Sowjetunion waren, mit sich brachte.[1]

Das formale Kriterium für die Analyse wird die Verbreitung und das Zitieren von sowjetischen und anderen Quellen sein, das inhaltliche Kriterium aber die Breite des Verständnisses des marxistischen Denkens, die eigene Einstellung zu anderen Diskursen und zu der einheimischen pädagogischen Vorkriegstradition. Die grundlegende Forschungsfrage ist, ob die Entwicklung der marxistischen Pädagogik in Jugoslawien auf dem sogenannten „Sowjetmarxismus“ (auch utopischer Marxismus genannt) oder auch auf dem Studium der marxistischen Klassiker und des sogenannten „Westmarxismus“ beziehungsweise Neomarxismus (oder kritischer Marxismus) beruhte. Der Schlüssel zur Bestimmung eines bestimmten Prozesses als Sowjetisierungsprozess wird die Kontinuität oder Diskontinuität in der Entwicklung der Pädagogik zwischen der Vorkriegszeit bzw. von 1945 bis 1950 sein. Es wird auch näher erforscht, wie sich die Informbiro-Resolution (28. Juni 1948), auf deren Grundlage Jugoslawien aus diesem beratenden Gremium der kommunistischen Parteien ausgeschlossen wurde, auf den Prozess der Sowjetisierung der jugoslawischen Pädagogik auswirkte, und ob wegen der Verschärfung in den Beziehungen der sowjetische Einfluss auf die Entwicklung der Pädagogik unterbrochen wurde.

Methodologisch basiert die Analyse der Sowjetisierungsprozesse auf der *Analyse von Inhalten und Referenzen* in Texten aus verschiedenen Perioden der Nachkriegsentwicklung pädagogischer Theorien und Ansichten in Jugoslawien. Am ausführlichsten werden wir uns mit Texten beschäftigen, die in den ersten Jahren der Nachkriegsentwicklung von 1945 bis 1952 entstanden sind. Neben Primärquellen aus der ersten Nachkriegszeit werden auch spätere Texte untersucht, in denen verschiedene Autoren ihre Ansichten zur Nachkriegszeit und den sowjetischen Einfluss vortragen.

---

1 Mehr dazu in Božidar Jezernik, *Titos Gulag auf der Insel Goli otok* (Hermagor: Hermagoras Verlag, 2014).

Die Pädagogik zwischen den beiden Kriegen ist ideologisch und theoretisch plural

Jugoslawien war in der Vor- und Nachkriegszeit durch große Unterschiede in der politischen, wirtschaftlichen und allgemeinen sozialen Entwicklung einzelner Regionen gekennzeichnet. Es gab Unterschiede zwischen wirtschaftlich und politisch entwickelten Teilrepubliken im Norden (insbesondere Kroatien, Slowenien, einschließlich Nordserbien) und denen im Süden. Unterschiede in der Entwicklung wurden auf vielen Ebenen zum Ausdruck gebracht, auch in der Kultur und Bildung. So wurde in Slowenien und Kroatien zu Beginn des 20. Jahrhunderts der Analphabetismus dank des österreichischen Schulgesetzes von 1869 nahezu eliminiert, während in den Gebieten des heutigen Nordmazedoniens 1945 75% der Bevölkerung im Alter von über zehn Jahren Analphabeten waren.[2] Šušnjara[3] findet einen ähnlichen Prozentsatz für Bosnien und Herzegowina, während Vujisić Živković 56,3% für Serbien angibt.[4]

Noch größere Unterschiede als in der Schulentwicklung und Bildung der Bevölkerung gab es zwischen den beiden Weltkriegen in der Entwicklung der pädagogischen Wissenschaft. Das akademische Studium der Pädagogik fand nur an den Universitäten Belgrad, Ljubljana und Zagreb statt. Es basierte auf dem Paradigma der Kultur- bzw. Geisteswissenschaftlichen Pädagogik.[5] Der Lehrstuhlinhaber in Slowenien war Karel Ozvald, in Kroatien Stjepan Pataki, in Serbien Miloš Milošević. Neben der akademischen Pädagogik

---

2 Suzana Miovska Spaseva, „Dostignuča i proturječja u razvoju obrazovanja i pedagogije u Socijalističkoj Makedoniji (1945–1990)," in *Razvoj i aktualne tendencije pedagogije i školstva na području nekadašnje Jugoslavije*, ed. Edvard Protner (Maribor: Universität von Maribor Press, 2020), 193.

3 Snježana Šušnjara, „Razvoj školstva u Bosni i Hercegovini nakon drugog svetskog rata do 1970-ih," in *Razvoj i aktualne tendencije pedagogije i školstva na području nekadašnje Jugoslavije*, ed. Edvard Protner (Maribor: Universität von Maribor Press, 2020), 136.

4 Nataša Vujisić-Živković, „Konstitutivni diskontinuitet: školstvo i pedagogija u socijalističkoj Srbiji (1945–1990)," in *Razvoj i aktualne tendencije pedagogije i školstva na području nekadašnje Jugoslavije*, ed. Edvard Protner (Maribor: Universität von Maribor Press, 2020), 155–156.

5 Tadej Vidmar, „Ključni vidici institucionalnoga razvoja pedagogije kao akademske discipline u Sloveniji," in *Razvoj i aktualne tendencije pedagogije i školstva na području nekadašnje Jugoslavije*, ed. Edvard Protner (Maribor: Universität von Maribor Press, 2020), 215–217; Zdenko Medveš, "Conflicting Paradigms in the Development of Slovene Pedagogy," *Journal of Contemporary Educational Studies* 66, no. 3 (2015).

waren zwischen den beiden Weltkriegen theoretisch auch die pädagogischen Bewegungen der Grundschullehrer sehr stark. In Slowenien waren dies die Pädagogische Zentrale und die Lehrerbewegung Učiteljski pokret (in der Fortsetzung die „Pokret"). Die *Pädagogische Zentrale* hat ihr liberales pädagogisches Programm auf der Grundlage der fortschrittlichen Reformpädagogik, Pädopsychologie und Pädologie[6] entwickelt. Die Lehrerbewegung „*Pokret*" orientierte sich eher an der gesellschaftlichen Rolle der Bildung mit charakteristischen Elementen des linken gesellschaftskritischen Diskurses. Dieser konzentrierte sich auf einen Begriff von Bildung als Emanzipation und als Weg aus einer gesellschaftlich bedingten Rückständigkeit.[7] Beide Bewegungen, insbesondere die Lehrerbewegung, waren auch in Kroatien und Serbien weit verbreitet. Sie hatten einen starken Einfluss in den 1920er und 1930er Jahren, in Serbien reichen die Anfänge mit der Bewegung „Zukunft" („Budučnost") bis vor den Ersten Weltkrieg zurück.[8]

„*Pokret*" wurde von links orientierten Lehrern organisiert und unterstützte offen die Kommunistische Partei (KP). Für unsere weitere Analyse ist wichtig, dass die „Sympathie" zwischen diesen Lehrern und der KP einseitig war, da die Partei „*Pokret*" aufgrund revolutionärer Illusionen nicht unterstützte, angeblich weil ihre „Bemühungen für eine gerechte Schule unnötig waren, da nach der Revolution sowieso alles ganz anders werden würde."[9]. Wahrscheinlich gilt die Hypothese, dass die zurückhaltende Position der Partei gegenüber „*Pokret*" nach dem Krieg ein Grund dafür war, dass einige pädagogische Theoretiker Zweifel darüber geäußert hatten, ob „*Pokret*" wirklich eine

---

6 Die Wissenschaft vom Studium der Kindheitsentwicklung ist wegen des naturalistischen Diskurses und dem Einsatz schlecht entwickelter Testmethoden umstritten (Stanley Hall); war deswegen auch im zaristischen Russland und der Sowjetunion(Wladimir Bechterew) durch den Erlass des Zentralkomitees der VKPb verboten („Über pädologische Verzerrungen im System der Volkskommissariate", 4. Juli 1936). Der Erlass hatte erhebliche Auswirkungen auf die Entwicklung der Nachkriegspädagogik in Jugoslawien, insbesondere auf das Verhältnis zur Psychologie; dazu mehr weiter unten.

7 Oskar Autor, *Intervju z Jožetom Jurančičem in Martinom Mencejem* (Maribor: Pedagoška fakulteta, 1988), 46.

8 Autor, *Intervju z Jožetom Jurančičem in Martinom Mencejem*, 46.

9 Autor, *Intervju z Jožetom Jurančičem in Martinom Mencejem*, 44–45.

angemessene Tradition für die „neue marxistische Pädagogik" sein könnte. Wie wir später sehen werden, artikuliert dieser Zweifel zum Teil das Paradox, dass nämlich bei der Entwicklung der marxistischen Nachkriegspädagogik sogar jene Lehrerbewegungen der Vorkriegszeit abgelehnt wurden, die die marxistische Orientierung deutlich zum Ausdruck brachten.

Trotz theoretischer Differenzen führten die *„Pokret"* und die *Pädagogische Zentrale* ein ähnliches Programm durch: „Für eine neue Schule". Das Programm war eine Alternative sowohl zur akademischen Geisteswissenschaftlichen Pädagogik als auch zu Zillers Herbartianismus, auf dem noch immer die Ausbildung von Grundschullehrern und auch die offizielle Schulpolitik basierten. Viele prominente Initiatoren waren Mitglieder des *Pädagogischen Zentrums*[10] und unterstützten das Programm „Für eine neue Schule", das sich auf eine methodische Erneuerung nach den Prinzipien der progressiven Pädagogik oder Reformpädagogik konzentrierte. Sie experimentierten mit pädagogischen Neuerungen wie Arbeitsschule von Kerschensteiner, Gaudig oder Blonsky, Dalton-Plan, Gesamtunterricht, Unterricht in der Natur, Selbsttätigkeit des Kindes im Unterricht[11], Lebensgemeinschaft Schule und Ähnliches.[12] Lehrer und auch Schulleiter, *„Pokret"*-Mitglieder, haben damals die ersten pädagogisch-soziologischen empirischen Studien in Sloweniens Geschichte durchgeführt.[13] Gesellschaftskritische Studien zum Einfluss wirtschaftlicher Rahmenbedingungen auf die Entwicklung junger Generationen verleihen der *„Pokret"* ihr eigenes Gepräge, in dem sich die sozialpädagogischen Ideen der europäischen Sozialdemokratie und auch der sowjetischen Pädagogik, vor allem von Blonskys Arbeitsschule, zweifellos *schon* vor dem Krieg nachweisen lassen. Ungeachtet dessen war der besondere Fokus beider

---

10 Autor, *Intervju z Jožetom Jurančičem in Martinom Mencejem*, 5.

11 Autor, *Intervju z Jožetom Jurančičem in Martinom Mencejem*, 22.

12 Autor, *Intervju z Jožetom Jurančičem in Martinom Mencejem*, 13. Jože Jurančič erzählt, dass er auf dem Lande den Bauern Mathematik an Beispielen aus dem Alltag beigebracht hatte – z.B. die Volumenberechnung des Rundholzes, sodass die Bauern sich dem Betrug der Holzhändler entgegenstellen konnten.

13 Franjo Žgeč, *Problemi vzgoje najširših plasti našega naroda*, 1923; Karel Doberšek, *Vpliv socialnih razmer na razvoj otroka na Prevaljah*, 1929; Jože Jurančič, *Iz šole za narod*, 1930; Miloš Ledinek, *Moj razred*, 1939.

Lehrerbewegungen auf die Erneuerung der Methodik dafür verantwortlich, dass in den ersten Nachkriegsjahren keine dieser Lehrerbewegungen als fortschrittliches Erbe und würdige Tradition für die „neue" sozialistische Schule und marxistische Pädagogik anerkannt wurde.

Der jugoslawische Raum der Vorkriegszeit, insbesondere Kroatien, Slowenien und Serbien, ist also von einem *Pluralismus* pädagogischer Ansichten und Paradigmen geprägt.[14] In anderen Regionen Jugoslawiens begann sich die Pädagogik dagegen erst nach dem Krieg zu entwickeln. Zorić stellt fest, dass es in Montenegro auch bis 1990 keine Bedingungen für die Entwicklung theoretischer und wissenschaftlicher Konzepte gab, sondern dass „Pädagogik" auf die Darstellung offizieller Bildungspolitik reduziert wurde.[15] In ähnlicher Weise behauptet Miovska Spaseva für Mazedonien, dass es „vor der Befreiung Mazedoniens und der Gründung der Philosophischen Fakultät (im Jahre 1946) in Skopje nur eine sehr bescheidene wissenschaftliche Forschungstradition auf dem Gebiet der Bildung [und] dass es in den ersten Nachkriegsjahren kaum Institutionen und qualifiziertes Personal gab, das wissenschaftlich forschen konnte."[16]

Über die Periodisierung der jugoslawischen Nachkriegspädagogik im Spannungsfeld zwischen Sowjetisierung und Autonomiebestrebungen

Die Periodisierung der Nachkriegsentwicklung der Pädagogik in Jugoslawien zeigt im Wesentlichen das Modell und die Genese der Sowjetisierung und – zugleich – die Autonomiebestrebungen der jugoslawischen Pädagogik. Die Periodisierung der Entwicklung wurde von vielen Autoren ähnlich vorgenommen (Schmidt 1982, Sagadin 1984 und 1987, Schmidt, Strmčnik, Medveš 1994, Damjanovski 1985, Potkonjak 1994, Radeka, Batinić 2020, Šušnjara, 2020, Vujisić Živković 2020). Die erste Phase in den Nachkriegsjahren (1945–1950) wird als die Periode der „etatistischen Pädagogik" bezeichnet, methodologisch ist sie aber durch die „Übersetzung der politischen Prinzipien in eine

---

14 Zdenko Medveš, "Conflicting Paradigms," 23–26.

15 Vučina Zorić, „Nastanek, delovanje in perspektive razvoja študijskega programa pedagogika v Črni Gori," *Sodobna pedagogika* 67, no. 3 (2016): 102–104.

16 Miovska-Spaseva, „Dostignuča i proturječja," 190.

pädagogische Sprache und mit der ausschließlichen Anlehnung an die sowjetische Pädagogik" gekennzeichnet (Sagadin 1987, Schmidt 1952, Schmidt 1954). Inhaltlich wird diese Phase am besten beschrieben durch den im Jahr 1945 erschienenen, äußerst einflussreichen Artikel *Leitlinien der modernen pädagogischen Arbeit* (im Folgenden: *Leitlinien*) von Vlado Schmidt (Schmidt, 1945), in dem er programmatisch die Besonderheiten der sozialistischen bzw. marxistischen Pädagogik definiert. Der Text wurde im Jahr 1946 ins Serbokroatische übersetzt und in der neu gegründeten zentraljugoslawischen pädagogischen Zeitschrift *Savremena škola* (*Moderne Schule*) veröffentlicht.[17]

Die zweite Phase (1950–1970), symbolisch eingeleitet durch Schmidts Beitrag *Wie wird die pädagogische Wissenschaft bei uns heute entwickelt* (1952), kennzeichnet die Entwicklung der empirischen Forschungsmethodologie und seine Forderung nach empirisch-wissenschaftlicher Evaluation politischer Schulideen in der Praxis, die er im folgenden Jahrzehnt immer wieder begründete.[18]

Der Beginn der dritten Phase (nach 1970) wird wiederum durch zahlreiche Schmidt-Texte, die seinem Beitrag *Sozialistische Pädagogik zwischen Etatismus und Selbstverwaltung* (1970) folgen, gekennzeichnet. Die gesamte

---

17 Vlado Schmidt war 1945 Professor an der Pädagogischen Hochschule in Ljubljana und nebenamtlicher Lehrbeauftragter der Pädagogik an der Philosophischen Fakultät, wo er 1954 fest angestellt wurde. Aufgrund seines hohen Ansehens, das er bald nach dem Krieg unter Pädagogen in ganz Jugoslawien genoss, spielte er eine entscheidende Rolle bei der Entwicklung der marxistischen Pädagogik in Jugoslawien. Alle seine programmatischen Texte, die Wendepunkte in der Entwicklung der jugoslawischen Pädagogik bedeuten, wurden ins Serbokroatische übersetzt: *Leitlinien der modernen pädagogischen Arbeit* (*Savremena škola* 1946), *Wie wird die pädagogische Wissenschaft bei uns heute entwickelt* (*Savremena škola* 1952) und *Sozialistische Pädagogik zwischen Etatismus und Selbstverwaltung* (Pädagogische Fakultät in Osijek 1985). Zwischen 1950 und 1970 widmete er sich dem Studium der pädagogischen Methodologie und der Bildungsgeschichte und veröffentlichte sein wichtigstes Werk, *Die Geschichte der Pädagogik und Bildung in Slowenien*, in drei Teilen mit 1166 Seiten.

18 Vlado Schmidt, „Metodologija šolske reforme," in *Socialistična pedagogika med etatizmom in samoupravljanjem*, ed. Mira Simon (Ljubljana: Dopisna delavska univerza Univerzum, 1966/1982), 99. (Die erste Zahl bedeutet das Datum der ersten Veröffentlichung des Textes, die Seiten sind aber nach der erneuten Ausgabe notiert; so schrieb Schmidt auch in „Metodologija" 1966/1982).

Phase wird durch die Zeit der Konstituierung einer autochthonen Pädagogik der Selbstverwaltung bestimmt.

Eine ähnliche Periodisierung der Entwicklung findet sich bei Pädagogen in ganz Jugoslawien, von einigen unterschiedlichen Schwerpunkten abgesehen.[19] Bei einigen Autoren bestehen die Unterschiede nur darin, wie lange die Dauer jeder Phase anzusetzen ist. Nikola Potkonjak etwa schreibt, dass die „Teilernüchterung in Bezug auf den Einfluss der sowjetischen Pädagogik und die Akzeptanz des methodologischen Erbes der empirisch-induktiven bürgerlichen Pädagogik erst in den späten 1950er und frühen 1960er Jahren eingetreten ist",[20] also zehn Jahre nach dem Meilenstein für die Neugewichtung (bzw. Gleichgewichtung) der slowenischen Theoretiker bezüglich der deduktiven und induktiven Methodologie.[21]

Diskontinuität Nr. 1: Auswechslung der Studienliteratur

Die elementarste Tatsache, die formal darauf hindeutet, dass das Jahr 1945 eine Diskontinuität in der pädagogischen Entwicklung darstellt, ist der Ersatz der Studienliteratur. Die akademische Pädagogik in Kroatien und Slowenien erfüllte ihre Aufgabe zwischen den beiden Weltkriegen auch mit entsprechender studienpädagogischer Literatur. An der Universität Zagreb sind dies die Werke von Stjepan Pataki *Probleme der Philosophie der Pädagogik* (1933) und *Pädagogische Wissenschaft und das Problem der pädagogischen Funktion* (1936) und

---

19 Vučina Zorić, „Obrazovna politika u socijalističkoj Crnoj Gori," in *Razvoj i aktualne tendencije pedagogije i školstva na području nekadašnje Jugoslavije*, ed. Edvard Protner (Maribor: Universität von Maribor Press, 2020), 170. Vučina Zorić teilt die Entwicklung der Pädagogik auf vier Perioden: Die Periode des administrativen Sozialismus (1945–1951), die Periode des Staatsuntergangs und der Anfang der Selbstverwaltung (1951–1963), die Periode der Korrekturen des Selbstverwaltungskonzepts (1963–1974) und die Periode der vollständigen Auflösung der Selbstverwaltung (1974–1990).

20 Nikola Potkonjak, *Teorijsko-metodološki problemi pedagogije* (Beograd: Prosveta, 1977), 185.

21 Janez Sagadin, *Nekateri glavni teoretsko-metodološki problemi v zvezi z ideološko preusmeritvijo povojne jugoslovanske pedagogike* (Ljubljana: Filozofska fakulteta, Oddelek za pedagogiko, 1984); Vlado Schmidt, „Povojni uspehi in stiske pedagoške teorije in prakse – intervju," *Sodobna pedagogika* 36, no. 7–8 (1985): 259–260; Franc Pediček, „Paradigme slovenske pedagogike – prikaz ideoloških nasprotij in obravnavanih vprašanj v slovenski pedagogiki (1945–1988)," *Sodobna pedaogika* 49, no. 7–8 (1990): 365–375.

an der Universität von Ljubljana *Kulturpädagogik* (1927), *Mentales Wachstum von Kindern und Jugendlichen* (1930) sowie die *Grundlegende Psychologie* (1932) von Karl Ozvald und *Die Grundlagen der allgemeinen Methodik* (1933) von Stanko Gogala. Nach dem Krieg wurden die meisten dieser Lehrbücher nicht mehr verwendet. Hauptgrund dafür ist ihr mangelhaftes Deutungsparadigma (Kulturpädagogik), das unmittelbar in den ersten Nachkriegsjahren als idealistisch und „germanisiert" kritisiert wurde.[22] Man kann davon ausgehen, dass das Lehrbuch von Stanko Gogala aus dem Jahr 1933 unmittelbar nach dem Krieg an der Philosophischen Fakultät in Ljubljana verwendet wurde, da Gogala im Studienjahr 1945/46 der einzige Pädagoge an der Fakultät war und 1951 das Lehrbuch *Allgemeine Methodik* (*Obča metodika*) veröffentlichte, das einige Teile des Lehrbuchs von 1933 wieder aufgriff und aufwertete. Dies ist im Jahre 1945 als ein Zeichen der Kontinuität mit der pluralen Vorkriegspädagogik aufzufassen. Viele Jahre nach dem Krieg gehörte Gogala der Geisteswissenschaftlichen bzw. Kulturpädagogik an, die er, wie er sagt,[23] in Richtung Persönlichkeitspädagogik, also in Richtung Personalismus, entwickelt hat. Nach dem Krieg wandte sich Gogala nicht der Entwicklung der marxistischen Pädagogik zu – im Gegensatz zum kroatischen Vorkriegsvertreter der geistlichen Pädagogik Stjepan Pataki[24].

Nach dem Krieg hatte die Pädagogik in ganz Jugoslawien so gut wie keine akademischen Ressourcen. In den Jahren 1947–1949 wurden einige Texte aus dem Russischen übersetzt, wofür die Bundesverwaltung gesorgt hatte. Die Bücher wurden auf Serbokroatisch veröffentlicht und nie ins Mazedonische oder Slowenische übersetzt. Sie galten als selbstverständliche pädagogische Studienliteratur für ganz Jugoslawien. Dies waren Übersetzungen sowjetischer Lehrbücher: *Pädagogik* (*Pedagogija* 1947) von B.P. Jesipov und N. K. Gončarev, das Lehrbuch *Pädagogik* (*Pedagogija* 1949), herausgegeben von P. N. Gruzdjev

---

22 Vlado Schmidt, „Smernice sodobnega pedagoškega dela," in *Socialistična pedagogika med etatizmom in samoupravljanje* (Ljubljana: Dopisna delavska univerza Univerzum, 1945/1982), 17–18.

23 Stanko Gogala, „Odgovor D. Frankoviću," *Sodobna pedagogika* 2, Nr. 2–3, (1951): 180.

24 Igor Radeka und Štefka Batinić, „Pedagogija in školstvo od završetka drugog svjetskog rata do kraja 1950-ih," in *Razvoj i aktualne tendencije pedagogije i školstva na području nekadašnje Jugoslavije*, ed. Edvard Protner (Maribor: Universität von Maribor Press, 2020), 114–118.

und die Sammlung *Über Erziehung* (*O vzgoji* 1947) sowie *Grundprobleme der Pädagogik* (*Osnovni problemi pedagogije* 1947) mit einer Auswahl pädagogischer Gedanken von Marx, Engels, Lenin, Plechanow, Stalin und Krupskaya.

Ansonsten stellt sich auch die Frage, welche Universitäten Übersetzungen sowjetischer Lehrbücher überhaupt als Studienliteratur verwendet hatten. Bald entstanden nämlich die einheimischen Texte der einflussreichsten Autoren einer „marxistischen Pädagogik", die in Serbien, Kroatien und Slowenien als Studienmaterial genannt werden.[25] Diese sind *Einführung in die Allgemeine Pädagogik* von Stjepan Pataki (1948), *Richtlinien für zeitgenössische pädagogische Arbeit* von Vlado Schmidt (in Slowenisch 1945, serbokroatische Übersetzung 1946 und 1947); *Politik und Bildung* von Dragutin Franković (1948), der Artikel von Vlado Schmidt *Wie man die pädagogische Wissenschaft in Slowenien heute entwickelt* (auf Slowenisch 1952, serbokroatische Übersetzung 1958). Für die Pädagogische Hochschule in Ljubljana veröffentlichte Schmidt 1948/50 ein Skript, das in vier Bänden das gesamte pädagogische Kompendium umfasst (*Allgemeine Pädagogik, Pädagogische Methodologie, Pädagogik- und Bildungsgeschichte*, Kapitel über *Bildungsziele* und das *System des öffentlichen Bildungswesens in Jugoslawien*, *Vergleichende Pädagogik – Moderne Kapitalismusbildung, Didaktik und Theorie der Bildung, Moralerziehung* und ein Kapitel über das *Kollektiv als Erziehungssubjekt*). Schmidts *Pädagogik* und Patakis *Einführung in die Allgemeine Pädagogik* sind das Ergebnis der akademischen Verantwortung beider Autoren, Studienliteratur für die neue marxistische Pädagogik bereitzustellen. Es sind originelle, eigenständige Werke. Die Autoren stützen sich zwar auf sowjetische Quellen, aber es überwiegen Schmidts Verweise auf einheimische Autoren der Vorkriegszeit, wobei die meisten seiner Verweise die kritische Behandlung der geisteswissenschaftlichen und reformorientierten Vorkriegspädagogik und die Bestätigung der Pädagogik als sozial orientiertes Paradigma umfassen.

---

[25] Radeka und Batinić, „Pedagogija i školstvo," 110; Vujisić-Živković, „Konstitutivni diskontinuitet," 159–161.

Diskontinuität Nr. 2: Die gesamte pädagogische Tradition der Vorkriegszeit wird als Element bürgerlicher Pädagogik abgelehnt

Schmidt kritisierte später sein Frühwerk[26] und sagte, die Pädagogik habe in den ersten fünf Nachkriegsjahren „nur die Aussagen unserer führenden Partei- und politischen Führer in die pädagogische Sprache übersetzt und die sowjetische Pädagogik übernommen."[27] Die Wahrheit ist aber, dass die *Leitlinien* und andere Texte in den ersten Nachkriegsjahren keineswegs nur das Übersetzen politischer Parolen (obwohl es ihnen auch daran nicht mangelt) und die Transkription sowjetischer pädagogischer Quellen waren. Alle diese Texte bedeuten vielmehr auch eine Abrechnung mit dem pluralistischen pädagogischen Denken der Vorkriegszeit, denn sie enthalten mehrere kritische Verweise auf einheimische Autoren der Vorkriegszeit, insbesondere auf die Autoren des „liberalen bürgerlichen Elitismus" (Geisteswissenschaftliche Pädagogik) und der „idealistisch-naturistischen" Pädagogik (Pädologie und Reformpädagogik). Die Grundlage der Kritik Schmidts ist die radikalisierte These des historischen Materialismus, dass die Ideologie der herrschenden Klasse immer und überall reaktionär sei. Wenn eine derart radikalisierte These auf die Pädagogik übertragen wird, erweist sich die gesamte pädagogische Tradition als ideologisch kontaminiert. Damit entwickelt sich eine Begründung der Diskontinuität, auf deren Grundlage Schmidt die slowenische pädagogische Tradition der Vorkriegszeit komplett ablehnte; nicht nur die (akademische) Geisteswissenschaftliche Pädagogik und die Reformpädagogik oder Pädologie (Pädagogische Zentrale), sondern auch das Programm der „Neuen Schule", obwohl es „*Pokret*" oder einigen der Hauptakteure dieses sozialkritischen pädagogischen Paradigmas der Vorkriegszeit nahe stand.

---

26 Unter den Studenten nannte er seine frühen Werke in seinen Vorlesungen Jugendsünden. Seine Offenheit für demokratische gesellschaftliche Prozesse zeigte er 1971, als er mit einem Vortrag zur Qualität des Studiums Studentenproteste und die „Besetzung" der Philosophischen Fakultät unterstützte. Auch in der Monografie *Sozialistische Pädagogik zwischen Etatismus und Selbstverwaltung* wurden 1982 Artikel aus den Jahren 1945–1952 in unveränderter Form abgedruckt, und dass sie, wie er selbst in der *Einleitung* sagt, vom Übergang von einer Pädagogik zur anderen zeugen.

27 Vlado Schmidt, „Kako naj danes pri nas razvijamo pedagoško znanost," in *Socialistična pedagogika med etatizmom in samoupravljanjem*, ed. Mira Simon (Ljubljana: Dopisna delavska univerza Univerzum, 1952/1982), 42. Schmidt, „Povojni uspehi," 259.

Schmidt lehnte das Programm der „Neuen Schule" ab, weil sie die Bedeutung sozialer Fragen vernachlässige: „Die Alternative entweder die ‚alte' oder die ‚neue' Schule war falsch, überhaupt leer, und innerhalb dieser Alternative bewegen wir uns heute nicht mehr. ‚Neue' und ‚Alte' Schule – beide standen im Dienst der volksfeindlichen Behörden."[28]

Die programmatische und personelle Verflechtung von *„Pokret"* und der *Pädagogischen Zentrale* und die gemeinsamen Auffassungen über die didaktische Modernisierung der Schule waren die Gründe, warum Schmidt den marxistischen Standpunkt bezüglich sozialer Fragen der Vorkriegsbewegung schlicht unterschätzte. Obwohl er in der *Pädagogik* die Bedeutung des sozialkritischen Ansatzes von *„Pokret"* in Hinsicht auf

> die konkrete Klassenumgebung [...] für die Entblößung der bürgerlichen Ausbeutung unseres Volkes anerkannte, steigt [seiner Meinung nach] die fortschrittliche Pädagogik in die politische Arena auf der Seite des Volkes und schafft damit Voraussetzungen für eine wirklich neue Schule. Die ‚Neue' Schule verlagerte jedoch den Schwerpunkt ihrer revolutionären Ideen auf die Einführung verschiedener methodischer Neuerungen und verkam so zu einem leeren, übertriebenen Methodisieren.[29]

Als Schmidt seine Kritik der Pädologie[30] auf ein Verständnis von Entwicklungsfaktoren, dem Einfluss der Vererbung und der Umwelt ausdehnte, wurden sogar die Sozialstudien der Vorkriegslehrerbewegungen kritisiert, und er argumentierte, dass Einsichten in widrige soziale Bedingungen die Lehrerverantwortung für den Erfolg von Kindern defätistisch beeinflussen könnten. Sie würden ihnen dazu dienen, das eigene Versagen mit den (negativen) Einflüssen des sozialen Umfelds oder mit den mangelnden Fähigkeiten von Kindern zu rechtfertigen. Schmidts negative Haltung gegenüber der *„Pokret"* und der Tradition wurde später, wie wir sehen werden, sogar von der Politik kritisiert.[31]

---

28 Schmidt, „Smernice," 19–20.

29 Vlado Schmidt, *Pedagogika – Skripta* (Ljubljana: Višja pedagoška šola v Ljubljani, 1948/1950), 20.

30 Vlado Schmidt, „Mladinoslovje – znak propadanja buržoazne pedagogike v dobi imperializma," *Popotnik* 67, Nr. 9–10 (1947): 257–260; auch Schmidt, *Pedagogika*, 23.

31 Franc Kimovec, „Pozitivna pedagoška tradicija in naša današnja stvarnost," in *Kongres pedagoških delavcev LRS na Bledu I*, ed. Vladimir Bračič (Ljubljana: DZS, 1950), 35.

Schmidt wusste sicherlich, dass in den ersten Nachkriegsjahren die ehemaligen Mitglieder von „*Pokret*“ sich sogar selbst von der Bewegung abgewendet hatten. Martin Mencej, einer der prominentesten Initiatoren der „*Pokret*“[32], veröffentlichte 1946 in der Zeitschrift *Moderne Schule* einen Artikel mit dem Titel *Arbeitsschule – eine fehlgeleitete Richtung in der Pädagogik.*[33] Die Arbeitsschule war vor dem Krieg ein geradezu erstrangiges didaktisches Moment von „*Pokret*“. Diese Wendung gegen die Arbeitsschule kommentiert Mencej in seinem persönlichen Geständnis von 1988: „Damals gab es in der Sowjetunion ein ‚*postanovljenje*‘[34], dass dieses pädagogische Experimentieren in der Schule eingestellt werden sollte [...] und dass man das Lernen in der Schule betonen sollte, weil es die Sache des Schülers ist zu lernen und sich Wissen anzueignen.“[35]

Mencej behauptet, dass er mit dem *Dekret* nicht einverstanden sei, weil „es die pädagogische Konzeption ablehnt, dass Psychologie und andere Momente zur Lösung von Problemen in der pädagogischen Arbeit eingesetzt werden.“[36] Diese Meinungsverschiedenheit lässt sich jedoch nicht aus dem Artikel ableiten, was bedeutet, dass die Redaktion der *Modernen Schule* von dem Autor gegen seinen Willen verlangte, das Dekret zu berücksichtigen. Aus dieser Aussage geht klar hervor, dass die Redaktion Beiträge aus der Sicht der sowjetischen Orthodoxie zensierte.

Schmidt schreibt die *Richtlinien* jedoch nicht per Diktat, sondern lehnt die pädagogische Tradition der Vorkriegszeit entgegen seiner vollen persönlichen Überzeugung ab. Geradezu süchtig nach einem militärischem Sieg behandelt er es in militaristischer Terminologie:

---

32 Mencej war in den 1950er Jahren politischer Häftling auf dem Goli otok, wo nach dem Informbiro echte und angebliche Sympathisanten der Sowjetunion oder des Stalinismus inhaftiert wurden.

33 Martin Mencej, „Radna škola – pogrešan pravac u pedagogici,“ *Savremena škola* 1, no. 1 (1946): 26–36.

34 Postanovljenje (Russisch) *Dekre*t; wir schließen daraus, dass Mencej auf den Erlass des Zentralkomitees der VKPb über pädologische Verzerrungen im System der Volkskommissariate für Bildung verweist, den auch Schmidt (in „Mladinoslovje“ und „Pedagogika“) zitiert. Beide Autoren führen nämlich als typische Formen der „Verzerrung“ laut *Dekret* „Methodisierung“ und „Experimentierung“ an.

35 Autor, „Intervju,“ 47.

36 Autor, „Intervju,“ 47.

> Der Kampf ist noch nicht vorbei [...] Der Kampf zwischen reaktionären und fortschrittlichen Kräften findet nicht nur auf wirtschaftlichem, politischem und militärischem Gebiet statt, sondern auch auf kulturellem, wissenschaftlichem und damit auch auf dem Gebiet der pädagogischen Theorie und Praxis. Viele Wissenschaften oder Wissenschaftsbereiche haben sich unter dem Druck der Reaktion von ihrer Grundaufgabe entfernt, um den Bedürfnissen der Menschen zu dienen [...], all dies gilt auch für die Pädagogik [...]. Daher wäre es unvernünftig zu erwarten, dass unter Bedingungen von menschenfeindlicher Macht [vor dem Krieg; Anm. des Verfassers] Pädagogik und Schulwesen reibungslos für die Bedürfnisse der Massen funktionieren würden [...] Es ist notwendig, unsere pädagogische Mentalität umzuerziehen. [...] Unsere pädagogischen Generationen sind unter dem Einfluss der deutschen Pädagogik aufgewachsen [...] All dies erfordert eine äußerst kritische Haltung gegenüber der deutschen Pädagogik. Das Studium der russischen und sowjetischen pädagogischen Literatur wird uns dabei von großem Nutzen sein.[37]

Das Studium der russischen und sowjetischen Pädagogik stellt Schmidt als methodologisches, theoretisches Werkzeug gegen die bisherige „Germanisierung" aller Richtungen in der jugoslawischen Pädagogik vor:

> Wir müssen die deutsche Definition des pädagogischen Gegenstandes, den sie sich abstrakt vorstellten, vollständig ablehnen; auch die Entfremdung ihrer pädagogischen Theorie gegenüber der Praxis wird abgelehnt sowie auch die, die Spekulation als Methode ihrer pädagogischen Arbeit, [...] die Leitlinien für ihre Arbeit von einer statischen Konzeption nimmt, aus der spirituellen Welt und nicht aus dem praktischen Leben (es handelt sich um das geistlich-pädagogische Paradigma; Anm. des Verfassers). Wir werden ihren Formalismus in der Lehre, Bürokratie in der Bildungsorganisation (das herbartianische Paradigma) verwerfen sowie ihre pedantische Einstellung gegenüber Kindern und das übermäßige Methodisieren ihrer ‚neuen Schulen' (reformpädagogisches Paradigma; Anm. des Verfassers).[38]

Es ist Ermessenssache, ob man diesen Text als ein Produkt der Sowjetisierung ansieht. Wenn ja, dann versteht Schmidt es als methodologisches, wissenschaftliches, theoretisches Werkzeug gegen die bisherige „Germanisierung". Die von ihm verwendeten Quellen weisen deutlich darauf hin, dass es einerseits darum geht, sich mit allen gängigen pädagogischen Paradigmen der Vorkriegszeit (Geisteswissenschaftliche Pädagogik, Herbartianismus, Reformpädagogik und sogar die sozialkritische Pädagogik von „*Pokret*")

---

[37] Schmidt, „Smernice," 17–18.
[38] Schmidt, „Smernice," 17–18.

auseinanderzusetzen, sich andererseits aber mit der jugoslawischen marxistischen Pädagogik, die er als ein historisch völlig neues pädagogisches Paradigma versteht, zu beschäftigen.

Schmidt weist auf drei Quellen marxistischer Pädagogik hin: a) auf die Verbundenheit mit den Interessen der Massen, den Bedürfnissen des Volkes und seinen Kampf, b) auf fortschrittliche, demokratische und humanistische Gedanken in der slowenischen Pädagogikgeschichte und c) auf das Studium der russischen und sowjetischen pädagogischen Literatur.[39] Interessanterweise wird 1945 als Quelle der marxistischen Pädagogik nicht das Studium der marxistischen Literatur angeführt. Diese Bezugnahme wird erst nach 1952 wichtig.[40]

Das „neue" Paradigma würde man heute als sozialkritische Pädagogik bezeichnen, wenn man Schmidts drei Hauptmerkmale der marxistischen Pädagogik betrachtet,[41]: das *Epistemologische* – das kritische Analysieren des ideologischen Diskurses und das Aufdecken der Hintergründe bei den Klasseninteressen von pädagogischen Praktiken; das *Normative* – das Erziehungsziel ist die individuelle Emanzipation, die aber nur durch die Emanzipation der Gesellschaft, durch die Aufhebung von Machtverhältnissen und die Bejahung der Bedürfnisse des Volkes bzw. der Masseninteressen durchgeführt werden kann; und das *Methodische* – wir erziehen das Individuum im Prozess der Kollektivbildung, *die Gemeinschaft ist das Medium der Erziehung.*[42] Schmidt begründet seine Zurückhaltung gegenüber Vorkriegsbewegungen damit, dass weder *„Pokret"* noch die *Pädagogische Zentrale* den Diskurs darüber führten, wem die „Neue Schule" diente. Dieser erkenntnistheoretische „Ausrutscher" wurde selbst von *„Pokret"*-Mitgliedern nach dem Krieg kritisch gewürdigt. In der Abhandlung von 1946 schreibt Mencej auch kritisch über die pädagogischen Richtungen der Vorkriegszeit und meint, dass „sie sich in der Regel auf das Gebiet der Methodik und Didaktik beschränkten, ohne den

39 Schmidt, „Smernice," 19.

40 Schmidt, „Smernice," 19–21; auch: Vlado Schmidt, „Kako naj danes," 44.

41 Schmidt, *„Smernice"* (1945/1982), Schmidt *„Vzgajamo mladino zmagovitega ljudstva"* (1947/1982); *die gleichen Einstellungen* finden wir in der oder einer anderen Form in Schmidts Beiträgen zum Thema „sozialistische Pädagogik zwischen Etatismus und Selbstverwaltung" (1970/1982) und in dem Artikel *„Značilnosti marksistične pedagogike"* (1974/1982).

42 Mehr über pädagogische Paradigmen in "Conflicting Paradigms" von Medveš, 14–17.

ideologischen Hintergrund dieser Strömungen kritisch zu analysieren."[43] Die jugoslawische Pädagogik hat nach dem Krieg als einen wesentlichen Schritt in der Entwicklung der marxistischen pädagogischen Theorie die ideologische Kritik etabliert, wobei sie aber wegen der Anwendung einer mechanischen Dialektik und eines verkürzten Verständnisses des historischen Materialismus', besonders in den ersten Nachkriegsjahren, an Schärfe und epistemischem Gehalt verlor. So konnte sie die materialistische (bzw. sozialkritisch fundierte) Kritik nicht als eine weiterführende hermeneutische Inspiration nutzen, blieb vielmehr in Dogmatismus und oberflächlichem Schematismus bezüglich des Verhältnisses von Gesellschaft und Bildung befangen.

Das Bildungsziel der Emanzipation ist nur in der Bindung der Pädagogik an das Interesse der Massen, des Volkes möglich. In der „*Menschenmenge*" und dem „*Volk*" könnten wir die Metapher dessen erkennen, was wir heute Zivilgesellschaft nennen. Angesichts des charakteristischen ideologischen Diskurses jener Zeit würde man erwarten, dass das Interesse des Proletariats statt des Interesses der Massen hervorgehoben würde. Aber für Schmidt war das Proletariat eindeutig nicht die „Quelle" seiner pädagogischen Vision auf dem Weg zu einer emanzipierten Gesellschaft frei von Machtverhältnissen, Klassen- und Parteikonflikten. Die ablehnende Haltung gegenüber der pädagogischen Tradition der Vorkriegszeit weist somit auf tiefgreifende theoretische Differenzen hin und nicht nur auf die Ablehnung von „Methodisieren" und „Experimentieren". Leider waren es gerade diese theoretischen Abweichungen, die die *Intoleranz des aufkommenden marxistischen Deutungsdiskurses gegenüber allen anderen pädagogischen Paradigmen schufen und statt einer fruchtbaren Vereinigung einen Traditionsbruch verursachten.*

Diskontinuität Nr. 3: Unterschiedliche Einstellungen zur Sowjetisierung (der Pädagogik) in Jugoslawien

Schmidt hebt in den *Leitlinien* dreimal die Notwendigkeit hervor, russische und sowjetische Literatur zu studieren. In Verbindung mit den *Leitlinien* sollte man eine für unsere Forschung relevante Episode analysieren. Die serbokroatische Übersetzung der *Leitlinien* wurde in der *Osijeker Sammlung* von Schmidts

[43] Mencej, „Radna škola," 26.

Abhandlungen und in der ersten Ausgabe der Zeitschrift *Moderne Schule* 1946 veröffentlicht, die in diesem Jahr als jugoslawische Bundeszeitschrift erschien. In den ersten Nachkriegsjahren (bis zur Umbenennung in pädagogische Fachzeitschrift *Pädagogik* 1962) spielte *Moderne Schule* eine zentrale ideologische Rolle, auch mit der Absicht, den sowjetischen Einfluss auf die Entwicklung der marxistischen Pädagogik zu sichern. Es ist indikativ, dass einige Schlüsselsätze der *Leitlinien* in der *Modernen Schule* in Kurzform veröffentlicht wurden. An allen drei Stellen, an denen Schmidt im Original das Studium der „russischen und sowjetischen pädagogischen Literatur" nannte, wurde in der Übersetzung das Wort „Russisch" weggelassen, sodass der entsprechende Satz in der Übersetzung immer lautet: „Studien der sowjetischen pädagogischen Literatur."[44]

Die offensichtlich mit der (falschen) Übersetzung verbundene dogmatische Korrektur gegenüber dem Original bietet Ansatzpunkte für manche Überlegungen, die für das Verständnis des Phänomens der Sowjetisierung der Pädagogik im jugoslawischen Raum wichtig sind. Wurde das Wort „russische Pädagogik" durch redaktionelle Selbstzensur oder gar durch externe ideologische Zensur entfernt? Auf jeden Fall zeigt uns dies, dass die Einstellung zur Sowjetisierung nicht im gesamten Territorium Jugoslawiens dieselbe war. Offenbar war in einigen Gegenden Jugoslawiens Schmidts Einschätzung in den *Leitlinien*, vorrevolutionäre russische Pädagogen aus der Zeit des zaristischen Russlands Belinsky, Dobrolyubov und Ushinsky als die „fortschrittlichsten Pädagogen der zweiten Hälfte des 19. Jahrhunderts" zu benennen, störend. Auch Batinić und Radeka sehen hypothetisch die Weglassung des Wortes „russisch" als Zensur, auch durch politische Kontrolle, die in diesem Umfeld (Belgrad, Serbien) stärker war. Dies wird auch durch die oben erwähnte Erfahrung von Mencej bestätigt.

Die oben erwähnte Hypothese ist tatsächlich wahrscheinlicher, also dass das Wort „russisch" vom Autor selbst weggelassen worden ist (Selbstzensur). Schmidt gab nämlich später einige Hinweise, die zeigen, dass die Bindung an die Sowjetunion auf der Ebene der zentraljugoslawischen herrschenden Elite und auch in Serbien, in Belgrad, besonders stark war.[45]

44 Vlado Šmit, „Smernice savremenog pedagoškog rada," *Savremena škola* 1, no. 1 (1946): 18, 20, 25.

45 Radeka und Batinić, „Pedagogija i školstvo," 111.

Diskontinuität Nr. 4: Die marxistische Pädagogik basiert auf dem diamatischen Marxismus

Der Referenzapparat dieser ersten pädagogischen Texte der Nachkriegszeit wirft heute die Frage auf, ob die Nachkriegspädagogik in Jugoslawien ihr marxistisches Interpretationsparadigma durch ein ernsthaftes Studium des Marxismus entwickelt hat. Wenn die jugoslawische Pädagogik von 1945 bis 1948 zu irgendeinem Zeitpunkt unkritisch die sowjetische übernommen hatte, so ist es gerade das Verständnis des Marxismus. Verweise auf übersetzte sowjetische Pädagogik-Lehrbücher sind in Schmidts Schlüsseltexten von 1945 bis 1949[46] nicht üblich. In der *Pädagogik* gibt es keine Verweise, nur im dritten Teil empfiehlt er den Studenten, sich mit den Grundkonzepten der Didaktik aus Goncharovs Lehrbuch für die Sekundarstufe vertraut zu machen.[47] Auch Verweise auf Texte aus der Zeitschrift *Sowjetische Pädagogik* (*Совéтская педагóгика*) sind selten. So zitiert Schmidt in seinen Veröffentlichungen 1945–1948/49 Ogorodnikov, Skatkin, Kornilov, Krupskaya, Rubenstein, häufiger Marx oder Engels, *am häufigsten* politische und philosophische Texte von Stalin, Lenin und die Schlussfolgerungen des Zentralen Ausschusses der VKPb. Dies lässt den Schluss zu, dass der Prozess der Sowjetisierung der Pädagogik unmittelbar nach dem Krieg eher von der Übertragung der politischen Ideologie und der sowjetmarxistischen Theorie als der Pädagogik selbst geprägt war. Die von 1945 bis 1949 als Studienmaterial entstandenen Werke sind von kurzer Dauer, wie Schmidt später selbstkritisch schrieb[48], und wurden bereits in den 1950er Jahren nicht mehr als Studienliteratur verwendet.

Bei der Entwicklung der „marxistischen Pädagogik“ stützten sich die Autoren in den ersten Nachkriegsjahren eher auf den sowjetischen Marxismus (Stalin, Lenin, Schlussfolgerungen des Zentralkomitees der VKPb), später von jugoslawischen Theoretikern diamatischer Marxismus[49] benannt als auf die Studien marxistischer Klassiker. In all den Nachkriegsjahren gab

---

[46] Vlado Schmidt, „Smernice“; tudi Vlado Schmidt „Mladinoslovje“ in Vlado Schmidt *Pedagogika – skripta* (Ljubljana: Višja pedagoška šola, 1948–1950).

[47] Schmidt, *Pedagogika*, 127.

[48] Schmidt, „Povojni uspehi,“ 264.

[49] Radovan Teodosić, *Основе научног педагошког наслеђа, декаденција буржоаске и ревизионизам совјетске педагогике* (Beograd: Znanje, 1952).

es in der Entwicklung der jugoslawischen marxistischen Pädagogik keinen sogenannten Neomarxismus oder kritischen Marxismus. Der Neomarxismus wird üblicherweise mit der sogenannten „Frankfurter Schule" für Philosophie (Theodor Adorno), mit der kritischen Gesellschaftstheorie, und mit Namen wie Herbert Marcuse, weiter mit György Lukács, Antonio Gramsci, Walter Benjamin, Jean-Paul Sartre und Louis Althusser, Jon Elster, Ernst Bloch und anderen in Verbindung gebracht. Im Skript *Pädagogik* wird das Vertrauen auf den „östlichen Marxismus" besonders im Kapitel *Philosophische Grundlagen der Pädagogik* deutlich. Bei der Definition des erkenntnistheoretischen und philosophischen Rahmens der Bildungstheorie verwendet Schmidt die folgenden Texte als grundlegende Quellen: *Über den dialektischen und historischen Materialismus* (von J. V. Stalin), *Eine kurze Geschichte der VKPb, Das VKPb-Programm* (März 1919). Die erkenntnistheoretische Grundlage der Bildungstheorie und die Gültigkeit und Legitimität von Erziehungszielen sind nicht das Ergebnis wissenschaftlicher Forschung der Gesellschaft, der Interessen der Massen oder des Volkes, sondern die Anwendung des historischen und dialektischen Materialismus, der der Erziehung nur eine gesellschaftliche Rolle zuschreibt. Die Einbettung in die Gesellschaft ist folglich das „absolute" Ziel der Erziehung. Als Dogma wurde die These entwickelt, dass jede Gesellschaftsklasse geschichtlich im revolutionären Machtkampf eine fortschrittliche Pädagogik fördert, bei Machteroberung jedoch ihre historisch fortschrittliche Rolle in der Bildung durch eine reaktionäre ersetzt. Im Kampf um die Macht betont Schmidt also die Bedeutung der ausbildenden Funktion, die für ihn immer fortschrittlich ist, aber wenn man an die Macht kommt, stellt man die erzieherische Funktion in den Vordergrund, um somit die bestehenden Verhältnisse und Beziehungen zu festigen.[50]

In dieser theoretischen Beweisführung könnten wir *schließlich den Hauptgrund für die Diskontinuität und für die Ablehnung aller pädagogischen Bewegungen der Vorkriegszeit im Königreich Jugoslawien erblicken*, da nach dieser harten Klassenlogik der Bildung alle Bewegungen mit der bürgerlichen Gesellschaftsordnung kontaminiert seien. Dieser theoretische Rahmen bildete die Grundlage für die radikalen Diskontinuitäten zwischen der

50 Vlado Schmidt, *Zgodovina pedagogike in šolstva na Slovenskem* (Ljubljana: Delavska enotnost, 1988), 176–178.

Vorkriegs- und der Nachkriegszeit. Dies ging so weit, dass die Autoren sogar ihre erfolgreiche fachliche Vorkriegsarbeit aufgegeben hatten.[51]

Diskontinuität Nr. 5: Pädagogik ist eine soziale, keine humanistische Wissenschaft; Bildung ist die Einbindung in die Gesellschaft und nicht die Entwicklung der Persönlichkeit

Die Wahrheit über die Erziehung kann man laut Schmidt nur durch das Erkennen des gesellschaftlichen Charakters der Bildung erreichen. Ihre expliziten und verdeckten Ziele werden immer vom sozialen Hintergrund diktiert. Sie ist deduktiv durch ideologische Kritik erreichbar. Diese radikalen Thesen zum Sozial- und Klassencharakter der Erziehung sind charakteristisch für die ersten Nachkriegsjahre. In den Jahren 1952 und 1966 plädierte Schmidt statt dieser einseitigen Erkenntnistheorie für ein Gleichgewicht von Deduktion und Induktion[52], *ideologischer Kritik und empirischer Forschung.*

Mit dieser erkenntnistheoretischen Wende beginnt eine neue Phase in der Entwicklung der jugoslawischen Pädagogik. Auf die erkenntnistheoretische Wende im Jahr 1952 folgte später eine Wende im Verständnis von Erziehungs- bzw. Bildungszielen, als Schmidt bei der Gestaltung der Selbstverwaltungspädagogik anstelle der bisherigen kollektivistischen

---

[51] Wie radikal Schmidts Traditionsbruch 1946 war, zeigt die Tatsache, dass er seine eigene berufliche Vorkriegstätigkeit völlig abwertete. Laut Vid Pečjak (*Nastajanje psihologije*, Ljubljana: Dopisna delavska univerza Univerzum, 1983; 372) war er der Pionier der angewandten Psychologie in Slowenien und beschäftigte sich von 1938 ab in der Berufsberatungsstelle der Region Banovina mit Psychotechnik und Testverfahren. Er hat sogar bei der slowenischen Anpassung eines Testes zur Messung der Intelligenz mitgewirkt. 1947 schrieb Schmidt über dieses eigene Werk: „Wenn wir berücksichtigen wie wir bereits darauf hingewiesen haben, dass die geistigen Fähigkeiten eines Kindes nicht nur eine Bedingung des Lernens sind, *sondern in erster Linie das Ergebnis des Lernens und* dass jede Fähigkeit ein Produkt der Entwicklung ist, fällt noch mehr die prinzipielle Unregelmäßigkeit des Prüfverfahrens auf. – Neben den Experimenten einiger Lehrer wurde diese falsche Methode auch von der ehemaligen Berufsberatungsstelle in Ljubljana unter der Leitung von Dr. Vlado Schmidt eingesetzt." (Schmidt, „Mladinoslovje", 263); Das Zitat wird 1949 in *Pädagogik* (*Pedagogika*, 56), wiederholt.

[52] Vlado Schmidt, „Kako naj danes," 52–54; so Vlado Schmidt auch in „Metodologija šolske reforme," 99–101.

Erziehung die Balance zwischen individueller Persönlichkeitsentwicklung und Einbettung in die Gemeinschaft hervorhob.[53] Die Vernachlässigung der Persönlichkeitsentwicklung des Einzelnen in den Jahren 1945–1952 könnte der Einfluss der Sowjetisierung respektive des Kollektivismus gewesen sein, ist aber, wie Schmidt selbst 1970/1982 schreibt, eher ein allgemein vorherrschender Glaube in der Nachkriegszeit. Es ist notwendig, diese Nachkriegszeit zu verstehen. Sie war von einem Glauben an eine bestimmte soziale und moralische Absolutheit durchdrungen, angetrieben von empathischen Gefühlen gegenüber Ländern mit einer verwandten sozialen Ordnung und durchdrungen von „Dankbarkeit gegenüber dem Befreier".

> Es war eine Zeit, in der allgemein akzeptiert wurde, dass sich der Einzelne diszipliniert und aufopferungsvoll den Bedürfnissen der Gemeinschaft unterwerfen sollte – dies ist auch das Beste für seine persönliche Entfaltung ... Das Engagement für eine neue Gesellschaft, die Begeisterung für den gerade errungenen Sieg und der damalige Arbeitselan wurden im Glauben an eine konfliktfreie Gesellschaft gestärkt, die bereits Harmonie zwischen dem Individuum und der Gemeinschaft erreicht hat und somit auch für das individuelle Glück durch die Erziehung in der Gemeinschaft gesorgt ist.[54]

Wenn auch Schmidt in seinen späteren Werken auf die Frage zurückkommt, ob das Ziel der Erziehung die Entwicklung der Persönlichkeit des Einzelnen oder die Einbettung in die Gesellschaft ist, wird er die Einbettung in die Gesellschaft an die erste Stelle setzen und auf seiner „jugendlichen" Kritik beharren, dass der idealistischen Pädagogik

> der Bildungsprozess nicht nur das Hineinwachsen in eine Gemeinschaft, also einen sozialen Prozess bedeutete, sondern auch einen kulturellen, der das menschliche Wesen verwirklicht, ‚humanisiert', und die Pädagogik die Wissenschaft von der Kultivierung des Menschen ist. [...] Das ist ein pädagogisches Konzept des liberalen bürgerlichen Elitismus. [...] Dem gleichen Irrtum sollte auch die idealistisch-naturalistische ‚Pädagogik' verfallen. Sie verlangt nämlich, dass das Kind seine eigene, sich immer wieder verändernde Natur verwirklicht. Hier haben wir eine vielfältige Sammlung von Ansichten und Richtungen – von Rousseaus Ansichten,

---

53 Vlado Schmidt, „Socialistična pedagogika med etatizmom in samoupravljanjem," in *Socialistična pedagogika med etatizmom in samoupravljanjem*, ed. Mira Simon (Ljubljana: Dopisna delavska univerza Univerzum, 1970/1982), 13–14.

54 Schmidt, „Socialistična pedagogika," 8.

> von individualistischer Erziehung des Übermenschen von Nietzsche, der existenzialistischen Erziehungskonzeption bis hin zur ausgefeilten Jugendwissenschaft, die pädagogisches Geschehen auf psychologische Gesetze reduziert [...] und so bekommt man eine klassenunbestimmte, sozial farblose Pädagogik.[55]

Das Zitat von Schmidt erschien zum ersten Mal 1974 in dem Beitrag *Charakteristiken der marxistischen Pädagogik*. Schmidt bezieht sich hier nicht mehr auf Stalins Diamat oder auf *Die kurze Geschichte* des *VKPb*, sondern auf Marx, Engels und Lenin und untermauert noch andere Ausführungen mit Hinweisen von Bogdan Suchodolski und von den sowjetischen Autoren Rubenstein und Makarenko. Dem Marxismus bleibt er durchwegs treu, doch in seinen späteren Werken findet sich keine Spur von westlichem Marxismus, obwohl sich seine Kollegin Milica Bergant schon in den 1960er Jahren vom ostmarxistischen Deutungsdiskurs abwandte. 1950 bekam sie eine Assistentenstelle an der Philosophischen Fakultät in Ljubljana. Zum zweiten Interpretationskreis gehört der Referenzkreis der Autoren, auf dem M. Bergant drei Studienrichtungen aufgebaut hat: Pädagogische Soziologie, Familien- und Vorschulpädagogik.[56] Ihre Wendung ist nicht nur methodologisch, sondern auch inhaltlich, und es ist wichtig, dass die Konzepte der pädagogischen Vorkriegstradition, insbesondere der progressiven Tradition der Jugendforschung mit dem Konzept der freizügigen oder demokratischen, nicht-autoritären und kinderzentrierten Bildung, in allen drei Studienbereichen zurückfinden. Hinsichtlich der Einstellungen zur marxistischen Pädagogik in Jugoslawien ist bedeutungsvoll, dass ihre *Themen aus der pädagogischen Soziologie* nur auf Slowenisch veröffentlicht wurden

---

55 Vlado Schmidt, „Značilnosti marksistične pedagogike," in *Socialistična pedagogika med etatizmom in samoupravljanjem*, ed. Mira Simon (Ljubljana: Dopisna delavska univerza Univerzum, 1974/1982), 206–207.

56 Milica Bergant hat 1970 die *Themen aus der pädagogischen Soziologie veröffentlicht* (Ljubljana, CZ, 1970). Das war auch ein Universitätslehrbuch, wobei man darin keine Referenzen auf Autoren jenseits des Eisernen Vorhangs findet. Wir Studenten mussten aber mindestens acht Jahre vor der Ausgabe des Lehrbuchs die Referenzautoren kennen (z. B. Herbert Marcuse, Erich Fromm, Benjamin S. Bloom, Orville Brimm, Helmut Schelsky, August Aichhorn, Anna Freud, Jacques Berna, Réné König, Cramer Brown). Die Theorie der Sozialisation von Peter L. Berger und Thomas Luckmann mussten wir aber schon im Studienjahr 1966/67 kennen, als ihre Arbeit mit dem Titel *The social Construction of Reality* in den Vereinigten Staaten erschien.

und in anderen Regionen Jugoslawiens völlig unbekannt blieben, sodass sie die Entwicklung des marxistischen pädagogischen Deutungsdiskurses nicht beeinflussten. Auch das 1985 von Pädagogen der jüngeren Generation in Ljubljana organisierte Kolloquium zur VRO[57] hatte in Jugoslawien keine Wirkung. Das Kolloquium zur VRO mit dem Konzept einer „allseitig entwickelten Persönlichkeit" bedeutete in Slowenien eine entschiedene Wende des pädagogisch-theoretischen Denkens hin zur Kritischen Theorie, zur Psychoanalyse und zum Strukturalismus. Dieses Ereignis im Jahr 1985 könnte zumindest in Slowenien ein *Symbol für das Ende der Orientierung auf die Entwicklung der marxistischen Pädagogik* sein. Gleichzeitig jedoch beginnt sich der angelsächsische Einfluss auf die slowenische und jugoslawische Pädagogik zu verstärken. Dies eröffnet neue allgemeine Dilemmata für die Entwicklung der Pädagogik, insbesondere das Dilemma der Pädagogik als integrale Bildungswissenschaft. An den jugoslawischen Universitäten begann der Zerfallsprozess der Pädagogik gegen Ende der 1980er Jahre, als sich die Andragogik von der Pädagogik in eine eigenständige Wissenschaft und ein eigenständiges Studium löste. Gleichzeitig begannen auch andere Wissenschaften sich mit der Forschung im Bereich der Bildungswissenschaft zu befassen.

Während der Informbiro-Periode wird die Verbindung zur sowjetischen Pädagogik nicht abgebrochen

In den Nachkriegsjahren hat sich die jugoslawische Pädagogik selbst ins Abseits gedrängt: Sie rechnete mit der „bürgerlichen Dekadenz" ab, lehnte die heimische pädagogische Tradition ab, und das Informbiro zeigte den revisionistischen Charakter der sowjetischen Pädagogik.[58] Wo sollte man jetzt die Fundamente für den Ausbau des eigenen Weges finden? Bisher wurde angedeutet, dass mit dem Informbiro der sowjetische Einfluss zwar nicht unterbrochen wurde, doch ist der ideologische Einfluss stalinistischer Prägung nach und nach verblasst. Von sowjetischen Politikern, schon gar

[57] „Vsestransko razvita osebnost," *Problemi*, Nr. 4 (1985). VRO = Vsestransko razvita osebnost – allseitig entwickelte Persönlichkeit).

[58] Radovan Teodosić, *Основе научног педагошког наслеђа*.

nicht von Stalin, begegnen uns keine Notizen oder Zitate mehr. Unter den zitierten sowjetischen Autoren tauchen die Namen der russischen Psychologen Rubenstein, Leontiev, Kornilov, Tjeplov, Smirnov, Skatkin und der Pädagogen Kairo, Goncharov, Jesipow und Medinsky auf. Nach den 1950er Jahren ist A.S. Makarenko hochaktuell. Auch Aussagen wie z. B., dass „die sowjetische pädagogische Theorie und Praxis die höchste Stufe der Wissenschaft erreicht haben“[59], sind nicht mehr anzutreffen.

Ein interessantes Beispiel für die Post-Informbirozeit ist die Schaffung der ersten „gemeinsamen“ jugoslawischen Pädagogik. Es handelt sich um eine umfangreiche Monografie, die auf Serbisch, Kroatisch und Slowenisch veröffentlicht wurde. Die slowenische Fassung erschien zwischen 1968 und 1969 in zwei Teilen, *Pädagogik I (Pedagogika I)* und *Pädagogik II (Pedagogika II)*, mit einem Gesamtumfang von 1162 Seiten. Die Autoren der Beiträge kamen nur aus drei Republiken, aus Serbien (von der Philosophischen Fakultät in Belgrad, wissenschaftlichen Instituten und Verwaltungseinrichtungen), aus Kroatien (von der Philosophischen Fakultät in Zagreb und in Zadar, von der Pädagogischen Akademie in Rijeka und von der Musikakademie in Zagreb) und aus Slowenien (von der Philosophischen Fakultät in Ljubljana), was erneut zeigt, wie ungleichmäßig die Pädagogik um die Wende der 1970er Jahre entwickelt war, wenn man den Norden und den Süden Jugoslawiens vergleicht.

Referenzen und Bibliografien in der Monografie *Pädagogik I und II* bestätigen die These, dass sowjetische Autoren immer noch stark unter den Quellen präsent sind, insbesondere bei Autoren aus einigen jugoslawischen Regionen. So finden sich etwa bei Ljubomir Krneta im Kapitel *Intellektuelle Bildung* mehr als 30 Prozent sowjetische Quellen, etwa ein Viertel der sowjetischen Quellen findet sich in Nikola Potkonjaks Kapitel *Das Thema Pädagogik*, auch bei Radovan Teodosić, Nikola Vučenov und Milan Mirković. Diese Autoren stammen aus dem serbischen Raum. Die Monografie bedient sich umfangreicher Quellen von Klassikern des Marxismus, häufig wird auf einheimische Politiker und Marxisten verwiesen, was in der Monografie die nach wie vor hohe Bindung der Pädagogik an die Politik zeigt. Auch englische,

59 Mencej, „Radna škola,“ 34.

deutsche und französische berufspädagogische Quellen erscheinen bereits in den Monografien, jedoch nur selten philosophische Werke aus diesen Sprachgebieten. Es ist rätselhaft, warum das zentrale theoretische Kapitel der Monografie *Zweck und Organisation des Erziehungs- und Bildungssystems in der Sozialistischen Föderativen Republik Jugoslawien SFRJ* nicht von akademischen Pädagogen verfasst wurde. Die Autoren sind ein wissenschaftlicher Mitarbeiter am Institut für Pädagogische Forschung Serbiens und ein stellvertretender Sekretär für Bildung in Serbien. Dies könnte als Zeichen dafür gewertet werden, wie sich die Pädagogik bei der Definition normativer Fragen nationaler Bildung einer (zentralistischen, etatistischen) Politik verpflichtet hat, was sich in den folgenden Jahrzehnten als einer der grundlegenden Brennpunkte des Jugoslawien-Konflikts vor dem Zerfall des Staates im Jahr 1991 herausstellte.[60]

In der Monografie beruht der interpretative Schwerpunkt noch immer auf dem historischen und dialektischen Materialismus (um die 20 Prozent der Quellen und Referenzen). Unter den verwendeten Quellen sind keine Autoren des sogenannten westlichen Marxismus, obwohl der Einfluss des westlichen marxistischen Diskurses insbesondere in Kroatien, Slowenien und Serbien im Bereich der Philosophie, Soziologie, Wirtschaftswissenschaften und anderen Sozialwissenschaften sehr stark war.[61] Es ist auch bekannt, dass Versuche, den Einfluss des westlichen Marxismus in den 1970er Jahren zu stärken, auf eine scharfe Reaktion der jugoslawischen Partei- und Staatspolitik stießen, die heute von manchen als Zeit der Restalinisierung[62] oder, wie Pediček sagt, „marxistischen Dogmatisierung“ bezeichnet wird.[63]

---

[60] Zdenko Medveš, „Socijalistička pedagogija uhvačena u mit pravednosti jedinstvene škole i kulturno hegemoniju,“ in *Razvoj i aktualne tendencije pedagogije i školstva na području nekadašnje Jugoslavije*, ed. Edvard Protner (Maribor: Universität von Maribor Press), 93–98.

[61] Weltberühmte Phänomene aus dieser Zeit sind die Korčula School mit dem Zagreber Magazin *Praxis*, *Perspektive und Revija 57* aus Ljubljana.

[62] Roman Uranjek, „*Intervju z Vesno Milek: Če hočeš postati klasik, moraš biti najprej sodoben*,“ in *Sobotna priloga. Delo 5. 12. 2020* (Ljubljana: Tiskarna Delo, 2020), 39.

[63] Pediček, „Paradigme slovenske pedagogike,“ 365.

Kontinuitäten: Alternativen zur marxistischen Pädagogik in der ersten Nachkriegszeit

1950 wurde die Entwicklung der jugoslawischen Pädagogik durch den ersten *Kongress der Pädagogischen Arbeiter der Volksrepublik Slowenien* in Bled geprägt. Die einzelnen Kongressveranstaltungen sind so entscheidend, dass einige Theoretiker[64] darin ein symbolisches Ende der diamatischen bzw. der etatistischen Pädagogik sehen.

Der Kongress als Ganzes ist eine komplexe Geschichte, daher beschränken wir uns hier auf drei für unsere Diskussion relevante Veranstaltungen. Das Einführungsreferat mit dem Titel *Positive pädagogische Tradition und unsere gegenwärtige Realität* von Franc Kimovec, ein Mitglied des KPS-Zentralkomitees. Die Grundthese des Beitrags lautet, dass die Nachkriegspädagogik unter dem Einfluss des sowjetisch-dogmatisch verstandenen Verhältnisses zwischen sozialen Schichten und dem Klassencharakter der Bildung die fortschrittliche pädagogische Tradition des „*Pokret*“[65] ungerechtfertigt ablehnte. Kimovec, ein aktiver Bewegungsteilnehmer der Vorkriegszeit, belebte in seiner Zeitung die Idee einer Arbeitsschule wieder. Ein Sprecher der slowenischen Parteiführung vermittelte die Botschaft, dass die „*Pokret*“ die Grundlage für die Entwicklung der marxistischen Pädagogik sein sollte, anstatt sowjetische Quellen und Autoren zu übersetzen.[66]

Noch dramatischere Geschichten werden auf dem Kongress durch zwei Beiträge ausgelöst, der erste von Stanko Gogala *Interne Bedingungen eines qualitätsvollen Unterrichts* und der zweite von Iva Šegula *Die Bedeutung der Psychologie für die Erziehungs- und Schularbeit*. Iva Šegula[67] steht der Pädopsychlogie mit dem Anspruch nahe, das Kind und seine Perspektiven zu

---

[64] Pediček, „Paradigme slovenske pedagogike," 365.
[65] Kimovec, „Pozitivna pedagoška tradicija," 35.
[66] Kimovec, „Pozitivna pedagoška tradicija," 35.
[67] Iva Šegula hat als Forscherin das Projekt der Programmüberprüfung für die reformierte einheitliche achtjährige Grundschule begleitet. Nach dem Projektabschluss war sie die Leiterin des Pädagogischen Instituts der Universität von Ljubljana.

berücksichtigen, Stanko Gogala gehört nach seiner pädagogischen Sichtweise zur Geisteswissenschaftlichen bzw. Personalistischen Pädagogik.[68]

Die pädagogischen Ansichten der Autoren beider Schriften waren damals in Slowenien bekannt und akzeptiert. Am Kongress von Bled nahmen auch Pädagogen aus allen jugoslawischen Republiken teil, unter denen die Schriften von Šegula und Gogala für große Aufregung sorgten. Dragutin Franković aus Zagreb hat in der Zagreber pädagogischen Zeitschrift *Pedagoški rad* einen ausführlichen Bericht über den Kongress verfasst. Für unser Thema Kontinuität und Diskontinuitat in der Entwicklung der Vorkriegs- und Nachkriegspädagogik ist Frankovićs Blick auf die Arbeiten von Gogala und Šegula interessant. Er sagt:

> Der Beitrag von Dr. Gogala leitet sich nicht aus der Analyse der Unterrichtsqualität ab, wie sie heute an den Schulen der Volksrepublik Slowenien vorliegt. Er verweilt bei einer ‚hohen' Theorie über jede gute Lektion, über eine ideale Lektion und war daher vage und unpolitisch. Anstatt das Thema Qualitätsunterricht mit dem sozialistischen Charakter unserer Schule zu verbinden, gibt sich Dr. Gogala mit der formellen Feststellung zufrieden, dass das Ergebnis einer qualitativ hochwertigen Lehre eine sozialistische Persönlichkeit ist. An einigen Stellen gibt es sehr genaue Beobachtungen und Empfehlungen, aber insgesamt ist das Referat wenig hilfreich, um die Probleme des qualitativ hochwertigen Unterrichts an unseren heutigen Schulen zu lösen … Theoretisch gesehen (Aufteilung der Qualität des

---

68 Stanko Gogala war 1945 der einzige Dozent für Pädagogik, als die Universität Ljubljana ein organisiertes Studium erneuerte. Nach dem Krieg entwickelte er die geistige Pädagogik weiter und wandte sich nicht der marxistischen Pädagogik zu. Als Dozent war er der Politik ein Dorn im Auge. France Strmčnik berichtet (Gehör, Menschlichkeit, Individualität, Gegenwärtige Pädagogik 51, Nr. 5, (2000): 24), dass im Studienjahr 1953/1954 Pädagogikstudenten, die Kommunisten waren, damit beauftragt wurden, den idealistischen und nicht-marxistischen Charakter Gogalas bei den Vorlesungen zu entblößen. Die Studenten haben es mit der Erklärung, dass in Gogalas Vorlesungen nichts Nicht-Sozialistisches sei, abgelehnt und meinten, dass seine Vorlesungen demokratisch seien und auf eine humane Weise den Menschen und die Gesellschaft vorstellen. 1964–1966 war Gogala Dekan der Philosophischen Fakultät in Ljubljana, und 1966 präsentierte er mit dem Beitrag *La mia pedagogia* die jugoslawische Pädagogik beim internationalen Treffen der europäischen Spitzenpädagogen der damaligen Zeit (u.a. Bogdan Suchodolski und Henri Irenne Marrou) an der Universität Padua. 1970 erhielt er den nationalen Preis für das Bildungswesen. In der Begründung wurden unter anderem seine Verdienste um die Kontinuität der wissenschaftlichen und pädagogischen Arbeit an der Philosophischen Fakultät in Ljubljana nach dem Krieg hervorgehoben.

Unterrichts in eine Reihe einzelner Qualitäten, worin didaktische Prinzipien und allgemeine Bildungsaufgaben definiert werden, was aber alles mit den Begriffen aus der Philosophie, Kulturpädagogik, Axiologie und geisteswissenschaftlichen Psychologie ausgedrückt wird) ist der Beitrag weit entfernt von marxistisch-leninistischer Pädagogik, die ihre eigene Struktur, ihre eigenen Begriffe und ihren eigenen Umgang mit den Problemen des Unterrichts beinhaltet.[69]

Bei den Fragen um die Kontinuität ist Gogalas kurze Antwort in der *Gegenwärtigen Pädagogik* noch interessanter als Frankovićs Kritik. Offen gibt Gogala zu, dass er die Pädagogik als humanistische Wissenschaft entwickelt. Die Kontinuität seiner Nachkriegs- und Vorkriegspädagogik bringt er unmissverständlich zum Ausdruck: „Vielleicht lassen sich die Einflüsse dieser Strömungen in meinem Aufsatz und vor allem in der Terminologie wirklich nachzeichnen …, aber meine pädagogischen Vorkriegsbemühungen gingen vorwiegend in Richtung personalistische Pädagogik."[70] Frankovićs Vorwurf, „das Wort sozialistische Persönlichkeit bedeute für Gogala nur ein Formalismus, mit dem er seinen Standpunkt verbergen wollte",[71] hat Gogala aufgewühlt und er schrieb: „Ich lehne seine Behauptung kategorisch ab, ich sei zufrieden mit der formalen Feststellung, dass das Ergebnis einer qualitativ hochwertigen Lehre eine sozialistische Persönlichkeit ist."[72]

Genauso direkt reagiert Gogala auf den Zweifel von Franković über die Terminologie. Er ist sich wohl bewusst, dass der Vorwurf unangemessener Terminologie unter anderem darauf abzielt, sowjetische Autoren nicht zu verwenden, was Franković bereits in anderen Beiträgen kritisiert hatte, da sie eine kritische Haltung gegenüber der sowjetischen Didaktik befürworteten.[73] Gogalas Antwort auf den Vorwurf ist für jene Zeit unglaublich aufrichtig:

Hauptsache, ich habe die Begriffe wissenschaftlicher Pädagogik verwendet, … an vielen Stellen konnte ich mich auf sowjetische pädagogische Literatur und Terminologie verlassen. Es stimmt aber auch, dass ich in meiner Arbeit viele Dinge

[69] Dragutin Franković, „Prvi kongres pedagoških radnika NR Slovenije," *Pedagoški rad* I, no. 9–10, (1950): 600.
[70] Gogala, „Odgovor D. Frankoviću," 103.
[71] Franković, „Prvi kongres," 600.
[72] Gogala, „Odgovor D. Frankoviću," 103.
[73] Franković, „Prvi kongres," 599.

> erwähnt habe, die in dieser und anderer pädagogischer Literatur nicht enthalten sind, und mich darin auf persönliche Weise ausgedrückt habe.[74]

Der Beitrag von Šegula ist ein Wendepunkt für die slowenische Pädagogik. Sie weist auf viele Thesen hin, die den damaligen Ansichten über die Bedeutung der Entwicklungspsychologie für die Pädagogik direkt widersprechen. Der Beitrag ist so herausfordernd, dass er später für einige Autoren zum Symbol für das Ende der Periode der diamatischen bzw. etatistischen Pädagogik wurde.[75] In seinem Bericht über den Bleder Kongress versteht Franković Šegulas Beitrag als eine theoretische Polemik gegenüber anderen Pädagogen. Er hebt besonders ihren Standpunkt hervor, dass der Einfluss der sowjetischen Pädagogik und der „inneren" Kritik der Pädologie zur Vernachlässigung der Psychologie und Pädopsychologie in der Pädagogik geführt habe. Šegula distanziert sich von der Pädologie, die als Anpassung der Erziehung an die Interessen des Kindes verstanden wird, und schreibt, wie auch Schmidt, die Pädologie sei in dieser Form Ausdruck der Krise der Verwirklichung bürgerlicher Bildungsziele im Imperialismus. Trotz dieser Distanz der Autorin weist Franković als wesentliche Botschaft des Beitrags darauf hin, dass die Forderung nach Berücksichtigung von Psychologie und Pädopsychologie in der Bildung und im Unterricht vor allem eine stärkere Rücksichtnahme auf das Kind bedeutet, was die Bedeutung gesellschaftlicher Ziele verringert.[76] Gleichzeitig erkennt Franković, dass im Hintergrund des Beitrags ein anderer interpretativer Diskurs existiert, der sich aus der Terminologie ergibt, die sich von der unter dem Einfluss der Sowjetisierung unmittelbar nach dem Krieg verwendeten pädagogischen Theoretiker unterscheidet. Der für Franković umstrittenste Punkt in der Arbeit ist der direkte Vorwurf des Autors, dass an dem „Vergessen" der Psychologie und des Kindes in der Nachkriegspädagogik der Einfluss der sowjetischen Pädagogik schuld sei, da sie mit ihrer Haltung zur Pädologie Misstrauen gegenüber der Kinderpsychologie verursachte, den gesellschaftlichen Zielen und Inhalten aber eine größere Wichtigkeit als den Perspektiven der Kinder zuschrieb.[77]

---

[74] Gogala, „Odgovor D. Frankoviću," 103.

[75] Pediček, „Paradigme slovenske pedagogike," 365.

[76] Iva Šegula, „Pomen psihologije za vzgojno in učno delo," in *Kongres pedagoških delavcev LRS na Bledu I*, ed. Vladimir Bračič, (Ljubljana: DZS, 1950), 115.

[77] Franković, „Prvi kongres," 601.

Franković bewertet Šegulas Beitrag als den besten auf dem Kongress und lobt, dass er

> konkret, materialistisch, auf der Grundlage der Praxis geformt ist und auch die Lösungen sind dialektisch ... Aber wir denken, dass mehr über die Pädopsychologie selbst gesagt werden sollte. Da ... Šegula vermutlich an die wissenschaftliche Psychologie des Kindes, die die marxistisch-leninistische Methodologie verwendet, gedacht hatte, hat sie weder dies klar genug formuliert noch Kritik gegen die bürgerliche Pädopsychologie, zu der sie kritisch sein sollte, geäußert.[78]

Der Franković-Bericht zeigt deutlich, dass der Kongress von Bled ein Beweis für die Pluralität des pädagogischen Denkens in den Jahren von 1945 bis 1950 war. Franković, der aus einem anderen Milieu kam, hat die Pluralität der pädagogischen Paradigmen schneller erkannt, da in Slowenien der Ideenpluralismus in den fachlichen Wissenschaftskreisen nicht als ein Problem gesehen worden ist. Franković war verärgert über die antisowjetischen Botschaften auf dem Kongress und auch über diejenigen von Kimovec, dem höchsten Parteifunktionär, der unter anderem die Arbeitsschule „lobte". Unter diesem Eindruck schließt Franković seinen Bericht über den Kongress von Bled dramatisch, fast im Stil eines „quo vadis Slovenien", ab. Er stellt ausdrücklich fest, dass eine Kontinuität mit der Vorkriegspädagogik nicht akzeptabel ist. Er schreibt:

> Der Kongress hat gezeigt, dass es in den theoretischen Ansichten zu den Problemen noch viele Unklarheiten gibt. In manchen Beiträgen und in Diskussionen sind die Überreste alter Vorstellungen und alter Terminologie (Hervorhebung vom Verfasser) trotz guten Willens, die Themen wissenschaftlich zu behandeln, klar erkennbar. Da es jedoch keinen ideologischen Kampf und keine Beseitigung solcher Fehler gab, könnten einzelne Kongressteilnehmer den Eindruck bekommen, dass wir in einigen Dingen zurück zum Alten, zur ‚Arbeitsschule'[79] und zur Pädologie, wie sie bei uns einst verbreitet war, zurückkehren. Ich sage nicht, dass dies eine Gefahr ist oder dass es absichtlich in diese Richtung geht (ich weiß nicht genug über die Situation in der Volksrepublik Slowenien), aber wir müssen darauf hinweisen,

---

78 Franković, „Prvi kongres," 602.

79 Nota bene: Franković war nach den Worten von Mencej (Autor, "Interview", 47) vor dem Krieg ein wichtiges Mitglied der „*Pokret*" in Kroatien und Befürworter der „Arbeitsschule". Sein Bericht zeigt klar die Wirkung von „postanovljenje" (*Dekret*) und die Vorstellung, dass ideologische Kritik und ideologischer Kampf Fehler in der Entwicklung von Wissenschaft oder Theorie beseitigen können.

um die Notwendigkeit intensiverer Arbeit für die Verbreitung der wissenschaftlich-pädagogischen Theorie hervorzuheben und den ideologischen Kampf im Geiste der Resolution III vom Kongress des Plenums des Zentralkomitees der Kommunistischen Partei Jugoslawiens zu entwickeln.[80]

Abschließende Gedanken mit einem Blick auf die Entwicklung bis zum Zerfall des Staates 1991

Die jugoslawische Pädagogik war in den ersten Nachkriegsjahren durch eine starke Abhängigkeit von der Politik, Philosophie und pädagogischen Theorie der sowjetischen Pädagogik gekennzeichnet. Die Übernahme sowjetischer Modelle war kein externes Diktat der sowjetischen Behörden, kein konkreter interner politischer Druck, sondern ein autonomer Prozess, der in der Gestaltung der jugoslawischen marxistischen Nachkriegspädagogik stattfand. In den ersten Nachkriegsjahren entstand diese Pädagogik nicht aus dem Studium der Klassiker des Marxismus, sondern als Ergebnis der Übernahme des interpretativen Diskurses des sogenannten diamatischen Marxismus'. In der Nachkriegszeit war der Prozess der Sowjetisierung der jugoslawischen Pädagogik am intensivsten. Man sah darin eine willkommene Alternative zur „Germanisierung" der Vorkriegszeit. Im Ergebnis brachte es eine erhebliche Diskontinuität mit der Vorkriegszeit, sogar die Ablehnung fortschrittlicher pädagogischer Bewegungen in Kroatien, Slowenien und Serbien.

Obwohl in Jugoslawien das Ziel der Entwicklung einer marxistischen Pädagogik in der Zeit nach dem Krieg bis in die 1980er Jahre vorherrschte, konnte in den ersten Nachkriegsjahren zumindest in Slowenien nicht von einer einheitlichen marxistischen Haltung gesprochen werden. Der Bleder Kongress 1950 beweist, dass das humanistische pädagogische Denken nach dem Krieg in ganz Slowenien ununterbrochen präsent war, und zwar in der personalistischen Pädagogik, die die Kultur- und Geisteswissenschaftliche Pädagogik der Vorkriegszeit nach dem Krieg am Leben erhalten hat, und in dem Engagement für die Pädopsychologie, d.h. für eine ausgewogene Berücksichtigung der Kinderentwicklung und ihrer Lebensperspektiven sowie für gesellschaftliche Bedürfnisse in der Bildungsplanung. Der Kongress bewertete die Übernahme der sowjetischen Pädagogik kritisch. Nach dem

[80] Franković, „Prvi kongres," 605.

Krieg war die akademische Pädagogik in Slowenien theoretisch plural und repräsentierte drei pädagogische Paradigmen:

(1) gesellschaftskritische Pädagogik mit marxistischem Deutungsdiskurs, (2) Geisteswissenschaftliche Pädagogik mit phänomenologischem Hintergrund und personalistischen Folgerungen und (3) Reformpädagogik, die sich in den 1960er Jahren mit dem Konzept der permissiven Erziehung beschäftigte sowie auch mit der Reform der Bildung von Menschen mit besonderen Bedürfnissen, insbesondere von Kindern und Jugendlichen mit emotionalen und Verhaltensproblemen.[81]

Die Politik in Jugoslawien sah die Pädagogik als ihr Eigentum – bis zum Zerfall des Staates. Ein glücklicher Umstand für die Pädagogik in den 1970er Jahren war die Ausrichtung der jugoslawischen Gesellschaft auf Selbstverwaltung. Die Orientierung eröffnete der Pädagogik zwei wichtige Perspektiven: zum einen die Möglichkeit, ein völlig neues, autochthones pädagogisches Konzept der Selbstmanagement-Pädagogik zu formulieren, zum anderen ermöglichte sie der Pädagogik eine kritische Haltung zum aktuellen Bildungsgeschehen und zur Gesellschaft im Allgemeinen. Die Politik beschuldigte das pädagogische Fachgebiet der Kontraproduktivität, des Negativismus, den sie mit einer angeblichen Kritik des Etatismus tarnen würde.[82] In den 70-ger Jahren ist Pädagogik-Etatismus zu einem Symbol für pädagogische Ideen und Programme geworden, die ohne Beteiligung der entsprechenden und eigentlich kompetenten Fächer als Produkt von Parteipolitik, Staatsverwaltung und Militär entstanden sind. Im Laufe der Geschichte zeigten diese Programme Tendenzen zur Homogenisierung des Bildungssystems, und sie tendierten zu einer kulturellen Hegemonie, die in den 1980er Jahren Bewegungen in Jugoslawien gegen Zentralisierung und Föderalisierung, leider auch mit deutlich nationalistischen Zielsetzungen, verstärkten. Das Motto „vom Etatismus zur Selbstverwaltung" wurde in den 1980er Jahren zu einem kritischen Dispositiv in der Pädagogik und im Schulwesen für die Beurteilung parteilicher und staatlicher Schulpolitik. Dieses demokratische Kriterium ermöglichte der Pädagogik, jede pädagogisch

---

81 Katja Vodopivec et al., *Eksperiment u Logatcu: pokušaj uvođenja novih koncepcija u vaspitni zavod* (Beograd: Savez društava defektologa Jugoslavije, 1974).

82 Emil Rojc, „Diskusija," in *Drugi posvet slovenskih pedagogov*, ed. Franc Pediček (Ljubljana: Zveza društev pedagoških delavcev, 1972).

relevante Entscheidung der Politik mit wissenschaftlichen Mitteln kritisch zu bewerten, und ggf. auch abzulehnen. Diese Rolle übernahm die Pädagogik in Slowenien bereits mit der Programmevaluation der achtjährigen Grundschule in den Jahren 1954–1965, und auch die Ablehnung des föderalen Schulreformprojekts von 1966 mit einheitlichen jugoslawischen Lehrplänen von 1984 ist eine Folge dieser kritischen Haltung. Genauere Forschungen könnten sogar der Hypothese nachgehen, ob die Pädagogik, die Erziehung, das Schulwesen sowie der Kampf um die Selbständigkeit der Pädagogik und des Schulwesens eine gewisse Rolle beim Zerfall Jugoslawiens gespielt haben.[83] Die radikale ideologische Kritik an der marxistischen Pädagogik in Slowenien beginnt mit dem interdisziplinären Kolloquium über die Allseitig entwickelte Persönlichkeit 1985[84], das die theoretischen Grundlagen für die Einordnung der slowenischen Pädagogik in die damaligen europäischen und weltweiten Trends legt. Das Kolloquium begründet die Pädagogik als empirische Wissenschaft und stellt damit eine Plattform für die umfassende Schulreform 1996, fünf Jahre nach der Entstehung des unabhängigen Staates Slowenien.

Primärliteratur

Autor, Oskar. *Intervju z Jožetom Jurančičem in Martinom Mencejem.* Maribor: Pedagoška fakulteta, 1988.

Franković, Dragutin. „Prvi kongres pedagoških radnika NR Slovenije.“ *Pedagoški rad* 1, no. 9–10, (1950): 597–605.

Gogala, Stanko. „Notranji pogoji kvalitetnega pouka.“ In *Kongres pedagoških delavcev LRS na Bledu I.*, editiert von Vladimir Bračič, 77–97. Ljubljana: DZS, 1950.

Gogala, Stanko. „Odgovor D. Frankoviću.“ *Sodobna pedagogika* 2, no. 2–3 (1951): 180–181.

Gogala, Stanko. *Izbrani spisi.* Ljubljana: Društvo 2000, 2005.

---

[83] Mehr in Medveš, „Socijalistička pedagogija,“ 68–71.

[84] „Vsestransko razvita osebnost,“ *Problemi*, no. 4 (1985).

Kimovec, Franc. „Pozitivna pedagoška tradicija in naša današnja stvarnost.“ In *Kongres pedagoških delavcev LRS na Bledu I*, editiert von Vladimir Bračič, 23–44. Ljubljana: DZS, 1950.

Krneta, Ljubo, Potkonjak, Nikola, Schmidt, Vlado und Pero Šimleša, ed. *Pedagogika I*. Ljubljana: Državna založba Slovenije, 1975.

Krneta, Ljubo, Potkonjak, Nikola, Schmidt, Vlado und Pero Šimleša, ed. *Pedagogika II*. Ljubljana: Državna založba Slovenije, 1975a.

Mencej, Martin. „Radna škola – pogrešan pravac u pedagogici.“ *Savremena škola* 1, no. 1 (1946): 26–36.

Pataki, Stjepan. „Akademija pedagoških nauka RSFSR v Moskvi – poročilo z letnega zasedanja 10–14. 9. 1945.“ *Savremena škola* 1, no. 1 (1946): 66–71.

Pečjak, Vid. *Nastajanje psihologije – knjiga pogovorov*. Ljubljana: Dopisna delavska univerza, 1983.

Pediček, Franc. „Vzgoja kot družbena funkcija.“ In *Drugi posvet slovenskih pedagogov, zbornik*, 99–111. Ljubljana: Zveza pedagoških društev Slovenije, 1972.

Pediček, Franc. *Pedagogika danes – Poglavja za antropološko snovanje slovenske pedagogike*. Maribor: Založba Obzorja, 1992.

Pediček, Franc. „Paradigme slovenske pedagogike – prikaz ideoloških nasprotij in obravnavanih vprašanj v slovenski pedagogiki (1945–1988).“ *Sodobna pedagogika* 41, no. 7–8 (1990): 363–396.

Potkonjak, Nikola. *Razvoj i shatanja u konstitutivnim komponentama pedagogije (1944/45–1991/1992*. Belgrad: Institut za pedagogiju i andragogiju Filozofskog fakulteta Univerziteta u Beogradu, 1994.

Potkonjak, Nikola. *Teorijsko-metodološki problemi pedagogije*. Beograd: Prosveta, 1977.

Rojc, Emil. „Diskusija.“ In *Drugi posvet slovenskih pedagogov*, editiert von Franc Pediček. Ljubljana: Zveza društev pedagoških delavcev, 1972.

Sagadin, Janez. *Nekateri glavni teoretsko-metodološki problemi v zvezi z ideološko preusmeritvijo povojne jugoslovanske pedagogike*. Ljubljana: Filozofska fakulteta, Oddelek za pedagogiko, 1984.

Sagadin, Janez. „Nekatere glavne teoretske in metodološke pomanjkljivosti naše poosvoboditvene pedagogike in njihovo premagovanje.“ *Sodobna pedagogika* 38, no. 9–10 (1987): 411–422.

Schmidt, Vlado. „Smernice sodobnega pedagoškega dela." In *Socialistična pedagogika med etatizmom in samoupravljanjem*, editiert von Mira Simon, 16–24. Ljubljana: Dopisna delavska univerza Univerzum, 1945/1982.

Schmidt, Vlado. „Vzgajamo mladino zmagovitega ljudstva." In *Socialistična pedagogika med etatizmom in samoupravljanjem*, editiert von Mira Simon, 25–41. Ljubljana: Dopisna delavska univerza Univerzum, 1947/1982.

Schmidt, Vlado. *Zgodovina pedagogike in šolstva na Slovenskem*. Ljubljana: Delavska enotnost, 1988.

Schmidt, Vlado. „Mladinoslovje – znak propadanja buržoazne pedagogike v dobi imperializma." *Popotnik* 67, no. 9–10 (1947): 252–267.

Schmidt, Vlado. *Pedagogika – Skripta*. Ljubljana: Višja pedagoška šola v Ljubljani, 1948–1950.

Schmidt, Vlado. „Kako naj danes pri nas razvijamo pedagoško znanost." In *Socialistična pedagogika med etatizmom in samoupravljanjem*, editiert von Mira Simon, 42–60. Ljubljana: Dopisna delavska univerza Univerzum, 1952/1982.

Schmidt. Vlado. „Pota naše pedagoške znanosti." *Naša sodobnost* 2, no. 9, (1954): 801–816.

Schmidt, Vlado. „Metodologija šolske reforme." In *Socialistična pedagogika med etatizmom in samoupravljanjem*, editiert von Mira Simon, 96–131. Ljubljana: Dopisna delavska univerza Univerzum, 1966/1982.

Schmidt, Vlado. „Socialistična pedagogika med etatizmom in samoupravljanjem." In *Socialistična pedagogika med etatizmom in samoupravljanjem*, editiert von Mira Simon, 132–146. Ljubljana: Dopisna delavska univerza Univerzum, 1970/1982.

Schmidt, Vlado. „Korak nazaj k starim zmotam." *Sodobna pedagogika* 21, no. 9–10, (1971): 353–357.

Schmidt, Vlado. „Značilnosti marksistične pedagogike." In *Socialistična pedagogika med etatizmom in samoupravljanjem*, editiert von Mira Simon, 205–218. Ljubljana: Dopisna delavska univerza Univerzum, 1974/1982.

Schmidt, Vlado. „Povojni uspehi in stiske pedagoške teorije in prakse. Intervju." *Sodobna pedagogika* 36, no. 7–8 (1985): 259–271.

Schmidt, Vlado. *Socialistična pedagogika med etatizmom in samoupravljanje*. Ljubljana: Dopisna delavska univerza Univerzum, 1982.

Schmidt, Vlado, France Strmčnik und Zdenko Medveš. „Pedagogika." In *Enciklopedija Slovenije*, 287–289. Ljubljana: Mladinska knjiga, 1994.

Strmčnik, France. „Posluh, človečnost, individualnost." *Sodobna pedagogika* 51, no. 5 (2000): 16–28.

Šegula, Iva. „Pomen psihologije za vzgojno in učno delo." In *Kongres pedagoških delavcev LRS na Bledu I*, editiert von Vladimir Bračič, 99–141. Ljubljana: DZS, 1950.

Šmit, Vlado. „Smernice savremenog pedagoškog rada." *Savremena škola* 1, no. 1 (1946): 17–25.

Teodosić, Radovan. *Основе научног педагошког наслеђа, декаденција буржоаске и ревизионизам совјетске педагогике*. Belgrad: Znanje, 1952.

Uranjek, Roman. „*Intervju z Vesno Milek: Če hočeš postati klasik, moraš biti najprej sodoben*." In *Sobotna priloga. Delo 5. 12. 2020*, 38–39. Ljubljana: Tiskarna Delo, 2020.

Vidmar, Tadej. „Ključni vidici institucionalnoga razvoja pedagogije kao akademske discipline u Sloveniji." In *Razvoj i aktualne tendencije pedagogije i školstva na području nekadašnje Jugoslavije*, editiert von Edvard Protner, 207–228. Maribor: Universität von Maribor Press, 2020.

Vodopivec, Katja, Bergant Milica, Kobal, M., Mlinarič, F., Skaberne, Borut und Skalar, Vinko. *Eksperiment u Logatcu: pokušaj uvođenja novih koncepcija u vaspitni závod*. Belgrad: Savez društava defektologa Jugoslavije, 1974.

„Vsestransko razvita osebnost." *Problemi*, no. 4 (1985).

Sekundärliteratur

Grupa autora. *Istorija Saveza Komunista Jugoslavije*. Belgrad: Narodna knjiga, 1985.

Jezernik, Božidar. *Titos Gulag auf der Insel Goli otok*. Hermagor: Hermagoras Verlag, 2014.

Kovač, Edvard. „Personalizem Stanka Gogale." *Sodobna pedagogika* 51, no. 5 (2000): 108–121.

Kroflič, Robert. „Avtoriteta in pedagoški eros" – temeljna koncepta Gogalove vzgojne teorie." *Sodobna pedagogika* 51, no. 5 (2000): 65–83.

Medveš, Zdenko. „Vzgoja kot doživetje absolutnega.“ *Sodobna pedagogika* 51, no. 5 (2000): 84–107.

Medveš, Zdenko. „Socijalistička pedagogija uhvačena u mit pravednosti jedinstvene škole i kulturno hegemoniju.“ In *Razvoj i aktualne tendencije pedagogije i školstva na području nekadašnje Jugoslavije*, editiert von Edvard Protner, 61–106. Maribor: Universität von Maribor Press, 2020.

Medveš, Zdenko. “Conflicting Paradigms in the Development of Slovene Pedagogy.” *Journal of Contemporary Educational Studies* 66, no. 3 (2015): 10–40.

Mollenhauer, Klaus. *Erziehung und Emanzipation*. München: Juventa Verlag, 1968.

Miovska-Spaseva, Suzana. „Dostignuča i proturječja u razvoju obrazovanja i pedagogije u Socijalističkoj Makedoniji (1945–1990).“ In *Razvoj i aktualne tendencije pedagogije i školstva na području nekadašnje Jugoslavije*, editiert von Edvard Protner, 187–206. Maribor: Universität von Maribor Press, 2020.

Radeka, Igor und Štefka Batinić. „Pedagogija i školstvo od završetka drugog svjetskog rata do kraja 1950-ih.“ In *Razvoj i aktualne tendencije pedagogije i školstva na području nekadašnje Jugoslavije*, editiert von Edvard Protner, 187–206. Maribor: Universität von Maribor Press, 2020.

Pirjevec, Jože. *Tito in tovariši*. Ljubljana: Cankarjeva založba, 2011.

Protner, Edvard. *Herbartistična pedagogika na Slovenskem: (1869–1914)*. Maribor: Slavistično društvo, 2001.

Šušnjara, Snježana. „Razvoj školstva u Bosni i Hercegovini nakon drugog svejskog rata do 1970-ih.“ In *Razvoj i aktualne tendencije pedagogije i školstva na području nekadašnje Jugoslavije*, editiert von Edvard Protner, 131–150. Maribor: Universität von Maribor Press, 2020.

Vidmar, Tadej. „Pedagogika na univerzi v Ljubljani od njene ustanovitve do začetka petdesetih let 20. stoletja.“ *Sodobna pedagogika* 67, no. 3 (2016), 32–48.

Vidmar, Tadej. „Oddelek za pedagogiko in andragogiko: krajša zgodovina oddelka in předmět Poučevanja.“ In *Slavnostni zbornik ob 100-letnici Filozofske fakultete Univerze v Ljubljani*, editiert von Barbara Pihler Ciglič und Gregor Pompe, 60–62. Ljubljana: Znanstvena založba Filozofske fakultete Univerze, 2019.

Vujisić-Živković, Nataša. „Konstitutivni diskontinuitet: školstvo i pedagogija u socijalističkoj Srbiji (1945–1990).“ In *Razvoj i aktualne tendencije pedagogije i školstva na području nekadašnje Jugoslavije*, editiert von Edvard Protner, 151–166. Maribor: Universität von Maribor Press, 2020.

Zorić, Vučina. „Obrazovna politika u socijalističkoj Crnoj Gori.“ In *Razvoj i aktualne tendencije pedagogije i školstva na području nekadašnje Jugoslavije*, editiert von Edvard Protner, 167–187. Maribor: Universität von Maribor Press, 2020.

Zorić, Vučina. „Nastanek, delovanje in perspektive razvja študijskega programa pedagogika v Črni Gori.“ *Sodobna pedagogika* 67, no. 3 (2016): 98–117.

Polytechnisation in the Hungarian Pedagogy: Learning from the Soviet Model

Lajos Somogyvári

Abstract: After Hour Zero new ideas and concepts spread in Hungary and transformed the public discourse about a desirable education in the post-WW2 situation. There was an overall consensus to create new content and methods of teaching in a democratic way, including bringing schools closer to real life. Working education or polytechnic education may be interpreted as a key tool in this development to establish a more egalitarian society for the future. My paper introduces the roots of polytechnic education in reform pedagogy and Marxist ideology, first appearing as an alternative approach after 1945, but during the communist takeover in 1948–1949, the whole pedagogy subordinated to the Party, which monopolized and exclusively defined the meaning of polytechnic education. I am going to present this transformation through Soviet translations, works of Hungarian scholars, and archival records: all of these illustrate the intention to indoctrinate the profession, aimed to follow the Soviet example directly. Mass media and propaganda played a crucial role in making a new language and world perception: polytechnic education was part of several mobilization campaigns from the late 1940s for more than one decade. The last important initiative of Stalin was to implement polytechnic education on a general level in 1952, but this first phase of polytechnisation was not a success story, because only a few, experimental trainings were introduced, without any coherence.

Keywords: polytechnic education, polytechnisation, propaganda, Soviet Union, Hungary, mobilization, democratic education

Introduction

Polytechnical education (in other words, education for work or labour education) as an umbrella term for the socialist education accompanied Soviet pedagogical discourses with varying intensity from 1917 to the late 1980s. This concept was originally elaborated by Marx when setting the programme of educating 'the whole man' (an old idea in a new exposition), combining the dimensions of *Bildung* of body and mind; adding technological or polytechnical training, the third element to this design.[1] The mixture of instruction and students' and teachers' participation in the productive

---

1 As Skiera cited Marx's triad: "Geistige Bildung – Körperliche Ausbildung – Polytechnische Erziehung", see: Ehrenhard Skiera, *Reformpädagogik in Geschichte und Gegenwart: eine Kritische Einführung* (München: Oldenbourg Verlag, 2009), 127. I can only refer here to the possible connections between Lebensreform, Reformpedägogik and working education, which need future investigation to discover in details.

work (the polytechnisation of schooling) had different phases in the Soviet Union: after the first period of experiments (labour schools) in the 1920s, the Stalinist direction opted for a return to a more traditional school system and stabilization; Khrushchev initiated the second wave of polytechnisation in the late 1950s.[2] The Zero Hour of 1945 created the opportunity to spread these notions all over the Central-Eastern European countries, based on the existing heritage of similar interwar initiatives, like sloyd (slöjd) education, using handicraft skills or reform schools. The present paper tries to describe the changing meanings of polytechnisation in Hungarian educational discourses between 1945 and 1953, from the new promise of democratic school in the transition period (1945–1948) through the communist takeover (1949) to the last Stalinist initiative and its direct aftermath (1952–1953).

My hypothesis is that the main characteristic of this development shows how the working education idea in the new democracy (including its various interpretations) capitulates when facing the political demands, and the discipline of the Party after the turning years of 1948 and 1949. The communist takeover took place parallelly in education, pedagogy, politics and other spheres, in which science became more and more dependent on the continuously changing decrees and directions of different central bodies of the State Party. In the first half of the 1950s, the practice and theory of education served the needs of the Party, lost most of its autonomy, restricted its operational area to translating the language of politics into the profession, fulfilling the expectations by transmitting and spreading the official messages through publications, conferences, meetings, seminars, training, propaganda, and so on.[3] The main focus of this process was learning from the Soviet Union, the role model of the transformation: different actors of education (politicians, scholars, teachers, etc.) used this reference as an argument to legitimise pedagogical interventions. There were different possibilities behind the surface of the monolithic structure to make such actions in everyday life under communism because the power was not as omnipotent as it wanted to

[2] Horst E. Wittig, *Die Marxsche Bildungskonzeption und die Sowjetpädagogik* (Bad Harzburg: Verlag für Wissenschaft, Wirtschaft und Technik, 1964). After the fall of Khrushchev, this topic lost its very significance, but remained an occasionally emerged reference point of the socialist education.

[3] The author sometimes feels a correspondence between *philosophia* as *ancilla theologiae* and the roles of every science during Stalinism, but this aspect leads us to another research field, namely, the political religion.

present itself to the subordinated society (my local research in Tab, Somogy County confirms this).[4]

Picture 1: The cover of the *Soviet Literature on Polytechnical Education.*[5]

---

4 To the „history from below" aspect, see: Larissa Zakharova, "Everyday Life Under Communism: Practices and Objects," *Annales HSS* 68, no. 2 (2013): 209–17.

5 *Szovjet irodalom a politechnikai oktatásról* (Budapest: Magyar–Szovjet Társaság Lap és Mozgalmianyag Kiadó Vállalat).

Sources and Methodology

The first picture shows the cover of a typical propaganda brochure, published sometime after 1949 by the *Magyar–Szovjet Társaság* (*MSZT, Hungarian–Soviet Society*), in the series *Our Ideal, the Soviet Union*. This handout offered translated summaries of articles and books related to the Soviet polytechnical education, gave detailed information and guide to presentations, curricular works, publications for instructors, teachers and other educationalists. The publisher was one of the many Friendship Societies from the Eastern bloc countries: in their definition, they worked on establishing cultural connections between the Soviet Union and the socialist countries, bringing Soviet culture closer to the audience, by organizing exhibitions, film festivals, theatre plays, and so on. At the same time, they were tools of Soviet cultural infiltration, designed to gain influence and manipulate public opinion in the satellite countries by demonstrating an attractive and desirable image of life in the Soviet Union.[6] As the citation from Rákosi (the general secretary of the Hungarian Workers' Party) stated at the top of the cover: "One of the biggest factors of our improvement is that we can use the immeasurable repository of the experiences of Soviet Union".

This is just an illustration of the first type of my sources, the introduction and translation of original Soviet pedagogical works, disseminating Marxist–Leninist (and Stalinist) beliefs about education, its goals and standards in the forms of books, booklets or articles. Writings by the Hungarian scholars, politicians, school inspectors, teachers, etc. constitute the second layer of the research corpus, printed in different volumes, newspapers (the most important one was *Szabad Nép/Free Nation*), pedagogical journals (*Köznevelés / Public Education*, *Pedagógiai Szemle/Pedagogical Review*) or in local dailies. One can interpret these reports as symbolic translations or transformations of the original role model, which tried to answer the following questions: How to use Soviet experience in Hungary? What could be the possible roles of parents, students and teachers during polytechnic implementation? A few archival records represent the first steps of polytechnisation – these documents belong to the third category of the analysed papers.

---

6 F. F., "Soviet Cultural Collaboration: The Role of the Friendship Societies in the Satellite States," *The World Today* 10, no. 5 (1954): 197–209.

Following the logic of Koselleck's famous concept of *Begriffsgeschichte*, I will outline the changes and continuities in the meanings of my basic ideas: polytechnisation, polytechnic education, and working education.[7] Notions like these established common activities, cultural practices, and identities, creating our social reality by words – that is one reason why we should understand their significance in the given historical context.[8] The starting point is the beginning of a radically new education, at the end of WW2; my study follows developments until the summer of 1955, in the era of re-Stalinization, just before the 1956 revolution, which was the other big interruption in the evolution of Hungarian education after 1945. Two main goals led my research through this study:

1. to describe the suggested meanings of polytechnisation/polytechnic education;
2. and to show the different ways of spreading this message to the public, revealing propaganda in action.

In this case, the biggest challenge to a present-day scholar is not to judge socialist education from a retrospective view, but seeing its characteristics through contemporary lenses: by doing so, polytechnisation becomes a term that may give a greater insight into a functioning communist system.

From the Uncertain Situation of Liberation and Occupation to the Total Communist Takeover (1945–1949)

1945, the end of the Second World War and the beginning of a New World brought ambivalent feelings to average Hungarian citizens: liberation from the Nazis and the brutal experience of occupation by the Soviet Red Army.

---

7 Reinhart Koselleck, *Futures Past: on the Semantics of Historical Time* (New York: Columbia University Press, 2004). Reinhart Koselleck, *Begriffsgeschichten. Studien zur Semantik und Pragmatik der politischen und sozialen Sprache* (Frankfurt am Main: Suhrkamp Verlag, 2006).

8 Peter L. Berger and Thomas Luckmann, *The Social Construction of Reality: A Treatise in the Sociology of Knowledge* (London, Penguin Books, 1966).

The first two years involved hope to achieve better education for a better world (albeit this utopia doomed to failure), and a possibility of democratisation in schools, but the rapidly intensifying sovietisation and cultural domination quickly extinguished these alternative pathways. The broader context of my topic is well-known thanks to the works of Viktor Karády and Péter Tibor Nagy: the changing ideas of polytechnisation and working education give a good lesson to us about how the ideological takeover of the social sciences and humanities took place in Hungary.[9]

Before 1949, the Marxist terms of polytechnical education or polytechnisation were unfamiliar in Hungarian discourses; working education or education for working appeared in sources with similar content. The ideal image of post-war education always contrasted new (modern, social, democratic) education and the old world (feudalism and/or Nazism): notions of community and working went hand in hand, in creating a new society everyone had to participate in production and reconstruction.[10] This model could be typified by liberal, humanistic, and nationalist views too in this early stage, but it turned out soon that real working education came true only in Soviet schools, on a high level of self-consciousness and individual motives.[11] The year 1949 was a turning point – both in Hungarian history and in polytechnic discourses; the communist takeover was completed in every sphere of life. In correlation with this, working education developed into a common topic of pedagogy in contrast to its receiving only the occasional remarks between 1945 and 1948.

---

9 Victor Karády and Peter Tibor Nagy, "Institutionalization and Professionalization of the Social Sciences in Hungary after 1945," in *Shaping Human Science Disciplines: Institutional Developments in Europe and Beyond*, ed. Christian Fleck et al. (Cham: Palgrave Macmillan, 2019), 289–325. Victor Karády and Peter Tibor Nagy, *Sociology in Hungary: A Social, Political and Institutional History* (Cham: Palgrave Macmillan, 2019), 65–92.

10 Zoltán Kiss, "Szociális nevelés, új módszerek," *Köznevelés* 1, No. 12 (1945): 13. Lajos Barankay, "A demokratikus nevelés történelmi hitele," *Köznevelés* 3, no. 5 (1947): 78.

11 György Szombatfalvy, "Nemzetnevelés vagy pártiskola?," *Magyar Nemzet* 3, no. 223 (1947): 1. László Faragó, "A Szovjetúnió nevelési rendszere," *Embernevelés* 5, no. 3 (1949): 128. Faragó was a faithful communist scholar, but in 1950, he was excluded from the Party and disciplinary work, and could only resume research in the late 1950s.

Legislation followed this change: the new regulations of teacher training included working education inside and outside of elementary schools (for example, in workshops); and using working education to build communities in special education.[12] In the afternoon, elementary students produced toys and other useful things to make a profit (which, according to the original idea, always referred to the precedent of Makarenko's pedagogical work), and the town hall of Budapest helped to support this new task with tools and work equipment.[13] The instructions were too general to implement the new activities, which is why lecturers and teachers did not exactly know how to interpret the term 'working education'. To resolve this problem, educational politics had to clarify its meaning through mass media and propaganda, suggesting that the only way is to follow the Soviet model.

Spreading the Message: Mass Media and Propaganda

Propaganda and mass mobilisation was an inherited characteristic of the Soviet-type systems, but this was true not just in the Eastern hemisphere.[14] In the Cold War context, both superpowers tried to convince the public about their own superiority by demonstrating advantage in the arms race, space race, or educational competition, to win the people's hearts.[15] In the polytechnisation process, the main issue was to advertise new indoor and outdoor school activities, showing only the positive side of working education, because many teachers worried about implementing polytechnics and feared a possible decline of quality in intellectual training.

---

12 "Melléklet a 65.500/1949. V.K.M. sz. rendelethez," *Köznevelés: A Vallás- és Közoktatásügyi Minisztérium rendeletei és közleményei* 5, no. 11 (1949): 72, 76.

13 "Városházi hírek," *Magyar Nemzet* 5, no. 157 (1949): 2.

14 Peter Kenez, *The Birth of the Propaganda State. Soviet Methods of Mass Mobilization, 1917–1929* (Cambridge: Cambridge University Press, 1985).

15 Gary D. Rawnsley, ed. *Cold-War Propaganda in the 1950s* (London: Macmillan, 1999).

Picture 2: "Get inspired and encouraged by the example of Soviet People!"[16]

The second picture is a small part of a two-page-long composition of different photos (like in a Western magazine), published in the Journal of the Hungarian–Soviet Friendship, *Új Világ* (*New World*). Different pictures presented the attractiveness of Soviet everyday life; this one depicts students in pioneer uniforms, visiting the Polytechnic Museum of Moscow to see the metallurgist exhibition. The girls are amazed by the exceptionality of Soviet technology (we should not forget here the emancipatory gestures of Stalinism in the currently topical gender issues, like women in heavy industry or mining, and so on). One cannot underestimate the effects of this symbolic culture in the early 1950s, inseparable from the modernisation narrative of the Soviet system.[17]

---

16 "Lelkesítsen és buzdítson a szovjet ember példája!," *Új Világ* 5, no. 39 (1952): 4.

17 Eric Schatzberg, "Symbolic Culture and Technological Change: The Cultural History of Aluminium as an Industrial Material," *Enterprise and Society* 4, No. 2 (2003): 226–71. Anna Krylova, "Soviet Modernity: Stephen Kotkin and the Bolshevik Predicament," *Contemporary European History* 23, no. 2 (2014): 167–92. Monica Mincu, "Communist Education as Modernisation Strategy? The Swings of the Globalisation Pendulum in Eastern Europe," *History of Education* 45, no. 3 (2016): 319–34.

Exhibitions and fairs provided good opportunities to demonstrate ongoing development in the new world; technology and technological training became important areas in the comparison between East and West and represented the defeat of capitalism.[18] In this sense, polytechnic education was very important for the decision-makers due to its propagandistic value – at least on the surface, since not reality, but its presentation counted.[19]

There were other channels to transmit the official message about polytechnisation: for example, Radio Petőfi broadcast a lecture about Krupskaia (Lenin's wife and famous protagonist of the new school) and working education on a Sunday afternoon, 18 September 1949.[20] By constructing a new pedagogical canon, contemporary heroes emerged into the centre of discourses, like Nadezhda Krupskaia or Makarenko, and were added to a selected tableau of old figures in education, which fitted into the concept of working education (Pestalozzi, Rousseau and Comenius).[21] Polytechnical education was given historic legitimacy by its portrayal: a progressive, leftist movement delineated from the Enlightenment, or even earlier periods.[22] Intellectuals and educationalists were the main target audience of this work, but the polytechnical propaganda tried to reach the whole of adult society

---

18 A seemingly distant parallel to the roles of (international) fairs in educational knowledge is: Joakim Landahl, "Aesthetic Modernisation and International Comparisons: Learning about Drawing Instruction at the Paris Exposition Universelle of 1900," *History of Education* 48, no. 1 (2019): 41–59. The connection to my topic: the so-called polytechnical exhibitions became popular in the 1960s in Central-Eastern Europe.

19 For a look at the special linguistic world and civilisation of the Soviet Union, see: Stephen S. Kotkin, *Magnetic Mountain: Stalinism as a Civilisation* (Berkeley: University of California Press, 1995).

20 "Magyar Nemzet rádiómelléklete," *Magyar Nemzet* 5, No. 215 (1949): 6. Radio and cinema, later the TV were strategic fields in the Soviet-type propaganda (in Hungary, the first TV-broadcasting was in 1957), Lenin and Stalin both pointed out the importance of radio, see: Boriszov, *A kezdő rádióamatőr* (Budapest: Népszava – SZOT Lap- és Könyvkiadó Vállalata, 1952).

21 A very important and interesting dissertation on developing pedagogical canon in Hungary: Attila Nóbik, *Klasszikusok és kánonképzés a magyar neveléstörténeti tankönyvekben, 1867–1956* (Szeged: Szegedi Tudományegyetem, 2010).

22 An imposing summary of such aspirations: Béla Jausz, Szilárd Faludi and Endre Zibolen eds., *A munkára nevelés hazai történetéből* (Budapest: Akadémiai Kiadó, 1965).

(including parents and teachers), thereby creating a shared responsibility for implementing polytechnisation and universal education.[23]

A crucial platform of propaganda was the so-called *Szülők Iskolája* (*School of Parents*), held by special local organizations, namely, *Szülői Munkaközösségek* (*Parental Work Communities*), with the patronage of *Magyar Nők Demokratikus Szövetsége* (*Democratic Alliance of Hungarian Women*), *Pedagógus Szakszervezet* (*Teachers' Trade Union*) and the *Fővárosi Népművelődési Intézet* (*Centre of Public Education in Budapest*).[24] That meant a series of obligatory lectures for parents in educational and political issues, under the control of the Party (related to the topics, syllabus, and so on); a kind of political training and indoctrination, which started in the capital city in the academic year of 1947–1948, but soon became nation-wide.[25] In the autumn of 1949, the *School of Parents* campaign arrived in small villages too, and planned to educate all parents, from all social classes, under the close control of the Magyar Dolgozók Pártja (MDP, Hungarian Workers' Party), which set the goal to learn from the educational methods of the Soviet Union. The curriculum included the topics of socialist patriotism, working education or the origins of life inaccordance with the science (this latter one was clearly against the religious beliefs), supported by the Ministry with full energy.[26] Other adult education associations also participated in this informative work: the *Társadalom- és Természettudományi Ismeretterjesztő Társulat* (*TTIT*, *Society for Dissemination*

---

[23] According to the Marxist-Leninist ideology, the first aspect in upbringing new generations was to educate the educators, because many teachers were not conscious communists. See: Michael R. Welton, "The Educator Needs to be Educated: Reflections on the Political Pedagogy of Marx, Lenin and Habermas," *International Journal of Lifelong Education* 33, no. 5 (2014): 641–56.

[24] "Jelentés a Nagybudapesti Szülői Munka Közösségek munkájáról," BFL XXXV.95.a, MDP Budapesti Pátbizottságának ülése, 1948. október 29.

[25] The *School of Parents* movement had interwar antecedents, originally coordinated by the Magyar Szülők Szövetsége (Association of Hungarian Parents) from 1917 to the end of Second World War, see: "A Magyar Szülők Szövetsége," *Magyar Paedagogia* 40, No. 1–2 (1931): 61–62. After 1945 the previously civil initiative transformed, and got filled with political content by the communist power, which was a typical process how the pre-war mass organisational forms were exploited and misused by the Party (another example is the unifying of scouts and pioneers in 1948).

[26] "A Szülők Iskolája mozgalom ankétjai," *Szabad Nép* 7, no. 254 (1949): 6. "Szülői Munkaközösségek hírei," *Köznevelés* 5, no. 22 (1949): 626.

of Knowledge for Social and Natural Sciences) gave lectures about ideology and polytechnical education, too; the *Hungarian–Soviet Society* did the same.[27]

Translations were natural tools of Soviet pedagogy; one over-advertised book by Petsernikova connected working education in family with achieving economic plans and the program of the Soviet Communist Party, in an easily intelligible way of telling everyday stories.[28] In this sense, the task of completing polytechnisation belonged to the whole society. This was another meaning of the political socialisation, trying to push the ideological directions into the deep structures of the population, sharing responsibilities, involving as many people as possible (more or less successfully). My other illustration of the translations addressed a narrower audience than Petsernikova, but theoretically established polytechnical education: it was the volume by Sergey Grigorevich Shapovalenko, one of the main ideologists of working education, and a corresponding member of the Russian Soviet Federated Socialist Republic Academy of Pedagogical Science.[29] Shapovalenko's publication strictly related to one of the latest Stalinist initiatives, worth to look at in details.

The Stalinist initiative and its aftermath

In September 1952, Stalin published his latest theoretical article in the journal *Bolshevik* (Economic Problems of Socialism in the U.S.S.R.); the following

27 "Jelentés a Társadalom- és Természettudományi Ismeretterjesztő Társulat munkájáról," MNL JNSzML XXXV. 39. 1. cs. 50. ő. e. MDP Szolnok Megyei VB, 1955. november 21. 25. "Jelentés a megye MSZT szervezeteinek munkájáról," MNL BéML XXXV. 27. 1. cs. 46. ő. e. 72. 1956. január 23. 72. Every organisation, trade union or association was a 'transmission belt' of the Party in the first half of the 1950s, with the main task to mediate official regulations, directives to the local levels.

28 I. A. Pecsernyikova, *Az iskolásgyermek munkára nevelése a családban* (Budapest: Hungária, 1950). Education in family was not a private issue, as the official standpoint stated, see: N. V. Naumov, "Az iskola és a család kapcsolata," *Köznevelés* 8, no. 8 (1952): 239.

29 Sz. G. Sapovalenko, *Tanulmányok a politechnikai képzésről* (Budapest: Tankönyvkiadó, 1953). Ten years later, UNESCO published a massive volume on polytechnic education, edited by Shapovalenko, which clearly indicated the impact of Soviet education on a global scale after the Sputnik shock, see: S. G. Shapovalenko ed., *Polytechnic Education in the U.S.S.R.* (Paris: UNESCO, 1963). About the influence in the US: Lajos Somogyvári, "Soviet Pedagogy and the American Educators (1957–1965)," *Rivista di Storia dell'Educazione* 5, no. 2 (2018): 133–55.

month (from 5 to 14 October) the 19th Congress of the Communist Party of the Soviet Union was held – both events signified the next turning point after 1949 in the story of polytechnisation in Hungary. Just after the Party delegation returned to Budapest, the Central Leadership of MDP made a decree that the pioneer work of Stalin (his writing) and the material of the Congress would be the guiding principles of politics and propaganda in the next period.[30] The paper summarised and closed a simulated debate about an official economics textbook, with different chapters: one about the reaction to Comrade Yaroshenko's views and mistakes, in which Stalin defined shortly what polytechnical education is:

> It is necessary, in the third place, to ensure such a cultural advancement of society as will secure for all members of society the all-round development of their physical and mental abilities, so that the members of society may be in a position to receive an education sufficient to enable them to be active agents of social development, and in a position freely to choose their occupations and not be tied all their lives, owing to the existing division of labour, to some, one occupation.
>
> What is required for this?
>
> It would be wrong to think that such a substantial advance in the cultural standard of the members of society can be brought about without substantial changes in the present status of labour. For this, it is necessary, first of all, to shorten the working day at least to six, and subsequently to five hours. This is needed in order that the members of society might have the necessary free time to receive an all-round education. It is necessary, further, to introduce universal compulsory polytechnical education, which is required in order that the members of society might be able freely to choose their occupations and not be tied to someone occupation all their lives.[31]

The main characteristics of the polytechnical idea were already evident:

- the Marxian vision regarding the all-round development of people,
- bringing closer physical and mental abilities with physical and intellectual training,

---

30 "Határozat" MNL OL M-KS 276. f. 52. cs. 21. ő. e. MDP KV, 1952. október 23.

31 Sztálin, *A szocializmus közgazdasági problémái a Szovjetunióban* (Szikra: Budapest, 1952): 68. The quotation in English is taken from here: Marxists Internet Archive (2005). Accessed August 20, 2021. https://www.marxists.org/reference/archive/stalin/works/1951/economic-problems/index.htm.

- radical changes in labour and society on the road to the communism,
- the utopia of communism as being free from traditional restrictions,
- implementing universal compulsory polytechnical education to achieve this stage.

The words and teachings of Stalin (and other communists) possessed a "magic" power: using ideological language meant transforming the world. The first step was to describe the required future, then realise it in actuality.[32] The 19th Congress enforced the Stalinist initiative; speeches of Bulganin and Suslov remarked the necessity of converting into compulsory polytechnical education in schools, and the principles of the new five-year plan fixed again the school-reform.[33]

The Soviet example was translated on two levels in Hungarian discourses: firstly from Russian to Hungarian; and secondly, from policies to possible actions in pedagogy (symbolic change).[34] Stalin's death interrupted the process in its tracks; polytechnical education was out of favour, and the last Stalinist initiative became a forgotten story: historiography remembered polytechnisation as part of the continuous reforms under Khrushchev. In the academic year of 1953–1954, polytechnical education was only implemented in Hungary in embryonic, experimental forms, without any regulation, schedule or other details.[35] The first period of polytechnisation did not have a successful history in Hungary.

Conclusions

During the so-called Rákosi Era (the hard-core communism from the communist takeover to the 1956 revolution), different periods followed each other in Hungarian educational politics:

---

[32] Nathan Leites, "Stalin as an Intellectual," *World Politics* 6, no. 1 (1953): 46–47.

[33] Fedor János ed., *Az SZKP XIX. kongresszusának anyaga* (Budapest: Szikra, 1952): 236, 285, 376.

[34] I. T. Ogorodnyikov, "A pedagógia kérdései I. V. Sztálin 'A szocializmus közgazdasági problémái a Szovjetunióban' című műve megvilágításában," *Pedagógiai Szemle* 3, no. 1–2 (1953): 1–13.

[35] "Jelentés az 1955/56. tanév előkészítéséről az Oktatásügyi Minisztérium felügyelete alá tartozó oktatási intézményekben," MNL OL XIX-A-83-b. Magyar Népköztársaság Minisztertanácsa, 1955. augusztus 11. 5.

- Fight against the enemy in the Ministry (1950), which excluded all other alternatives from the pedagogical discourses (liberal, humanistic, social-democrat, etc.), described these directions as a bourgeois reaction to the only real revolutionary movement, which is Marxism-Leninism. This processed through like a purification in the field of management and scholars, including the emergence of a dogmatic interpretation of the official ideology in education.
- New Phase of de-Stalinisation (1953–1954), or the Imre Nagy Era: the new prime minister represented the idea of national communism, which was defined later as revisionism. It allowed more freedom and eased the strict application of Soviet principles by emphasizing the national characteristics of schooling. The ideological framework remained but with wider boundaries.
- Re-Stalinisation in 1955 meant a counter-attack by the orthodox Party members and educationalists against the Imre Nagy direction to re-occupy the main administrational and political positions. The control strengthened in ruling the education and the advocates of a more liberal and patriotic way to establish socialism were expelled from the leadership.
- The first half of 1956 was the period of pre-revolutionary turmoil. Vibrant and real debates, criticizing the political practice and various reforming intentions characterized these months. Rákosi had to resign, the discussions of Petőfi Circle (which was a debating society for young students and intellectuals) and the Educational Congress in Balatonfüred clearly showed the possibility of renewing the schooling system.[36]

These rapid turns were in accordance with the political changes, that is, the struggle between Rákosi and his Stalinist supporters, and the reform Communists, led by Imre Nagy. In this debate, the Soviet leadership provided the *ultima ratio* in every decision, which caused wavering discussions about polytechnisation and working education. The stake had always been the same:

---

[36] Kardos József, "Fordulat a magyar iskolák életében: a Rákosi-időszak oktatáspolitikája," *Iskolakultúra* 13, no. 6–7 (2003): 73–80. To the broader context, see: György Gyarmati, *A Rákosi-korszak. Rendszerváltó fordulatok évtizede Magyarországon, 1945–1956* (Budapest: ÁBTL-Rubicon, 2011).

Who interpreted Marxist-Leninist ideology by monopolising educational knowledge and how?[37]

Bibliography

"A Magyar Szülők Szövetsége." *Magyar Paedagogia* 40, no. 1–2 (1931): 61–62.

"A Szülők Iskolája mozgalom ankétjai." *Szabad Nép* 7, no. 254 (1949): 6.

Barankay, Lajos. "A demokratikus nevelés történelmi hitele." *Köznevelés* 3, no. 5 (1947): 75–79.

Berger, Peter L. and Thomas Luckmann. *The Social Construction of Reality: A Treatise in the Sociology of Knowledge*. London: Penguin Books, 1966.

Boriszov. *A kezdő rádióamatőr*. Budapest: Népszava – SZOT Lap- és Könyvkiadó Vállalata, 1952.

F. F. "Soviet Cultural Collaboration: The Role of the Friendship Societies in the Satellite States." *The World Today* 10, no. 5 (1954): 197–209.

Faragó, László. "A Szovjetúnió nevelési rendszere." *Embernevelés* 5, no. 3 (1949): 109–130.

János, Fedor ed., *Az SZKP XIX. Kongresszusának anyaga*. Budapest: Szikra, 1952.

Gyarmati, György. *A Rákosi-korszak. Rendszerváltó fordulatok évtizede Magyarországon, 1945–1956*. Budapest: ÁBTL-Rubicon, 2011.

Jausz, Béla, Faludi Szilárd, and Zibolen Endre eds. *A munkára nevelés hazai történetéből*. Budapest: Akadémiai Kiadó, 1965.

Karády, Victor and Peter Tibor Nagy. "Institutionalization and Professionalization of the Social Sciences in Hungary after 1945." In *Shaping Human Science Disciplines: Institutional Developments in Europe and Beyond*, edited by Christian Fleck, Matthias Duller and Victor Karády, 289–325. Cham: Palgrave Macmillan, 2019.

Karády, Victor and Peter Tibor Nagy. *Sociology in Hungary: A Social, Political and Institutional History*. Cham: Palgrave Macmillan, 2019.

[37] Géza Sáska, "Igény az igazság monopóliumára I-II. A politikai és világnézeti marxizmus-leninizmus a sztálini kor pedagógia tudományában," *Pedagógiatörténeti Szemle* 4, no. 1–2 (2018): 1–52.

Kardos, József. "Fordulat a magyar iskolák életében: a Rákosi-időszak oktatáspolitikája." *Iskolakultúra* 13, no. 6–7 (2003): 73–80.

Kenez, Peter. *The Birth of the Propaganda State. Soviet Methods of Mass Mobilization, 1917–1929*. Cambridge: Cambridge University Press, 1985.

Kiss, Zoltán. "Szociális nevelés, új módszerek." *Köznevelés* 1, no. 12 (1945): 12–13.

Koselleck, Reinhart. *Futures Past: on the Semantics of Historical Time*. New York: Columbia University Press, 2004.

Koselleck, Reinhart. *Begriffsgeschichten. Studien zur Semantik und Pragmatik der politischen und sozialen Sprache*. Frankfurt am Main: Suhrkamp Verlag, 2006.

Kotkin, Stephen S. *Magnetic Mountain: Stalinism as a Civilisation*. Berkeley: University of California Press, 1995.

Krylova, Anna. "Soviet Modernity: Stephen Kotkin and the Bolshevik Predicament." *Contemporary European History* 23, no. 2 (2014): 167–92.

Landahl, Joakim. "Aesthetic Modernisation and International Comparisons: Learning about Drawing Instruction at the Paris Exposition Universelle of 1900." *History of Education* 48, no. 1 (2019): 41–59.

Leites, Nathan. "Stalin as an Intellectual." *World Politics* 6, no. 1 (1953): 45–66.

"Lelkesítsen és buzdítson a szovjet ember példája!." *Új Világ* 5, no. 39 (1952): 4.

"Magyar Nemzet rádiómelléklete." *Magyar Nemzet* 5, no. 215 (1949): 6.

Mincu, Monica. "Communist Education as Modernisation Strategy? The Swings of the Globalisation Pendulum in Eastern Europe." *History of Education* 45, no. 3 (2016): 319–34.

Naumov, N. V. "Az iskola és a család kapcsolata." *Köznevelés* 8, no. 8 (1952): 239–240.

Nóbik, Attila. *Klasszikusok és kánonképzés a magyar neveléstörténeti tankönyvekben, 1867–1956*. Szeged: Szegedi Tudományegyetem, 2010.

Ogorodnyikov, I. T. "A pedagógia kérdései I. V. Sztálin 'A szocializmus közgazdasági problémái a Szovjetunióban' című műve megvilágításában." *Pedagógiai Szemle* 3, no. 1–2 (1953): 1–13.

Pecsernyikova, I. A. *Az iskolásgyermek munkára nevelése a családban*. Budapest: Hungária, 1950.

Rawnsley, Gary D. ed. *Cold-War Propaganda in the 1950s*. London: Macmillan, 1999.

Sapovalenko, Sz. G. *Tanulmányok a politechnikai képzésről*. Budapest: Tankönyvkiadó, 1953.

Sáska, Géza. "Igény az igazság monopóliumára I-II. A politikai és világnézeti marxizmus-leninizmus a sztálini kor pedagógia tudományában." *Pedagógiatörténeti Szemle* 4, no. 1–2 (2018): 1–52.

Shapovalenko, S. G. ed. *Polytechnic Education in the U.S.S.R.* Paris: UNESCO, 1963.

Schatzberg, Eric. "Symbolic Culture and Technological Change: The Cultural History of Aluminium as an Industrial Material." *Enterprise and Society* 4, no. 2 (2003): 226–71.

Skiera, Ehrenhard. *Reformpädagogik in Geschichte und Gegenwart: eine Kritische Einführung*. München: Oldenbourg Verlag, 2009.

Somogyvári, Lajos. "Soviet Pedagogy and the American Educators (1957–1965)." *Rivista di Storia dell'Educazione* 5, no. 2 (2018): 133–155.

Szombatfalvy, György. "Nemzetnevelés vagy pártiskola?." *Magyar Nemzet* 3, no. 223 (1947): 1.

Szovjet irodalom a politechnikai oktatásról. Budapest: Magyar–Szovjet Társaság Lap és Mozgalmianyag Kiadó Vállalat [No Data Avalaible about the Date of Publication].

Sztálin. *A szocializmus közgazdasági problémái a Szovjetunióban*. Szikra: Budapest, 1952.

"Szülői Munkaközösségek hírei." *Köznevelés* 5, no. 22 (1949): 626.

"Városházi hírek." *Magyar Nemzet* 5, no. 157 (1949): 2.

Welton, Michael R. "The Educator Needs to be Educated: Reflections on the Political Pedagogy of Marx, Lenin and Habermas." *International Journal of Lifelong Education* 33, no. 5 (2014): 641–56.

Wittig, Horst E. *Die Marxsche Bildungskonzeption und die Sowjetpädagogik*. Bad Harzburg: Verlag für Wissenschaft, Wirtschaft und Technik, 1964.

Zakharova, Larissa. "Everyday Life Under Communism: Practices and Objects." *Annales HSS* 68, no. 2 (2013): 209–217.

Sources

"Határozat." MNL OL M-KS 276. f. 52. cs. 21. ő. e. MDP KV, 1952. október 23.

"Jelentés az 1955/56. tanév előkészítéséről az Oktatásügyi Minisztérium felügyelete alá tartozó oktatási intézményekben." MNL OL XIX-A-83-b. Magyar Népköztársaság Minisztertanácsa, 1955. augusztus 11.

"Jelentés a megye MSZT szervezeteinek munkájáról." MNL BéML XXXV. 27. 1. cs. 46. ő. e. 72. 1956. január 23.

"Jelentés a Nagybudapesti Szülői Munka Közösségek munkájáról." BFL XXXV.95.a, MDP Budapesti Pátbizottságának ülése, 1948. október 29.

"Jelentés a Társadalom- és Természettudományi Ismeretterjesztő Társulat munkájáról." MNL JNSzML XXXV. 39. 1. cs. 50. ő. e. MDP Szolnok Megyei VB, 1955. november 21.

Marxists Internet Archive (2005). Accessed August 20, 2021. https://www.marxists.org/reference/archive/stalin/works/1951/economic-problems/index.htm.

"Melléklet a 65.500/1949. V.K.M. sz. rendelethez." *Köznevelés: A Vallás- és Közoktatásügyi Minisztérium rendeletei és közleményei* 5, no. 11 (1949): 68–78.

The Book Reviews of The Library of Socialist Education 1950–1957. Biographical and Content Analysis

Zoltán András Szabó, Erzsébet Golnhofer, Éva Szabolcs, Zsuzsanna Polyák and Bence Ruzsa

Abstract: In the 1930–40s, educational sciences in Hungary showed a dynamic development and reflected upon several scientific trends of pedagogy. Between 1945 and 1949, it seemed that the continuity and the renewal of educational theories and practices could be on the agenda. Yet the pluralistic approach to educational ideas was gradually eliminated and the propagation of Stalinist ideology became the most important issue in educational sciences. The educational books ("A Szocialista Nevelés Könyvtára" – "The Library of Socialist Education") were published for teacher education colleges and university courses for in-service teachers and for teachers in general. In this paper, we intend to review this particular series, and analyze the content characteristics of reviews of the ideologically driven educational textbooks. We performed a deductive content analysis that concerns the following subject matter: science (profession), politics, and ideology. These elements were extended with the examination of the attitudes (positive, negative, other) towards the referred categories. In addition, we also deal with problem of continuity and discontinuity by analyzing the books' and the reviews' authors' professional careers. The results of the empirical examinations indicated that the variables (geographical origin of the books' authors, chosen journal, the intensity of professional, ideological and political content and attitudes) have considerable interconnection with the appearance of the content categories.

Keywords: book reviews, content analysis, professional periodicals, socialist education

Introduction

In common with other countries in Eastern and East Central Europe,[1] the political changes after WWII had considerable effects not only on the political landscape of Hungary, but on the institutional background of science, arts and education as well. The gradually forming one-party system, the violent spread of the dominant ideologies of Marxism-Leninism and Stalinism resulted in reorganizing scientific institutions with aggressive personnel

1 Monica E. Mincu "Communist Education as Modernisation Strategy? The Swings of the Globalisation Pendulum in Eastern Europe (1947–1989)," *History of Education* 45, no. 3 (2016): 319–334.

changes: scientists, university professors were labelled as "enemies of the Communist Party" and were fired while politically reliable but professionally not necessarily appropriate persons gained leading positions in the cultural and academic life.[2]

Parallel to the significant works about this period within the disciplines of history, educational historians have also played a key role in investigate these changes in social sciences,[3] public education and in the science of education that emerged after 1945, especially after 1949 in the era of the exclusively dominant Stalinist ideology.[4] Research focused on these pivotal years attempted to show how education as a science was interpreted within the ideological constraints; how drastic institutional and personal changes affected scientific research.[5]

One of the greatest concerns associated with the changes in these years was how science and ideology could be reconciled, how scientific norms and

---

2 Melinda Kalmár, *Történelmi galaxisok vonzásában. Magyarország és a szovjetrendszer 1945–1990* (Budapest: Osiris Kiadó, 2014). Vilmos Erős and Ádám Takács, ed., *Tudomány és ideológia között. Tanulmányok az 1945 utáni magyar történetírásról* (Budapest: ELTE Eötvös Kiadó, 2012).

3 Victor Karády and Péter Tibor Nagy, "Institutionalization and Professionalization of the Social Sciences in Hungary Since 1945," in *Shaping Human Science Disciplines. Socio-Historical Studies of the Social and Human Sciences*, eds. Christian Fleck, Mathias Duller and Victor Karády (Cham: Palgrave Macmillan, 2018), 289–325.

4 There had been two research projects led by András Németh in this field: between 2004–2008 *Trends in the development of the Hungarian Science of Education in the Second Half of the 20th Century;* between 2012–2016 *The History of Hungarian Science of Education in the Light of Professional Journals 1945–1989*. A running research project led by András Németh *The Past and Present of Hungarian Educational Science – Development of a Discipline, Scientific Communication 1970–2017* is further contributing to understand and interpret the changes of educational science during these decades.

5 Erzsébet Golnhofer, *Hazai pedagógiai nézetek* (Pécs: Iskolakultúra könyvek, 2004). Géza Sáska, "A reformpedagógia alakváltozásai az 1945-ös kis és az 1947 utáni nagy rendszerváltást követő időszakban," *Magyar Pedagógia* 106, no. 4 (2006): 263–285. András Németh, "A magyar egyetemi neveléstudomány szocialista paradigmájának kialakulása az 1945–53 közötti időszakban," in *A magyar neveléstudomány a XX. század második felében*, ed. András Németh and Zsuzsanna Hanna Biró (Budapest: Gondolat Kiadó, 2009), 26–56. Erzsébet Golnhofer and Éva Szabolcs, "Lázár György és a magyar pedológia – mítosz és valóság," *Magyar Pedagógia* 113, no. 3 (2013): 133–151; András Németh, Imre Garai and Zoltán András Szabó, eds., *Neveléstudomány és pedagógiai kommunikáció a szocializmus időszakában* (Budapest: Gondolat Kiadó, 2016).

the exclusive ideology of Marxism-Leninism and Stalinism could coincide. The intertwining of educational science and ideology can be well researched by analyzing the contemporary educational press. Our previous research in this field showed the dominance of ideology-controlled educational science but we could also see the professional elements as well.[6] This line of research led us to analyse the history of a series of professional books: The Library of the Socialist Education[7] published between 1950–1957, with the aim of founding the socialist pedagogy in Hungary. According to the intentions of contemporary representatives of the ideologically biased educational policy, the series was established to help teachers and other professionals to understand and accept socialist pedagogy, thus breaking with the old, ideologically unacceptable prewar issues in education. 133 volumes of the series were published in the mentioned period. In our former analysis we focused on the development of the series, on the question of how education as a science and socialist ideology were intertwined. This latter problem was investigated through the biographies of writers and editors, whether they represented continuity or discontinuity in the different subdisciplines of education. We also showed how Soviet education served as a norm in the volumes of the series and how the influence of Soviet educators decreased after 1956. According to our previous research, the series was both an ideologically driven product and an experiment to include scientific and professional knowledge.[8]

As outlined above, these particular series are considered as important sources regarding the development of educational science(s) after World War II. Although prior research focused on the books and their authors/editors of

---

6 Golnhofer and Szabolcs, "Lázár György," 133–151. Erzsébet Golnhofer and Éva Szabolcs, "Pedagógia a tankönyvekben az ötvenes évek első felében," *Könyv és Nevelés* XVI, no. 4 (2014): 88–101.

7 The series also appears under the names "A Szocialista Nevelés Könyvtára" and "Szocialista Nevelés Könyvtára". In the present study, we used the longer version.

8 Erzsébet Golnhofer and Éva Szabolcs, "A Szocialista Nevelés Könyvtára: törekvés a szocialista pedagógia kialakítására 1950–1957," in *A Borsszem Jankótól Bolognáig. Neveléstudományi tanulmányok*, ed. Anikó Fehérvári (Budapest: L'Harmattan, 2018), 62–73. Erzsébet Golnhofer and Éva Szabolcs, "A Szocialista Nevelés Könyvtára 1950–1957: politikai termék vagy tudományos produktum?," in *Mestermunka. A neveléstudomány aktuális diskurzusai*, ed. Imre Garai, Katalin Kempf and Beatrix Vincze (Budapest: L'Harmattan, 2020), 160–173.

these above-noted series, the analysis of reviews concerning these works was less emphasized. We thus aim to bridge this gap by investigating these writings in two of the most important pedagogical journals of the age, Köznevelés and Pedagógiai Szemle (Public Education and Pedagogical Review). We will analyze to what extent the book reviews served professional, ideological and political purposes, and how political changes affected the role and content of the reviews. Apart from that, we examine the extent to which the authors of the reviews represented a professional continuity or discontinuity in terms of their professional socialization.

In this article, we aim to move towards a more holistic approach in interpreting and understanding the nature of contemporary educational science by analyzing some reviews on the volumes of the above outlined series.

To examine this, we formulated the following research questions:

1. How can the authors of the book reviews be characterized in the context of continuity and discontinuity?
2. What are the differences between reviews about Soviet and Hungarian authored books regarding their content?
3. What are the differences between the two journals' reviews regarding their content?
4. How can be the intensity of scientific (professional), political and ideological content described in the different book reviews?
5. What types of attitudes (positive, negative, other) can be observed towards the different content categories in the reviews?

Sources and Methods

In our approach, we sought to apply a complex social and cultural-historical orientation[9], using both quantitative and qualitative analysis; the computer-assisted content analysis is complemented by historical source analysis and biographical data analysis.

[9] Németh, Garai and Szabó, eds., *Neveléstudomány és pedagógiai kommunikáció a szocializmus időszakában*.

Primary sources

As outlined above, among the various education related journals, we have chosen two decisive professional periodicals, namely the Public Education[10] and the Pedagogical Review.[11] These were the two most relevant educational journals for professionals in the respective period (1950–1957/1958), when the series were published or reviewed. These sources are also available in an online database, the Arcanum Digitheca (ADT).[12] Besides this online source, we have digitalized some of the two journals' volumes in a former project – these were also used in this examination.[13] We used the following search expression in the ADT to find the relevant book reviews:

SZO = ("szocialista nevelés könyvtár") AND DATE = (1950–1958)

As it can be seen, we did not use the first and last character of the series' title ("A Szocialista Nevelés Könyvtára"), because of the possible faults of the optical character recognition (OCR) technology (see below). Accordingly, this search technique resulted in more detections. After that, we have used the built-in functions of the database in order to filter our data. Only those records were chosen, which were published in the two examined journals (sort by date).

By using this technique, 99 records appeared on our list. However, it was very difficult to identify the relevant writings of the volumes. Sometimes the book review does not mention the series itself, or the title of the review does not contain the title of the book. Additionally, the OCR – which was applied in the aforementioned database and also in our own collection – may have resulted in altering characters. Because of these reasons, we found additional manual search necessary.

In this extended set of book reviews, we have excluded the debates on published books, those texts which only mentioned the books or the series, and that short news that only informed the readers about the publication of a new book in the series without any significant comment.

---

[10] Köznevelés.

[11] Pedagógiai Szemle.

[12] Arcanum Digitheca, accessed December 15, 2020. https://adt.arcanum.com/en/.

[13] *The History of Hungarian Science of Education in the Light of Professional Journals (1945–1989) – scientific communication, professional discourse* (granted by the National Research, Development and Innovation Office). Grant No.: 100496.

With this above-described method, we were able to identify 47 different book reviews (including one about the whole series). However, depending on the search technique and the inclusion/exclusion criteria, other lists can be composed. The list of the book reviews can be found in the References.

Methods

In this paper, two different methods will be presented that were applied with the overall aim of examining the chosen phenomena. Regarding the authors of the reviews, the combination of historical source analysis and biographical analysis were used to examine the relevant individuals of the scientific/professional community.

In respect of the book reviews, we performed a deductive content analysis with the help of ATLAS.ti software.[14] Our sample consists of the different book reviews of the previously mentioned periodicals (namely the Pedagógiai Szemle and the Köznevelés). Within this, we attempted to compare the various groups of the book reviews (i. e. Soviet vs. Hungarian author, Köznevelés or Pedagógiai Szemle). The coded segments were the references to the examined topics (see below) within the respective primary documents.[15] The context unit – the largest amount of information from which we made decisions about the coding – was a book review.

The coding process was divided into three main phases.[16] The aim of the first phase was to support the development of the coding frame. In order to do this, we chose to examine book reviews which are similar to the analyzed ones, but they are not the part of the corpus. This phase enabled us to attach example quotations to the previously developed, deductive codes, which then was grouped into three categories, namely *Science, Politics* and *Ideology*.

During the second phase, we selected a random sample from both periodicals (N=6) in order to calculate the reliability of the coding process. The reliability of the content analysis was ensured by two independent coders. The preparation of the coders included one training, the introduction of the corpus and the qualitative data analysis software. For both coding, reliability

---

[14] Klaus Krippendorff, *Content Analysis. An Introduction to Its Methodology* (SAGE Publications: Thousand Oaks, CA, 2004).

[15] The reliability analysis was character-based. Cf. Klaus Krippendorff, "On the Reliability of Unitizing Continuous Data," *Sociological Methodology* 25, no. 47 (1995): 47–76.

[16] For more details on the coding process, please contact the authors.

statistics and analysis ATLAS.ti 9 were used. Although some of the dimensions showed very high reliability (1 or close to 1), a considerable amount of the variables has been excluded. We have chosen those categories which showed higher reliability.

In the third phase, the two independent coders have received the modified coding manual, and performed the coding on the whole corpus. As the result of this phase, 809 (Coder A) and 1197 (Coder B) quotations has been created by the coders. These serves as the basis of the reliability statistics.[17] The results of this examination are summarized in Table 1.

Table 1: Reliability statistics of the third coding phase.
Note: n. r.: not relevant i/e: included/excluded

Variable	c-Alpha-binary	Cu-Alpha/ cu-Alpha	Note	Decision
Attitude	0,606	(1) N/A (2) 0,17 (3) 0,774	Due to the lack of mutual exclusiveness, we were not able to calculate the Cu-Alpha/ cu-Alpha value at the first attempt. After the removal of three problematic documents (ID: 8, 26, 29) the value changed to 0,17. After that, the non-indicated and the neutral attitudes were merged into the "others" category. This is how reached the third (reliable) result.	i
Ideology: individual	0,604	n.r.		i
Hungarian political individual	0,153	n.r.		e
Hungarian political organization	0,643	n.r.		i

(Continued)

[17] Andrew F. Hayes and Klaus Krippendorff, "Answering the Call for a Standard Reliability Measure for Coding Data," *Communication Methods and Measures* 1, no. 1 (2007): 79.

Table 1: (*Continued*)

Variable	c-Alpha-binary	Cu-Alpha/ cu-Alpha	Note	Decision
Professional organization	0,347	n.r.		e
Professional individual	0,582	n.r.	Since a considerable amount of the differences can be traced back into one single problem (namely coding the authors of the book reviews), we decided to include this variable, which was very close to the critical value.	i
Soviet political individual	0,768	n.r.		i
Soviet political organization	0,767	n.r.		i
Total	**0,609**	**n.r.**		**n. r.**

During the above-mentioned reliability measurements, we have calculated the relevant Alpha values. According to Landis and Koch's work[18] – and taking into account the similarities of Cohen's Kappa and Krippendorff's Alpha – we used a slightly lower limit (0,61) than Krippendorff's recommendation (0,667).[19]

After the removal of the unreliable codes, we aimed to finalize the coding pattern. There are several ways to eliminate the differences of the two codings in order to get a final pattern – even if there are two coders' in the final phase – (e. g. discussion by the two coders, third coder's decision etc.). As the majority of the differences came from the fact that Coder A identified a smaller set of quotations, but they have a considerable intersection, we decided to use Coder B's results (thus this served as the basis of the final

[18] J. Richard Landis and Gary G. Koch, "The Measurement of Observer Agreement for Categorical Data," *Biometrics* 33, no. 1 (1977): 165.

[19] However, Krippendorff also emphasized that these levels should be adjusted to "the costs of drawing wrong conclusions" – Krippendorff, *Content Analysis*, 242.

coding) in order to avoid the exclusion of possible detections. A third coder checked this pattern in order to exclude the possible errors. The results of this examination are based on this final code structure and coding pattern.

Findings

The Book Reviews and Their Authors – Professional Continuity or Discontinuity

In the 1950s, political and professional public documents expressed the expectation that a new, socialist pedagogy was needed, which would be created by a "new and/or socialist intelligentsia". This issue has been incorporated into the discourse of continuity and discontinuity in social science and pedagogical history analyses after the change of regime.[20] Accordingly, we investigated whether the authors of these reviews can be considered as members of the intellectual elite before 1945, based on their educational attainment and academic degree[21]. From the data available to us, we can see that two-thirds of the authors obtained a university degree before 1945, a quarter of them had a doctorate and published mainly in relation to their doctoral studies. One tenth of the authors did not have a higher education degree before 1945, but all gained one after 1945. Similarly to the authors in the series, the professional -and academic socialization of the majority of the reviewers began before 1945 and continued after 1945 under the conditions of the one-party state.

---

20 Golnhofer, *Hazai pedagógiai nézetek*. András Németh, Zsuzsanna Hanna Biró and Imre Garai, *Neveléstudomány és tudományos elit a 20. század második felében* (Budapest: Gondolat Kiadó, 2015). Sáska, "A reformpedagógia alakváltozásai az 1945-ös kis és az 1947 utáni nagy rendszerváltást követő időszakban," 263–285; Éva Szabolcs, ed. *Pedagógia és politika a XX. század második felében Magyarországon* (Budapest: Eötvös József Könyvkiadó, 2006).

21 1. There are many different interpretations of the concepts of intellectual elite and intelligentsia, and in our study we used the categories of university degree and academic degree accepted in elite studies. 2,87% of the reviews in Köznevelés and Pedagógiai Szemle were published with the authors' names, but we do not have sufficient information on the professional socialisation of all authors.

According to our data, at the time of the review's publication, nearly one third of the reviewers were working close to those in power. That is, they obtained employment in the Communist Party apparatus, the Ministry of Education, Party-controlled pedagogical institutes, or in higher education institutions, and publishing houses. One third of them worked as college and university teachers, one tenth as primary and/or secondary school teachers. The degree of integration of the reviewers who socialized before 1945 into socialist professional and scientific life is indicated not only by the appearance of reviews, but also by the fact that in the 1950s they all appeared with various publications in the Hungarian pedagogical and professional press. Between 1950 and 1957, some of them received a candidate's degree and/or an academic doctorate in the Soviet-style academic classification, and one of them was an academic member. However, the integration process was not without conflicts, for example, one reviewer was deprived of his academic membership, others had their teaching license revoked or were expelled from their church school in the context of nationalization of schools. Nevertheless, they were allowed to remain in employment.

Based on the overview of the socialization processes, we cannot discuss the elite exchange among the reviewers, respectively the dominance of the "new intelligentsia". Review writers who had begun their professional socialization before 1945, were allowed to continue their academic and professional careers, and to contribute to increasing the enhancement of the social base of the party-state through their writings. Further research and more information are needed in order to gain a deeper understanding of the phenomenon of continuity and discontinuity, especially with regard to the individual life paths and identification processes of the review authors to be examined.

The Books and Their Authors. The Comparison of the Reviewed Books with Soviet and Hungarian Authorship

Among the various features of the authors of the books, we focused on their geographical origin, because we expected that this peculiarity influences the distribution of the content categories, especially the individual and collective (institutional) reference points.

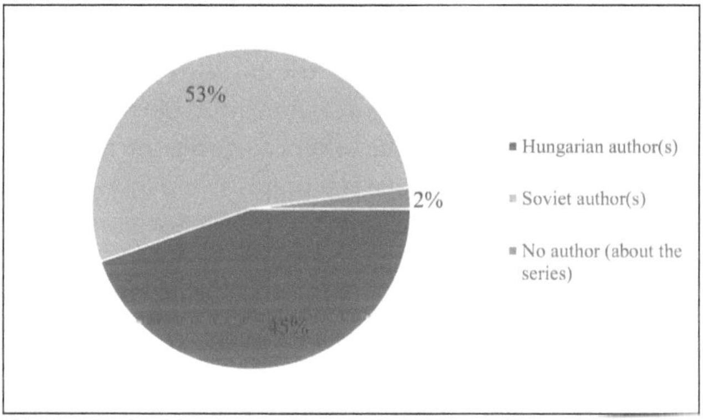

Figure 1: The geographical origin of the authors of the books (%).

The origin of the book authors shows a balanced ratio; 53% of the books have Soviet authors, while 45% of them have Hungarian ones, as can be seen in Figure 1. There is also a review about the whole series, which is the 2% of the examined corpus. Besides this, the inner ratio of the respected journals (Hungarian: 71% from Köznevelés and 29% from Pedagógiai Szemle – Soviet: 72% from Köznevelés and 28% from Pedagógiai Szemle) is similar to the 72/28 ratio of the corpus (excluding the review about the whole series). This suggests that there is no significant difference between the two journals' book reviews regarding the selection of Hungarian or Soviet authors.

We also examined whether the geographical origin of the authors influenced the distribution of the different content categories.

Figure 2: The distribution of the different categories within the geographical origin of the authors.

Making distinction between the Soviet and Hungarian book authors also resulted in some differences between the number of the applied codes (Figure 2). While the references to professional individuals shows smaller relative distance (HU: 787/SU: 659), the other categories are more imbalanced. Although the references to Hungarian political organizations are higher in the case of the Hungarian authors (35/11), the Soviet-related categories appeared more frequently in the case of Soviet authors (individuals: 27/51; institutions: 5/35). Besides the geographical variables, the ideology-related individuals can also be detected more often in the case of the book reviews with Soviet authorship (27/125). However, it has to be emphasized that the references of the books themselves may have influenced the citations in the reviews; since the latter often repeated the books' references to the representatives of an ideology:

> *The last, larger chapter, which is 60 pages long, deals with the theory and the practice of Soviet pedagogy. First of all, it gives a summary of the education-related thoughts of Lenin and Stalin. Lenin and Stalin are introduced as the further developers of Marx and Engels's pedagogical teachings, who raised a lot of new question regarding the building of socialist and communist society.*[22]

The Comparison of the Two Journals' Book Reviews' Content

Figure 3: The distribution of the different categories within the two journals.

With the aim of further investigation, we compared the content of the two journals (see Figure 3). According to the results the most balanced ratio can be observed in the case of the most frequent category, namely the

[22] "Medinszkij: A nevelés története," *Köznevelés* 7, no. 17 (1951): 746.

professional individuals (504/593). The other variable which was higher in the Pedagógiai Szemle is the Hungarian political organization (8/24). The authors of the reviews often referred to existing political organizations, however, the historical perspective was also important. The most referred Hungarian political organization was the Magyar Dolgozók Pártja (MDP) (Hungarian Working People's Party), the state party in Hungary between 1948 and 1956, which was often represented in a strong ideological context, as can be seen in the quotation below:

> *Today, teaching of literature educates our children to become workers who are led by great ideas and the love of their country, who will build our people's happy future with trust, and they can protect it from the enemy selflessly. The development of our textbooks tracks this way, which follows the Soviet experiences and the MDP's imposition.*[23]

The other three features were more frequent in the case of the Köznevelés, so both ideology-related individuals (107/38), Soviet political individuals (41/29) and institutions (31/7) were higher. Although in certain cases the ratio was found to be unbalanced, the absolute differences of the respected values are not significant in the two journals.

The Intensity of Professional, Ideological and Political Content of the Book Reviews

Besides the above-mentioned code system, the two coders evaluated the intensity of the scientific (professional), ideological and political content in the book reviews. They used a 5-point Likert scale in order to indicate the intensity of these components. The rating of the two independent coders was compared by using Krippendorff's Alpha (for interval scale) – for further details, see Appendix A. Two components did not reach the critical value (scientific: 0,14 political: 0,36), but in the case of *ideology*, the coding was consistent (0,79). Thereafter, the average of the two codings was calculated for each document, and subsequently for the two journals too (see Figure 4).

[23] Lajos Illés, "Golubkov: Az irodalomtanítás módszertana," *Pedagógiai Szemle* 1, no. 1–2 (1951): 173.

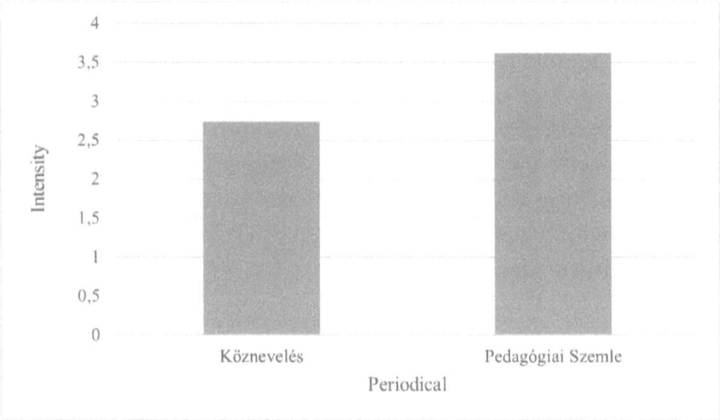

Figure 4: The comparison of the intensity of the ideological content in the two examined professionals.

Result indicated that there is a considerable difference (0,88) between the two journals regarding the intensity of the ideological content. The Pedagógiai Szemle's value is higher (3,62) and also has a smaller standard deviation (1,10). This implies that the Pedagógiai Szemle emphasized the ideological content in a more intensive (and more balanced) way.

The Different Attitudes (Positive, Negative, Other) towards the Content Categories

Figure 5: Attitudes towards the coded material.

As Figure 5 shows, a considerable amount of the references regarding the professional individuals are positive, while the ratio of the negative references is remarkably low concerning the same category. Besides that, we could identify a negative attitude only in one dimension, but for the other variables (that can be found on the right side of the figure) out of the other two attitudes (other or positive) the latter one was more frequent. One of the examples of negative references can be seen below:

> *Herbart was the representative of this reactionary trend in the field of educational science. But we can witness the same mistake in the case of Plato too.*[24]

This quotation highlights the fact that negative attitudes not only appeared in relation to the modern ages' intellectual flows, or in the cases of philosophers of antiquity. This phenomenon can be interpreted as the application of the contemporary ideology on the figures of the past.

The respected c-coefficients, which show the intensity of the relationship between the two codes, can be found in the Appendix B.

Conclusions

With regard to the authors of the book reviews, we can emphasize that although the dominance of the 'new intelligentsia' cannot be stated, further research is needed in order to understand their socialization processes (Q1). As well as the authors of the book reviews, we also examined the origin of the authors of the books themselves, which showed a relatively balanced ratio (Q2). It is worth mentioning that although the references to ideology-related individuals were definitely higher in the case of the Köznevelés (Q3), both coders – with a significant reliability – allocated higher intensity of ideological content for the Pedagógiai Szemle (Q4). This phenomenon underlines the fact that a large number of references to ideological individuals itself does not enable a book review to become more ideological in comparison with the other ones. The attitudes towards the different content categories (Q5) showed the preference of the 'positive' and the 'other' classes.

Our results showed that the analyzed book reviews cannot be categorized only as ideological works. Although the literature emphasizes the dominance (or even exclusiveness) of ideology in the 1950s, our examination highlighted that markers of other dimensions can be identified in the corpus. Moreover, the presence of ideology is not constant; it appears in varying extents –and

---

24 Gyula Bizó, "Medinszkij: A nevelés története," *Pedagógiai Szemle* 1, no. 1–2 (1951): 165.

variability. This underscores the complexity and diversity inherent in the literature of the examined period, challenging general categorizations and encouraging a more comprehensive exploration of the multifaceted elements shaping the discourse surrounding The Library of Socialist Education from 1950 to 1958.

In this paper, two Hungarian core pedagogical periodicals were examined. Nevertheless, our findings serve as an entry point into further research on the analysis of other – rather peripheral – professional journals as well, the collection and digitalization of which has been started in recent times. We would also like to conduct a deeper examination concerning the context of the multifarious references. We have to emphasize that the style of the reviews' author (i. e. the number references by name) strongly influences the results.

Bibliography

Erős, Vilmos, and Ádám Takács, eds. *Tudomány és ideológia között. Tanulmányok az 1945 utáni magyar történetírásról*. Budapest: ELTE Eötvös Kiadó, 2012.

Golnhofer, Erzsébet, and Éva Szabolcs. "A Szocialista Nevelés Könyvtára: törekvés a szocialista pedagógia kialakítására 1950–1957." In *A Borsszem Jankótól Bolognáig. Neveléstudományi tanulmányok*, edited by Anikó Fehérvári, 62–73. Budapest: L'Harmattan, 2018.

Golnhofer, Erzsébet and Éva Szabolcs. "A Szocialista Nevelés Könyvtára 1950–1957: politikai termék vagy tudományos produktum?." In *Mestermunka. A neveléstudomány aktuális diskurzusai*, edited by Imre Garai, Katalin Kempf and Beatrix Vincze, 160–173. Budapest: L'Harmattan, 2020.

Golnhofer, Erzsébet and Éva Szabolcs. "Lázár György és a magyar pedológia – mítosz és valóság." *Magyar Pedagógia* 113, no. 3 (2013): 133–151.

Golnhofer, Erzsébet, and Éva Szabolcs. "Pedagógia a tankönyvekben az ötvenes évek első felében." *Könyv és Nevelés* XVI, no. 4 (2014): 88–101.

Golnhofer, Erzsébet. *Hazai pedagógiai nézetek 1945–49*. Pécs: Iskolakultúra könyvek, 2004.

Hayes, Andrew F. and Klaus Krippendorff. "Answering the Call for a Standard Reliability Measure for Coding Data." *Communication Methods and Measures* 1, no. 1 (2007): 77–89.

Kalmár, Melinda. *Történelmi galaxisok vonzásában. Magyarország és a szovjetrendszer 1945–1990.* Budapest: Osiris Kiadó, 2014.

Karády, Victor and Péter Tibor Nagy. "Institutionalization and Professionalization of the Social Sciences in Hungary Since 1945." In *Shaping Human Science Disciplines. Socio-Historical Studies of the Social and Human Sciences*, edited by Christian Fleck, Mathias Duller and Victor Karády, 289–325. Cham: Palgrave Macmillan, 2018.

Krippendorff, Klaus. "On the Reliability of Unitizing Continuous Data." *Sociological Methodology* 25, no. 47 (1995): 47–76.

Krippendorff, Klaus. *Content Analysis. An Introduction to Its Methodology.* Thousand Oaks, CA: SAGE Publications, 2004.

Landis, J. Richard and Gary G. Koch. "The Measurement of Observer Agreement for Categorical Data." *Biometrics* 33, no. 1 (1977): 159–174.

Mincu, Monica E. "Communist Education as Modernisation Strategy? The Swings of the Globalisation Pendulum in Eastern Europe (1947–1989)." *History of Education* 45, no. 3 (2016): 319–334.

Németh, András, Biró, Zsuzsanna Hanna and Imre Garai, eds. *Neveléstudomány és tudományos elit a 20. század második felében.* Budapest: Gondolat Kiadó, 2015.

Németh, András, Garai, Imre and Zoltán András Szabó, eds. *Neveléstudomány és pedagógiai kommunikáció a szocializmus időszakában.* Budapest: Gondolat Kiadó, 2016.

Németh, András. "A magyar egyetemi neveléstudomány szocialista paradigmájának kialakulása az 1945–53 közötti időszakban." In *A magyar neveléstudomány a XX. század második felében*, edited by András Németh and Zsuzsanna Hanna Biró, 26–56. Budapest: Gondolat Kiadó, 2009.

Sáska, Géza. "A reformpedagógia alakváltozásai az 1945-ös kis és az 1947 utáni nagy rendszerváltást követő időszakban." *Magyar Pedagógia* 106, no. 4 (2006): 263–285.

Szabolcs, Éva, ed. *Pedagógia és politika a XX. század második felében Magyarországon.* Budapest: Eötvös József Könyvkiadó, 2006.

Sources

Arcanum Digitheca, accessed December 15, 2020. https://adt.arcanum.com/en/ and own digitalization.

[Sine nomine]. "A természetrajztanítás módszertana." *Pedagógiai Szemle* 2, no. 1–2 (1952): 173–181.

[Sine nomine]. "Az orosz nyelvi kiejtés, írás és olvasástanítás módszertana." *Köznevelés* 10, no. 5 (1954): 120.

[Sine nomine]. "Fizikai kísérletek gyűjteménye II." *Köznevelés* 10, no. 5 (1954): 120.

[Sine nomine]. "Medinszkij: A nevelés története," *Köznevelés* 7, no. 17 (1951): 745–746.

[Sine nomine]. "Vaszkó Mihály: Komensky Ámos János világnézete és pedagógiája." *Köznevelés* 10, no. 7 (1954): 168.

Áfra, János. "A helytörténeti kutatások módszere és feladatai az oktató-nevelőmunkában." *Köznevelés* 13, no. 8. (1957): VII.

Ágoston, György. "Jeszipov-Goncsarov: Pedagógia." *Köznevelés* 6, no. 19 (1950): 605–606.

Bálint, Sándor. "Perényi László: Áz énektanítás pedagógiája." *Köznevelés* 14, no. 2 (1958): 45.

Banó, István. "Csisztyakov módszertanának felhasználása az orosz nyelv tanításában." *Köznevelés* 8, no. 11 (1952): 361–362.

Bihari, József. "Harcban a reakciós pedagógiával. Vincze László – Vincze Flóra: A gyermek fejlődésének és nevelésének kérdései." *Köznevelés* 11, no. 3 (1955): 71–72.

Bíró, József. "Faragó László: A koordináta-geometria módszertana." *Köznevelés* 13, no. 8. (1957): 195.

Bizó, Gyula. "Medinszkij: A nevelés története" *Pedagógiai Szemle* 1, no. 1–2 (1951): 163–166.

Bizó, Gyula. "Megjegyzések Vincze László – Vincze Flóra: 'A gyermek fejlődésének és nevelésének kérdései' című könyvhöz." *Pedagógiai Szemle* 5, no. 1 (1955): 109–120.

Cs[eke], G[ábor]. "Fizikai kísérletek és eszközök." *Köznevelés* 7, no. 13 (1951): 605–606.

Cs[er], A[ndor]. "A koordináta-geometria tanításának módszertana." *Pedagógiai Szemle* 7, no. 3 (1957): 92–96.

Fenyő, István. "A Szocialista Nevelés Könyvtára két új kötete." *Köznevelés* 11, no. 14–15 (1955): 351.

Fenyő, István. "Abramovics: Bevezetés az irodalomtudományba. Fordította: Kosaras István." *Köznevelés* 11, no. 20 (1955): 479.

G. Méhes, Vera. "Bleher: Szervezett foglalkozás az óvodában." *Köznevelés* 6, no. 22–23 (1950): 737.

Garami, Károly. "Vegytani kísérletek technikája és módszertana az iskolában." *Köznevelés* 8, no. 4 (1952): 127.

Garami, Károly. "Verhovszkij: Vegytani kísérletek technikája és módszertana az iskolában." *Pedagógiai Szemle* 2, no. 6 (1952): 573–581.

Gy[öngyösi], J[ózsef]. "Bragyisz: A középiskolai matematika-tanítás módszertana." *Köznevelés* 7, no. 19 (1951): 817.

Gyöngyösi, József. "A. SZ. Pcsolkó: A számtantanítás módszertana." *Köznevelés* 7, no. 18 (1951): 787.

H[uszár], P[ál]. "Az osztályfőnök nevelő munkája." *Köznevelés* 7, no. 15–16 (1951): 707–708.

H[uszár], P[ál]. "I. K. Novikov: A Az oktató-nevelőmunka megszervezése az iskolában." *Köznevelés* 8, no. 11 (1952): 365–366.

Hahn, István. "Karcov: A történelemtanítás módszertana az alsó osztályokban." *Köznevelés* 7, no. 15–16. (1951): 706–707.

Harsányi, Zoltán, "Tóth Béla: A gyermek és az irodalom." *Köznevelés* 11, no. 22 (1955): 527–528.

Huszár, Pál. "Nagy Sándor: A tanítási óra felépítése és elemzése." *Köznevelés* 9, no. 23–24. (1953): 558–559.

Illés, Lajos. "Golubkov: Az irodalomtanítás módszertana." *Köznevelés* 7, no. 14 (1951): 654–655.

Illés, Lajos. "Golubkov: Az irodalomtanítás módszertana." *Pedagógiai Szemle* 1, no. 1–2 (1951): 166–178.

Károly, Sándor. "A Szocialista Nevelés Könyvtára." *Köznevelés* 6, no. 19. (1950): 587–588.

Kontra, István. "'Érik a szőlő'. 91 magyar népdal énekhangra, zongorakísérettel. Közreadja: Bárdos Lajos." *Köznevelés* 11, no. 20 (1955): 479.

Kovács, Péter. "V. I. Szelivánov: A falusi iskola." *Köznevelés* 9, no. 16 (1953): 390.

M. Zemplén, Jolán. "Gorjacskin: A fizikatanítás módszertana (I–II. kötet.)." *Pedagógiai Szemle* 2, no. 3 (1952): 273–279.

Makay, Gusztáv. "Golubkov művének felhasználása irodalomtanításunkban." *Köznevelés* 7, no. 15–16 (1951): 684–687.

Makay, Gusztáv. "Széljegyzetek egy irodalomelméleti tankönyvhöz. Abramovics: Bevezetés az irodalomtudományba." *Pedagógiai Szemle* 5, no. 5–6 (1955): 555–563.

Margócsy, József. "Helyesírástanítási segédkönyvek." *Köznevelés* 12, no. 5 (1956): 120.

Mérei, Ferenc. "A szocialista embernevelés. N. K. Krupszkája: Válogatott pedagógiai tanulmányok." *Köznevelés* 6, no. 1–2 (1950): 39–41.

Nyilas, Dezső. "Gorjacskin: A fizikatanítás módszertana." *Köznevelés* 8, no. 2 (1952): 63.

Péter, Rózsa. "Nyikityin: Szöveges feladatok megoldása az általános iskolában." *Köznevelés* 6, no. 20 (1950): 644.

Ravasz, János. "Vincze László: Táncsics Mihály pedagógiai nézetei." *Pedagógiai Szemle* 5, no. 5–6 (1955): 572–575.

Simon, [?]. "N. A. Petrov: A tanító tekintélye és személyes példaadása." *Köznevelés* 7, no. 14 (1951): 655–656.

Székely, Endréné. "Ágoston György: A közösségi nevelés és az Úttörőmozgalom című könyvének vitája." *Pedagógiai Szemle* 2, no. 6 (1952): 622–627.

Szoboszlay, Miklós. "Az idegen nyelvek oktatásának időszerű kérdései (SZNK 128. sz.)." *Pedagógiai Szemle* 8, no. 3 (1958): 277–282.

V[aszkó], M[ihály]. "Állathatározó." *Köznevelés* 7, no. 3 (1951): 119–120.

Vág, Ottó. "A tanító kézikönyve. I—IV. kötet." *Pedagógiai Szemle* 3, no. 1–2 (1953): 178–187.

Váli, Dezsőné. "Hogyan alkalmazom Nyikityin könyvét a III. osztály tanításában." *Köznevelés* 7, no. 7 (1951): 293–295.

Wéber, Mihály. "Gelei Gábor: Állattani kísérletek és gyakorlatok." *Pedagógiai Szemle* 2, no. 6 (1952): 581–582.

Appendix A: Statistical data for Q4 (The intensity of professional, ideological and political content)

	Krippendorff's Alpha (interval scale)	LL95%CI	UL95%CI	Critical values (left) and the probability of failing (right)	
Ideological	,7873	,6994	,8659	,8000 ,6700 ,6000	,5876 ,0055 ,0002
Political	,3570	,0672	,6196	,8000 ,6700 ,6000	,9999 ,9912 ,9589
Scientific (professional)	,1404	-,1714	,4238	,8000 ,6700 ,6000	1,0000 1,0000 ,9999

Number of bootstrap samples: 10000

Appendix B: Statistical data for Q5 (The different attitudes towards the content categories)

	ideology: individual		politics: Hungarian organization		politics: Soviet individual		politics: Soviet institution		profession: individual	
	n	c	n	c	n	c	n	c	n	c
attitude: negative	0	0,00	0	0,00	0	0,00	0	0,00	55	0,06
attitude: other	33	0,05	12	0,02	11	0,02	13	0,02	510	0,49
attitude: positive	104	0,18	15	0,03	52	0,09	24	0,04	418	0,37

n: number of co-occurrences c: coefficient

Acknowledgement

The paper has been supported by the National Research Development and Innovation Office (NKFIH/OTKA), grant number: 127937.

We would like to say thank you to Emese Schiller for her valuable suggestions regarding the text of the manuscript.

Position of Pedagogy in Bosnia and Herczegovina during the Period of the Soviet Influence

Snježana Šušnjara

Abstract: After the Second World War, Bosnia and Herzegovina (BiH) became a part of the newly formed state of Yugoslavia. The new Communist regime followed the Soviet model of making policy in all spheres of life. Therefore, as education was seen as an important part of spreading a new ideology, the school policy was organized in this spirit. The promotion of Marxist-Leninist perspective was evident and seen as the only correct approach in the science and practice of pedagogy. Consequently, BiH pedagogy was uncritically modeled on the Soviet socialist pedagogy. This could be seen through the articles published in the journal *Prosvjetni radnik* (1946–1949). Pedagogical texts of that time were full of quotations from speeches made by Tito or Stalin and from the works of other Soviet pedagogues who glorified a universally education man, the 'New Soviet Man'. For the most parts they referred to "new education that forms the communist consciousness of the masses".[1] My attempt is to analyze post-war socialist pedagogy, based on the state-defined ideology that was submissive to that of the USSR. Bosnia and Herzegovina was a specific republic without higher educational institutions. The first University in this country was established in 1949. Therefore, it was the era when Yugoslavia decided to be distanced from Soviet Union. However, ideological influences in education lasted much longer and were practiced in years that followed.

Keywords: Bosnia and Herzegovina, socialism, pedagogy, Soviet influence, Titoism

Introduction

Bosnia and Herzegovina (BiH) as one of the republics of the newly established state after the Second World War, Yugoslavia, started to re-build its society on a new ground in a challenging postwar situation. New political concepts were introduced to the people who were mostly illiterate. The only political party, communist one, controlled every aspect of people's life and activities. As children were seen as important factor in building the new way of thinking, the party's ideological influences were concentrated on education. Therefore, they were educated to detest enemies, those who lost the war and disagreed

---

1 Boris Petrovič Jesipov and Nikolaj Kirillovič Gončarov, *Pedagogika* (Beograd: Prosveta, 1947), 36.

with newly established regime. In the Yugoslav society private ownership was replaced with state one, care for children became state privilege and public matter.[2] In this way, children stopped to be family possession and became possession of the state.[3] Josip Broz Tito was the president of the Yugoslavia. He was presented as the great son of the nation and children were taught that he loved all of them and he was the one to whom they showed gratitude for their freedom and prosperity. They were following Tito's revolutionary paths, e.g. annual ceremony promoted in schools in order to remember Tito's war achievements. Every student needed to know poems and novels devoted to Tito's life. The cult of Tito was publicly proclaimed and functionated as a system of values, political practice and political system.[4] The new educational politics were created in a manner that "school becomes the institution for entire society and serves to its progress and liberation."[5]

BiH as the one of Yugoslav republics, was organized as a multicultural and multiethnic republic. It served as a good example for advocating 'brotherhood and unity' that was a generally used slogan referring to the arrangement of a multi-ethnic Yugoslavia.[6] The period after 1945 meant a "new beginning", a "zero hour", when the previous existing political tradition was "rewritten" by those who won in World War II. Social, cultural and scientific discussions were under the Soviet influence, which aimed to ensure the utmost guidance and control in every aspect of people's life. This required unconditional obedience and devotion to the Soviet communist representation of the time. Education was an important area in which new ideas were transferred through the teaching process. "Key to the regime's policy of brotherhood and unity were the education, industrial, leisure, security, military and medical sectors. It was in factories, hospitals, schools, army barracks and football pitches that

---

2 Marko Fuček, "Konsolidacija jugoslavenskoga socijalizma kroz ideološke aparate države," *ČSP*, no. 3. (2014): 523.

3 Igor Duda, *Danas kada postajem pionir – Djetinjstvo i ideologija jugoslavenskoga socijalizma* (Zagreb – Pula: Srednja Europa, 2015), 13.

4 Ivo Goldstein and Slavko Goldstein, *Tito* (Zagreb: Profil knjiga, 2015), 576.

5 Ljubomir Krneta, *Prilozi nastavi pedagogije* (Beograd, 1966), 184.

6 Vanja Lozić, "(Re)Shaping History in Bosnian and Herzegovinian Museums," *Culture Unbound* 7, (2015): 307–329.

loyal citizens and Tito devotees were molded."[7] All actions were promoted *in the name of people*.

Impacts of the USSR on the New State's Functioning

As it was mentioned above, the new Yugoslav state followed the model of the USSR in political, social and economic aspect. The Soviet example was a pattern to follow in finding solution for a complex national problem that this country inherited from the past. Therefore, modeling USSR, Yugoslavia was divided to national republics and autonomous regions, legitimizing and promoting national principle as the basis of its constitution. Schooling and education were intensely covered by the Soviet pedagogy in the years after the war. Communist pedagogical discussions made the efforts to sovietize pedagogical science after 1945. Soviet authors' books were strongly recommended. Even the educational staff were co-opted into the Trade unions following the model of the USSR. These two countries, Yugoslavia and USSR that adopted the communist ideology collaborated closely until 1948. Later on, a conflict occurred between the two leaders, Tito and Stalin, and completely changed the relations between them. After the split, the Soviets were no longer idealized, but seen as an enemy. An overview of the relationship between two countries and influences in the sphere of culture and education will be brought forth.

The USSR created an image of super state using the symbols and institutions which served for people's everyday indoctrination. Hammer and sickle, military parades, comrades, heroic results were symbols of their victory. The Yugoslav impressions of the Soviets were made in a special social and political conditions. Policy influenced a lot to understanding of the Soviet Union and relation among them. Yugoslav culture took a great deal from the Soviet culture but did not ignore its specificities. At the time of immediate post-war centralization, Tito asked permission from the Soviets for every act but his own historical battles and victories, as well as support from Great

7 Cathie Carmichael, *A Concise History of Bosnia* (United Kingdom: Cambridge University Press, 2015), 108.

Britain, gave him an idea to rule over the Yugoslavia alone.[8] The Communist party built its success on the synthesis of common interest of the all Yugoslav peoples and the utopian ideas of the society without rich and poor.[9] The new country gave a priority to the state ownership, took economy and production following the Marxist theory. It also promoted agrarian reform and colonization and this influenced common people's way of living. For often, this was not welcomed by people, but politicians used their methods to make them obedient. The planning economy and first five years plan, as it was in the Soviet Union, were implemented. The ideas of liberty, social rights, brotherhood and unity, female rights, empowerment of education and better life for villagers and workers were constantly promoted. In accordance to the Soviet model, intelligence services and Yugoslav army were established. The state acted as the regulator of the construction of social reality. Education of a "New Man", as a responsive and organized process was a big task of the party.[10] Education was under the Soviet influence, as well as journalism, literature, art, film and theatres.[11] After the split in 1948, the Yugoslav authority wanted to find an alternative to the ideological postulates based on the Marxism. Banac defined such an intention as "ideological revisionism".[12] The one-party system did not tolerate any democratic process in the society. The special office for agitation and propaganda, *agitprop*, was formed within the Central Committee of the Communist party of Yugoslavia (KPJ) with an aim to promote ideological messages of the regime. The term *agitprop* was created in USSR-u and served as an abbreviation for state department for agitation and propaganda originating from the central and regional committees of the Soviet Communist party. The main idea of the Soviet Communist party was to connect agitation and propaganda in order to create a powerful weapon in spreading leading ideology. Namely, propaganda affected minds while agitation stimulated emotions. Agitprop had a goal to spread out the

---

8 Ivo Banac, *Sa Staljinom protiv Tita. Informbiroovski rascjepi u jugoslavenskom komunističkom pokretu* (Zagreb: Globus, 1991), 27.

9 Duda, *Danas kada postajem pionir*, 13.

10 Radovan Papić, "Ministar prosvjete o NR BiH o nekim pitanjima prosvjetne politike," *Prosvjetni radnik*, No. 11 (1948): 7.

11 Maja Novak, "Predodžbe o Sovjetskome Savezu u jugoslavenskoj kulturi prije i nakon 1948. godine," *Jat – Časopis studenata kroatistike*, No. 3 (2017): 44.

12 Banac, *Sa Staljinom*, 138.

communist ideas and propagate achievements of the communist regime.[13] As it was case in USSR, the agitprop observed political education and mass media in Yugoslavia and initiated people's support for the party program.[14] The activity of this powerful apparatus of agitation and propaganda of Yugoslavia was determined by the party monopole at each level of society. Propaganda and indoctrination had an important role in preserving power presenting to people that the ruling policy worked for their benefit. The mission of propaganda was to manipulate symbols in order to limit freedom of choice and to influence others to behave in a way they would not normally have done, believing that their decisions were achieved by themselves.[15]

The state offices and agitprop apparatus promoted ideological indoctrination among the population at all levels through official and unofficial channels. The Communist party was in charge for spreading the Yugoslav ideology among children. Amongst various ideological apparatus that state ensured for children the basic place was reserved for education. School was the only institution that took children from their families at the most vulnerable age and offered them knowledge colored by ruling ideology.[16] Therefore, school became the most important state institution that enabled the regime to promote its ideas and messages. The staff that worked in the ministry of education, councils for education, science and culture, schools and educational boards were ideologically trained and instructed to transfer information through school books and lectures during a long period of children's schooling. Therefore, Tito and party could easily control the educational process, regulated and modified children's minds. Children were trapped between family and the state that influenced school policy, between traditionally patriarchal society and the new one promoted by the state and its apparatus.[17] As the dominant institution, the state inculcated

---

[13] Branko Petranović. *Istorija Jugoslavije 1918–1988, Treća knjiga – Socijalistička Jugoslavija 1945–1988* (Beograd: Nolit, 1988), 121.

[14] Britannica, Agitprop. Accessed July 16, 2021. https://www.britannica.com/topic/agitprop.

[15] Reana Senjković, "Propaganda, mediji, heroji, mitovi i ratnici," *Polemos*, No. 8 (2001): 34

[16] Siniša Malešević, *Ideologija, legitimnost i nova država* (Zagreb: Jesenski i Turk, 2004), 38.

[17] Duda, *Danas kada postajem pionir*, 13.

and eradicated family influence, religion and traditional values as patterns of identification and import its official versions.

The Educational Situation in Bosnia and Herzegovina

Throughout history, educational efforts made in BiH were always framed in accordance to the prevailed regime and educational institutions merely followed orders given by the authorities. When BiH was a part of the Austrian-Hungarian Empire, teachers who worked in teacher training schools, established by the new government, dealt with pedagogical issues attempting to prepare future teachers in the best manner. They were promoters of the European pedagogical achievements, transferring Herbart's ideas, especially German, e. g., *Arbeitsschule* (labor school) methods or *Reformpädagogik* (Progressive or New School Education) approach. Almost all of those teachers were educated abroad and were experts in the field of their interest. When the Austrian-Hungarian Empire collapsed, the new state was formed in the Balkan region, the Kingdom of Yugoslavia. This state was much more centralized and politically incorrect towards majority of its regions except Serbia. Therefore, education was not seen as a priority. Conversely, there was a trend of closing down teacher training schools despite the enormous amount of illiteracy (72%). The minister of education from Belgrade even claimed that there was a hyper production of intellectuals. Therefore, he ordered that teacher schools and gymnasia had to be closed down and teachers fired or pensioned off. This was considered as an anti-cultural and anti-social action among intellectuals of that time.[18] Up to 1941, BiH was at the last position regarding culture and education in the Kingdom of Yugoslavia. Only 1.043 elementary schools with 2.321 teachers and about 150.000 pupils were available for BiH population.[19]

After World War II, there was an increase in the birth rate in BiH. The number of children who needed to attend schools was bigger than the available

---

18 Mladen Bevanda, *Pedagoška misao u BiH, 1918–1941* (Sarajevo: Filozofski fakultet, 2001), 80.

19 Radovan Papić, "Ministar prosvjete o NR BiH o nekim pitanjima prosvjetne politike," 7.

school's space which was mostly devastated during the war.[20] A lack of teachers was evident and a part of the pre-war teachers was not ready to accept and follow the new-fangled ideas. BiH did not have any university or faculty before World War II except theological faculties.[21] The Catholic Church had three higher theological schools: Vrhbosanska high theological school, founded in 1890; Franciscan theology in Mostar was founded in 1895, and the Franciscan seminary in Sarajevo in 1909.[22] "Austrian authorities recognized theological studies in monasteries and placed them in the rank of faculties."[23] There were 1354 elementary schools with 2750 teachers and about 300.000 pupils in 1948. Only 811 school buildings were functional with 1629 classrooms while 566 schools with 765 classrooms were placed in private buildings that were not suitable for school work.[24] The lack of teachers forced the new regime to organize short-term courses for those who had finished some classes of gymnasium or teacher training school. This resulted in inadequately trained staff. It was estimated that three quarters of teachers had finished a basic course instead of attending teacher training school.[25] The words of Lenin, leader of the Russian Bolshevik Revolution, were transferred among educational staff with an aim to encourage them to act properly. "A teacher should be put at such a high position where he never stood up before and could ever stand in the bourgeois society."[26]

The entire country was in a phase of reconstruction, but educational process was not conducted in a proper way. Because of this, numerous children were left out of school. Many adults were illiterate, as well. The authority planned to modernize society, decreasing the number of illiterate people

---

20 Snježana Šušnjara, *Special Education Contained in Educational Magazines and School Practice in Bosnia and Herzegovina and Croatia, 1958–1990* (Joensuu: University of Joensuu, 2009), 29.

21 Snježana Šušnjara, "Pedagogy of Bosnia and Herzegovina between Past and Future," *Journal of Contemporary Educational Studies*, no. 3 (2016): 90.

22 S. M. Džaja, *Bosna i Hercegovina u Austrougarskom razdoblju (1878–1918)* (Mostar-Zagreb: Ziral, 2002), 72–73.

23 Anđelko Barun, *Svjedoci i učitelji, povijest franjevaca Bosne Srebrene* (Sarajevo-Zagreb: Svjetlo riječi, 2003), 383.

24 Papić, "Ministar prosvjete", 8.

25 Snježana Šušnjara, "Bosnia and Herzegovina under the Communist Regime: an Outlook on Educational policy," *Historia scholastica* 7, no. 1 (2021): 118–120.

26 Papić, "Ministar prosvjete", 8.

(70%). Therefore, the University of Working People organized evening schools for adults.[27] The triumph in the war allowed the communists to work on building of a society with a special political strategy. The Marxist standard and its world's view were an example to follow. New creators of education prized physical work as the only way that would contribute to formation of a proper socialist man. Prominent politicians fought for expelling intellectualism from schools by including more practical work for a "real" laborer. The educational policy was made uniform and full of normative trends.[28] "There is no new school without proper political instructions of teachers. All teachers need to adopt the Marxist-Lenin science in order to promote it in their everyday work."[29]

There was a journal called *Prosvjetni radnik* (Educational Laborer) published in Sarajevo from 1946 to 1949. Its authors dealt with the situation in education, quoting Lenin and Stalin immensely, attempting to introduce school practice from the USSR. One of the authors quoted Lenin who claimed "it is not possible to work without a plan, the longstanding plan for a serious success. Do not be afraid of longstanding plans: without them we cannot promote economic change. You should put all your strength in every place to fulfil this aim."[30] In accordance to this proposition, a five years plan in education was promoted in USSR as it was mentioned before. The same plan was accepted in Yugoslavia and practically promoted in all republics. The main task was to eliminate illiteracy among people in the age below 45. At the same time, it was necessary to propagate "proper" ideological attitudes spreading them broadly. The ready-made structure of the Soviet socialist approach to education was applied without critical observation. The Ministry of Education created a series of courses to train and educate youth and potential teaching staff. There were numerous difficulties in holding of these courses. Local resistance was apparent at both the administrative and

---

27 Snježana Šušnjara, *Razvoj specijalnog školstva u Bosni i Hercegovini od 1958. do 1990. godine* (Zagreb–Sarajevo: Synopsis, 2013), 43.

28 Snježana Šušnjara, "Development of School Systems and Pedagogy in Bosnia and Herzegovina from the Period after World War II to the 1970s," *Journal of Contemporary Educational Studies*, no. 2 (2015): 64–80.

29 Papić, "Ministar prosvjete", 9.

30 N. N. "U SSSR i škole postavljaju svoj petogodišnji plan," *Prosvjetni Radnik*, no. 1 (1946): 27.

individual level. One of the main obstacles was the attitude of the Regional People's Committees which had frequently not joined the "mobilization of youth" and had not sent the required number of course participants.[31] Government administrators blamed older generations for this resistance of youth. They considered that youth inherited the primitive attitudes from them as well as negative standpoints towards education. In addition to this, between 1945 and 1946, large numbers of youths had been taken away to work in the labor battalions in order to be involved in the reconstruction process of new country that was devastated during the war. As well as learning about basic hygiene and health conditions, how to read and write, trainees were also required to know the Yugoslav socialist system, and the statements of Lenin and Stalin on education and social justice.[32]

The five years plan determined to remove all remnants of bourgeois history as soon as possible and to undertake steps to literate adults in a big manner. The winter campaign of struggling with national illiteracy was promoted, as well as the organized courses in companies, in constructing fields and in the most distanced regions. The main role in this process was taken by teachers.

> Their pioneer role at the field of labor class literacy in our country is the outstanding record of the high patriotic awareness of teachers, their firm determination and constant wish to contribute with their cultural and educational work towards a prompt construction of the powerful building of socialism. With their unselfish efforts and sacrificial work, they only confirmed the actual thought of the great Stalin who pointed out the importance of the Soviet teacher: 'Falange of people's teachers is the most important part of the great labor class army that builds our country on the socialist basis'.[33]

According to the efforts made in order to attract adults to education in 1946, those courses served for recuperation, and physical strengthening developing understanding of life in collective, comradeship, culture and manners. Their achievements were interpreted as important for building of socialism,

---

[31] Rory Yeomans, "From Comrades to Consumers: Holidays, Leisure Time and Ideology in Communist Yugoslavia," in *Yugoslavia's Sunny Side: A History of Tourism in Socialism, 1940s–1980s*, ed. Hanes Granditz (Budapest: Central European University Press, 2010), 75

[32] Yeomans, "From Comrades," 75.

[33] Hasan Đikić, "Za upis omladine u učiteljske škole," *Prosvjetni radnik*, no. 4 (1948): 1.

which demonstrated that the Yugoslav worker was entering a new era.[34] "The proletarian was idealized; he was depicted as being the driving force of the future, the ultimate criterion for determining the truth."[35]

A New Type of Teacher

Bosnian and Herzegovinian authorities promoted an idea that youth education had an enormous importance in building of socialism in the country. This task needed to be supported by culturally and politically responsive people that teacher training school was expected to produce. In the post-war period, a lack of professional teachers was evident. Therefore, the authority took the decision to re-open teacher training schools in places of their previous existence and to organize short courses for those who already possessed some knowledge or had finished few years of gymnasium. As a result, teacher training schools were opened in Travnik, Sarajevo, Banja Luka, Mostar and other larger towns and cities in the republic.[36] Tito's messages were broadcast all the time in order to encourage people to action: "Our youth is our future. From the way of someone's upbringing depends the future of all people." Teacher training school main task was to educate youth in the spirit of socialism and "in accordance with the wish of the great leader and teacher of our peoples, comrade Tito," who clearly revealed this wish with the words: "A teacher in the new Yugoslavia will be on a higher position that he never experienced before."[37] It was evident how Soviet ideas were transferred through public speeches. Hasan Đikić, teacher and regional education officer was in charge of opening a wider meeting of all currently available intellectual forces that was held in Mostar in 1945, with the aim of forming the Society for Cultural Cooperation with the USSR.[38] Later in his contributions to the Prosvjetni radnik, he constantly mentioned the great instructors of socialism, Lenin, Stalin, and Tito, emphasizing in every occasion that a condition for building

---

34 Yeomans, "From Comrades," 75.

35 Kosta Nikolić and Ivana Dobrivojević, "Creating a Communist Yugoslavia in the Second World War," *Balcanica*, No. XLVIII (2017): 265.

36 Šušnjara, "Bosnia and Herzegovina," 121.

37 Đikić, "Za upis," 1–3.

38 N. N. "U Mostaru je formirano Društvo za kulturnu saradnju s SSSR," *Sarajevski dnevnik* (1945).

of socialism in one country meant working on the enlightenment of laborers from villages and towns. Tito's messages were echoing: "It is necessary to send a great number of youngsters to teacher training schools in order to create a future generation of teachers"[39]. However, teachers who used to work before the war and were accustomed to another way of working and believing were not readily accepted by the new regime. The prosecution of political opponents was at stake. The mass displacement of people from rural to urban areas was encouraged and promoted. All of these changes and in particular mistrust towards intellectuals marked the first years after the war.[40]

The main goal of the state politics was to completely divide education from previous influences, especially religious one. The Communist party's intention was to found a new state as independent, socialist and secular. "School is free of the church and religious influence and its educational activity are based on the Marxist theory. The whole society is involved in the process of upbringing and education. Through its representatives, it supports school to maintain this task."[41] However, the party agents brought not very much encouraging information from the country regarding this issue. They reported that students and teachers were absent from school during the religious holidays. "The damaging phenomenon of superstition and the absence of students and even teachers during the religious holidays have to be diminished. Teachers as educators who served as an example to youth must not support the remnants of the clerical sort and back ward behavior in our schools."[42] It was apparent that people were not recognized for their individual qualities apart from social circumstances. Communists did not want to face any deviation in religious matters. They considered their party as sacralized and as the only religion that should be followed in the new state, as happened in the Soviet Union. Different form of obedience had been transferred through a new religion, communist atheism.[43] The most

---

39 Đikić, "Za upis," 6.

40 Ivana Dobrivojević, "Od ruralnog ka urbanom, modernizacija Republike Bosne i Hercegovine u FNRJ 1945–1955," in *Identitet Bosne i Hercegovine kroz historiju*, ed. H. Kamberović (Sarajevo: Institut za historiju, 2011), 7–8.

41 Krneta, *Prilozi nastavi*, 184.

42 Midhat Begić, "O radu i zadacima naših srednjih škola," *Prosvjetni radnik*, no. 9 (1948): 9.

43 Nikolić and Dobrivojević, "Creating a Communist," 263–265.

effective tool of proclaimed atheism laid in fact that the Communist Party of Yugoslavia had a leading role in society guaranteed by the Constitution. As atheism was the main pre-condition for membership in the Party, the atheists were at all leading position in the society. State atheism had its most extreme manifestation immediately after the war and during the consolidation of the communist order. Priests were liquidated or imprisoned, believers were exposed to violence. Later on, the complete secularization of public life was promoted. The teaching of religious subjects in schools was forbidden. School books did not contain any religious content and critique of religious was stimulated instead.[44] According to the Law on National Schools, which was adopted on November 26, 1951, the school received the status of a social institution whose employees became public social workers with the task of raising children in a socialist spirit.[45] In the fight against the influence of religion in general, the government wholeheartedly counted on the support of the school staff, and in this sense, it tried to "control" teachers either by gaining in the political sense, or by admonitions, threats or dismissals from work. Examples of teachers who lost their jobs or lost certain privileges clearly testify to the attitude of the new government towards religious teachers. The dismissal of teacher Alojzia Ulman with the explanation that "she did not adopt a materialistic view of the world", or the exclusion from the teacher's association of Hela Žnidarčić, a teacher in Bosanski Brod, which was explained by "her expression of religious feelings".[46]

New Type of Science

The communists saw the Marxist-Leninist model of economic, political and social life as the only one that was able to bring freedom and prosperity to people. The creators of the new country really believed that such an approach could be applied into common people's practice. Nothing was equally important as the new ideology promoted through the "Marxist-Leninist science", as they used to call. A person could be an expert in his profession but without

44 Hrvoje Matković, *Povijest Jugoslavije – Hrvatski pregled* (Zagreb: Naklada Pavičić, 2003), 283.

45 Ivana Beus, "Prosvjetna politika u službi ideološkoga pre/odgoja u Hercegovini (1945–1952)," *Hercegovina*, no. 2 (2016): 281.

46 Beus, "Prosvjetna politika", 277.

a proper political base, s/he would be treated as an intruder. Therefore, they were persistent in promoting this model in every occasion. They were quoting Stalin who emphasized the importance of studying the Marxist-Lenin literature in his report on the 18th congress of SKP, 1939:

> Education and forming of the young staff are usually made by their grouping around some sort of scientific and technical discipline in accordance to their professions. It is important and meaningful. It is not necessary to be an expert in medicine and in the same time an expert in botanic or physics and vice versa. But there is one discipline of science that must be obligatory for all Bolsheviks of any scientific discipline – it is the Marxist-Lenin science of society, social development, development of proletarian revolution, socialism structuring development, victory of communism. A real Leninist cannot be the one who called himself a Leninist but who is attached to his own profession and nothing else. Leninist cannot be only a specialist in one discipline of science that he loves – he must be at the same time a political and public worker who is vividly interested in his country's destiny… Of course, this will be new burden for Bolshevik specialist but the burden that would be paid multifunctionally.[47]

The author Begić commented that these words were very much appreciated by those who worked on the production of such experts, teachers in the first place. The same author claimed that it was necessary to start an ideological battle of progressive forces within the working class against slavery and the reactionary bourgeois forces of the world. "The neutral path cannot exist because the science itself and scientific facts are never politically neutral."[48] He mentioned Copernicus, Galileo and Darwin as models to follow in order to discover the relationship of science and party which is always linked with the social position of one epoch.

> A teacher who did not accept the Marxist-Leninist science cannot properly explain problems of a subject he taught. Teaching must be based on the Marxist-Leninist science in our working-peasant state which is in a phase of building socialism. Only a teacher with this attitude would be qualitative and effective. Opposite to this is a teacher who does not believe in these scientific truths but in clerical lies and deceptions. The teacher who is a believer cannot teach biology because his

47 Begić, "O radu," 24–25.
48 Begić, "O radu," 24–25.

> attitudes and belief show that he does not believe in the power of nature. There are still teachers who oppress students with their prejudices and bourgeois ideology.[49]

Evidently, religion that was expelled from schools was changed to a new religion – dogmatic Marxism. Marxism was not only the school subject but also the state ideology and prescribed world view. Therefore, every teaching subject had to include Marxist ideology.[50] This was a typical example of the procedure that led to "empty" educational science by "stealing" its basic professional pedagogical questions while trying to "publicize" the educational image of the "New Man".

The position of the "new communist elite" in the field of educational science was occupied by the new 'experts' whose main characteristic was participation in the National Liberation War[51] and membership in the Communist party. Denunciations or removals of domestic scientific pedagogical experts from the interwar period proceeded. Thus, key positions in educational policy were occupied by people who also held high positions in the Communist party. The party used to send loyal and prosperous members to additional education and this was a way of spreading and promoting its own ideas. This was the case with the newly established faculties in Bosnia and Herzegovina and the necessary personnel. Most of the future professors studied in Belgrade or Zagreb and after that became the promoters of the ideas of self-managed socialism. There was no other way to progress. Thus, pedagogical theory and practice were created in this spirit and developed gradually under the open eye of the party.[52]

The establishment of Bosnian-Herzegovinian higher institutions after 1945 could only be understood within the context of country extensive transformations. The first university was founded in BiH in 1949 as a part of the Yugoslavian education system.[53] "The avant-garde of the working class", the Communist Party, became the highest authority that made decisions on "what

49 Begić, "O radu," 26–29.

50 Jadranka Čačić-Kumpes, "Odgojno-obrazovni sustav i etnički konflikt," *Migracijske teme*, no. 8 (1992): 8.

51 The People's Liberation Struggle or the People's Liberation War (abbr. NOB, NOR), the name given to the to the liberation struggle (1941–45) under the leadership of the Yugoslav Communist Party in socialist Yugoslavia.

52 Šušnjara, "Development of School Systems," 92–93.

53 Šušnjara, "Bosnia and Herzegovina," 120.

was considered scientific and what was not, thus making the universities and academic elites directly dependent upon the party-political apparatus."[54] Academic education had a significant importance and served as a path towards social upgrading ensuring better social status and professional position. "During the immediate post-WWII period the demands of an expanding leadership in politics, state administration, and the economy meant that the universities were filled with people seeking formal qualifications retroactively – graduating with a 'Party diploma'."[55] However, a university education was important but not the only requirement for social improvement at that period of time. Additional pre-conditions, such as politico-ideological loyalty and social ties were crucial.[56] The communist regime obviously mobilized public education system with schools as the instruments for propagation of specific interests to support political power.

Postwar Socialist Pedagogy

The socialist pedagogy in the postwar period, as it was already mentioned, passively accepted and re-interpreted a concept of the Soviet socialist pedagogy in the first phase of its development. In the second phase it followed a new politically proclaimed doctrine of the Central Committee of KPJ.[57] Medveš claimed that the term 'socialist pedagogy' was not "internally differentiated as was used to characterized both education policy and pedagogical science"[58] in the period after 1945. The consolidated practice immediately after the war was the classification of pedagogical orientation by the socio-economic formations such as feudal, bourgeois, socialist. "The use of the adjective 'socialist' to characterize a scientific paradigm or current of scientific thought

---

[54] Bodo Weber, *Kriza univerziteta i perspective mladih naučnika u Bosni i Hercegovini* (Sarajevo: Zaklada Friedrich Erbert, 2007), 82.

[55] Weber, *Kriza*, 87.

[56] Weber, *Kriza*, 87.

[57] Štefka Batinić and Igor Radeka, "Pedagogija i školstvo u Hrvatskoj od završetka Drugoga svjetskog rata do kraja 1950-ih," in *Razvoj i aktualne tendencije pedagogije i školstva na području nekadašnje Jugoslavije*, ed. Edvard Protner (Maribor: University of Maribor Press, 2020), 110.

[58] Zdenko Medveš, "Socialist Pedagogy: Caught between the Myth of the Fairness of the Unified School and Cultural Hegemony," *Journal of Contemporary Educational Studies*, no. 2 (2015): 15.

and research could only mean the forcible subjection of pedagogical science to education policy."[59]

Pedagogical theory as well as pedagogical practice were under the strong influence of the dominant ideology. In the first years after the war the space for maneuvering was not large. Loyalty was proved by supporting of the Soviet examples and dividing from the pre-war cultural pedagogy and *Arbeitsschule* (labor school). This meant a division from the main protagonists of this pedagogy and school, especially from those who were determined in their professional and ideological orientation. Political domination of one party confirmed education as a source for promoting its goals.

> Socialism was a process in which the past and present were deconstructed in order to make room for the construction of the future. Constructed by the 'enlightened vanguard', this bright future was to be built in opposition to the present and the past. Hence, the forces of the past and present, 'retrograde elements' and 'conservative forces' are the main enemy of socialism. The stronger they are, the more brutal the violence against them must be. Violence is justified if it serves 'social progress'.[60]

Curriculum of compulsory education was a tool for the state to accomplish its goals. Therefore, education "is used – and perhaps manipulated –in an effort to create particular kind of citizens who suit the national stories and imaginations that governments and other agents hope to foster."[61] Some distinguished professors and teachers from the interwar period were isolated and excluded from the official pedagogical community. At the time of ideological assessments, the competences of theorists of pedagogy were determined with the quality of their interpretation and application of the Soviet socialist pedagogy. The words of teacher Salih Ljubunčić who became aware of new rules in education clearly picture the status of educational science at that time:

> Pedagogues-authors used to write under a direct influence of cognition, while now they write in accordance with their position. There is a significant difference there: previous writers on pedagogy always revealed knowledge and experience, a

---

59 Medveš, "Socialist Pedagogy," 15–16.

60 Nikolić and Dobrivojević, "Creating a Communist," 262–263.

61 Lynn A. Staeheli and Daniel Hammett, "Educating the New National Citizen: Education, Political Subjectivity, and Divided Societies," *Citizenship Studies* 14, no. 6 (2010): 668.

> great extent of being well-read and scholarly, whereas today's authors write without insight. With the exception of those who had written before, the present-day authors writing about pedagogy show they have not read widely and if they mention any bibliography, it only reveals their shallowness. By applying the 'socialist stance' to their discipline, they erase everything non-scholarly, 'scholarly' in their opinion being only the Marxist. Thus, they free themselves of reading and working with anything outside that particular framework.[62]

The analysis of changes in schooling in the first five postwar years discovered inadequately arranged intervention into school system and practice based on "trial and error". As expected, the biggest achievement was made in restoring school buildings and fostering courses for the illiterates while the modification of entire school system requested a better professional organization.[63] It seemed that new educational system ignored the fact that the main rule regarding properly positioning of the educational goals required to be evaluated from the exact posed conditions as John Dewey suggested. Opposite to this, educational goals of the new school system were produced from the ideological interpretation of the existing conditions and requirements of the state ideology.[64]

Apart from teacher training schools that were influential in developing pedagogical thought and practice, there was no other scientific and educational structure in BiH.[65] The absence of the development of pedagogical theory and research in education was evident in the period from 1945 to 1950s. These processes were linked to the contemporary development of education and pedagogical thought in Yugoslavia, but the shortcomings of this pedagogy continued longer in BiH. The Soviet pedagogy was put at the forefront and at the same time the accomplishments of the civic pedagogy, civic-oriented education[66], were excluded and seen as negative. Later on, when the first University was established in Sarajevo, and first experts in pedagogical

---

62 Salih Ljubunčić, *Dnevnički zapisi* (Zagreb: Arhivska zbirka Hrvatskoga školskog muzeja, HŠM A 3753 Ljubunčić, Salih, 1952).
63 Batinić and Radeka, "Pedagogija," 120.
64 Čačić-Kumpes, "Odgojno obrazovni," 7.
65 Bevanda, *Pedagoška misao*, 17.
66 Vučina Zorić, "Fundamentals of John Dewey's Concept of Civic Education," *History of Education and Children's Literature*, no. 10 (2015): 445.

field were produced, they started to work on a preferred educational discourse in accordance to the current ideology.[67]

Translations of Russian editions on pedagogy shaped the theoretical basis for pedagogues in the postwar period. The manuals with pedagogical heritage of Marx, Engels, Lenin, Plekhanov, Stalin and Krupskaya were translated as well as Soviet papers from pedagogical psychology.[68] Pedagogical theory was learnt from the textbook *Pedagogika* (Pedagogy, 1947) by Jesipov and Gončarov, collections of essays *O vaspitanju* (On education, 1947) and *Osnovni problemi pedagogije* (The main problems of education, 1947), the book *Pedagogija* (Pedagogy, 1949) edited by Gruzdjev and other Soviet texts on pedagogy.[69] Lenin triad of awareness, "from vivid observing to abstract thinking and from the last one to the practice",[70] became the theoretical basis of the Soviet didactic that prevailed in Yugoslav educational system.[71] "The methodological approach emphasized phrasemaking, 'citatology' apologetics, dogmatism and speculative deductivism."[72]

Consequently, the previous dominance of German pedagogy was strongly criticized as well as any reference to preceding pedagogical achievements. The Marxist-Lenin approach was seen as the only one valued to be used in the pedagogical science and practice. The era of the Soviet domination left a significant ideological impact in Yugoslavia that lasted much longer after the split with Soviets in 1948. School books were treated as an instrument of the revolution, the basic tool of education as well as influence to people consciousness.[73] Post war lecturing needed to be based on the combination

---

67 Šušnjara, "Pedagogy of Bosnia and Herzegovina," 91.

68 Nataša Vujisić Živković, "Konstitutivni diskontinuitet: školstvo i pedagogija u socijalističkoj Srbiji (1945–1990)," in *Razvoj i aktualne tendencije pedagogije i školstva na području nekadašnje Jugoslavije*, ed. Edvard Protner (Maribor: University of Maribor Press, 2020), 159.

69 Batinić and Radeka, "Pedagogija," 110.

70 Ladislav Bognar and Milan Matijević, *Dvadeset godina jedne didaktike – Kako smo stvarali Didaktiku* (2014), 9–10. Accessed August 30, 2021. http://ladislav-bognar.net/files/Kako%20smo%20stvarali%20Didaktiku%20%284%29.pdf.

71 Bognar and Matijević, *Dvadeset godina*, 5.

72 Mile Ilić, "Periodizacija razvoja pedagoške nauke u BiH (1945–1980)," *Naša škola*, no. 3–4 (1989): 104.

73 Ljubodrag Dimić, *Agitprop Kultura. Agitpropovska Faza Kulturne Politike u Srbiji 1945–1952* (Beograd: Radna organizacija Rad, 1988), 153.

of the Marxism, Leninism, Stalinism and at the end Titoism.[74] Consequently, from 1948 new way of communist ideology appeared under the name Titoism, in accordance to the main leader of the country – Tito. Titoism was the totalitarian ideology of communism, the way of managing one party communist country that was opposite to Soviet and Stalin domination. This variation of communism theory had an independent position in foreign policy and moderate ways of communist system (labor self-management, free travel, bigger independence of the federal units) in accordance with the Constitution from 1974.[75] Titoism existed from 1941 to 1980 and functioned as a system of value, political practice and organization named by Tito who was its main protagonist and the author.[76]

New Way – Socialist Self-management Pedagogy

On the third Plenum of the League of the Communist Party of Yugoslavia (SK KPJ), in 1949 an explanation on dogmatism in science and pedagogy was indicated. It was strongly stated that the goal of education should be "[…] the forming of universally educated free constructor of socialism, who is distanced from bureaucracy and narrow mindedness".[77] This announced new potentials in theoretical thinking and a liberation from the USSR's control and influence. Consequently, this political settling of accounts with Stalinism was also produced by the pedagogues and their articles concerning the Soviet pedagogy, which highlighted the negative aspects of this soviet pedagogy approach and related delusions in political and theoretical concepts. They the mentioned pedagogues contributed with this to, "an affirmation of dialectic and materialistic opinions in pedagogy".[78] In the 1950s, new winds started to blow. Namely, it was suggested that a school of the socialistic society should

---

74 Snježana Koren, *Politika povijesti u Jugoslaviji (1945–1960)* (Zagreb: Srednja Europa, 2012), 120.

75 Hrvatski jezični portal, Titoizam. Accessed July 11, 2021. http://hjp.znanje.hr/index.php?show=search.

76 Goldstein and Goldstein, *Tito*, 576.

77 Gavrilo Subotić, "Pedagoške misli Rodoljuba Čolakovića," *Naša škola*, no. 3–4, (1985): 232.

78 Nikola Filipović, "Odnos pedagogije i politike u vremenu od 1945–1970," *Naša škola*, no. 9–10, (1971): 514.

predominantly concentrate on modeling character "to raise active laborers for the socialistic country."[79] The Pedagogical society of BiH was established in 1950 and promoted the pedagogical magazine *Naša škola* that published articles related to educational issues. Tito's cult was constantly developed and leading pedagogues used to idealize him and his work. For example, Nikola Filipović, very influential person in BiH policy and professor at the Chair of Pedagogy that was established in 1963 stressed that Tito was an expert in making firm connections between the party's policy and pedagogy.[80] He also emphasized "[…] the domination of policy over pedagogy was 'cultivated' and accepted as a normal fact which had a positive effect towards understanding the behavior of political and professional employees in ministries, committees and boards, as well as pedagogues in different institutions."[81]

Conclusion

In accordance with all information presented above, it is evident that education in Bosnia and Herzegovina during the Yugoslav period was a combination of propaganda, ideological messages and slogans. All educational contents served to glorify and promote war victories and individuals that gave their life for freedom and better future. Through the years that followed, this ideological approach did not lose its strength. In the immediate postwar period, the theory and practice of pedagogy were profoundly influenced by the dominant political ideology. Faithfulness was proven by loyalty to Soviet models and dissociating from cultural pedagogy and the German labor school that prevailed before the war. The prominent protagonists of that pedagogy were forbidden to mention if they were persistent in their professional ideological orientation. Pedagogy and a school system were seen as a appropriate area for promoting a new ideology led by the communist party that had a strong political influence. School books and reading materials were translations of the soviet pedagogical experts. In regard to school theory and practice, everything was done and organized following the model of Soviet Union. It is noticeable that larger promotion of socialism appeared after split

---

79 Subotić, "Pedagoške misli," 240.
80 Šušnjara, "Development," 86.
81 Filipović, "Odnos pedagogije," 512.

with Soviets in 1948. Yugoslavia and its republics struggled to find a new way searching for the system most adaptable to laborer – self-management. The authority transferred its own values in different manners attempting to create children's characters in accordance to its ideological intentions. The Communist pioneer and youth associations were good examples of its action. Education was seen as a fertile soil for promotion of Tito's cult and his ideological strategies. Teachers were promotors of political ideas and were completely subordinated to the regime. Their main mission was to teach children transferring to them an ideological concept proposed by the educational authority that were devoted to the communist party and its aims. The state made the crucial impact on the construction and reconstruction of the mechanisms to create a social reality and educational process. Nevertheless, BiH did not promote any complete theoretical or empirical pedagogical research or study in this period of time. Up to 1960s the pedagogists dealt with current issues of pedagogical practice and educational policy. That had a great importance in a situation of school system reconstruction and insufficient development of pedagogical theory.[82] "In comparison to social action on the development of culture and education, investments in pedagogical research in BiH were still modest [...]. Comparing social relations towards pedagogy with relations towards other discipline, one could conclude that pedagogy was neglected, not only in terms of funding but also in terms of importance."[83]

Literature

Banac, Ivo. *Sa Staljinom protiv Tita. Informbiroovski rascjepi u jugoslavenskom komunističkom pokretu*. Zagreb: Globus, 1991.

Barun, Anđelko. *Svjedoci i učitelji, povijest franjevaca Bosne Srebrene.* Sarajevo-Zagreb: Svjetlo riječi, 2003.

Batinić, Štefka and Igor Radeka. "Pedagogija i školstvo u Hrvatskoj od završetka Drugoga svjetskog rata do kraja 1950-ih." In *Development and Current Trends of Pedagogy and Education in the Former Yugoslavia*, edited by Edvard Protner, 108–130. Maribor: University of Maribor Press, 2020.

---

82 Šušnjara, "Development," 91.

83 Mile Ilić, *Savremeni tokovi u pedagogiji* (Banja Luka: Novi glas, 1994), 31.

Begić, Midhat. "O radu i zadacima naših srednjih škola." *Prosvjetni radnik*, no. 9 (1948): 5–37.

Beus, Ivana. "Prosvjetna politika u službi ideološkoga pre/odgoja u Hercegovini (1945–1952)." *Hercegovina*, no. 2 (2016): 249–285.

Bevanda, Mladen. *Pedagoška misao u BiH 1918–1941*. Sarajevo: Filozofski fakultet, 2001.

Bognar, Ladislav and Milan Matijević. *Dvadeset godina jedne didaktike – Kako smo stvarali Didaktiku*. 2014. Accessed August 30, 2021. http://ladislav-bognar.net/files/Kako%20smo%20stvarali%20Didaktiku%20%284%29.pdf.

Britannica, Agitprop. Accessed July 16, 2021. https://www.britannica.com/topic/agitprop.

Carmichael Cathie. *A Concise History of Bosnia*. United Kingdom: Cambridge University Press, 2015.

Cipek, Tihomir. "Stoljeće diktatura u Hrvatskoj." In *Hrvatska politika u XX. Stoljeću*, edited by Jelena Hekman. Zagreb: Matica hrvatska, 2006.

Čačić-Kumpes, Jadranka. "Odgojno-obrazovni sustav i etnički konflikt." *Migracijske teme*, no. 8, (1992): 5–13.

Dimić, Ljubodrag. *Agitprop Kultura. Agitpropovska Faza Kulturne Politike u Srbiji 1945–1952*. Beograd: Radna organizacija Rad, 1988.

Dobrivojević, Ivana. "Od ruralnog ka urbanom, modernizacija Republike Bosne i Hercegovine u FNRJ 1945–1955." In *Identitet Bosne i Hercegovine kroz historiju*, ed. H. Kamberović. Sarajevo: Institut za historiju, 2011.

Duda, Igor. "Svakodnevica pedesetih: od nestašica do privrednog čuda." Način u jeziku/Književnost i kultura pedesetih. In *Zbornik radova 36. seminara Zagrebačke slavističke škole*, edited by Krešimir Bagić, 69–85. Zagreb: Filozofski fakultet – Zagrebačka slavistička škola, 2008.

Duda, Igor. *Danas kada postajem pionir – Djetinjstvo i ideologija jugoslavenskoga socijalizma*, Zagreb – Pula: Srednja Europa, 2015.

Đikić, Hasan. "Za upis omladine u učiteljske škole." *Prosvjetni radnik*, no. 4 (1948): 1–6.

Džaja, S. M. *Bosna i Hercegovina u Austrougarskom razdoblju (1878–1918)*. Mostar-Zagreb: Ziral, 2002.

Fuček, Marko. "Konsolidacija jugoslavenskoga socijalizma kroz ideološke aparate države." *ČSP*, no. 3. (2014): 515–534.

Goldstein Ivo and Slavko Goldstein. *Tito*. Zagreb: Profil knjiga, 2015.

Filipović, Nikola. Odnos pedagogije i politike u vremenu od 1945–1970. *Naša škola*, no. 9–10, (1971): 511–525.

Hebrang, Branko. "Politička promidžba kao socijalna pojava." *National Security and the Future*, no. 1–2 (2012): 11–126.

Hrvatski jezični portal, Titoizam. Accessed July 11, 2021. http://hjp.znanje.hr/index.php?show=search.

Ilić, Mile. "Periodizacija razvoja pedagoške nauke u BiH (1945–1980)." *Naša škola*, no. 3–4 (1989): 104.

Ilić, Mile. *Savremeni tokovi u pedagogiji*. Banja Luka: Novi glas, 1994.

Jesipov Petrovič Boris and Nikolaj Kirillovič Gončarov. *Pedagogika*. Beograd: Prosveta, 1947.

Korenčić, Mirko. *Stanovništvo i naselja SFRH 1857. – 1971*. Zagreb: JAZU, 1979.

Koren, Snježana. *Politika povijesti u Jugoslaviji (1945–1960)*. Zagreb: Srednja Europa, 2012.

Krneta, Ljubomir. *Prilozi nastavi pedagogije*. Beograd, 1966.

Lozić, Vanja. "(Re)Shaping History in Bosnian and Herzegovinian Museums." *Culture Unbound* 7, (2015): 307–329.

Ljubunčić, Salih. *Dnevnički zapisi*. Zagreb: Arhivska zbirka Hrvatskoga školskog muzeja, HŠM A 3753 Ljubunčić, Salih, 1952.

Malešević, Siniša. *Ideologija, legitimnost i nova država*. Zagreb: Jesenski i Turk, 2004.

Matković, Hrvoje. *Povijest Jugoslavije – Hrvatski pregled*. Zagreb: Naklada Pavičić, 2003.

Medveš, Zdenko. "Socialist Pedagogy: Caught between the Myth of the Fairness of the Unified School and Cultural Hegemony." *Journal of Contemporary Educational Studies*, no. 2 (2015): 14–41.

N. N. "U Mostaru je formirano Društvo za kulturnu saradnju s SSSR." *Sarajevski dnevnik* (1945).

Nikolić Kosta and Dobrivojević Ivana. "Creating a Communist Yugoslavia in the Second World War." *Balcanica*, No. XLVIII (2017): 261–267.

Novak, Maja. "Predodžbe o Sovjetskome Savezu u jugoslavenskoj kulturi prije i nakon 1948. godine." *Jat – Časopis studenata kroatistike*, no. 3 (2017): 40–59.

N. N. "U SSSR i škole postavljaju svoj petogodišnji plan." *Prosvjetni radnik*, no. 1 (1946): 26–27.

Papić, Radovan. "Ministar prosvjete o NR BiH o nekim pitanjima prosvjetne politike." *Prosvjetni radnik*, no. 11, (1948): 7–10.

Petranović, Branko. *Istorija Jugoslavije 1918–1988, Treća knjiga – Socijalistička Jugoslavija 1945–1988*, Beograd: Nolit, 1988.

Senjković, Reana. "Propaganda, mediji, heroji, mitovi i ratnici." *Polemos*, no. 8 (2001).

Staeheli, Lynn A. and Daniel Hammett. "Educating the New National Citizen: Education, Political Subjectivity, and Divided Societies." *Citizenship Studies* 14, no. 6 (2010): 667–680.

Subotić, Gavrilo. "Pedagoške misli Rodoljuba Čolakovića." *Naša škola*, No. 3–4 (1985): 232–240.

Šušnjara, Snježana. *Special Education Contained in Educational Magazines and School Practice in Bosnia and Herzegovina and Croatia, 1958–1990*. Joensuu: University of Joensuu, 2009.

Šušnjara, *Snježana. Razvoj specijalnog školstva u Bosni i Hercegovini od 1958. do 1990.godine*. Zagreb–Sarajevo: Synopsis, 2013.

Šušnjara, Snježana. "Development of School Systems and Pedagogy in Bosnia and Herzegovina from the Period after World War II to the 1970s." *Journal of Contemporary Educational Studies*, no. 2 (2015): 64–80.

Šušnjara, Snježana. "Pedagogy of Bosnia and Herzegovina between Past and Future." *Journal of Contemporary Educational Studies*, no. 3 (2016): 86–103.

Šušnjara, Snježana. "Bosnia and Herzegovina under the Communist Regime: an Outlook on Educational policy." *Historia scholastica* 7, no. 1 (2021): 111–132.

Yeomans, Rory. "From Comrades to Consumers: Holidays, Leisure Time and Ideology in Communist Yugoslavia." In *Yugoslavia's Sunny Side: A*

History of Tourism in Socialism, 1940s–1980s, edited by Hanes Granditz, 69–106. Budapest: Central European University Press, 2010.

Vujisić-Živković, Nataša. "Konstitutivni diskontinuitet: školstvo i pedagogija u socijalističkoj Srbiji (1945–1990)." In *Razvoj i aktualne tendencije pedagogije i školstva na području nekadašnje Jugoslavije*, edited by Edvard Protner, 152–166. Maribor: University of Maribor Press, 2020.

Zorić, Vučina. "Fundamentals of John Dewey's Concept of Civic Education." *History of Education and Children's Literature*, no. 10 (2015): 427–445.

Weber, Bodo. *Kriza univerziteta i perspective mladih naučnika u Bosni i Hercegovini*. Sarajevo: Zaklada Friedrich Erbert, 2007.

About the Authors

Ass. Prof. Dr. Imre Garai, garai.imre@ppk.elte.hu, Associate Professor at the Institute of Education, Eötvös Loránd University (Hungary).

Prof. Hon. Dr. Erzsébet Golnhofer, erzsebetgolnhofer@gmail.com, Honorary Professor at the Research Group on Historical, Theoretical and Comparative Pedagogy, Faculty of Education and Psychology, Eötvös Loránd University, Budapest (Hungary).

Prof. Dr. Tomáš Kasper, tomas.kasper@tul.cz, Professor of History and Theory of Education at the Technical University of Liberec and Charles University in Prague (Czech Republic).

Ass. Prof. Dr. Dana Kasperová, dana.kasperova@tul.cz, Associate Professor of History and Theory of Education at the Technical University of Liberec (Czech Republic).

Prof. Dr. Iveta Kestere, iveta.kestere@lu.lv, Historian of Education, Professor at the University of Latvia (Latvia).

Prof. Dr. Blanka Kudláčová, blanka.kudlacova@truni.sk, Professor of History of Education at Trnava University in Trnava and Head of the Department of Educational Studies (Slovakia).

Prof. Dr. Zdenko Medveš, zdenko.medves@gmail.com, Emeritus Professor of Education, University of Ljubljana (Slovenia).

Prof. Dr. András Németh, nemeth.andras@ppk.elte.hu, Professor of History of Education, Eötvös Loránd University, Budapest (Hungary).

Ass. Prof. Dr. Attila Nóbik, nobik.attila@szte.hu, Associate Professor at the University of Szeged (Hungary).

Dr. Zsuzsanna Polyák, polyak.zsuzsanna@lisztakademia.hu, External Member of the Research Group on Historical, Theoretical and Comparative Pedagogy, Faculty of Education and Psychology, Eötvös Loránd University, Budapest (Hungary).

Dr. Carla Liege Rodrigues Pimenta, email to co-author: garai.imre@ppk.elte.hu, PhD in Education (2023, ELTE Budapest). Thesis: "Attributes of Higher Education and Quality of Institutional Strategies in Times of Globalization in Hungary and Germany."

MA. Bence Ruzsa, ruzsa.bence@ppk.elte.hu, Member of the Research Group on Historical, Theoretical and Comparative Pedagogy, Faculty of Education and Psychology, Eötvös Loránd University, Budapest (Hungary).

Ass. Prof. Dr. Lajos Somogyvári, tabilajos@gmail.com, Associate Professor and Head of the Education Science Institute at the University of Pannonia, Veszprém (Hungary), Vice-Dean at the Faculty of Humanities.

Ass. Prof. Dr. Dariusz Stępkowski, dariusz_stepkowski@sggw.edu.pl, Associate Professor of General Pedagogy at the Warsaw University of Life Sciences (Poland).

Prof. Dr. Snježana Šušnjara, snjezana.susnjara@ff.unsa.ba, Professor of History of Pedagogy and Education; Pedagogical Advisory Work; Pedagogical Anthropology; Basic Teaching Skills and Teaching Communication at the University of Sarajevo, Faculty of Philosophy (Bosnia and Herzegovina).

Dr. Zoltán András Szabó, szabo.zoltan.andras@ppk.elte.hu, Head of the Research Group on Historical, Theoretical and Comparative Pedagogy, Faculty of Education and Psychology, Eötvös Loránd University, Budapest (Hungary).

Prof. Dr. Éva Szabolcs, szabolcs.eva@ppk.elte.hu, Professor Emerita at the Research Group on Historical, Theoretical and Comparative Pedagogy, Faculty of Education and Psychology, Eötvös Loránd University, Budapest (Hungary).

Prof. Dr. Ulrich Wiegmann, u.wiegmann@imail.de, Adjunct Professor (retired) of History of Education at Humboldt-Universität zu Berlin, Associate at DIPF | Leibniz Institute for Research and Information in Education (Frankfurt a.M./Berlin, Germany).

Prof. Dr. Alida Zigmunde, Alida.Zigmunde@rtu.lv, Historian of Education, Professor at Riga Technical University (Latvia).

STUDIA EDUCATIONIS HISTORICA

Bildungsgeschichtliche Studien/Studies in the History of Education/
Estudios de Historia de la Educación

Herausgegeben von/edited by/editado por
Marcelo Caruso

Vol. 1 Anna Larsson/Björn Norlin (eds.): Beyond the Classroom. Studies on Pupils and Informal Schooling Processes in Modern Europe. 2014

Vol. 2 Marcelo Caruso (ed.): Classroom Struggle. Organizing Elementary School Teaching in the 19th Century. 2015.

Vol. 3 Cristina Alarcón/Martin Lawn (eds.): Assessment Cultures. Historical Perspectives. 2017.

Vol. 4 Sónia Vaz Borges: Militant Education, Liberation Struggle, Consciousness. The PAIGC education in Guinea Bissau 1963–1978. 2019.

Vol. 5 Marcelo Caruso/Daniel Maul (eds.): Decolonization(s) and Education. New Polities and New Men. 2020.

Vol. 6 Till Eble: Gelehrter Eklektizismus und Schulpolitik. Ideologie und Unterrichtsorganisation im Spanien des konservativen Liberalismus (1834–1900). 2020.

Vol. 7 Ingrid Miethe/Jane Weiss (eds.): Socialist Educational Cooperation and the Global South. 2020.

Vol. 8 Marcelo Caruso: El espíritu o la mecánica. La enseñanza mutua y la culturalidad del orden de la enseñanza (Prusia, Dinamarca/Schleswig-Holstein, España, 1800–1870). 2021.

Vol. 9 Luis Carlos Morales Zúñiga: Paraíso Cívico. Politicidad Nacional y Transnacionalidad Político-Educativa en la Educación Cívica en Costa Rica (1886–2015). 2023.

Vol. 10 Tomáš Kasper, Iveta Kestere and Attila Nóbik (eds.): Hour Zero – Educational Sciences in Central, Eastern and Southeastern Europe. 2026.

www.peterlang.com

www.ingramcontent.com/pod-product-compliance
Ingram Content Group UK Ltd.
Pitfield, Milton Keynes, MK11 3LW, UK
UKHW041826100926
8556IPUK00002B/39

9 783631 890615